IN THOSE OTHER LANDS

Survival, hope, and redemption

Caroline Mertens

OTHER BOOKS BY CAROLINE MERTENS

Amsterdam Serenade

A Splendor Among Shadows

Lights on Banderas Bay

Sambal and Spice in Amsterdam

The Road from Java: East of Thousand Islands

Tulips for Lotte: A Dutch Florist in WWII Amsterdam

Dedicated to my tenacious, joyful Oma & steadfast,
cherished Opa.
I love you both with all my heart.

TABLE OF CONTENTS

PART ONE

CHAPTER ONE
BATAVIA, JAVA, DUTCH EAST INDIES, 1925

Diny Dekker's curious Mam loved to lounge on the front portico, dreaming long beyond their four o'clock tea time, resting in a creamy gown, leaning back on the soft orange and yellow swirled cushions set against her round-back wicker bamboo chairs. Cornelia Dekker stirred a cube of sugar into her black tea with a silver spoon, then quietly sipped. She glanced at her boisterous four-year-old daughter Diny, eyes full of love, closing them into an almost squint, with a dimpled smile and a nod of her head, a gesture of deep, unswerving love between them.

"A double-wink," Mam called the act of affection.

Diny tried to wink back, but usually closed both eyes and giggled, and her mahogany eyes lit with enthusiasm, eyebrows raised as if she considered some mischief. She spun around, her white linen dress fluttering, and bent down to pull her socks higher. Diny's earliest memories contained family moments surrounding their wicker rattan table, resting on bamboo chairs, sipping tea, and eating meals outdoors.

Mam took little *Diny* (as they affectionately called her) into her arms and rocked her gently, whispering, "A little D, on my knee, this is my *Dee-knee*." She straightened Diny's large black bow atop her head. Diny's eyes searched the expansive sky for colorful birds, her brown cocoa eyes gently twinkling.

"You live in Batavia, *buh-tah-fee-ya*," Mam sang, "in the Dutch East Indies, *In-dees*," and Diny's eyes were transfixed on Mam, the serene face hovering cozily above her each day. In the unflappable early morning tranquility, Mam transported Diny for a pull-along walk in the *kinderwagen*, the little cart rumbling along as she introduced her daughter to garden paths near their home, flourishing tropics surrounding them.

The air still cool and unsullied, Mam delighted in the simplicity of the morning, remarking, "The day has only just started, *Meisje!*" She was her mother's sweet little girl and felt the hospitality of Mam's radiant gaze. "Remember, Diny, all of God's wonderful adventures await us each new day!" Mam spoke into the cerulean sky.

In her buoyant endeavors, Cornelia assumed the return of daybreak each morning precluded any conflicts, trials, and inevitable frustrations, an unavoidable part of any life, even life in a paradise landscape. While she knew troubles would come, her infectious optimism pervaded.

Diny's father Pieter Dekker labored in his lieutenant leadership role in the police department, a task suited to his loyal, reliable nature, in a career with great prospects. Cornelia adored her devoted husband, and Pieter affectionately whispered, "My dear Cora," as he left for work each morning. He wore a crisp white linen suit, shiny brown shoes, and carried a leather attaché case filled with newspapers, reports, personal correspondence, and books. Their home steadied into a quieter hum after Pieter's daily departure, but Cornelia was determined to generate special time nurturing Diny's mind and soul.

Their garden offered shade and respite from balmy tropical heat, as the front of their home contained their *voorgalerij*, a covered open veranda. The three-sided enclosed covered patio offered an open texture of the outdoors, accompanied by a coziness to replicate the comfort of the more formal Dutch sitting room in their home. This opportunity to embrace outdoor living coupled with al fresco air revitalized Mam's spirits and Diny's liveliness.

Mam strolled the veranda, slid a round record from its paper covering, and meticulously placed it in the gramophone. She moved the arm onto the disc and aligned the vertical needle with the beginning of the record. As classical music played, Mam clapped joyfully while Diny alternately danced around the front yard and ran to her for a hug.

In the sultry warmth, and in keeping with the traditions of the island women, Mam wore a light colored *kebaya*, the traditional Javanese blouse-dress, which provided flowing coolness paired with comfort. Some kebayas were made of silk or thin cotton, with a brocade or floral stitchwork. Mam embroidered her clothes, laboring meticulously over a simple yet elegant piece, demonstrating her intricate needlework to Diny.

While strolling in the market, Mam tried to dress according to custom and paired the kebaya with a *sarong* covering, carried her accordion fan, and waved the pretty paper at her smooth, round face. She fashioned her long caramel-colored hair into a sweeping bun, to offer respite from the heat. Her arms were thin but strong, and her frame curvy from blossoming into womanhood, from carrying, birthing, and nourishing two children. Her fragrance of lavender came from small glass bottles lined on her vanity. Mam allowed Diny a drop of lavender perfume on her neck for Sundays they attended church service.

During morning tea and coffee break, called *koffietijd, Mam* sipped tea, while using a fork and knife to eat ripened fruit or jelly toast on a delicate porcelain plate, as the bamboo chandelier swayed gently above her.

Diny played on the stoop and hummed or sang, her tiny fingers swirling shapes into the dirt, with her companion a stuffed teddy bear, or a waving baby doll, which she pulled around in a bamboo cart-on-wheels. Little brother Huibert napped in his pram in the shade, beside a wooden-carved room divider. He smiled as he slept, still a tiny boy at the fresh age of two, a singular moment in his busy day to cease his lively demeanor. Their living room was an open extension of the front of their home, set outdoors, to experience the grandeur of lush mountain views and blue sky.

In their Dutch East Indies homes, verandas opened to the front of a home, for inhabitants to observe the life ahead of them; assembled with scattered wicker chairs, colorful cushions atop, and bordered by roll-down bamboo mat draperies meant to enclose the room during monsoon season. Covered, enclosed porches with carved wooden dividers provided a cooling respite from heat and served as their main living quarters and their primary gathering area for entertaining guests. Morning and afternoon *koffietijd* coffee and tea breaks were taken on the veranda, together as a family, along with evening meals.

Diny's Mam preferred local foods and teas, fish and produce, all of which were readily available at the local markets in town. Stalls lined with canvas overhangs threaded chaotic city streets, and each stall was colorful, with unique orange and red vegetables, greens like lemongrass, chili peppers, fruits, and scents of the bunches of aromatic herbs and intense spices: all the specific fragrances of this region of southeast Asia simmered in the air.

Food vendors silhouetted the edges of markets, offering hot flame-grilled kebabs, seafood and noodle soup, or wok-steamed meats, and an intermittent dance. Only on special occasions were the children permitted to sample food from one of the vendors, as Mam was not certain their tiny stomachs could handle spicy delicacies.

Each morning after breakfast, the tall and impressive Pieter Dekker exited their home following a round of kisses from Cornelia, Diny, and little Huib.

Pieter's commanding frame towered over others, his dark hair curled on the sides from humidity, his bright blue eyes danced underneath dark eyebrows while his mouth smiled below a thick, caterpillar-like mustache. Cornelia pulled him into a gentle embrace, her green eyes shining as she smiled him off to work.

Each morning he journeyed into town for his role as a Lieutenant of Police, Second Class. After laboring all morning at his police work, in meetings and business, reviewing cases, reports, and investigations, he returned home for lunch, to join the family for the daily hot meal at 12 o'clock noon, followed by a nap. A habitual nap time was a custom in the humid tropics; it meant respite and refreshment for their spirits, as oppressive, tropical heat exhausted them. Then, after his nap, Pieter returned to work from 2-4 o'clock, at least, sometimes later, or perhaps worked on correspondence and reports at home in the evening.

During monsoon season, constant sultry dampness hung above them with heaviness, and the rains were a welcome release from humidity. Amidst the dry season of July through November, the heat remained consistent without storms. And at 4 o'clock, the children took turns enjoying an invigorating bucket-shower in the garden, using the large butter tin to pour cool water over them, cascading as a wonderful and refreshing reprieve!

Pieter's promising beginning in the police department gained momentum, his love with Cornelia swelled solid and accomplished, their affection blossoming in marriage. Pieter's greatest joy each day encompassed spending time with his beloved wife and their two children.

During dinner times within their peaceful veranda, they used glass plates, placed on a freshly-ironed tablecloth, and Diny held the white cloth with her small hands, tracing blue floral patterns around the edge, an embroidery project from Cornelia's newlywed days. Diny's parents spoke quietly yet affectionately, while using their blue porcelain teapot, cups, and saucers.

The delicate flavor of the yellow orange mango — a pungent and fragrant explosion within her mouth, coupled with syrupy undertones — was one of Diny's favorite fruits to enjoy in the shade on those delicate plates, a sweet and aromatic fruit an interval from the tropical air of the Dutch East Indies. Or Dad offered Diny *hagelslag*, chocolate sprinkles, on her buttered toast, but only for breakfast. They always dined with forks and knives to remain cultured, Mam reminded her, as civilized citizens.

The Dekker family emigrated from the Netherlands to the Asian Pacific nation of the Netherlands East Indies, cultivating their love for the *Emerald Girdle*, as the verdant island nation was affectionately called. Their country's location was a series of 17,000 islands, only about 6,000 of which were inhabited, situated north of Australia and south of countries bundled together by land borders: Siam and countries combined to inhabit Indochina, and across another sea to the northeast, the Philippine Islands.

The Dutch East Indies was situated amidst a paradise of ecosystems of sea and coast with expansive beaches, seagrass beds, coral reefs, coastal mudflats, and mangroves. The country was one of the Coral Triangle countries with the world's greatest diversity of coral reef fish with more than 1,600 species found exclusively in the eastern islands. Living near the equator afforded year-round balmy temperatures, lush forests, and fertile fields. Volcanic ash dispersed for millennia, expressed into the air from more than one hundred active volcanoes interspersed in mountain ranges, pushing soil upward, heaving fields in the volcanic ring of fire.

This colorful, vibrant culture felt unpioneered, undeveloped, and preserved in beauty and enchantment. It was tucked away from the rest of the world at times, as untamed wilderness. Academic, cultured Europeans pursued the uncultivated habitats of tigers, birds, reptiles, elephants, orangutans, leopards, and rhinoceroses and cut through thick forests, with playful monkeys spotted roaming along shorelines and splashing in the water.

The multitude of tropical islands served as a backdrop for enterprising advancement in the long-successful spice trade, government work, public service, or education, among other endeavors. Some Dutch were traders, sailors, colonialists, or adventurers. Perhaps they considered themselves sojourners, setting forth to procure a fortune before returning to Europe. Others fashioned a life of service in the tropics, enthralled with the people and charmed by the islands but determined to live with goodness. Some had been born and raised on the islands, although their skin tone revealed a different heritage, a lighter skin, more like the color of crushed ginger or turmeric, their roots in Europe. Those raised on the islands, their bloodline traced back to Java's early days, appeared the color of cloves or cinnamon.

The privileged spice and shipping trade of the Dutch East India Company, *Vereenigde Oost-Indische Compagnie*, VOC, originally held a monopoly on procuring spices like cinnamon, cloves, nutmeg, and mace, exporting at a high price to Europe and beyond. Later, the company added other financially profitable crops: tea, tobacco, coffee, rubber, cacao, and sugar, which encroached on the surrounding territories with influential dominance. They added canals, trading systems, and a new government, and if they missed Holland, the islands provided consistent balmy warmth and relief from the long, cloud-filled Dutch winters in northwestern Europe.

As a matter of words, the Malay language was studied intensely by Dutch scholars, then adapted and transformed during the earlier days of the Dutch arrival; they added key words, phrases, and colloquialisms. Prior to the earliest Dutch settlement, little of Malay was formally understood beyond the islands (outside of traders and academics), but always aiming for success, the Dutch realized the need to learn the language and culture.

The Dutch took to spelling Malay words with a phonetic recognition, in which the words were written exactly as they were spoken, providing easier training for their children. The language "Melayu Pasar," interpreted as "Market Malay," was the common language during colonial times and indirectly influenced many of the other island languages. In general, the Dutch East Indies consisted of a layered society and social status was dependent upon one's heritage and skin coloring, which consistently astounded the Dekkers.

In the early evening hours, following work and tin-bucket shower, and after 4 o'clock *koffietijd* tea and coffee break in the veranda, Pieter meandered around their extensive backyard garden, near the anthurium plants and mossy rock walls, smoking a pipe. His time alone was usually outdoors; in moments of serenity or refuge he spent pondering, in substantial thought.

"These gardens are my sanctuary," Dad reminded them, "and a holy place to meet with God."

Their garden, which housed a sense of adventure among the flowers and trees, was their playtime delight, and an escape for their father: a place of refuge and haven within his yard. His greatest moments of inventiveness, along with an invigorating rest, he told them, were found amidst the swaying flamboya trees with red blossoms, bougainvillea sparkling forth with violet blooms, or other florals of crimson or cobalt.

Waringins — banyan trees — looked like beige ropes woven together. The thin contorted branches twirled and meshed together, sometimes a dozen branches wrapped as one unit, as though a twisted vine. The claws of those ropes pressed down into the leafy soil, rooting into a lumpy mass. The banyan branches spread farther in scope, roots knobby and reaching heights stretched out to the heavens, as though they were praising their Creator.

Rubber trees swayed nearby, stretchy and bouncy in the tepid breeze. Bamboo, orchid, teakwood, sandalwood, and ebony lined forests and the perimeters of homes. Banana trees, with thick green trunks and wide-leafed palm branches, served as a verdant canopy over the growing clusters of green banana fruit, with a red blooming flower below as a velvet bow adorning the newest crop. Diverse gardens greeted them, blooming about their world with remarkable enthusiasm, and Pieter was drawn to the sanctuary he discovered in his gardens.

Pieter's considerable height carried him above crowds, with stunning blue eyes a surprising contrast to his olive-colored skin. His thick, wide mustache sometimes hid his mouth's expression, or offered an additional mysterious disposition to his commanding presence.

An embrace from Pieter encapsulated Mam's frame, his bellowing voice whispering, "Cora!" to his beloved; his large ears heard the tiny rustling of Diny's running on the fallen palmetto fronds in the yard, and his broad arms easily held Diny, bouncing her on his knees, or his expansive hands grasping her tiny hand for a leisurely neighborhood walk.

In the garden, he silently meandered through the tranquil, muted estate, and from the coolness in the back of their home, Diny barely pictured his tall, sturdy frame through the greenery, his dark, thick hair swirling high and puffy on his head. Each step was full of confidence and certainty: a steady, poised presence.

Sometimes she quietly followed him, tiptoed behind his long strides, and her bare feet smacked loudly on the stepping-stone path. He undoubtedly heard her pursuing, and playfully pretended to not pay attention, allowing her the delight in a game.

Then, almost dramatically, Pieter spun around, surprised Diny with a roaring chuckle, and with a nod, tipping his pipe in the air, a small salute to his eldest child. His laughter could be heard throughout the estate, another joke allowed for amusement. Diny squealed jovially at her gentle bear of a father, revealing her dimpled cheeks, with her wavy hair twirling in the breeze, as she returned to the table to play *bikkelen*, her jacks game, and *touwtje springen*, jump rope. Later, Pieter invited her to fly their colorful kites in the breezes of sunset. The sky opened to their entire world of Batavia, and for Diny, these were the happiest moments a childhood could contain.

Within the coziness of their veranda, if the weather was mild and welcoming, they lingered beyond their evening meal, watching the languid sun drop behind the trees and into the horizon. Their veranda echoed with joy, and served as a portal into the beguiling wilds of the tropical rainforests. Behind their dining table, an expansive bookshelf lined one wall and housed stacks of books. There were imported Dutch hymnals and ancient European poetry, various religious tomes by Chesterton or Moody, and cultural books about the Dutch East Indies by Louis Couperus. One searing book criticized the exploitation of the Indies, entitled *Max Havalaar*, by Eduard Douwes Dekker (no relation to their family, for all they knew), or his pseudonym *Multatuli*, along with Dutch poetry by P.C. Boutens, and children's story books for Diny and Huib.

Cora collected a few painting book compilations from Rembrandt, Van Gogh, and Cezanne. On the top shelf, housed bottles and decks of playing cards and games intended for lively evenings entertaining guests. On a lower shelf, stacks of records served as background music to their lives. Musicians like Schubert, Handel, Bach, Mozart, and Brahms felt like traveled friends, alongside Wagner's operatic movements, Beethoven's dramatic overtones, and Vivaldi's cheerful violin melodies in *The Four Seasons* orchestrated their activities.

"Come, my friends, 'tis not too late to seek a newer world." — Alfred, Lord Tennyson

When Pieter Dekker and Cornelia Chiela van den Bout were married by-proxy on 17 March 1920 in the Netherlands, Pieter had already journeyed ahead on a ship to *Nederlands Oost Indie* — which was also called Netherlands East Indies — for his job as a police officer, his career there launched on the islands two years prior. From their first meeting in Cornelia's hometown of Hardinxveld, to their riverside courtship and eventual engagement, Cornelia demonstrated her fondness and devotion toward Pieter with her embrace.

Cora's unconventional courtship with Pieter was brief and full of promise. He was a visionary and risk-taker, loved to dream of their future together, and his passion for serving others evident. He was a natural leader, decisive, and determined. These character traits appealed to her — the ability to traverse the world with her strong, able husband and explore the Indies together. Cora knew their lifestyle there would differ from the Netherlands. While they were each raised in quiet, bucolic settings within a modern, efficient country, their upbringings were wholesome and sweet. The gentleness of living away from bustling city life had afforded daily wooded walks for Pieter in Friesland, and riverside meanderings for Cornelia in Hardinxveld.

Pieter hailed from the northern Friesland village of Kollum, and was born 2 August 1893. He was brought up by exacting, traditional parents — Reverend Jan and Gerdina Dekker — in a meager farming community, small hamlets of farms strung together in the sparsely populated landscapes of the far northwestern province, the outer stretches of the Netherlands. Sea water etched the rugged land, and farmers navigated temperamental weather forming off the North Sea. Livestock grazed in the green and fleeting summer, then bore down under the burden of a heavy and dreary winter.

The Frisian language contained eight dialects with varying intonations, so even within Friesland at times, language became a barrier, an isolating prospect unless citizens knew Dutch and their native Frisian language. Pieter was raised by a successful Christian Reformed Church pastor Jan and his gentle wife Gerdina. Elevated expectations were placed on a pastor's family, and Pieter knew well the responsibility and privilege of leading a family as examples in the community.

Reverend Jan Dekker originally hailed from a small northern Frisian village called Andyk, had lived and served in Kollum as a Reformed Church minister since 1896, and published numerous short theological works alongside a pair of poetry collections. He became a noted member of the Frisian Forests, as for 25 years he wrote the lead article for *The Free Frisian*, the weekly newspaper of the Anti-Revolutionary Party.

Meanwhile, Cora was raised in a strict and thriving Protestant family, quickly learning a sense of duty, loyalty, hard work, and tradition in the family. Her steady father Huibert van den Bout and her compassionate mother Pieternella Jannigje den Breejen raised Cornelia along the Merwede River in Hardinxveld (east of Rotterdam, near Zwijndrecht), an idyllic location for serene picnics. Villages contained brightly-colored buildings and red roofs, and meticulously maintained public gardens for the enjoyment of all citizens.

Cornelia's parents married on 19 May 1893, at ages 26, and 22. Cornelia was born ten months later, on 15 March 1894, the oldest of five children, with Adriana, Jannigje, Rokus, and Piet; two, four, six, and fourteen years after her. Cornelia's outgoing, boisterous mother raised their five children to explore the world with a natural curiosity. Tranquil, introverted father Huibert van den

Bout happily captained a riverboat along the Merwede River, navigating his own sense of adventure on the waterways.

The Merwede originated as the Rhine River in the Swiss Alps before flowing through Germany, passing along the metropolis of Cologne, westward toward the Netherlands, and funneled into various smaller rivers, like the Merwede, before emptying into the North Sea near Rotterdam. Wooden ships creaked and groaned, serviced by strong, iron-like men. Just as windmills captured a breeze to funnel water up and away, ships like the 1904 Flying Dutchman harnessed wind via canvas sails, with a skipper and his mate for sailing. That same drive for exploration Cornelia inherited would undoubtedly inspire her own journeys.

Pieter Dekker seemed to inherit a sense of restlessness from previous generations, from his forefathers who searched for heritage through traveling new landscapes. With the cessation of fighting and The Great War ending in 1918 came renewed hope for rebuilding Europe. The Netherlands had escaped devastation by remaining neutral in the war, allowing both sides to access land and resources. Pieter's original ambition was to work as a Forest Ranger, but he found few opportunities in that field. After the war, resources were limited, and the government's budget would not allow for many jobs in the Forest Service. However, careers in the police force were plentiful and offered a new adventure abroad. With the war's completion, Pieter secured a police job and ventured via boat to the Dutch East Indies as the first Dekker to relocate to Indie.

After their by-proxy wedding, Cornelia bravely traveled alone on a ship sailing across the world to join Pieter. Her only suitable cause for venturing forth in a far-flung manner was marriage, and as she boarded the ship bound for Pieter, she was already married to him — indeed, felt connected to him, her gold ring moved from her left engagement hand to her right wedded hand. However, Pieter Dekker was sadly unable to attend his own wedding. Instead, in his place, his brother Jan Wolter served as his stand-in. Jan Wolter contributed to the "by-proxy" aspect of Pieter and Cornelia's union by arriving at the City Hall and answering all the questions in lieu of Pieter.

The ceremony appeared polished and formal, as other Dutch weddings: a bride, and a groom, accompanied by an officiant and handful of witnesses. Both Pieter and Cornelia's families were present, attending two wedding ceremonies: the first in front of a judge in City Hall and the second in front of

God within a Church. Yet the primary difference was merely that the groom was thousands of kilometers away, absent from his wedding.

The simplicity of the matter was Pieter's new career was Cornelia's singular boat passage to join him. A young woman could hardly travel alone to Indie unless married and her husband employed in the location of her arrival, prohibited from a lengthy solo journey to the Far East. Their by-proxy wedding remained sufficient until she arrived for the Indie church wedding when Pieter would stand opposite of her and profess his love.

During the City Hall wedding reception in the Netherlands, Cornelia visited with the van den Bout and Dekker families and placed a framed photograph of Pieter on the table next to her dinner setting, as her husband certainly belonged at his own wedding reception! Gazing at Pieter's photograph reminded Cornelia of the peculiar adventures they would embark upon in their life together. Batavia, as their lively Dutch East Indies capital city had been named in 1616, offered all they could possibly desire: mystery, a fragrant tropical climate, education, opportunity to succeed, and Dutch innovation through canal systems and culture; yet was remiss for the presence of their immediate families, and most modern conveniences.

Several months later, when she arrived in the Dutch East Indies, Cornelia and Pieter were married before God in the Kwitang Church (*Gereformeerd Kwitang*) in Batavia. In moving to Indie, Cora's lofty expectations soon encountered a difficult reality. Their life there would not be perfect, as the culture, climate, and lifestyle held many differences from the Netherlands. Moreover, Cora was a naïve new bride, had never left Europe, or even visited Indie before, and apart from Pieter, had no family there! These true steps of faith were modeled in her upbringing, and she was required to live in that faith in marrying Pieter. Their first year of marriage was filled with settling into a simple, yet hearty life in a place they affectionately called "Indie," a location in which neither Pieter nor Cornelia had been raised. They grew accustomed to the Dutch social structures and government policies, including lavish celebratory galas for the police force. As Pieter advanced in his career, his social responsibilities would increase.

The northwestern country of the Netherlands was the land of their bloodline and heritage. They held dear memories and relationships with family who remained there. For a diminutive country of only 300km long by 200km wide, the spirit and perseverance of her people compensated. For a pyramid of generations, the convention of marriage and life near the family had been a customary way of Dutch life, with each son inheriting his father's vocation. The Dekker and van den Bout families and heritage stretched back into the Netherlands, long settled in places in the northwest like Amsterdam and Hilversum, south like Hardinxveld, west in Rotterdam, to the north in Groningen, Kollum, Friesland.

Pieter's exit from Friesland became disconcerting to his father, but he soon learned his brother Gerrit would receive the mantle and retain their farm, bringing relief to all. Likewise, Cora's brother Rokus was expected to carry forth the riverboat captain career of their father Huibert. Pieter and Cora's relief from the tropics would be to the Netherlands, a furlough once every six years, for a six-month period of rest, bookended by three-week boat journeys to and from their destination.

Their love traveled over stormy seas, and into an adopted, yet affectionate land, which required as much improvisation and faith as any prior challenge. They respected opportunities and cherished this life together, with Batavia as their new home. As a port city, Batavia's importance was steep, serving as the capital of the Dutch East Indies and a location central to the police force. Teeming with possibilities and vibrant enthusiasm, Batavia's streets were filled with half a million people, including more than 30,000 Europeans. With 17 cities boasting populations over 50,000 and their combined populations numbered 1.87 million of the Dutch colony's 60 million scattered throughout thousands of islands, the Dutch influence remained strong.

Some Dutch settled in the islands for trade or governmental employment, and others for the languid year-round tropical atmosphere. After being raised in Kollum, Friesland by loving parents Jan and Gerdina, who were married 3 Nov 1892, at ages 34 and 20, respectively, Pieter left the docile farming community of his youth. His parents were gentle and hardworking, farming their land from sunrise until sunset, yet they welcomed the rural, bucolic lifestyle afforded them. Their large age difference never seemed a problem to his well-matched parents, both of whom remained faithful and dedicated Christians, unified as a team and dedicated to the church in their community where Jan was also a minister.

As the oldest of five boys, Pieter assumed the leadership and responsibilities he was required and gladly secured. His four brothers Jan Wolter, Cornelis, Gerrit, and Nicolaas were younger by 3, 5, 14, and 21 years, respectively. Cornelis and Gerrit sought a life in farming while Pieter headed south for further education. At age 21, Pieter received excellent police training at Amsterdam's Police Academy and was later appointed as a contender for Head Commissioner of Police. He relocated to Dutch East Indies in 1918 and attended the Soekaboemi Police Training Academy in the Javan mountains before being stationed in Batavia.

Pieter and Cornelia were married before God in the Kwitang Church in Batavia on 17 March 1920, ages 27 and 26. Both had matured beyond youth and eagerly settled into domestic felicity, keen to begin a family. Their firstborn child Gerardina Margaretha Dekker was born on 20 July 1921, named after Pieter's mother Gerdina, and they hoped *Gerardina* would someday grow into her loquacious name. *Diny*, as they called her, was born into a balmy ambiance during the clipping winter trade winds of July, in an environment which witnesses insignificant variation of season. Diny belonged to a new era of growth, change, and discovery, in the generation springing forth after The Great War.

Batavia purred as a dense and congested city on Java. Crowded market stalls lined colorful, busy streets, with vibrant vendors, animated people full of life and ideas, offering delicious fragrant food, or exquisite bright fabrics. In the complicated labyrinth of streets and side alleys, men on bicycles drove customers around on pedaled taxi carriages called *becaks*, to work, school, and meetings. Within this economic, cultural, and political center, a variety of Dutch families lived, happily transported to this world. Their hearts intermingled with the islanders, and they were content with their lot.

Diny soon preferred exploring outside and local monkeys amused her. Black colored Siamang Gibbon monkeys frolicked on shorelines, splashing in the waves like eager toddlers. They were prevalent on Java and neighboring island Sumatra. Diny searched for monkeys jovially swinging in trees, long limbs balancing on thin branches, swaying in forest tops, and accelerating into the wind on the uppermost breezes between jumps and arm stretches, as though flying. Monkeys mingled with local crowds, searched for food, and scurried through the markets. Diny could hear tigers roar in the evenings as Mam tucked her into bed, and comforted her with the reminder they were safely inside. Some evenings, Diny watched tiny yellow butterflies flicker as a canopy in the sky as the sun gently set into the trees.

On 12 August 1923, Diny's little brother Huibert was born, and her love and pride for her dear younger *broertje* swelled as they grew together. Named after Cornelia's resolute father Huibert, she called him *Huibje*, and he blended well with the family unit, his easy-going temperament a calming balance to Diny's passionate countenance. Mam often commented on what a tranquil baby her Huib was, full of peace, with luminous hair and a round face; his ears stood profoundly from his head, much like his amiable same-named grandfather.

Huib's pleasantness offered Mam a sense of equilibrium in her home and life with two small children. Mam's morning habit involved sitting in the shade at their wooden picnic table across from her children, keeping her kebaya cool before the heat of the day. She situated their table on the lawn amid flowering bushes, away from the house, a place of learning and delight.

"Today will be glorious, my little *Grietje!*" Mam stroked Diny's cheek and indeed, she was her mother's little doll. When Huib was old enough, joined them, and Mam held out her hand for her son as they settled into study. By the time he was two, Huib started out on Mam's lap in her wooden armed chair, before he fully awoke to the day and joined Diny on the learning bench.

The dew comforted and cooled them, their school lessons in the shade of the trees a blessing before the air of the day became too humid and sticky. At times the children remained in their night clothing, long sleeves and pants a comfort against the momentary morning chill. Huibje and Diny leaned forward, propping their arms on the table, listening as their Moeder read Bible stories telling them about Jesus and all the heroes from the Bible, like Abraham, Moses, David, and Samson. Mam excitedly relayed stories with facial expressions and animated voices to convey emotion behind each lesson.

Cornelia steadily sat beside them, her frame poised at the edge of her wooden chair, legs crossed neatly at the ankles, simple indigo slip-on shoes barely covering her toes and extending underneath her feet like elegant slippers. Soft house shoes kept their marble floors clean. She pulled her hair back neatly into an upswept bun and gently reminded her children of God's goodness and grace toward their family, urging Diny and Huibje to place their trust in Jesus, as he would take them on life's greatest adventures.

Mam's endearing look and smile provided Diny her deepest encouragement, as her total enrapture with Diny evidenced each day. Diny felt no memory of loneliness in her first years, only the warm face of Mam, the buoyant laughter of Dad with his caterpillar mustache, and tenderness of connection with soft, temperate Huib. Mam and Diny adored Huib's hugs and deep voice, sweetness and gentle spirit pervading.

When Mam shared the story of baby Moses found in the river bushes, spared by God's grace in Egypt, she told them each baby was a miracle, and they agreed. Some afternoons, while Mam watched Diny and Huib play together, she sewed their clothes, her foot pacing quickly on the pedaled sewing machine, the carved wooden stand swaying merrily with each row stitched. Mam bought colorful material from the Batavian stores, woven by local women, and created masterpieces for her children. Evenings were filled with gatherings around the piano, as Pieter sang Psalms, while Cornelia played the piano. The children were captivated by Mam as she played and sang for their enjoyment.

Batavia, Java, Dutch East Indies, 1925

Pieter Dekker's work as Lieutenant of Police provided amply for their family, and his job required spending time in the *Stadhuis*, their stately Batavian City Hall, where the spice and shipping trade of the Dutch East India Company, *Vereenigde Oost-Indische Compagnie*, VOC, administered their empire for two hundred years. The era which encompassed the domain of the spice trade was affectionately called *The Golden Age*, and the building swelled with a sense of history, perspective, and place. Pieter strolled along the south-east sections of the ancient port, with the old cobblestone square under his feet. Sometimes as he arrived at the *Stadhuis*, the City Hall, the bell tower rang noisily, as he arrived for his meeting at the top of the hour.

In other moments of entrance, the sturdy white building stoically and silently towered above: formal and imposing on those who entered. Tall palm trees lined the front of the building, swaying amicably toward the red-tiled roof, and Pieter felt regal while entering past white columns into the building. Sometimes his hands clammed, and his breath quickened as he proceeded to the offices where he conducted his business. An uneven sense of nervousness manifested deep inside, often without proper escape. The whirlwind of an emotion swirled within Pieter's chest, yet his stature remained confident and steady, his nervous demeanor unnoticed by others. His eyes masked doubt, remaining perceptive. Pieter matured into his leadership roles. Sometimes merely observing others provided an opportunity for new knowledge.

During his meetings, Pieter's shining blue eyes scanned the room, viewing awards and photographs. Events marking the influence of the VOC lined the walls, and provided witness to the era, even to the dissolution of their monopoly, signaling the end of the Golden Age, and the remnants scattered into their current government. Pieter saw beyond the corruption and moral bankruptcy in the prior system of the VOC, which brought ruin and defamation at a time when their power might have yielded charity, goodness, and aid for others in need. Yet the financial fluency and success which elevated their status eventually became a hindrance to the VOC as they stumbled through the veils of prosperity, blinded by greed, and hypnotized by the illusion of power.

Later, in empty rooms after police officers exited meetings, Pieter lingered, scanning photographs, staring into the eyes of the men who lived a generation prior, those whose efforts at growing an industry resulted in the ability to empower those Dutch leaders to raise up a country of their own imaginations. He speculated, *where was the selfless leadership of these generations?*

Shipping enterprises and spice and tea fortunes were built on the backs of natives. Every worker deserved recognition, no matter their position in the company, or race, or ethnic origin. The undeniable thorn, a hindrance Pieter would surely battle his entire career, was an imbalanced ethnicity on the islands. There was the superficial politics of color, one Pieter wished to break away from and transform into tolerance, kindness, and freedom for future generations. He heard rumors of those in leadership before him, cruel and dishonorable actions surfacing every generation, without decency toward fellow humans.

Pieter wholly opposed slavery, favoring equality, forging strong friendships with Indie coworkers along with other foreign travelers of many other ethnicities. He observed a fellow human, not a race; a person, a soul, a life filled with joy and hope. Pieter enjoyed friendship with a Siamese man who lived up the street, along with a Filipino fellow who lived near his office. Friendships developed out of an organic sense of companionship, and Pieter sought to discover the personalities of his companions, as they were all connected as humans, no matter their race. He knew those men were strong leaders in their communities, yet the current Dutch government would never elevate a non-European's status to any senior leadership position, due to ethnicity; the inequalities were unjust, blatant examples of discrimination.

As Pieter surveyed the awards and accomplishments on the walls of the government buildings, the tidy offices, he hypothesized at his predecessors' ability to establish an infallible outer shell, a sense of entitlement stemming from perfectionism and pride; a sheen, a veneer. Those before him established dominance, a monopoly, without compromise with those who carved their lives and homes on these islands for generations preceding the first Dutch ships entering the rustic ports.

Those enterprising Dutch transplants from two hundred years before succeeded in numerous ways ultimately benefiting the world. They were worthy of applause, as they sought to abolish cannibalism, slavery, widow-burning and head-hunting, and provided valuable assistance by means of education and healthcare. The VOC created a railway system, utilized steamships, designed a suitable postal delivery, and fashioned telegraph services.

They created various government agencies, all of which served to introduce a degree of new uniformity across the colony, and specialties included an intricate port trading system. The VOC invented stock and a new form of coin, chartered a spice trading authority, and established treaties with the rulers of Asian nations. Early Dutch settlers formed a privileged upper social class of soldiers, administrators, managers, teachers and pioneers. They lived together with the "*natives*" as some derogatorily called them, but the white Dutch Europeans were always at the top of a rigid social and racial caste.

Treaties were at the cost of local customs and culture, and decimated the lives of these local islanders. Certainly, Indies were the casualties of power forces, their joyful lives invaded by commanding Dutch explorers. Pieter shook his head sadly, disappointed for the actions of his fellow countrymen and the tension often felt with locals. His daily life was surrounded by lessons for any who would enter a leadership role, if only he listened to the stories and learned from poor judgment, while amply praising humble leaders who lived gracefully.

After Pieter's business at the Stadhuis, he wandered down the hill to his police station, the feel of those old, worn stones from the Dutch settlement a tangible link to the past. On his journey back, the Hall of Justice loomed nearby, and he guessed at the hearings and justice of current trials. During an afternoon *koffietijd* break, Pieter traversed sidewalks along market stalls, stopping in Cafe Batavia for an unhurried cigarette and coffee with boiled milk with a dash of local cinnamon. He might have a jovial discussion with his Malaysian friend who worked at the Cafe. Pieter sat across the counter while they discussed family, activities, and plans for the month, his mind actively seeking to form a Malay joke.

Outside, while enjoying an after-coffee cigarette, Pieter gazed into the distance at the thriving city filled with twisted curves; the Ciliwung River cut through the middle of the city, surrounded by spaces of poverty from an unseen distance, only a patchwork collection of colors. Before him huddled a mass of commerce. Thick mangrove forests and humid swamps lined down through the end of the valley, which spilled the Ciliwung River into the Tanjung Priok — Batavia's bustling western harbor — and the sparkling sea beyond.

The Ciliwung River originated on the highlands of the volcano Mount Gede, West Java, and flowed down through the Javanese village of Puncak, along villages, and into the bay. Each summer, for a luxurious month away from the bustle of the swelling city, the Dekkers escaped to those mountains for a family holiday, and when Pieter pointed to the area where the Ciliwung River sprang up, Diny asked ride a swimming tube on the river down through Batavia and out to the Java Sea.

CHAPTER TWO
HILVERSUM, NORTH HOLLAND, THE NETHERLANDS, 1925

On 4 March 1925, the Dekker family arrived in the Netherlands to enjoy six months of respite and renewal. Once every six years, companies offered their staff a Furlough, which included a trip to the Netherlands via a three-week boat journey, a six-month holiday, and a three-week boat return back to Indie, all paid by the company. This generous gift of an extended holiday was a respite for employees, escaping a humid environment, and as they left their families in the Netherlands, they rarely saw loved ones. Cornelia's parents retired from Hardinxveld to Hilversum, while Pieter's family relocated from Kollum to Amsterdam after his brother Gerrit took over the farm. Neither family could afford a long, expensive trip to the Dutch East Indies, so they all eagerly anticipated the Dekker family's arrival.

Upon their return to Batavia, Pieter would be transferred elsewhere, as the Dutch government liked to move police officers into new promotion roles immediately following Furlough, as though the refreshing holiday invigorated their senses and capabilities. The Dekker family received leave, and Pieter would return ready to bring all his energy into the new job. Before they left, Pieter organized his office, typed lengthy reports, and met with the man who temporarily covered for him on the police force. Cornelia readied their home to be vacant for six months, and gathered gifts for their family, like elegant linens and colorful fabrics, carved wood, and spices, which were more expensive to ship across the seas. In anticipation of their arrival, Cornelia's dear mother faithfully knitted much of the winter clothing they would need in the Netherlands during their Furlough, like winter hats, mittens, and scarves.

The three-week boat trips to their holiday, and later back again, were a highlight. They all loved those boating voyages and would reminisce about them with nostalgia. What a marvelous and wonderful childhood their children were afforded! And having the opportunity for extended time with their families was a special benefit, away from the stress and daily routines of work. Their route away from the port in Batavia entailed crossing the Indian Ocean to the Red Sea, through the Suez Canal, up through the balmy Mediterranean, through the narrows of the Strait of Gibraltar. From there they sailed up the sun-drenched coasts of Spain and France and past Belgium to the far northwest corner of Europe. This was their means of travel, as there were no commercial airplane journeys.

The Dutch cities they encountered were new and foreign to Diny, as she encountered her first experience in her parents' homeland. The Netherlands offered cities with towering, crooked, gabled houses, warehouses, masts of ships entering port, manicured landscapes, and bucolic villages, flat lands with windmills harnessing the air and water on farms. In Amsterdam, trees were lined along clean, straight streets and winding canals. The first several days required acclimation to the frigid temperatures, meeting with family, and for Diny and Huibert, and introduction to Dutch culture. Their lives varied with extremes of tremendous depth of friendships and lifestyle from one continent to the other.

The Dekkers began their holiday at a refreshing break at the North Sea, where Diny lounged on a blanket spread on the sand in Den Haag, watching bicyclists move smoothly along the paved paths beside the soothing water. As winter yielded to springtime, they relished picnics at Hilversum's Boombergpark: bread, meats and cheeses, fruits and sweets, and tea. As spring's thaw arrived, her capstone and signature style of tulips bloomed gloriously. Those varieties of tulips radiantly gleamed with distinctive blush and vibrancy, each indigo, cerulean, and scarlet petal a unique blend of swirling colors, vermillion shaded with ambers and yellows. They spent Saturday afternoons in March and April in friends' fields filled with expansive patchwork quilts of colors, arranging the rainbow in hues unseen before in flowers, except in Indie, with flowers Diny found no names for, and birds which fluttered closely to them and then away, their feathers and songs unlike other birds she discovered in Indie.

Diny and Huib loved the little *snoepjes* Oma Dekker stored in her Amsterdam cupboard, treats like *Hopjes* (coffee-flavored hard candies), *babbelaars* butterscotch candies, spiced cookies, and *spekkoek*, a thinly layered spice cake, made with many thin layers of cake and creamy butter fillings. Oma called her beloved grandchildren to her side, and their hair snarled underneath her embrace, which smelled of jasmine and mothballs.

Meanwhile, Opa Dekker could be heard from down the hallway, upstairs, or even outside in the townhome's courtyard gardens, with a loud, booming voice and gregarious laughter, his hand coarse from decades of farming, knees calloused from prayer, his arms still strong and capable, his back straight, his legs ready for racing. Oma prepared the *koffie* and tea, with Diny begging Opa for a full cup of coffee. She was resigned to drink a child-appropriate tea instead.

Times with grandparents emitted a *"gezellig"* time — a "warm, cozy togetherness" — which was more of an inviting, welcoming feeling, than a word to explain the action, always with talking and laughing. She felt *gezellig* in a friendship, during a meal, or in church. The word transcended place. Feeling *gezellig* could translate into any experience drawing people together in convivial togetherness.

Pieter and Cornelia embarked upon an interlude of escape to the Swiss mountains for a chalet retreat, and then a few nights in Paris while the children stayed with Opa and Oma Dekker in Amsterdam. During those special times together, Oma taught her eldest grandchild to sew. Diny wanted to assist Mam with creating clothing for the family, and someday, for a family of her own. As they sat together on a wooden bench, Diny could not reach the pedal of the foot-cranked sewing machine, but Oma helped pump the pedal, slowing during difficult turns, allowing Diny mistakes in stitches while she embroidered a pillowcase, flowers and vines swirling around the edges.

Oma Dekker was gentle and patient, her voice quiet, pleased with Diny's first sewing creation. She reminded her they had the entire summer to gain preciseness and a feel for the machine, to learn the personality of sewing. As Diny matured, her hands would expand, and her mind would come alive with sewing ideas. Oma's tender love and praise encouraged Diny and provided enough confirmation to continue sewing.

While Diny sewed with Oma, Huib played ball or read with Opa Dekker, drawn to his vibrant enthusiasm and zest for life. Both Diny and Huib loved to sit on Opa's lap as he read books to them with a lively voice, animating each character. Huib tried to mimic Opa's booming vitality, as they both shared some vivacious effervescence and joie *de vivre*. They were inseparable during their visit; Opa smelled of pipe and soap and carried Huib on his shoulders outside to offer him a unique look at the world.

When Dad and Mam returned rejuvenated, the family continued visiting others, including Mam's parents, Huibert and Pieternella van den Bout, who lived in Hilversum. Oma van den Bout always kept stroopwaffels and Queen Wilhelmina peppermints close by, and they baked together on snowy days, Huib scooping in the flour at just the appropriate time. Diny cracked eggs delicately, yet bits of shell escaped her hand and settled into the mixture. Oma scooped them out swiftly, moving on from a small error. She heartily reminded them a bit of egg shell just added fiber to the mix, and they giggled together. Oma instructed them on how to bake a brown sugar nut tart and almond cookie-cakes with vanilla, which reminded them of Sinterklaas Day celebrations every 5th and 6th of December. The *gezellig* family togetherness warmed Diny.

Cornelia's father Huibert van den Bout offered to play with his eager grandchildren in the backyard, kicking a ball or helping them learn to ride a bicycle. If Oma needed the children more actively entertained, Opa walked them to the park, where running through fields in brisk spring weather brought bright spirits and rosy cheeks.

Their summertime was languid and fiery; the heat of the sunshine was humid but not oppressive. They escaped to the coast for an afternoon, the refreshing sea air calming and soothing them. Diny splashed Huib in the North Sea, and they created villages made of sand, using a bucket and shovel Mam brought along, either under the umbrella or in the full scope of the sun.

They ran together along the thin layer of life where the foamy water churned in bubbles on the beige sand, fleeting moments which constantly changed and altered. Sea creatures effervesced layers of water, scuttling down into the sand when water receded. Even messages of love written from Dad to Mam were erased with the water's high tide velocity, yet joy beamed upon Mam's glittering face.

A distinctive feature of remaining in the country for summertime on Furlough included an opportunity to visit Pieter's younger brother Cornelis and his wife Sietske in the north, in the province of Groningen. Dad was born in Kollum and marveled at the quaint villages and family farms in the surrounding countryside. While brother Gerrit and his wife Etje had only recently inherited the family farm in Kollum, it was too small for overnight visitors.

While Tante Sietske and Oom Cor did not yet have children, their nurturing love brought encouragement and delight. As farmers in Groningen, they raised a variety of animals, including horses, which Dad and Mam relished riding together. Diny's excitement escalated, as she thought about how her younger brother Huib, just a toddler, would appreciate chasing chickens, watching sheep grazing the pasture, and observing pigs eating slop in their stalls.

Dad said Diny was too young and small to ride a horse alone, so she watched her parents ride. She leaned along the wooden fence, while Huib sat on a stool next to her and politely folded his hands, contentedly watching. Each time Dad showed off his equestrian skills and brought his horse to a standing, commanding position, Huib clapped joyfully, cheering and whooping from the fence. Dad rode a horse as a police officer, and it seemed he could maneuver the spirits of even the wildest horse, demonstrating to his brother some new methods on taming horses. They later ate dinner together, esteeming Tante Sietske's delicious cooking, and relished leisurely meals of savory cheeses and smoked meats — salmon, herring, and eel — before saying "so-long for now" and returning to the city.

Amsterdam held interest for the family in addition to Opa and Oma Dekker's house. The metropolis of 90 islands with 400 bridges connecting them held more than 100km of canals to navigate. Pieter arranged for a canal boat cruise, navigating through the various narrow alleyways of water, as Pieter described historic monuments, churches, and squares along the way. Marled red bricked businesses with white window frames and cherry-colored tile roofs on townhomes appeared as a radiant contrast to gray days. Homes boasted bright pops of colored shutters, with ground-floor cafés sporting dazzling colored awnings and crimson umbrellas, quaint coffee shops situated at the intersection of canals, bike paths, and tree-lined trails.

Diny was mesmerized by the gliding canal boat, a smaller version of their sea-voyage, canopy overhead, protecting them from rain. They sashayed under arching trees reaching above the black wrought iron fencing and parked bikes, and cruised underneath distinct canal bridges. Even gray days were colorful with the surrounding greenery. A breeze fluttered her hair, bringing intrigue. So many streets and waterways to explore and discover! Each gabled home stood stately, decorated with unique façades and ornate accents, pillars and spheres and spires.

Also, in Amsterdam, the Dekkers attended church to hear Pieter's father Jan preach again. While recently retired from being a Christian Reformed Church preacher, he was often invited to guest speak at churches in Amsterdam when their preacher was away on business or other engagements. During those times when Opa Dekker preached, Diny was expected to sit with Dad, Mam, and Huib in the front row. She had to remain alert and pay attention since he would watch her closely during the entire sermon.

The pews were straight and wooden and painful, without any cushion, and Diny felt miserable about the requirement. Sitting up close to watch a sermon! Mam allowed Diny to keep a plum pit in her mouth during the sermon to stay awake and concentrate so boredom and pain would not overcome her. Diny could not smile with the pit in her mouth, but at least she remained a good little girl for her Opa Dekker.

In September, they journeyed to the Merwede River in Hardinxveld (east of Rotterdam), to enjoy the peaceful river setting for a picnic and tour Cora's place of childhood. They sailed through De Biesbosch National Park, a wetland area full of scenery and birds to discover. Cornelia's father, Huibert van den Bout piloted their riverboat along the Merwede River for a cruise as the sun lowered into the western edges of the North Sea.

Huibert's role as a river captain had proved successful and offered him many opportunities. Now in retirement, he relished time to visit his old boating friends. Opa van den Bout gathered Huib on his lap for the last stretch of river toward the shore, and allowed Huib to hold the steering, which brought hearty giggles and smiles from his sunny grandchild.

As the summertime splendor was ending, the heath in the Hilversum countryside transformed from purple to golden ocher. Fields faded from amber to tawny, and later, chestnut brown. Their furlough nearly finished, in November they said so-long to beloved family and friends. Huib seemed downhearted to depart from Opa Dekker, as a bond had developed during their visit, their shared effervescence and true joy for living, the "*joie de vivre.*"

Dad placed sealed packages of Gouda and Edam cheese in his luggage, attempting to preserve the flavors of the Netherlands after Furlough, enjoying a taste of Europe while living in the tropics, if they could keep the cheese cool long enough once opened. Mam packed her extra suitcase with Maja soaps from Spain and lavender soaps from France, and small jars of rosewater and lavender, with Tosca 4711 to manage migraines. Scents of jasmine, bergamot, and orange blossom with a dash of patchouli comprised the distinct Tosca perfume.

Furthermore, she gathered peppermints, licorice, and spice cookies as gifts for their servants. Upon return to Batavia, the family celebrated Sinterklaas Day. On 5th of December, children placed their wooden shoes ready for Sinterklaas, with carrots for his horse, then awoke on 6th December to an array of goodies and gifts inside their wooden shoes: presents with jokes and poems attached, alongside candies and treats. After the holiday, they packed their home for moving. Pieter was transferred west on 29 December 1925 to another city on the island of Java called Bandung, where he was promoted to the role of First-Class Police Commissioner.

Bandung, West Java, Dutch East Indies, 1926

Tropical rainforests surrounded them, with nearby walks to waterfalls, and in the Dekker's backyard gardens birds chirped and crooned with songs Diny never imagined, glorious musical melodies never heard before. Near the flowing rivers were homes on stilts with palm-frond roofs; fruits dripping with syrupy sweetness like maroon guava, bright yellow mango, purple passion, spiny reddish rambutan, golden papaya, lime breadfruit, bright pink drops of dragon fruit, and carambola, those yellow star-shaped fruit. There were vibrant flowers unseen except for on these islands. Orchids abounded in thousands of varieties. This was a place as wild as possible, even more so than Batavia. There were rubber tree plantations in Bandung, and at market one morning, Cora heard from a neighbor that tigers roamed freely.

One Sunday evening, the Dekkers entertained friends from church on the front veranda, and tigers roared in the distance. The roars grew as they neared, bellows echoing through palm fronds and the river valley, while families socialized on the veranda. The distinctive roar of the tiger turned faces aghast. Diny's hairs on her arms stood on end, and she raced to Mam's lap, breathless, and buried her face in Mam's dress.

"Paps and Moesje!" Diny cried for her parents.

Their housekeeper *Baboe* dashed to the porch, screaming. The tiger was spotted preying upon their village, and ate a dog, the fateful pup's yelp sounding the alarm for shelter. Mothers scuttled their children into the safety of their homes, and Diny heard whispers.

"Perhaps they might construct a trap for the ferocious animal!"

"We must group together to hunt for the beast!"

As soon as the danger arrived, skilled warriors struck down the tiger.

Upon these islands, betel nut trees were used by men as chewing tobacco, as the deep red substance originated from the *sirim* tree, and leaves were used with an addictive seed wrapped inside the leaves. Mam warned Diny away from those betel nut trees. All the Indie men smoked their own local tobacco called *Kretek*, which had significantly higher amounts of nicotine. The blend was tobacco, cloves, and other various spices, like nutmeg and cumin, wrapped in banana leaves. The word "*Kretek*" was derived from the actual sound of cloves crunching and burning in the cigarette. Most Dutchmen who smoked were already addicted to their own European brands of cigarettes.

Dad cut a sliver off the bark and told Diny a story about the 1883 arrival of rubber plantations on the island of Java 60 km south of Batavia and 100km west of Bandung. When the city of Buitenzorg introduced the wonder of rubber to the world, rubber plantations quickly spread through the Indies. Workers harvested the extract, called sap, in a process called rubber tapping. They created a descending, circular cut into the bark, like ribbons running down and around the trunk, and thick rubber oozed out, slowly channeling through the groove, into a metal cup at the bottom of the tree.

Diny's fascination by the murky, earthy scent of rubber tapping grew as she watched Pieter peel tree bark, removing white substance from a vein in the tree, a material he called *latex*. Then he squeezed it, manipulating the material into a small roundish ball. The strands of rubber wound tightly into a ball, worthy of bouncing. Children peeled the bark of rubber trees, collecting the marrow and rolling it into sticky, bouncy balls.

During the mid-1800s Buitenzorg developed into a city of beauty, a leading area for industries, scientific institutions, a library, museums, and laboratories for biology and chemistry. The large botanical garden drew the Governor-General, who ruled over all the Dutch East Indies, and whose summer home was in Buitenzorg. Diny hoped to collect enough rubber to vault to school on a giant ball. Their recent relocation to Bandung proved profitable, and the children settled into another happy routine 150 kilometers southeast of their previous home in Batavia.

Cornelia's face displayed exhaustion, as caring for two children seemed to invite daily headaches. Soon her weariness was explained, as on 8 January 1926 a little sister, Pieternella Jannegja was born. They called her *Nelly*. Again, Diny fell in love with *her* new baby. Nelly had a creamy face, wisps of curly brown hair, and hazel eyes. Diny helped Mam as much as possible, as days at home were busier with three children to tend, and Mam needed Diny's assistance finding a cloth diaper, helping Huib with a game, or stroking Nelly's cheek to soothe her. Cornelia placed Nelly into the bamboo crib on the *voorgalerij* and sat Diny beside her sister in a wicker chair. Nelly settled into sleep, and later, when fussy, Huib's calming demeanor settled her, as Nelly demonstrated fussiness during evening meal time. Huibje was tender and cautious with his little sister Nelly, protective of her and proud to be her brother.

Cornelia breezed into the room wrapped in her dark *kebaya* covered with flowers, parasols, and butterflies. She leaned over the bamboo crib, her hair twisted up, face radiating the love she carried for her children. She glowed in pregnancy, the vibrancy of motherhood bringing great delight to her heart. Similarly, Pieter's gaze of love and admiration soared, and Mam set a pillow underneath their *voorgalerij* tablecloth, then placed Nelly atop, to take photographs as a family. Pieter leaned over, his arms resting upon the cloth, broad hands holding Nelly's delicate fingers, his face pleased with his daughter. Diny glanced up at her father, her face full of trust and love, as Huib obediently stared at Mam for the photograph. Under Dad's watchful eye, they were permitted to hold Nelly.

Each new morning, after Dad kissed them so-long enroute to work, the children spent hours outdoors, learning about God's creation. Mam pulled wicker chairs to the edge of the veranda, adjusted the cushions, and welcomed her children to their chairs for a lesson. They shared memory verses, prayed together, and Huib sang his own little song. His low, deep voice harmonized sweetly together with Diny.

In April, the family vacationed north of Soekaboemi for a month at Selabintanah Resort (a retreat center for Europeans, a holiday spot in the mountains of Mt. Gede and Mt. Pangrango), with crisp mountain air and quiet peace. The popularity of this place surged after a title for a classical *'keroncon'* song was released years prior: "Musim Bunga di Selabintana" (*Springtime in Selabintana*). Cooler mountains offered a place of leisure from work. The Dekker family toured expansive gardens, played in banyan tree groves, splashed in the swimming pool, hiked hilly areas, and rested away from Pieter's draining work schedule and politics.

Huib felt older and did not stay close to Mam. His mischievous demeanor surged, and he became a "real boy", though he was never truly naughty or ugly, as he avoided that which brought grief. After acting unruly and recalcitrant, he readily asked forgiveness, always contrite. His sweet demeanor remained *hartelijk* (hearty) and thankful. Diny carried a parasol everywhere they journeyed, and after Huib's apology, he removed his hat and his face turned scarlet in the sunshine, so she provided shade for him. He was always very sorry for his disobedience.

Dad joined a few other Dutch transplant fathers and took a men's trekking tour along a river, and walked across a long, rope-lined suspension bridge, narrow enough for only one person at a time. Meanwhile, Cornelia handed Diny and Huib round white hats to shade their faces and took a pony ride along the road to Wanasari. The shaded, stony path provided laughter for Cornelia, who commented on the rocky road ahead of them and the tremendous jostling ponies beneath them. Each pony required the guidance of a local boy who held the reins and walked ahead of them. The Dekker holiday in Selabintanah as a family further cultivated wonderful memories.

The entire year before Diny began her formal education in *big school*, Mam aimed to prepare her. They worked on schooling while Nelly napped. Huib insisted on joining them, as a big boy, so Mam taught Scripture verses and songs. Huib was four and learned quickly and soon knew long texts without mistakes. He seemed fond of spiritual pursuits, his dazzling blue eyes lit up with pleasure. Mam was amazed Huib could remember lengthy verses, and he delighted in the contentment he offered her. While Diny's temperament was full of spice and passion, Huib remained a peaceful, sunny child, the perfect companion for her animated antics.

Together, they played in the sandbox, created sand tarts, and fashioned a village for their sand world; he coaxed birds from hiding, and implored them to sing their jovial songs, as each bird carried a tune inimitable to their own expression. As summer ended and Diny's first school experience began, she awoke each morning excited to learn, honored for Dad to walk her to school.

Dad brought Diny to school right after breakfast, and Huib loved to come along as company. They lived five minutes walking distance from school, not far for Huib to walk too.

"*Dag*, Paap, *Dag, broertje!*" Diny called to them and waved.

"Bye!" They cheered. Huib walked proudly next to his tall father and as they journeyed back home, and remarked, "Man by man, huh Pap?" His hearty laughter was contagious.

Pieter rummaged in his pocket before squatting next to Huib and pressed a Wilhelmina peppermint into his hand. "This mint is a souvenir of our time in the Netherlands, son, and happy memories from our Furlough."

Huib smiled broadly at his dad and thanked him, then tucked the coin-shaped mint into his cheek. He reached for Pieter to carry him the rest of the way home.

Huib sat still and played contentedly with his blocks for hours. His soft heart for everything small extended to a tenderness and caution with Nelly, gently smoothing her wispy hair as she napped in the pram on their veranda. One afternoon during tea break as he caressed Nelly's hair, Huib caught sight of a yellow butterfly flickering nearby, and chased it until he caught and played with it, stroking the butterfly's wings.

"Gently, Huib! Play with butterflies tenderly, *Broertje*!" Diny shrieked.

"Yes *Dien*. I will try to be tender," Huib murmured, as a fragile yellow wing broke off the butterfly. Huib raced to Mam, holding the fractured insect in his tear-stained hand, begging her to help. "Mam, please fix the wing! Tenderly!" he cried.

She set aside her *koffietijd* teacup and saucer, then pulled a wailing Huib upon her lap. Mam warned, "*Lieverd*, this tiny butterfly is in pain now, so you must be careful next time when playing with little animals." She softly cupped his face and brushed away his tears, then encouraged him, "My dear, you must watch butterflies with your *eyes*, and follow their delightful fluttering that way, instead of petting their wings."

He cried, "Will the butterfly die?"

Mam's face became solemn as she set the butterfly aside on the floor of the veranda, underneath her chair, but she would not answer his question; instead, she enveloped Huib in her arms as she sang to him. He calmed and slept on her lap.

The next morning, Huib again saw a small yellow butterfly resting on a bush in the misty garden and called Diny over, exclaiming, "Look *Dien*, there is the butterfly again, and the Lord made a new 'leaf' on it!"

The yellow insect stretched into the sunlight and fluttered away. Then off Huib danced in the garden, near the low-hanging banyan trees, with his arms in the air, reaching toward the craggy-knob branches of the tree, under which the butterflies gathered, his cheery face lifted to the heavens.

Diny tucked her legs under her in the shadows of the veranda while watching him dance, and a bright yellow leaf tumbled at her feet, wafting in the wind. Huib's butterfly from the day before, which he lovingly and "tenderly" touched now lay crumpled before Diny. It was a brittle shell, which flittered along on the veranda ground in a gust of wind. Huib did not notice as Diny scooped up the soft yellow wings and tossed the remains into a bush beside the veranda. Unable to deflate his enthusiasm, she raced to join him under the airy canopy of butterflies.

Bandung, Dutch East Indies, 1927

Diny knew little of her father's job, of the challenges surrounding his role on the police force. From her cozy bed, Diny overheard her parents on the veranda, whispering each evening.

"Communist revolts are surging in cities, and will undoubtedly arrive here in Bandung," Pieter said. "It seems like the start of a greater uprising."

"And there have been many riots over the last year," her Mam said. "So how is this one different? What do they want?" She coughed sharply.

"Well, Cora, rebel insurgencies cost us all a lot of pain and money. The violence, destruction, and subsequent arrests, with over one thousand imprisonments… they require more police officers as a result."

"Pieter, money is not the problem. Think of their goal. Of what the riots mean."

"We have a budget to maintain, Cora. And the country's morale falls in times of unrest."

"The morale? How so? We live in a time of relative peace."

"The Dutch government still rules as a colony here. White European men oversee everything. Asian citizens hold limited rights and no chance for promotion. Cora, the fight for the Dutch East Indies will be bloody… the battle for freedom is inevitable…someday."

Their voices muffled and silenced; Diny fell asleep wondering about rebels and revolts.

Due to violent uprisings, the government expanded the police department, hiring many more police officers — both European and Indie — enlarging the organization, further brainstorming the best methods of refining their principles. The police force needed to sharpen their vision and create some order concerning their methods.

In the previous summer of 1926, the family vacationed for a month in Selabintanah Resort. On 12 August 1927, Huib turned four while on an overnight holiday, and they planned to honor him with a great celebration. He asked for an outdoor picnic and family walk, so they left early in the morning for Mount Gede Pangrango National Park for the day, to run through open wilderness and explore the mountain foothills. Diny marveled at the wild field of Javanese Edelweiss. The Edelweiss was an alpine flower Mam associated with great cheer and joy, and together they frolicked through the abundance of Edelweiss, which flourished and bloomed each August.

During his birthday picnic celebration, those flowers fully prospering into maturity, Huib found burnt orange and bright yellow Edelweiss. He picked flowers, and Mam assembled them into a bouquet, although Dad cautioned, "These flowers are momentary, and cannot grow away from their roots!" The children were horrified to learn those flowers would wither and crumble.

Mam shook her head and laughed. "Yes, as your father says, these flowers are temporary, but they will dry neatly at home, where we will keep the dried bundle safe in a vase."

Huib's birthday was a *leuk*, happy occasion with presents. They were only small gifts, but not in his eyes. When the family returned to their home and routines the next day, Mam attached a string to the bundle of colorful Edelweiss and hung the flowers upside down to dry.

After their return, Huib went with Mam to church on the 16th of August. His arrival at church marked his first time in a service, and he was so proud! It was on a weekday, and Diny attended school. The church gathering was a marriage ceremony — a short service — and when the money bag came by for the collection, Huib placed his hand inside to take something out, because he thought they were offering something to him for attending. Mam chuckled and explained they were collecting money, not giving it away.

Ten days after their return home from holiday, Huib was not his cheery self, but lethargic and exhausted. It was clear their beloved Huib was ill, and his condition deteriorated within hours. Dad took Huib to hospital, where he remained several days, but his fever exacerbated. Because of his youth, delicate condition, and a lack of treatment for his sickness, which the doctors called *meningitis*, the doctors said he must fight the meningitis fever on his own. The family prayed for Huib's healing, for comfort, and for his little body to regain its own momentum.

When her parents visited Huib in the hospital, Diny and Nelly remained with a couple she called "Tante and Oom," even though they were not her real aunt and uncle. Diny was prohibited from visiting Huib, due to the contagious nature of meningitis. During her days at their home, Diny listened to Tante and Oom's only child perform on the piano, their daughter's red hair bouncing aflame, her shoulders lifted with playing. Her kindness soothed Diny's fears and distracted her from doubts. Still, at night, Diny could only think about her beloved Huib with anguish.

On 27 August 1927, Huib's fighting spirit waned. The terrible angst of the meningitis proved too difficult an enemy to overcome, and Huib was carried to his Heavenly home. Their sweet Huibje died of meningitis; he would never again return to tenderly care for his animals or brighten their home.

Now their home was filled with grief and sorrow, darkness with windows closed, bamboo shades shut, an eerie stillness, each family member despondent in their own way. Six-year-old Diny cried into her bed, her pillow flattened and wet with bitter tears, full of loneliness, crying loudly for her *broertje*, as she missed Huib. Her tears increased as Diny learned she would not be permitted to see him, to say goodbye, or attend his funeral at church — the same church which housed incredible happiness only days before with the wedding Huib and Mam attended. Now their Bandung church held misery and grief, and no one was to ever mention him again. Huib's life became a forbidden memory, one of those *Tempo Doeloe* old times which faded eventually.

"No use ruminating on *Tempo Doeloe*, Diny," her Mam sternly reminded her. "We have no power to change the *past*."

After weeks of tears, every day awakening and thinking it was only a nightmare, followed by the realization he was gone, Diny discovered her mother collecting all Huib's toys: a carved wooden train, a rubber ball made from those bouncy rubber trees, metal spinning tops, and bright paper kites they flew in breezy evenings. Mam gathered all his tiny clothing, and his rock, leaf, and butterfly collections into a stack of possessions which comprised his life. It was a small grouping of items, all ordinary and without meaning, which only held value because her dear brother inhabited them. He brought them to life with his enthusiasm.

Mam took Huib's possessions and placed them into a basket, to keep in her closet. However, she removed the dried Javanese Edelweiss and placed it into a vase in her room, high up on a shelf, away from tiny hands, unable to bear losing a valued gift from her lost son.

Nelly remained Diny's solitary sibling, but her age precluded her from being a real playmate. Mam noticed vivacious Diny playing or reading, and paused, swollen with tears, to hold her daughter, whispering kindness, offering the loving comfort of a mother's soft hand stroking her daughter's hair, but unable to provide insight or understanding of Huib's death.

Dad's preoccupation at work or in his garden led to him walking down the road for air, for respite from pain. Mam remained quiet and reserved, resolved to accept this new reality, yet wrote memories of *Huibje* in a little book, and Diny felt in doing so her mother preserved Huib's memory. "Aan onze vroeg gestorven lieveling" – after her dear son passed away. The title: "In memory" (Ter Gedachtenis): He often sang, with a deep voice, so sweetly, the song:

"Klokje klinkt, vogel zingt,
Iedereen op zijne wijs.
Kind, ook gij. Zingt daarbij
Tot des Heren lof en prijs.

Bid en zing, want geen ding
Gaat er zonder bidden goed.

Leder kind, dat God mint,
Zingt hem met een blij gemoed.

Leer, O leer, tot de heer
Zingen, bidden elke stond.
God geniet graag een lied,
Stijgend uit der kindren mond."

* * *

"Clock sounds, bird singing,
everyone on his point.
Child, also shall sing therefore
To the glory and praise of God.

Pray and sing, because nothing
goes without praying well.
Each child God created,
Sing it with a happy heart.

Learn, O learn, to God
We sing, we pray where we stand,
God loves to enjoy a song,
Rising out of the children's mouths."

With Diny, together they sang so sweetly. He often played with Diny the little game called "Handkerchief Lay":

Zakdoekje leggen,
Niemand zeggen,
"Ku-kele-kuu," zei kraait onze de haan.
Ik heb mooie schoentjes ann,
Twee paar schoenen heb ik aangedaan
één van stof en één van leer,
Hier leg ik mijn zakdoekje neer.

Handkerchief lay,
Never say,
"Kukeleku" as the rooster crows.
I only have two pairs of shoes:
Of a fabric and a leather,
Here I put my handkerchief down.

A few months before Diny went to the "big" school, Mam played "school" with Dien and Huib, teaching from Luke 2:14, "Ere zij God in de hoogste hemelen, vrede op aarde, in de mensen een welbehagen." "Glory to God in the highest, and peace on earth, good will toward men." Huib knew the text without a mistake and Mam shared from the Bible and sang with them. He liked that so much — his eyes would light up with pleasure.

* * *

Mam's eyes were wild and her countenance despondent for a time. Who can fathom the depth of pain, the emptiness of soft arms which once held a vivacious child? Her hands had soothed and bathed Huibert as a newborn and held his wiry body in the cleft of her arm to pacify him. He nuzzled her neck as she burped his tiny back after a nighttime feeding, then wiped warm milk from his cheek. After bath time, she gently combed his soft hair. As he grew into a toddler, and then a boy, Huib became sunnier and more amiable. His smiles brightened her soul, his deep voice sang so sweetly. Diny thought if she could see Huib's photographs and read stories about his life, perhaps he would remain alive in her memories. The door sealed on Huib's life on Earth, as his brief time here seemed simple, depraved of the fullness an expanse of seventy years afforded.

With Huib's life complete, the family realized his healing had come, and their prayers had been answered — yet healing through Huib's death. Death never held the final, absolute answer, the last word. Huib was offered Real Life, which began the moment he breathed in Earth, a final moment out, and traded his body for a perfect one, in Heaven with Jesus. This truth brought peace and hope, although they realized profound wounds never healed within a lifetime.

Pieter assured them that while Huib's life was precious, and his kind compassion and gentleness a rare treat, his time here was finished. Any dream or hope for the future, ambition or promise, was not intended for Huib's life. This was a difficult reality to accept.

Some late afternoons, beyond tea and the lighting of candles, and again refusing music on the gramophone, following the moments their daughters settled into sleep, Pieter and Cornelia nestled silently together in wicker chairs on the veranda, each settled into their own cushioned seat, separate from the other, simmering in memories.

Together they watched the orange sun lower into the tall clusters of mangrove and banyan trees, burnt golden air billowing through sturdy bamboo and fragrant orchids. That evening, a dazzling, hypnotic light refused to dim before reluctantly lowering and succumbing into surrounding darkness.

Before the dark engulfed them, Pieter whispered, "My dear Cora," and reached across the divide to grasp Cornelia's hand. They held each other during frail, brief minutes, fading seconds, a hesitant breath, the temporary golden moment of sunset remained magical and almost tangible, the thick yellow haze of peace and tranquility edible, yet short-lived. After those amber moments, the sunlight, the sparkle, faded. The most brilliant colors are for a short season. After the brevity of light seeps into the evening, and beyond, shadows surround; only a memory can invoke the inimitable interlude.

Time, which faded sunlight, and brimmed new seasons and cycles, might lessen the pain of wounds. And over galloping seasons, time delivers other changes: like a broken bone which has been painfully injured, too wounded on the inside and requiring a new setting to mend properly. The marrow heals, sealing together, yet always leaves a seam of inward scarring, of a break and a subsequent restoration. The split edge of brokenness may have healed, but fracture line remains visible, even if only through judicious examination. The bone regenerates, as the body learns to adapt to an agonizing alteration. Yet an approaching storm can instigate an unexpected ache, a swell of humidity or heavy memory, and the wound — once closed and cared for — requires additional tending.

Chapter Three
Batavia, Dutch East Indies, late 1927

Time pressed forward for the Dekker family. In late 1927, Pieter again transferred back to Batavia — promoted with distinction as Commissioner in the Cities Police Investigations Department, supporting Governor General Master Cornelius. Just a few months after Huib's death, they packed their belongings and journeyed. Diny sorrowfully left Huib's grave in Bandung, her grief compounded by the pain of Opa Dekker, who, upon receiving the sad telegram of Huib's death, ran from the house, seeking refuge in his garden, the Reverend in his sanctuary.

For a time, Pieter also found respite from grief in his gardens, and wandered back to the veranda for tea before drifting to the gardens again for sunset. Nelly napped in her pram near the divider wall and cooed occasionally. Diny sat stiffly in a new linen dress as Mam handed her the prepared tea.

"Where is Huib now?" Diny asked her parents. She picked at the hem of her dress and pulled at a ragged string. Mam cleared her throat to prevent Diny from unstitching the hem and unraveling the sewing. Dad sipped his tea and stared at the ground.

Diny continued, "And, what is Huib doing?"

Her dad shook his head, his tea cup rattled, and he gazed at her with a sorrowful face.

"Does Huib have someone to play with in Heaven?" She raced to her bedroom to find *bikkelen*, her jacks game, and brought the bag of jacks and balls back to the veranda. Diny's brown eyes lit up with hope, as she felt eager to play with a friend as cheery and happily dispositioned as her dear *broertje* Huib.

Pieter placed his teacup on the tray, then held Diny's hands and a *bikkelen* game. For a moment it seemed he would speak, and he opened his mouth, but no words emerged. He could only embrace her. They all sat in silence on the veranda for the remainder of tea time. Diny's parents could not offer her any answer which eased her grief. They all lingered Somewhere beyond the Already and on the road to the Not Yet. She knew Huibert dwelled in Heaven and she would someday reunite with him. She believed he was happy and safe and not alone.

After several months, the Dekker family found a new rhythm for their life in Batavia, and Diny asked to take a boat on the waterways, hoping to ride on the Ciliwung River to explore their city. At seven years old — an age of discovery — Diny longed to stretch outwards, the mysterious existence her parents had not yet enlightened her about concerning the world beyond. Her growth at school felt exhilarating, she matured in reading and writing and new cultures through her studies. Her friendships at school smartened her astute ability to learn. Yet, Diny longed for genuine experience, to encounter directly, not through a story.

Mam and Dad rode the *becak*, pedaled carts powered by strong local men, which ferried passengers through bustling Batavian streets and alley passageways, easily maneuvering and shifting. One could just as effortlessly complete the ride on the becak as walk to the destination. Likewise, Diny expressed her delight for a leisurely afternoon touring the inner-workings of Dutch villages they explored during Furlough three years prior. She had few memories as a four-year-old, but a photograph assisted her in remembering. She relished the afternoon cruising an Amsterdam canal boat with her family and expected a Batavian boat to match the enchanting Dutch journey.

After much persistence, Pieter and Cornelia agreed to take Diny on a boat ride. Early into the Colonial Age of the Dutch East Indies, canals were created. The Dutch were oblivious to the possibility of mosquitoes bringing malaria and other water-born illnesses plaguing balmy countries like the Indies. The tropical climate prevented the deep hard-freeze with which those in the Netherlands were familiar.

While the canals delivered beauty, light, presence and place to their lives, the Ciliwung River was a major access waterway, and cargo boats squeezed through with merchant fare, leaving the country for distant ports, or entering the city to deliver shipments. Remnants of old sugar cane factories scattered the shorelines, leaving behind discarded a hollowed-out frame of a factory, long-since burned, polluting the river.

Dotting the way along the Ciliwung lay vestige villages consisting of metal patchwork shanty homes haphazardly pieced together, and huts composed of banyan knobby tree branches. Many islanders could only afford a medley of jumble homes, an array of discarded metal scraps as a mismatched puzzle consisting of rusted, precarious items. Next to soldered, patchwork shanty homes balanced withered furniture sets, including frayed wicker chairs like the chairs Diny's family housed in their veranda. Yet these chairs were piled, broken and splintered, discarded remnants from colonial homes. Beside the homes stacked a pair of woven baskets, used for daily chores. Diny watched a woman heap dirty linens into a woven basket and place it on top of her head. Then with a steady head, she hazardously made her way down the banks into the murky water to wash the laundry in the darkened pools of the river.

Farther downstream, another woman squeezed out wet clothing, heaping it into a woven basket, then hoisted the basket on her head for the rickety hike upslope toward her patchwork shanty hut and the tattering line to hang her laundry. Children bounded about between homes, providing alternating noises of crying or laughing. Lines of rope hung between homes, and wet laundry dried in the wind like colorful flags fluttering on fraying rope. Those huts seemed fragile, unsteadily placed close to the shoreline, restricted to polluted shorelines.

Meanwhile, cramming the banks of the Ciliwung River, other women bathed children in the busy water. And in other portions of the canal (and up the river, their driver told them), children trapped animals or dumped waste. The filth introduced to the river intermingled with attempts at cleaning and bathing, resulting in a swirling of bacteria and filth. Coughs, disease, mosquitoes, and general sickness pervaded. The Dutch charm and idealism of a tidy canal system was lost in the tropics. Waringins and rubber and banana trees populated the lush landscape, and provided minimal privacy from those navigating the waters.

Beyond, along those same shores, on the opposite, manicured banks of the Ciliwung River, homes of the money-making elite built up around existing mangrove and palm trees, conveniently obscuring the river poverty with trees and bushes, evading the deficiency on the opposite side of the river. The length of the backyard provided separation from the river people, stretching farther away from the water's edge. They all shared the Ciliwung River, but with class distinctions and prejudices. Diny's group sailed past the *Tokar Merah* (Red House) with its red bricks and painted façade, which housed a luxurious indoor setting with dark mahogany wood.

The connectivity of port with portal, traversing boats and other water taxis offered Indie locals a paddle to work on canal systems or daily income in ferrying others through murky waters. A woman wearing a bell-shaped straw hat sat in a long open rowboat in the brown water, palms together as she smiled, bowing a respectful hello. Her boat was a floating store, with buckets of merchandise, baskets filled with shoes, bins of hats, folded blankets, parasols: a livelihood in a rowboat, hovering along the water.

Through each effort of physically transforming Batavia, erecting stately buildings or carving out a waterway, those same elites required efforts of those hard-working islanders. Those locals were never offered the opportunity as the highest-paid employees or the president of the company. Dutch colonists created a privileged upper social class of all Dutch: pioneers, soldiers, administrators, teachers and managers. Their daily lives intermingled with islanders, but at the top of a rigid social and racially determined caste system remained white European males. This noticeable inequity — the social system of cultural inequality — concerned the Dekker family, unable to favor societal mandates rather than sidestep their Christian beliefs of God's love for all. They could live a more insulated, secluded lifestyle if necessary, but not at the cost of their commitment to Jesus.

Soekaboemi, Java, Dutch East Indies, late 1928

The Javanese jungle consisted of untamed, wild expanse and tropical mazes. It was a place roaming with tigers, monkeys, and rhinos, or so Diny heard. She relied on her vivid imagination to catapult daydreams, and their hired servants possessed natural story-telling abilities, sharing magical myths along with mystical folklore, of bloody expeditions seeking extinct animals or rare flowers, swampy explorations to discover ancient religious stone structures, or lava-spewing volcanoes their ancestors had conquered, living in the shadows of towering angry mountains.

The Dekker family now lived in a different section of the thin, horizontal island of Java, 100km south of Batavia, inland, amidst jungles, near their vacation spot of Selabintanah. Pieter was promoted to assist with creating an official Soekaboemi Police Training Academy. His role multiplied in becoming the Adjunct-Chief Superintendent of Police, and Inspector, and he accepted this monumental task with enthusiasm and charisma.

Within the police force, Pieter's reputation blossomed with strong values, courage under pressure, and decisive composure. His steady work ethic — integrity coupled with discernment and optimism — provided unique opportunities. Forming the Police Academy served as a challenge, developing the next generation of policemen to lead and manage the country within the traditions of integrity coupled with moral courage. Although the Police Academy was established in 1914, it carried little prestige among all ranks, as some believed the entire premise involved elder men telling stories from their experiences without textbooks or curriculum. Instead, only upper-class police officers attended, learning mostly moral and situational ideals.

In the early 1920s, the academy opened for nearly all ranks of police, at which time Pieter attended, yet the leadership had not established a centralized core of curriculum; thus, alumnus Dekker and others were called in to develop a curriculum. Pieter had been hired to refine principles and create order concerning policing methods.

The Police Academy program would be composed of three areas. First, they would teach new recruits the use of arms (rifles, pistols, and sabers), along with semi-military discipline with physical exercise and mental constancy, observing and reporting. They learned methods of acting professionally — in a robust, controlled, and dignified way. This training required ongoing regulation and consistency.

Second, recruits would learn in-depth principles of a constitutional state, criminal law and justice, and methods and rules of civilized modern policing — including restrictions on police power, and instructions on the use of physical force — issues of temperance to delay the use of violence when handling public safety concerns.

Third, police officers were instructed in "cultivation and progress," to bring order, decency, safety, and cleanliness into every society. The modern police were trained in how to act professionally and "in a strong, constrained, sedate way, and to postpone violence as long as possible while dealing with any public security problem." The central idea remained of *"rust en orde"* (law and order) and *"zaman normal"* (normal times). Rank was determined via row, line, series, military standing, and social class.

The Association for Inspectors and Head-Inspectors of Police in the Netherlands Indies began in the early 1920s and reflected the requirement for police professionalization and civilization from within the police force. The image of police should be presented in a firm, upright and effective way to provide the social need for safety, and to illustrate police as a tool of the colonial forces of civilization: *oom agent* (Uncle Agent) in the *desa* (village), who reports infectious diseases, ensures everyone keeps their yards neat and tidy, and behaves well.

Dekker's colleagues, Tacoma and Smith, were men of valor, whose characters had matured into their current roles. Johan Hendrik Smith arrived in the Indies in 1921 after an already-decorated career in the Netherlands, showing his promise in the police force. His zeal was contagious, and he began teaching at the Police Academy in 1923, providing a refreshing change of pace and atmosphere, and developing a written curriculum. Smith instructed on Scientific Research, Dactyloscopy (fingerprinting), and Signalement Doctrine (navigation). His colleague S.H. Tacoma joined in the writing of the handbook, beginning in early 1929. Their writings included ideas shaped over centuries of policing into a handbook for police officers.

The handbook included government policy concerning laws, ethical practices, manners of behaving, and police practices and tactics, all of which was of interest for upper administration and judicial power. It was an overall collection of administrative prescriptions and general regulations. The handbook opened with government policy, and commissioned students to become a force of "men of high principles of life, strong moral and character traits." The academy graduates would serve "as a tool of 'civilization' to bring order, safety, cleanliness, and decency into colonial society." With J.H. Smith, Dekker created a quick guide for officers, education on ordinances for entry-level staff. Smith could use this curriculum as he taught new academy recruits.

The Dekker family grew accustomed to living without modern conveniences their family in the Netherlands and other affluent Europeans afforded, although their homes from one Indie village to another were similar, with pillars and an entry gate. Homes featured a *voorgalerij* (veranda) at the front, with lush gardens surrounding the home, and inside the home, cool marble floors. The same designs were alike from one location to the next.

In distant conversations in the evenings, while lingering on the cusp of sleep yet still attuned to the noises of daily life, Diny overheard her parents speaking of the Depression which gripped the world, even the Netherlands. They mourned jobs lost alongside hopes for recovery.

However, Dad's employment training recruits at the Police Academy afforded the family to hire servants who helped their household, providing an allowance for a lack of modern machines for washing and cooking. Hiring paid servants to assist in managing the household remained a several-centuries-old customary practice in the Indies, and Pieter always paid them above a fair wage. His salary helped local families provide for their children.

Cornelia eagerly anticipated beginning a new season of their lives with their move to Soekaboemi. She set out to assemble a celebration for Pieter's new role at the Police Academy and to become acquainted with other staff members and their families by hosting a festive party at their home. Perhaps extending outwardly could help the Dekkers celebrate the cultures of the Indies and become better adjusted as community leaders. Cora decided upon a welcoming *rijsttafel* (rice table), an elaborate collection of forty man dishes representing the different islands. Rijsttafel consisted of meats, vegetables, salads, and fruits, with garnishes of pickles, nuts, and egg rolls served as sides in smaller portions. White steamed rice was the central canvas for adding flavors and side dishes.

For the week leading up to the banquet, their staff prepared prevalent Dutch East Indies dishes like Nasi Goreng (fried rice), vegetarian meals of Gado Gado, Lodeh (jackfruit and vegetable coconut soup); Javanese dishes like peanut Saté Babi (skewered grilled pork) with Katjang Saus (peanut sauce), Kip Saté (skewered grilled chicken), and Babi Kecap (pork in sweet soy); Balinese Chicken; Sumatran dish Rendang (dried meat, coconut milk, chili, and spices, which preserved the meat for weeks). They made Saté Daging (marinated chicken on bamboo sticks), fusion foods like Filipino-influenced Loempia (meat/vegetable egg rolls) and Bamie (Chinese wheat noodles with meat); ubiquitous but fragrant Pisang Goreng (fried banana fritters), Atjar, a cool, crunchy cucumber salad to soften the spicy Sambal bite (a spicy relish), and kroepoek emping crackers (shrimp chips).

The dishes were served on white glass plates, lined precisely on a banquet table with crisp white linens, fragrant dishes surrounding the versatile clean base of white rice. The various textures, flavors, spices, and temperatures of foods provided a rewarding — and colorful — dining experience to enhance all the senses.

Dad held a prosperous future in police work, and Mam optimistically determined to settle into their life quickly, as she was pregnant and expecting another child. Mam never mentioned little Huib, although Diny noticed her face pale when they drove past the Selabintanah resort. While Diny's mind fixed upon her disappointment at leaving her school friends in Bandung, Pieter and Cornelia appeared eager to set out on an adventure, as their mindset was always upon the next challenge.

Mam seemed thankful to settle into their home before her next child arrived, as she surmised any move deemed easier while pregnant than while tending to a newborn. Diny started a new school, a quaint walk just down the lane, which had a welcoming feel. It was full of local community opportunities and cheerful Dutch families. Several students also had fathers in leadership roles at the Police Academy.

Soekaboemi, Java, early 1929

On 7 February 1929, Diny's brother was born. They decided to call him *Jan*, after Dad's father, and he was Diny's "yawn," as his name was pronounced. "His name rhymes with *fawn*," Diny whispered to her Mam. Right away Diny felt Jan was "her baby," as she was almost 8 years old, and Nelly 3 years old. For a moment, Diny was afraid to love Jan, wondering, "What if he becomes sick, like Huib? What then?" He did not answer her questions. Diny helped bathe Jan and smiled at him. Jan held a special place in her heart right from the beginning. His face was pleasant, and he looked like Diny's mirror image, a pleasant and hearty baby.

"He is beautiful and healthy, *Moesje*," Diny reassured her Mam.

While Diny loved the challenge of school and the opportunity for creating groups of diverse friendships, she missed her little sister and brother, and as soon as she returned home each afternoon, she raced to their sides for kisses. Mam fed Jan while managing her children, urging Diny toward a chore or a book they were reading. Diny preferred running outside, strengthening her legs and breathing the air, staring at the sky, feeling the sun welcoming her, remembering Huib and his love of nature.

At other times, Diny was as absorbed in reading books as in any personal task, especially as her teacher encouraged students to read as much as possible. Mam urged Diny to remain in bed at night so Diny might receive the rest needed for the following day. Yet her desire to read about the lives of others was entirely too compelling. Evenings consisted of family time, and the dreams glimmering in Diny's father's eyes and in her mother's smile, of possibility. Pieter brought home a radio one Sunday afternoon and told them, "This radio receives broadcasts all the way from the Netherlands!"

Eight-year-old Diny was awed to consider that a wooden triangular box created noise. "Mr. Halkema told me about the Happy Station Show on

Sundays, so I thought we could join in and listen, to see if we like the story," Pieter said, checking the clock for the appropriate time Sunday evening.

Cornelia examined the brown box and shook her head. "I heard Mrs. Maseland talk about the first international radio broadcast last year, but I had no idea what she meant!"

Pieter plugged the box into the outlet in the wall, and a zap of static circulated, much like the beginning of a record playing. There were noisy levels of humming and distorted, blurred scratches, then the anticipation of a song. Dad looked through the instructions, found a volume adjustment knob and a station-tuning knob, and evened out the static until finding the Philips shortwave station PHOHI: *Philips Omroep Holland-Indië.*

Suddenly, a voice came from the box. Eddie Startz introduced them to the *Happy Station Show*, and the family sat together, entertained, while music and comedy resounded from the radio. Another *leuk* — jolly — happy, daily tradition grew within their family.

In the hollow of the night, the earth sometimes shook, and Diny felt great fear. Her home was her world, and she misunderstood the grander world around her. She and Nelly raced to their parents' bedroom, and Dad reminded them of God's grace and mercy. Tiny Jan never rustled from his slumber in the bassinet, but slept through earthquakes, as though dreams drew him away from reality. Diny wished to have the same peace.

During daytime earthquakes, Mam said, "look out the window at palm trees bending over, palmetto fronds touching the grass. They look like flamingos, their heads touching the ground, long necks bent. The palm trees sway not by wind but by the shaking ground!"

In daytime earthquakes, Diny closed her eyes and covered her ears, or sometimes crouched in a ball on the ground. Perhaps during the next daylight event, she would glance out the window at dancing, bending trees.

The day after night earthquakes, enroute to school, Diny observed the broken ground, with new cracks and fissures. The street lurched with each quake and as she jumped over the crevices, hopscotching, she realized the world was fractured. This fertile soil, which produced spices and bird songs, undoubtedly remained unpredictable and undomesticated. Diny also feared volcanoes. The volcanoes Mount Salak, Mount Kiaraberes-Gagak, and Mount Perbakti-Gagak were observed from their home and alternatively emitted vapor. Heavy steam escaped from the mountain like smoke ascending from a fire.

Mam called the most predominant, menacing volcano "Mount Merapi," and Diny felt the rumbling wrath roaring through their home, with pulsations pounding in her chest. The thundering volcano's force magnified as it groaned and grumbled, and they watched the eruption spew at night, crimson lava exploding upward, churning some agitated force on sharp black rocks. Vermilion poured from the mountain, scalding its way down valleys.

In past holidays, they visited decimated, barren fields, lands black from volcanoes now set with solid volcanic rock, and her parents assured Diny the ground had cooled. On nights when she watched the fury unfurl from a safe distance, Diny's mind returned to the changes of the earth, the capricious momentum to which they all were subjected.

The next morning the air hovered thick with ash, and their servants arrived wearing facial masks, shaking their head about the bad omen of the red sun and smoke-filled air. By evening, the sky paled into a white haze, the air blank and obscure. As Diny tried to sleep, the smoldering sun descended beyond trees, casting flickering shadows on the wall. In between black shadows were orange flutters dancing upon the wall like flames, a silhouette of shaking leaves through the smoke-hazed sun.

Dad's new assignment in Soekaboemi required months to research the highest levels of policing. He interviewed police officers and commanders, and wrote at night next to a lantern. They trained new police recruits in becoming a police officer, with the character and personality requirements needed for a successful career. Pieter completed the police manual with co-authors Smith and Tacoma. The book was entitled, *De politie in nederlandsch-indie; hare beknopte geschiedenis, haar taak, haar bevoegdheid, organisatie en optreden* (*The Police in Dutch-Indie: Her Brief History, Mission, Competence, Organization and Action*), published in Soekaboemi in 1929. The shortened title: *The Standard Operating Manual for Police Officers.*

This assignment also provided a new financial opportunity to hire paid helpers in their home. Diny noticed their helpers did not have the same color of skin as she did.

"Mam, my skin is like the bark of a lighter colored tree, or maybe a bamboo plant," Diny told her laughing mother. "Or like ginger, where my friend's skin is cinnamon." She had heard the analogy before, and enjoyed using spices as comparisons. "But our helpers' skin is dark, like cloves or ground cumin, or as the sea looks at midnight."

Mam smiled at eight-year-old Diny's dramatic description. "Remember Diny, every person is just as unique and loved by God as every other person." Mam was correct, and until she scrutinized their hired helpers, Diny never considered the coloring of her skin.

Their family hired various helpers to assist their lives. They employed a "*Djongos*," a man butler, who dusted and cleaned rooms (except bedrooms), and mopped the big, white square marble floors every afternoon.

"The white marble floors date from the times when the Portuguese were in the Indies," Dad said, "and those smooth stone floors keep our house cool from heat, and mopping keeps it fresh from dust."

Their family employed an excellent cook, "*Kokki*," whose laughter echoed through their home. Mam discussed the menu in advance, so Kokki and Djongos shopped at the market according to anticipated meals.

Storing food without spoiling remained a challenge, yet they owned an ice box where they stored small quantities of items in their kitchen. A large block of ice sat in an upper region of an insulated compartment, in which frigid air circulated down to the food. Each day a fresh block of ice was delivered, and the box was only large enough for a few days-worth of food. Underneath the four legs of the ice box, Kokki placed *bakjes* (trays) with carbolic, so ants stayed out. Simple staples like cheeses, milk, meats, butter, and eggs could be stored in the ice box.

As evening approached, Djongos prepared the veranda table with a tablecloth, cloth napkins, silverware, and glasses, and an arrangement of blooms in a vase, then welcomed the Dekkers to the diner table. He carried glass dishes filled with fragrant food to the table, then cleared dirty dishes to the kitchen, where Kokki washed and stored them. In the evening, Djongos sprayed the rooms against mosquitoes and prepared netting over the beds, then lit torches around the perimeter of the veranda.

They employed a "*Baboe*," the maid, who washed and ironed clothes, made the beds each morning, and kept bathrooms and bedrooms clean. Baboe cleaned their clothes and sheets on a washing board, with nicer clothes washed delicately by hand. Baboe seemed a constant bustling of energy, never slowing or lacking in activities to accomplish. She said there were always chores and tasks which dictated her day.

Some Dutch families hired a nanny Baboe for bathing, dressing, and grooming all the children and keeping them presentable, but Cora decided to accomplish those tasks on her own, personally caring for her children. She delighted in nurturing her small children, feeding them at the veranda table, bathing them, and singing while dressing them, taking them on walks, and teaching them about God. Mam assumed responsibility and felt honored for the marvelous opportunity to weave stories of the Lord's unswerving grace and goodness and to raise her children to know God.

Finally, they hired a "*Kebon*," a gardener who kept precise maintenance of the yard. The *Kebon* efficiently kept their gardens tidy, healthy, and thriving, encouraging the flowering orchids, bamboo, teakwood, or rambutan to flourish, clipping and pruning. When Pieter meandered in the lush estate to speak to Kebon, they discussed the plants and flowers of the estate and the simple pleasures of a well-situated garden.

Diny learned from her parents to pay a fair wage and respect the servants, and to extend goodness, benevolence, and grace. She learned to say "*minta*" (please), when asking for something. Their Indie helpers were caring, respectful, and welcoming. The servants were faithful and loyal, devoted to Pieter and Cora, and fond of the children.

The presence of helpers also brought comfort to the family, as Mam lived with what Dad called "fragile health." Mam occasionally felt sick due to oppressive heat, and when she had terrible, debilitating headaches, Diny did not know what to do to help her. Mam's severe pain sometimes combined with vomiting and she would rest in bed. Cora closed her bedroom door so the children would not be subjected to her condition. The tropical humidity often brought pain and angst to Cornelia.

When Diny entered the house after school, she knew if Mam was sick simply from the aroma. If the air permeated cooking spices, she found Mam sewing on the veranda. Yet if their home smelled of jasmine, bergamot, and orange blossom, she knew just where to find Mam: in bed. For her headaches, Mam used Tosca 4711 perfume, with a distinctive floral-citrus scent to mask the sickness and provide a fresh fragrance in her head. That aroma represented illness, in Diny's mind.

In Pieter's new role heading the Police Academy, the only car they owned was the company car, and they could not use it for family travel. Only her dad used it for his work. Dad arrived home from work for lunch, to join family togetherness for the daily warm meal at 12 o'clock, followed by a nap for the entire family. Then, Pieter went back to work from 2-4 o'clock. At 4 o'clock they took turns and enjoyed a refreshing bucket-shower, using a large tin (which previously held their butter). Djongos cleaned out the tin, then fastened a wooden handle to the tin from side to side, the *"gajong."* They scooped water out of a deep-water basin with the *gajong* and poured the water over their heads. Wonderful! And so invigorating! After the bucket bath, they enjoyed tea on the veranda, feeling refreshed and cooled. For tea time, *Djongos* brought the tea and cups, and *Kokki* made something delicious and sweet, like fried bananas with powdered sugar, a chilled coconut drink, or cookies made from tropical fruit. *Lekker!* It was so delicious!

As a small toddler, when Diny used her own teacup and saucer, Mam prepared her tea with some milk and sugar. And Mam stirred it. All Diny had to do was drink the tea and enjoy it, which did not sound fun to her. Diny wanted the spoon to stir, the milk to pour, and the sugar to scoop and swirl, and sometimes eagerly grabbed these items and made a mess. Dad did not allow for untidiness, even though Diny simply wanted to learn.

Dad softly tapped her hand and warned, "No, no, Diny, just drink your tea."

She simply waited awhile and watched her dad, and slowly but surely her hand went back to the spoon. More taps followed, every time a little bit stronger, and although Diny would not give up fast, Dad always won. As she matured, Diny prepared her own tea.

Later, when they ate their evening meal, Diny was not fond of a warm meal, but just wanted dessert. Talking instead of eating did not help her with the task of finishing her meal, so Dad placed her at a small table in her bedroom, alone, with her dinner.

"*Duduk* in your chair until you are finished. *Sit* in your seat, Gerardina."

She slumped into the chair.

Many times, he stood at her doorway, asking, "Are you finished?"

She replied, "Diny wants dessert."

He sternly reminded her to eat dinner and lectured her on the benefits of moderation in life, then left her alone. Soon, the sky outside became dark, and Diny grew scared and promised to eat her (now-cold) dinner. She did, sitting on her father's lap, a cozy place to remain. And then the dessert tasted sweeter than ever. Diny was refractory and obstinate, not an easy child for her parents. But she was surrounded by a lot of love.

Another time, weeks later, she spoke disrespectfully, sassy in her tone toward her father. As she talked back, he slapped her in the face with his big hands. (Big hands, big ears!) Her reading glasses went flying off, onto the ground.

"Huh! Well! They did not even break!" Diny said, which further infuriated her father.

While being raised by loving parents, Diny also realized Dad was the disciplinarian, and his word was law. As his daughter, her complete obedience was required. Since she was unable to see God in the flesh, she settled for her father's example in life, of a Heavenly Father unseen but realized through the imperfect relationship of father and daughter.

Diny felt great admiration for her dad, and he was an optimist, with a compelling, booming laugh. He would bend over, tears of joy seeping from his eyes. Pieter was a humble hard worker and although he reached an extremely prominent position in the police force, he never boasted about his position. She felt thankful that although she could not commune with God over a cup of tea, her earthly father spent time with her, playing, laughing, taking walks, and investing in his family for their spiritual, social, and emotional needs.

At home, Mam was a wonderful hostess and housewife. The servants loved her, and she never had a problem with them where they would quit their job and leave. They would stay, they promised, just as long as the family was stationed in Soekaboemi. Their hired staff held differing religious beliefs than the Dekkers, but Mam only discussed God with her children and not their household staff.

"Jesus' greatest command is to love the Lord with all our heart, mind, soul, and strength," Mam reminded Diny and Nelly. "And secondly, God calls us to love others. If we seek to accomplish those important tasks, then everything else will fall into place." If they concentrated on those two principles, Mam was certain their entire world would be a more loving, thriving environment.

Monsoon season emitted rivers of rain water running off from homes and thirsty palm trees, mangroves, banana trees and banyans, gathering momentum and roaring down hills toward the Java Sea. Foliage slowed the rate of pace, yet rain expelled from the heavens, unleashing torrents of water. Local children splashed in undulating monsoon waters, anticipating the thrill of floating down streets amid the rainwater.

Banana trees, with thick long green trunks, and wide-leafed palm branches served as a canopy over growing clusters of green banana fruit, water pouring through to soak the crops. Diny anxiously stood under their veranda, watching islander children splash in the water, squealing with delight. Mam warned her of the sudden fury of unpredictable rivers, along with the filth within the waters, and Diny was forbidden to join the children in their rain dance. Their open veranda on the porch was a number of steps up from ground level to avoid flooding.

Each night, as she drifted to sleep, sounds of the jungles traveled into Diny's room, of creaking rubber trees, chirping crickets, and reverberating frogs. Those sounds stayed with her always and brought her comfort.

In a nightmare, however, she found Huib again, several years after his death, both entangled in thick, muddy branches of swampland mangrove trees near the docks, their bodies saturated in fear, engulfed in disbelief. Huib never escaped the snarled nonsense, but urged her to swim onward, all while smiling and sinking underwater.

When she awoke sweating, panting from her dream, she remembered Huib's head above water as her nightmare ended, yet her mind was disturbed at his calm presence in her nightmares. She expected the Java Sea to be a wavy mess of black ink, luring her further out toward Surabaya, and sea creatures, and the unknown beyond.

In August 1929, Pieter received a brief telegram from a younger brother, telling him the dreadful news his dear father Jan had died. He knew the day would arrive when he received sad news but hoped for a longer stretch of life with him. After all, Father Dekker seemed healthy and robust, content at age 71, nearly fourteen years older than his wife Gerdina, now a widow at 57. They experienced nearly 37 years of marriage, serving as an example.

When Pieter told the children of Opa's death, Diny was most visibly upset, as she was close to her grandparents, being the eldest Dekker grandchild, and Huib surely would have remembered Opa and their lively reading adventures together, but Huib was also gone, and his death had greatly affected Opa Dekker. Nelly and Jan were born in the meanwhile and never met Opa.

Diny remembered their visit four years before, and he smelled of pipe and soap. Opa Dekker read books aloud with a lively voice, animating each character, which Huib had tried to replicate. They were so similar in personality, boisterous and excited, and now both Huib and Opa Dekker were gone.

She was full of questions as Pieter processed the news with grief and stared at Jan, who at seven months old would never know his grandfather, his namesake. Diny wondered where her Opa Jan went, and would she see him again? Pieter shared about Jan's entrance into Heaven and the promise of Hope for those who love God. He explained the message as clearly as possible for her to understand. She was eight years old, and suddenly, hearing about Opa Jan and his welcome into Heaven, the message of God became real and alive in her heart.

Soekaboemi, Java, 1930

Pieter's handbook *The Standard Operating Manual for Police Officers* had been completed for a year and found great success. All police civil servants received the handbook, in addition to the code for criminal law, and Pieter remained Inspector and Adjunct Chief Superintendent of Police. His love for Cora matured, and his delight for his children flourished.

Jan matured into a rambunctious toddler, and Nelly grew into an active five-year-old, and attending school improved her growth and maturity, so Diny sought to know Nelly and befriend her. After all, they were sisters! Diny longed to know her sister closely as a best friend. At age ten, Diny's world expanded, her exploration matured, and she brought dolls to Nelly, to play together, but Nelly ran to her room and slid a chair in front of the door, sealing away any connection to Diny. Diny knocked and called out, but Nelly said she wanted to play alone. Sometimes, Nelly ran outside to hide in the garden, away from the family home.

On Sunday mornings they either attended church or remained home to rest. The spiritual tone was secular in Indie, and some Christians met in more of a social gathering, like *SOOS*. Their *SOOS* club was a Dutch social club, the name shortened from "Society." They gathered together, spoke Dutch, and ate delicious food with their families. Churches employed no pastor, yet someone always volunteered to share a message. Occasionally Pieter spoke, as did other men in the community, on the occasions they attended church. Afterwards they entertained company at their home or journeyed to a friend's home for coffee or a meal.

In remaining respectful to God and honoring her family by taking a Sabbath day, Diny was not permitted to swim or ride her bicycle on Sundays. Instead, Mam and Dad invited a group of friends to arrive on Sunday afternoons after their nap and tin-bucket bath, for a "*gezellig*" time, a "warm, cozy togetherness."

Some evenings, their friends stayed for dinner, lingering together on the veranda, as many hours passed with lively conversation and enjoyment. Friends shared stories along with general conversation. One friend thought he saw a rare Javan Rhinoceros, which usually fled in fear when humans drew near, as they were secluded animals. Afterwards, the children grew tired. Some were asleep on parent's laps, and families left to return home, cheerful songs of so-long echoing in the valley as they shuffled off, carrying sleeping children in their arms.

When the evening of 25 November arrived, after a Sunday afternoon entertaining friends from church, the family lay sleeping in their beds. Mount Merapi suddenly churned again, rumbling along as a series of violent earthquakes, signaling the culmination of the volcanic eruption by thundering its fury. Diny raced into her parents' bedroom, eager to embrace them and find comfort. They peered out their window, their faces serious and tired. Diny gasped and covered her mouth with her hand as Merapi exploded with fury, sending red lava bubbling and spewing against the inky night sky, down the fractured mountain, and into valleys, erupting over the lives of those who lived in those surroundings.

Although they lived a considerable distance from the mountain, she felt afraid of the volcano. Her parents reassured Diny of the safe distance from their home, yet in this instance, Mam admitted there may be many who were unable to heed the admonition of evacuating in time. Atop the "Mountain of Fire," smoke unfurled daily, so they knew the eruption would be visible from home. Eight earthquakes rattled their nerves for days, even weeks.

The next few evenings, Dad listened to radio updates and Diny overheard a report of thirteen villages destroyed, killing one thousand people. No visitors were permitted to the evacuated lava-filled land for months until the ground cooled and roads reopened. The volcano continued to spew for more than ten months, cutting through fields, jungles, and valleys, then emptying into the sea.

Those Sunday evenings whenever their family hosted company, Mam delivered Diny to her bed at the appropriate time. Diny lay in bed and listened, feeling warm and surrounded by pleasant noises as her parents' friends remained, the golden glow of a lantern moving through the house, shadows extending and later extinguished. She heard frogs ribbiting, creaking voices intermixing with breezes blowing across waterlogged rice plantations and through waterfalls, fresh trade winds singing through flamboya trees, calling her name as the air wound through effervescent rubber trees. Diny imagined glittering splashes of water cascading on staircases of palm fronds, shimmering down, trickling along the path.

Her ears detected the melodic harmonies of the *Tokay* gecko from outside, counting how many times he rolled his "r" sounds, and then called his "*tokay*," like a sequence of "Toh-Keh."

Her mother said, "If you hear the Tokay make its 'tokay' sound seven times in a row, it is considered good luck, so make a wish!" Too enamored with the mystery and song, she often forgot to count the number of "tokay" sounds in a row.

Then she noticed Tokay geckos in their yard the next morning, surprised by their size and appearance, some measuring about 30 centimeters in length, with splotchy circles on their scaly body, colored with wild varieties of light yellow and bright red. Mam reassured her these lizards were harmless and native to the islands. The Tokays ate insects like mosquitoes and other pests like beetles and spiders. Diny must get used to the Tokay and try to befriend them.

Diny's favorite Tokay was blue like the sky with small orange splotches. He could camouflage in green scenery or colorful flowers, the patterns of which ranged the entire rainbow. She chased the Tokay around the yard but could never catch him. His large yellow eyes frightened her as he dashed around, staring at her with a vertically slit pupil. He froze in place with his mouth open, as though prepared to speak, awaiting the enemy's attack, before scampering away, slipping into hidden grasslands. She hoped those animals would not bite or bother her. Mam said their bite was unrelenting, as they rarely let go once clamping onto a finger with a sturdy jaw.

At night, Diny also listened to the sound of the little "*tjitjaks,*" sounding like "chit-yaks," their nails tapping along in clippity sounds as they walked inside homes, making "tji…tji…tji…" sounds. Smaller tjitjaks appeared like mini-Tokays but were merely a common island lizard. Small tjitjaks scurried on walls, scratched their presence on ceilings and floors, enjoying their feast of mosquitoes and bugs.

From bed while drifting into sleep, Diny heard echoes of the tjitjaks and then the *Saté Man*, pushing his food cart past her house. He called out, "*Saté!*" with various grilled food options:

"*Saté ajam* (chicken)!" "*Saté babi* (pork)!" "*Saté gambing* (goat)!"

The distinct smell of the fire on which he roasted his sate drifted into her room. Diny could almost taste the salty nuts of the caramel-colored peanut saté, with *sambal* spice-infused relish, the fire-laden flavor lingering, and coconut milk creamy in her mouth to balance the spice. The scents and sounds of the islands launched her into a dreamland filled with food, vendors calling, tjitjaks scuttling walls, frogs creaking, branches swaying in the canopy of trees, and the tenderness of their breezy home.

Chapter Four
Hilversum, The Netherlands, February 1932

The Dekker family again prepared for Furlough to the Netherlands, for a change of pace and food, Mam's recovery from tropical heat, and Pieter's relaxation away from his challenging and demanding role at the Police Academy. They traveled across the seas to the Netherlands, and at age ten, Diny looked forward to adventures, a lovely farm visit, and colorful fields of tulips.

Nelly was six years old and learned about the furlough through Diny's stories, and begged for a horse ride. Small brother Jan at age three loved the idea of traveling on a boat. Dad cautioned them as Mount Merapi began erupting again the previous September, emptying ash and lava, so they would remain inside the boat while the air was thick with smoke when the boat sailed past the volcano.

The three-week boat trips from Indie to the Netherlands, and later back again, were a highlight. They loved those boating voyages and pondered them with nostalgia. They had a marvelous and wonderful childhood in Indie! And having the opportunity for extended amounts of time with their family was a special benefit. On the boat ride, activities kept the children busy, with craft and singing contests. Diny joined a group of children who learned various songs throughout a week, then performed a show on the main deck for their cheering parents at the end of the week.

Dad rented a three-story gabled house in Hilversum, a charming home which showed its age and wear. The home's appearance was unadorned and clean, with creamy outer walls and tan and charcoal accents and red shutters. Inside the furnished rented home, efficiency reigned, practically serving the Dekker family with little clutter and still plenty of enchantment to attend to their needs.

While the structure of their home was decorated in an uncomplicated way, the inside became their own, a signature of their cozy and welcoming nature. The Dekkers hosted friends and family, with grace at once effortless and yet sensibly planned. Cornelia established their family within a greater community in Hilversum and Amsterdam with each Furlough, enjoying the six-month stretches as though their family transplanted permanently back into the Netherlands. Mam meant to create a safe place of respite for Pieter, a haven from the preceding years, shedding the rigorous challenges of police work. The quaint country of the Netherlands brimmed full of determined, optimistic people with impeccable work ethic, a prosperity of which, founded on trade, thrived with each generation.

Tales of ancestors who reclaimed land from the sea transfixed the Dekker children. Opa van den Bout recounted the fortitude of the Dutch people. They bore the brunt of the sea upon their sturdy backs, fashioned a wall, and reimagined a soggy landscape into a solid fertile country. They rebuilt with each flood, assembling the land according to their delight. Expansive green fields were neatly arranged, and cottages were built with delicate glass windows and colorful panes, layered atop with thatched roofs, and yards lined with stone paths. There were meticulously designed gardens honed in by fences, where cinnamon-colored horses galloped beside hardy farmers who charmed the land. Their ability to harness ferocious wind power through windmills directed water away from homes and unleashed it back into the North Sea.

From afar, windmills turned gracefully — quietly, or rapidly — on pace, brown structures situated beside fields, panels glimmering in sunlight, swirling while inner workings of the oak mill spun, constant tension steady upon the solid foundation. Standing closer to the windmill afforded an intimate view of the four turning panels connected in the center to create a winding unit, lattice wood and canvas sail panels attached with ropes, sometimes pulled snug, other times unfurled into the zephyr.

Their family knew wind millers who clomped oak floors in wooden shoes and maneuvered their windmills like proficient sailors, pulling at ropes and shouting into the wind, as though their vessel barreled headlong into a seawall of water, some gale-wind squall. In those wooden structures, Diny marveled at the roofed sides, solid oak mills, stairs leading up to the "captain's quarters," some seven levels high, and various chains and anchors required to channel the watercourse by using locked connecting gears.

The miller spun the spoked wheel — a wench sliding horizontally on roller bearings — like turning a ship, which spun the cab of the windmill to face the breeze, for windmill sails to spin. When he found the wind, the miller anchored the spot with a heavy chain and a cross-shaped pin, locking into place. Outside near the river, Diny watched a large planked metal screw constantly spiral water up and away from the land.

How curious for a country to build canals and fortresses to protect from water, while hardy workers drained the water behind, emptying it into the North Sea. As they built those large sea walls, they claimed new land and restrained the water, turning roaring rapids into placid ponds, with green willows lining its banks. This portrait of rural Holland seemed old and quaint, with each village a personality, a life force.

On furlough, they again became acquainted with their grandparents. Opa and Oma retired to Hilversum for a change of pace, just blocks away from the Dekker's rented home, which proved an easy location for grandchildren to visit. Diny gazed intently at her grandmother, a woman her own mother Cornelia would someday undoubtedly resemble. Oma van den Bout's lace curtains open, revealing large bay windows in their Hilversum entry room, allowing an occupant to observe busy happenings in their street. The gray skies remained steadily foggy and cloudy for weeks each winter, with frequent snow showers since their arrival. Diny liked to watch people speeding on bicycles with packages attached on the back, or mothers strolling prams which held bundled babies.

Oma called the entry room "the sitting room," which, to Diny, seemed stuffy and reserved, with stately, aged couches and precious Delft porcelain dining dishes in lofty enclosed glass-fronted cabinets of a dark mahogany. The cabinets matched their stately formal dining table, also a deep grain of the same sturdy wood. One enclosed hutch was built into the sitting room's wall, and a cupboard door opened to reveal a built-in bed. The sitting room became a bedroom each evening and chairs were shuffled to the corners.

Dutch real estate and land remained a prime price, with gabled homes built narrow and tall, sometimes four stories high, so they utilized all their horizontal living space. Shops like merchant buildings were situated on the ground floor. Families lived on the middle two floors, and attics were a warehouse. Land was expensive, and seventeenth century homeowners were required to pay taxes according to the home's width, which contributed to skinny homes.

Some evenings, Diny slept in the sitting room. In the morning, she closed the cupboard upon her bed, rearranged the chairs, and resumed the sitting room again. Oma promised plenty of togetherness with cousin Anje Stencher, a girl several years older than Diny and a faithful pen pal across the miles. Just three years prior, when the Dekkers lived at Soekaboemi, Cornelia's sister had visited them in Indie, bringing along her husband and four daughters, the cousins from Haarlem.

She remembered her Dad's brother Cornelis, the farmer in Groningen, who built two bunk beds into the corners of their children's bedroom, with closing panels to allow up to four children to sleep, the floor utilized for playing and school work around a central table during the day. Oom Cor's two children were five and three.

As Diny looked further up Oma van den Bout's walls, past paintings and portraits, she observed royal-blue-on-creamy-white Delft tiles lining the upper walls near the ceiling, with dozens of tiles serving as tidy wall decorations for their kitchen. The tiles began as a blank canvas of creamy white square tiles, measured and fired in the kiln, then cooled and hand-painted into heirlooms.

They visited the Delft factory and watched the masterpieces created, crafted by skilled artists who utilized a rich royal blue paint to depict rural Dutch country scenes, windmills, a sleepy summer respite, burgeoning ships venturing boldly on the seas, or some other cheery event, like a horse-and-carriage taking a newly-married couple onto a life of bliss. Some tiles marked the realities of everyday farm life: oxen pulling a cart, animals grazing, a woman churning butter. A few tiles were in full color, a stark contrast to the uniformed patterns of blue-and-white. All the Delft tiles lined up with events symbolizing the changing of seasons in their own lives, with marriages, births, anniversaries, and important remembrances.

In Amsterdam, they visited newly-widowed Oma Dekker, who welcomed them. She graciously adjusted to her new life. With ice skating season nearly over, they anticipated springtime thaw and the opportunity for countryside outdoor adventures. Spring arrived, so Pieter took them out on a bicycle day, touring canals via paths, tires clunking over drawbridges crossing the Amstel River. A dam was built on the Amstel in the thirteenth century, Oma Dekker told her grandchildren, as they marveled at the moss and dark stones encompassing the canals. Alternately, Oma Dekker took the train to stay in Hilversum for a few days, and the family picnicked at Hilversum's Boombergpark. Diny's body chilled from breezes at Laapersveld Park, yet she delighted in the sensation of wearing a sweater, something she never needed on the islands. Leisurely moments away from routine felt like a celebration. They arrived in time for spring, but the change in temperatures brought Diny a fever, chills, cough, and stuffy head.

Mam kept her in bed for several days and tended to her, bringing hot chicken soup to her room. She smoothed a layer of menthol ointment along Diny's neck and wrapped her in flannel cloth, to loosen muscles and release the sickness. After a few nights of this routine, coupled with oranges and plenty of water, Diny found her voice again; the fever lifted, and she resumed her everyday life.

As springtime yielded to warming sunshine, they ventured to the North Sea, salt air an invigorating change, and scents of sea-life: oysters, mussels, clams. They searched for cod, haddock, sole, mackerel, and herring. Circling overhead were loons, turns, and gulls. Dolphins, whales, and seals could be seen in the distance. In nearby fishing villages, hardy men set out in boats, launched into the North Sea at night to collect their catches early in the day, entertained by white seagulls swooping low to nip at their earnings.

The atmosphere, picnic areas, and food stalls during the summer attracted families and tourists to the coast. Wind gusts rippled gray-blue waves and pushed through tall seagrass, which billowed like feathers, pointing with the wind before submitting to the air and laying down into the sand. Dunes provided ample opportunity for running, while older children scaled up the shifting sand of the dune and slid back down.

Frequent walks along the shore offered a renewed perspective, the opportunity to observe with an altered viewpoint. Diny spread a blanket along the shore and watched waves cycle through their crashing and foaming, swelling routine of a sequence; approaching forward, toward her, then retreating backwards, into the shimmering sea. Water billowed and surged like a looming presence, or a person, some shadowy figure, storming toward her, a frothing breaker approaching to swallow her whole.

Diny remembered the Bible story of Jonah, the prophet who tried to outrun God and escape his calling. She wondered, in the moment he was swallowed, did Jonah sense the fish advancing? Was he aware of his plight before spending three miserable days inside the fish's belly? Did he recognize his fate before it consumed him?

"The Great Depression consumed our country bit by bit, and able men are out of work. Mothers are struggling to feed their children," Opa van den

Bout said late one evening as the adults huddled at the kitchen table. Diny, unable to sleep, tiptoed down and sat on the stairs, listening to muffled voices discussing the Dutch stance of neutrality during the Great War.

After a few minutes, the tone shifted to optimism.

"We think the banks and markets will eventually return to a stable, normal level," Opa assured the other adults. "But we need to help each other through this grim time."

Dad attempted to encourage Oma and Opa, who had a lifetime of accomplishments and disappointments behind them, steering them in the direction of happiness. Those discussions held no clarity to Diny, except to realize most of her family had little money to spend on extras. Instead, time together with loved ones was valuable. If they ate a meal in a restaurant, Dad paid for the family meals, as he felt thankful for a job which afforded rare occasions for dining outside of their home.

One of Diny's appetizing indulgences was the thick, amber maple syrup layered in a sandwich of two waffles, called *stroopwaffels*. Oma baked a brown sugar tart or chocolate cakes, also an indulgence. Cafes served a *yoggie* drink, the luxurious creamy treat, a welcome respite from coconut milk. Diny suddenly realized some young children had hungry stomachs when falling asleep, while Diny had a selection of desserts which kept her full.

Diny and Nelly attended school each day, and after school Diny would write letters to Indie friends, keeping them updated on her adventures. They spent evenings visiting family for meals and talking while lingering in the sitting room around the fireplace. Opa van den Bout tended the fireplace lined with Delft tiles. He set aside his stoking poker, inviting his grandchildren to challenge him at a chess match to test his skill.

Diny and her cousins played jacks-and-ball games or roller skated on metal skates with wheels, tied on their feet with leather straps, a new invention her cousins loved. The boys raced their small wooden cars around the paths, or if the weather was fine, they flew kites. Diny held tightly to the string, bracing against the wind, and remembered Dad's suggestions to keep the kite aloft. Usually, cousins surrounded her with intense animation; by the time their parents gathered them in the evening, all were exhausted. On weekends they played outdoor games: croquet, badminton, or darts; or if inside, around a table for games of *Sjoelbak*. The Dutch shuffleboard game employed a flat wooden game board about 16" by 80" with raised sides, using 30 wooden pucks to slide across the *Sjoelbak* board, into any of the four-slotted divided scoring zones, or goals.

During their time in Holland, they ventured on cobblestoned streets next to canals, and in the city's open central squares, they awed at the scope of adorned churches and historical structures, few of which existed with intricate care for detail in Indie. A visit to Haarlem with cousins featured another highlight of bold and intricate seventeenth century architecture, cafés surrounded a bustling market square, abutting a stately cathedral with turrets, buttresses, and easements.

Food stands spanned the square, with vendors selling favorite foods, like herring brined in salt, a way of preserving. Pieter held a whole herring high above his head, leaned back, then lowered the fish into his mouth, eating the entire fish in two bites. Cornelia requested a knife to slice the herring into pieces, accompanied by onions and pickles, to eat herring with a fork, claiming, "This is far more elegant and refined, Pieter." Herring stands sold sandwiches, drinks, herring by the pound, and jarred herring for customers to carry home.

Nelly was fond of potato fries served with mayo sauce, and Jan chose *kroketten* — cylindrical croquettes made of meat ragout, breaded, then deep-fried. While *kroketten* were sold in restaurants and bakeries, they were a popular Dutch street food and filling to eat. The creamy texture of cheese allured Diny, and she fancied Gouda cheese, with a pale yellow — almost white — coloring, and a smooth yet hearty texture. It had a smoky aftertaste and a savory delight but best eaten in moderation, as the rich cheese could incur a stomach ache if eaten in too large a quantity. Some Gouda was often accented with anise seed or other spices. Gouda tasted like a holiday.

Mam used a mixture of Gouda and Edam with local farm cheeses to blend together for fondue meals, a Switzerland specialty. She shredded cheese, simmered and stirred it over low heat, and gathered bread, meat, and fruit to dip in the cheese sauce. Alternately, chocolate melted to perfection became a swirling ribbon of goodness. If they could endure life away from family and without modern conveniences, European food was a portion of their heritage they missed living on the islands.

The Dekkers visited the fields of tulips outside Leiden, near ancient castles and foggy, dreamy fields. They bundled jackets, galoshes, and scarves to slosh through vibrant fields, which farmers allowed for visitors late March through May. During Furlough evenings, the Dekkers visited family and ate meals together, coffee and cards in the sitting room while children played with cousins. Diny marveled at the paintings in her Oma Dekker's home, of artistic Dutch masters, men who made the Golden Age indeed magical. Exquisitely detailed images of food symbolized wealth and expertise.

Family stories, heritage, and ideas inspired artists as each generation of Dekker held at least one skilled painter. Galleries in Amsterdam were exciting, and Diny marveled at the visible, famous displays of these Golden Age painters. Yet only a few small, local galleries carried any of her family's paintings, and she was unaware of anyone's uncle supporting a hungry family on the meager income of an artist.

Amsterdam, The Netherlands, early May 1932

In Hilversum, townhouses were crowned with fancy gables. In the fall they planted tulip bulbs all through front and back gardens, as Cora was determined to have her own personal fields of tulips every spring, and Pieter told her they would be a pleasant surprise! Pieter drove her to the countryside fields and gardens northwest of Amsterdam where farmers opened their tulip fields fully in bloom, row after row of splendid color, rainbows of fluttering flowers. Windmills churned and welcomed visitors. As summer matured, they enjoyed morning markets and food stalls, and evenings in Amsterdam were relaxed, charming, and scenic, gentle canal boat rides under lamps glowing on bridges. Time together was unhurried.

Pieter took Cora alone on a trip to Switzerland to see the Matterhorn, cows grazing in meadows, experience waterfall hikes, and eat cheese fondue. Homes in the cleft of the hills were snug and charming. The sun rose slowly, illuminating the tall mountain peaks and lowering down to those homes. The children stayed one week with Oma Dekker while her parents were in Switzerland. Diny gathered tea cups, saucers, and crocheted lace cloths on a serving tray as a place setting. She arranged silver spoons for stirring, and a few *snoepjes* treats assorted on a glass serving plate. The sitting room was cozy and prepared for church guests who visited every Sunday afternoon.

When the guests departed later, Diny and Oma sewed, sitting on the wooden bench. Diny finally reached the pedal of Oma's foot-cranked sewing machine, revealing her growing efforts. She had developing skills in some areas. Oma observed from afar while clearing dishes, humming in the kitchen as she offered space for Diny's masterpiece, allowing her granddaughter mistakes in stitches while bringing an embroidered dress into a shapely form with flowers and vines swirling around the borders. Oma's gentleness permeated her countenance, her voice quiet, patience extending, head dancing in rhythm to the whirling machine.

Oma seemed pleased with Diny's progress at sewing, reminding her they had the entire summer to gain preciseness with certain stitches and designs. Oma chose three patterns for Diny to master and Diny promised to finish them by July. Again, Oma's tender praise encouraged Diny, and provided enough confirmation to continue.

A few days later, after Pieter and Cornelia returned from Switzerland, the family held a party to honor Moeder Dekker, who would turn 60 years old in August — long after Pieter and Cornelia returned to Indie. They chose to hold the birthday party in May and invited all the family. Oma Dekker's Amsterdam neighbors and church friends would also join them for the feast, along with Oma and Opa van den Bout.

Dad bought a fine three-piece suit, a thick woven fabric with a patterned tie, and his watch chain connected to a fancy watch his father long-ago bequeathed him. He visited a barber early in the day for a haircut and shave.

Mam found a modern skirt set at an Amsterdam department store, a peach, pink, and white outfit with a belt. Diny had never attended a party with her parents so smartly assembled! Diny and Nelly wore woolen skirts and sweaters with poms on the end of the strings. Jan wore tights with shorts and scratched at his leggings. His top with stripes similarly displayed a string bow, and he cried when Mam placed him in saddle shoes. Diny felt warm and cozy as Mam styled their hair, and all seemed appropriately prepared for Oma Dekker's birthday party.

Cornelia assembled a *rijsttafel*, an elaborate collection of Indie dishes prepared weeks ahead of time, and several church friends helped cook their home kitchens to create lavish dishes. The Omas had settled on twelve *rijsttafel* dishes surrounding the canvas of white rice. With all the culinary pleasures, Diny's anticipation mounted. Cora baked a three-layer chocolate birthday cake.

The night of the party, dozens of friends ascended upon Oma's home. Oma Dekker's five tall sons all joined them, including Jan Wolter and his wife Josephina, with their two children; Cornelis and his wife Sietske, with their two young sons; Gerrit and wife Etje; and Oma's youngest son Nicolaas. The adults gathered around the outside portico, fancifully decorated with bright white lights, with long tables covered in a lacy tablecloth and Oma's finest dishes and cutlery; the food table overflowed with selections, and all the children dined on the grass on blankets.

The late afternoon air warmed the backyard, with sunshine and conversation; indoors they continued the celebration. Cornelia brought out the chocolate cake, and Pieter lined six candles on the frosting, then lit the candles while the family sang the birthday song to Oma Dekker. As friends and neighbors returned to their homes, the family remained, unwilling to depart, uncertain of when they might all gather again for a delightful celebration.

Pieter cleared the sitting room for dancing, and Oma cued up the gramophone to play her favorite waltzes. Cora swayed in Pieter's arms, lifted on her toes as he twirled her, and they spun. Later, Dad pulled his girls toward him, while Cora held her son for their moment of dancing. Before the night concluded, Oma gathered Diny in her arms, her thin body warming with Diny's embrace, Oma's neck smelling of licorice and spice, kissing her *Meisje* and thanking her for the most glorious celebration of life possible.

"So-long, my little *Grietje*. This must be all for now."

The Dekkers drove home into the dark coolness of the spring night.

Less than one week later, in May 1932, Pieter was visiting his youngest brother Nicolaas when his dear mother Gerdina suddenly died. A telephone call from Cora explained the details. Oma Dekker had complained of exhaustion and passed away with her son Jan Wolter beside her. With the expressions, "Everything is good," and, "The Father takes care of me," their very calm and dearly beloved mother and grandmother, Gerdina — widow of Jan Dekker, emeritus pastor of the Reformed Church of Kollum — was gone at the age of 59 years.

Diny felt distraught at the loss of her beloved Oma Dekker, for whom Diny was named, especially as they had just visited with her a few nights before her death, and she offered Diny no indication of sickness. Her home would no longer be filled with Oma's loving-kindness. Pieter, not even forty years old, was now an orphan, encumbered as the eldest with caring for his four younger brothers, all of whom lived in the Netherlands, and overwhelmed by the obligation to manage two homes. Pieter contacted the Indie police department and received an extension on his already six-month Furlough, to liquidate his mother's home and care for the financial and personal matters surrounding her death.

Diny considered the enormous loss of both Dekker grandparents, those who went before her, who loved God and set an example of faith and hope. All four grandparents were rooted in the Lord, and their durable heritage broadened robustly despite difficulties, the importance of prayer tantamount to their core, their wellbeing.

They were oaks of righteousness, these generous, steady, optimistic grandparents, who extended their love past their front door to those in need, rooting their faith in God, and stretching out beyond comfort to bless others. The expression of her grandparents' faith was learned first from their parents, reinforced at church, and practiced in their community; they were for their neighbors a spiritual fortress or haven. As oaks of righteousness, they sheltered the needy, and their leaves of grace provided shade from the scorching heat of judgment. To rest under their refuge was indeed a solace and respite.

Oma Dekker's memorial service in Amsterdam's Reformed Church brought Diny little consolation but provided closure, and Diny sat straight in the hard pew, listening closely to the preacher's message of hope through loving God. Diny proudly wore the dress she and Oma had sewed together only days before and stared at the flowers swirling around the edges of her hem. She considered, *what fleeting beauty is our mortal life and the delicate flowers we tend!* Diny contemplated how Gerdina Margaretha Moen Dekker's life had resembled Christ in forgiveness, generosity, and grace. Although her beloved Oma had died, Diny rested knowing she had trusted in Jesus as her Savior and secured the promise of Heaven. *Such a far-away place*, she considered through tears.

Pieter handled Oma Dekker's estate, dispersing belongings and selling her home. He was most concerned for his youngest brother Nicolaas, only 18 years old. As the youngest boy in the family, Nicolaas Dekker admired his eldest brother Pieter. In a bold, determined family, as all five children were sons, their active home always remained animated, hectic, and energetic. After birthing four sons, Mother Dekker desperately wanted a daughter.

When Nicolaas was born a boy, seven years after the fourth son was born, Mother refused to accept Nicolaas as a boy, and dressed and treated him as a girl for the first five years of his life, all of which deeply affected him. Nicolaas was 15 years old when his father died. Suddenly, at age 18, he was a young adult and an orphan. Pieter spent considerable time visiting Nicolaas and was determined to cultivate a strong friendship with his youngest brother, loyal to him as family. He hoped to provide guidance and maturity as the eldest son of the family.

The rivers all empty into the sea, and larger built heartily with oak and timber were fashioned to withstand surging waves and swells and launched eastward. Dutch merchant ships set sail with eager explorers and returned with spices, bringing Amsterdam riches and notoriety during the Netherland's Golden Age, and tulips and the spice trade both fueled the progress of that economic boom. The city evolved internationally and socially, and those qualities carried through several centuries to launch the Dutch into the modern era.

The Dekkers delighted in visiting Friesland. Pieter's younger brother Cor and his wife Sietske were farmers in the northern countryside in Groningen, and in 1925 on their previous Furlough they visited with them. Dad promised to take Nelly on a walk in the woods, which softened her disappointment at not riding a horse. Their two delightful cousins had been born since the last furlough: five-year-old Jan Cornelis and three-year-old Nicolaas.

On this trip, nearly eleven-year-old Diny eagerly asserted her readiness to ride a horse, and recognized the shiny chestnut colt as he galloped. The charming thatched roofs, windmills, and tulips were an allure of the countryside, but raising horses seemed the most fantastic aspect of farm life. The colt was her favorite horse and she watched him grazing under the willow near the front fence. He lifted his head as their car turned up the road slowly toward the farm.

Diny embraced Tante Sietske, who held her close and ushered her inside, to sit at the kitchen table and devour bread and drink fresh milk. Sietske started the percolator to brew coffee for Pieter, and hot water for Cornelia's tea. After coffee and tea break, Diny brushed crumbs from her face and tugged at Mam's sleeve. "We are ready to ride the horse, Mam!" Her mouth was full of crusty bread, but she pulled on a sweater and ran to the horse, bounding with a brightness.

"He just started training for riders," Sietske called to Diny.

The horse grazed nearby, and trotted toward them, his muscles rippling with youthful exuberance. Diny's uncle fed the horse a carrot, then helped Diny mount the horse, and firmly reminded her of the riding instructions. Oom held the reins as Diny grasped the shiny saddle horn and he offered steady direction like an old, trusted friend. Oom led the way for the chestnut to become acquainted with Diny and her scent, posture, and voice.

"Even when our chestnut was a yearling, he bucked at hoof trimming, and cantered away to the front fields," Oom said. "He always needs my pursuit."

Diny nodded and spoke calmly as they walked in the fragrant spring air, a verdant carpet under his merry hooves. She hugged the colt's neck, rested her head on his rust colored mane, and sang her school songs. After her ride, Dad helped Diny dismount, and they thanked Oom for the ride. As he trotted along to the barn, the chestnut colt's hooves seemed to glint in the light like bricks of gold galloping on waves of grass. Oom Cor gathered the horses together into the barn, cooled them down, and Diny helped groom the horse, brushing his hair gently with a hand brush.

Inside the farm house, all was quiet. Her cousins settled down for a nap, and Pieter and Cornelia had taken Nelly and Jan for their promised long walk in the woods. As they were alone with some time to visit, Tante handed Diny a cup of tea and a plate of cookies and explained her role on the farm. Tante and Oom employed seasonal workers to plant seeds in the fields, and months later to harvest the crops, but their neighbor's sons assisted once a week before and after school. The season ahead would prove especially productive as they would hire more helpers to clear fields, gather hay for cattle feed, chop down a tree and split wood, paint the house or barn, and other maintenance tasks.

Tante served as her husband's assistant and kindly accepted the tasks required in raising her family. Her disposition was light and cheerful, and ultimately welcoming. After several minutes of visiting and showing Diny her inventive indoor greenhouse for growing fruit, Tante said she needed to begin the process of preparing lunch.

She and Diny began the process of lunch arrangements.

"What career would you like when you grow up?" she asked as Diny sliced strawberries.

"Well, *Tante,* I have always wanted to be a nurse," Diny beamed.

Sietske smiled as she rinsed a few apples under the streams of water, then sliced them into wedges. "Why do you hope to become a nurse?" she asked.

"I want to help sick people heal, and assist doctors at repairing broken people."

Tante paused, nodding sympathetically. "A wonderful career, Diny."

"I plan to have a job in the city," Diny said, "in Amsterdam if I am lucky." Diny said.

"But how about being a farmer's wife — and a mother?" Tante's eyes gleamed. She seemed content in her role, dedicating herself to the vital tasks children presented.

"Yes, Tante, farming is valuable as well."

Tante considered her words. "My choice of vocation may seem simple, basic, and full of routine, but I love being able to live in the countryside. I consider this lifestyle a calling, in how God has encouraged us to live. We are blessed to spend time with our children and feel a farm is a significant place to raise them. If we need to buy a bigger household purchase or fancy clothing, we take the train to Amsterdam."

"This sounds like a wonderful life, here Tante, really. Maybe I can help with my cousins if I visit you in the summer…." Diny trailed off, remembering she lived a three-week boat ride away — halfway around the world — when the next European summer time would arrive.

"You are always welcome to stay here with us, my *lieverd* — darling — niece, but at least we can write to each other and continue to share our thoughts on paper."

Diny gleamed.

Tante continued, "Before I met your uncle, I was raised by very strict parents in a setting like this, our countryside farm, farther south. All I wanted to do after school was ride my horse. She was a loving and pretty Frieswhite mare and frolicked in the meadow. But I was unwilling to groom her, clean her stall, or help with the barn, and my father was angry. I had to learn to work through those challenges, those differences with my parents, and I realized they were right!"

"Surely they should let you ride the horse," Diny said.

"My father reminded me that if I wanted the benefit of a horse, I needed to take responsibility for the privilege. I became more gentle and completed my chores because I knew the labor and work required. I had to remember my parents were doing the best they knew how, while looking to God for help and guidance. They loved me, so they disciplined and directed me."

Diny nodded. "I do understand, Tante, and I want to be open to what the Lord is teaching me — and how He speaks through my parents."

Sietske hugged Diny close. "Here, Diny, let me show you how to make a loaf of bread, from the beginning." This process started before Diny's arrival, as Tante had to work throughout the day, planning for a dinner feast.

As they spoke and worked with food together, Tante explained the process of turning wheat into flour, of waiting the allotted amount of time to allow the dough to rest, remain covered, and rise, all while the baker might fret over the patience required for waiting. But the yeast always worked in the same method, if the baker remained faithful to the instructions.

Then, later, Tante kneaded the dough on the countertops, adding a dash of flour, rolling out the dough. On the counter next to her, beyond the ready baking pans, were lists of chores Tante still needed to accomplish. Diny guessed at how she attempted those farm duties alone, with additional errands in town, and other family responsibilities, like caring for tiny children.

"Many necessary farm duties cannot be completed today, so they go on the top of my list for tomorrow," Tante explained. "Everything depends on what is urgent and important. If I can plan, then I am thankful."

Diny counted the tasks in her mind as Tante spoke.

"But caring for my children is important, and I must be present for them all the time and daily invest in their character." Tante said, "My boys bring joy and I am truly blessed."

The dough was ready to bake and transformed into crusty bread. Soon a fragrant bread emerged. As they cleaned Tante's kitchen while working to the smell of bread, Diny contemplated a life on the farm, one she always viewed as carefree and untroubled. She realized she still had much to learn about the realities of the lives and world surrounding her.

Diny's own extended family assemblies were not always as merry as Oma van den Bout's sitting room Delft tiles evoked, with happy village life and bucolic scenes of felicity. But while living in Indie, Diny often longed for the closeness of cousins and aunts and uncles, something this Furlough provided, even despite the pain of Oma Dekker's death. During their months in the Netherlands, Diny quarreled with cousins and with her parents, in front of her grandparents, who were bewildered at Diny's strong will which mirrored their own.

After Diny argued with her parents, she would retreat to her bedroom and look out the window at the city and sky, and marvel at the way the Dutch light illuminated everything. She would fall asleep on her bed with the curtains open to the glory of the skies, and dream about thick colorful paints swirling into a Van Gogh masterpiece.

July arrived, and Dad arranged for a proper Dutch holiday. They escaped for a weekend break at the North Sea in Den Haag, where Mam lounged on a blanket and read books, as Diny hummed and watched bicycles zoom along the paved paths beside the water. Nelly and Jan held hands and dipped their feet into the water, then ran back to build sandcastles, while Dad walked for kilometers, up and down the coast; up for a kilometer, then back to them, then down the coast another kilometer before turning around and arriving again in Den Haag.

Diny's eleventh birthday was celebrated at Hilversum's Boombergpark over picnic food. The grandparents joined them, and relished time together flying diamond-shaped kites. Dad noted the contrasting colors against the sky, with brightly colored paper birds soaring in the air, stringing tightly so the kites would not escape their hands. Ribbons cascaded from the bottom of the kites, floating in the air, suspended like wind-blown candies, content to fly. One kite twirled fiercely and escaped her hands into a brisk gust of wind. Diny watched it fly away, speeding into the horizon, a diamond flashing away into nothingness.

A yellow haze rests over large fields and dips into streams, traverses along canals, and veils the rivers. It permeates translucent air, invading crisp clarity, delivering opaque mystery and charm. The golden Dutch atmosphere envelops, enchants, and hypnotizes dreamers into a realm of incredible possibility. For centuries before, light inspired painters, artists, and undaunted visionaries.

An air like this intermingled reality with expectation, shimmering promise into the life while infusing hope, unlatching opportunity to unburden the weary. It offers an atmosphere where manifestations of vigor sparkle in bright sunshine, and solemn contemplation and stillness within the fog of a river's early morning. Bright days of sunshine, with clear skies, devoid of clouds, beckoned soaring birds and newness. The optimism of shimmering glory illuminated the goodness of grace, a vision of rays beaming down in generous approval. Those days where sunshine prevailed were unmatched days of grace.

During a gentle August evening in Den Haag again, Diny removed her shoes and raced Jan down the coast, much to Mam's dismay at her toddling young son frolicking too closely to the water's edge at high tide. Puffs of sand tracked behind them as they sprinted, footprints leaving a trail for Nelly to follow. Small flowers on long green stems among the sand dunes provided materials for Diny and Nelly to create flower necklaces and crowns, for their pretend kingdom. As darkness settled around them, Dad carried Nelly and Jan to the car. Diny felt fond of the Dutch seaside, which was so different from Batavia!

Summer gave way to a cooling autumn, with yellowing trees lining Amsterdam's canals, smoldering a golden hue to the air. Foggy mornings faded into bucolic afternoons, a white filter muting the world and then releasing into the mist. Weeks later, the trees were bare amidst a rain storm, and the canals swollen with water. Skies grew gray and darker earlier those days, and the same cheery golden canal lanes and walkways were now littered with wet, soggy leaves interspersed like cobblestones. They soured to dullish yellow black and scraggly trees creaked in the wind, knobby arms outstretched.

Cora visited with friends and family in Hardinxveld during Furlough and discussed Pieter's prospects on the police force in the Dutch East Indies. Their families didn't always understand their lives in Indie, but she tried to explain the unique burdens of the police force, moral regulations, and the racial tensions which galvanized deeply-set divisions. They couldn't fathom the challenges police families faced, nor the economic and political changes surrounding them, swirling about Asia. They all noted the economic downturn in the Netherlands and Europe, and the struggle to retain money, jobs, and progress. As farming, shipping, and pastoral families, they felt the economic impact at the basic level.

The beginning of December 1932 hearkened celebrations of Sinterklaas Day. Pieter purchased treats at the candy store, like coffee-flavored candies called *Hopjes,* butterscotch candies named *babbelaars*, and Queen Wilhelmina peppermints. Their carved wooden shoes were cheerily placed at the fireplace hearth with carrots for Sinterklass' horse on the evening of 5th December. The morning of the 6th of December, they awoke to plump oranges, bags of chocolate coins, and new toys in their shoes, and a feast for the family to share together at supper time. Presents were offered with jokes and poems attached, alongside candies and treats.

Sinterklaas Day 1932 seemed best celebrated amidst family. Diny, Nelly, and Jan loved the little *snoepjes* — delicate cookies and cakes — their Oma Dekker had created from simple ingredients in her cupboard, so Oma van den Bout baked and cooked treats for her grandchildren.

At the bakery, besides the flaky pastry treats available throughout the year, they sampled spiced cookies (speculaas), lace, stroopwaffels, and Jan Hagel cookies — buttery cinnamon and sugar cookies, sprinkled with sliced almonds. Together, they enjoyed savory cheeses and smoked meats, like salmon, herring, and eel.

The days leading up to Christmas Day was full of decorating, adorning frosted windows with golden candles, the verdant, fragrant tree with bells, shiny embellishments, and velvet ribbons, creating wreaths from greenery bushes and tying with twine, and assembling them together. The trimming of the home enhanced their celebration..

During the New Year's Eve celebration, Mam played classical records, and everyone danced along as well. The family snacked on *oliebollen:* powdery, sugary fried dough balls filled with raisins, and the bells of Christmastime still echoed in their memories.

Amsterdam townhomes were different colors, one to the next, with red brick predominantly and white edging, steeply slanted tile roofs. Some homes were brown, white, or black. Ornate façades added character and whimsy. Later, they walked in the frosted air and enjoyed the brisk, crisp refreshment. Then they went inside a cafe for a hot cocoa and coffee break. Even in the snow, the bicycles sailed through the streets. Cobbled brick roadways arched over canals and offered a prime view of the water below. As they walked back home from one outing, Cora waved at three children piled into a front cart, covered with blankets, as their mother bicycled behind, pushing the cart, a *bakfiets* for the family ride.

Ice skating on a canal in a Dutch winter was a frigid engagement: groves of frozen trees on the side of the bank, swaying together in a dark, damp heap. An empty, vast canal, the frosted expanse of an icy waterway covered with fresh snow. Cold air froze Diny's throat and hair, her nostrils were icy, and her lungs burned. People huddled in clumps, pressed forward skating, mingled together for warmth, and clustered as a group to reach home.

Skaters were in store for the special *Elfstedentocht* skating tour if their winter continued as frigid as was predicted. They journeyed up to Friesland for the event to stay with Pieter's brother's family at their farm. There was something cheery about a roaring fireplace near a large-paned window, where one could watch snow pour down from the heavens and pile heavily onto fields, from inside the cozy confines of the home.

The *Elfstedentocht* would no doubt be frigid and windy in Friesland. The Elfstedentocht was an "eleven cities tour," the 200-km ice skating race event through all eleven villages in Friesland. As lakes and ponds turned solid with ice, they strapped on skates to test the ice and hope for the infamous race. An ominous, overcast day generated a colder temperature. Brisk, wintry days slowed their senses, sending them inside for the warm fireplace or stove, the bundled comfort of heavy coats, hats, scarves, and mittens. Yet as winter intensified, it was time to leave the Netherlands and return to the tropics.

Upon their return to Dutch East Indies from their Netherlands Furlough in January 1933, the Dekker family transferred to Semarang, as Pieter was promoted to Adjunct-Chief Commissioner/ Superintendent of Police. The Head Chief Commissioner was WFG Stein. As the capital of Central Java district,

Semarang was on Java's northern coast and emerged as a major port town. Old Town overlooked the sea, and the southern cooler area was in the hills. The Dutch created tobacco plantations and built roads and railroads, transforming Semarang into an important colonial trading center.

Chapter Five
Semarang, Central Java, Dutch East Indies, early 1933

Cornelia's fingers worked her needlepoint project with a shiny threaded needle, and her strong hands flattened the thick, starchy fabric. She shifted into sunshine on the veranda to better illuminate her work, concentrating on tiny, exact stitches. Her mind filled with patterns and she excitedly recreated those images in embroidery. Cora happily sighed as her green spool of thread neared its end, along with a sense of delight for her artistic outpourings, her mind always brimming with imaginings for projects.

Late afternoons spent sewing or creating a cross-stitch pattern of swirling reds, blues, and greens were a worthy challenge for Cornelia. With her girls at school, and little boy Jan napping, she sometimes joined him. Yet today she felt revitalized. A reborn energy exploded within her, as though the twirling greenery surrounding their home inspired her to fashion a likeness on fabric. Swaying flamboya trees poured out bright red blossoms, bougainvillea sparkled forth violet blooms, and other stunning florals ranged from crimson to cobalt. Cornelia's needlepoint projects were often endeavors to embroider a pillowcase, construct doilies for tea and coffee breaks, create a modern style of dress for her girls, or a wall decoration, a piece of art inspired by nature.

Banyan trees looked like beige ropes woven together, as thin contorted branches twirled and meshed together. Sometimes a dozen parallel branches wrapped together as one unit, as though a thicker, more permanent vine. Branches spread farther in scope, reaching heights stretched out toward the heavens, as though knobby roots praised their Creator. Some afternoons as Cornelia stitched, little Jan climbed banyans, or hid inside the wide hollows of their knotty bark. The large embrace of the tree's trunk was just the right size for his frame.

As her daughters' school day neared an end, Cornelia placed her cross-stitch on an upper shelf as Jan awoke from his nap, then carried him along the shaded path on their brief walk to school, until he was awake enough to walk alone. On the journey home, Diny and Nelly excitedly discussed what they learned in school, things they read or wrote, or about friendships.

After arriving home from school each day, as twelve-year-old Diny anxiously awaited Dad's return from work for their tin-bucket bath and four-o'clock tea on the veranda, she joined Mam to read or work on school lessons. She tried to read Dad's newspaper, but Mam always cautioned her, stating Diny's efforts would be better employed in other projects better suited to her age level — and not newspapers — until she was older.

Mam returned to her wicker chair and to her colorful needlepoint project. Diny intently watched Mam's fast fingers accomplish their goals, and asked Mam about her friend at school. One of her neighborhood friends had a Dutch father and a Javanese mother. When Diny asked about things like skin color, those conversations took longer than a few minutes to explain.

Without looking up from her work, Mam used a confusing word "mixed."

Diny's voice broke as she probed, "So where do mixed people belong? Is my friend 'Dutch-and-Javanese,' or is she 'Javanese-and-Dutch'?"

She wondered, if her heritage split into two extremes, two diverse cultures, countries and places thousands of kilometers from each other in the world — where was her home? Was her true bloodline from their land of birth and roots, or nurturing and education? Were her roots from some combination of bloodline and birth collectively?

The complications surrounding intricate thoughts baffled Diny, so Mam sought to delicately navigate those questions. She stopped stitching and looked at her anxious daughter. Many of the people of mixed-blood were part-Dutch and part-islander, called Dutch-Javanese, Dutch-Sumatran, or Dutch-Balinese. Some Dutch men married islander women. The joining of many backgrounds and customs provided the mingling of both flavors and cultures. Yet the marriage of spices and scents was often complicated and uncomfortable to discuss.

Diny leaned on her arms on Mam's chair, her damp hair snarled, her mouth open, eyebrows raised. Her eyes were wide with questions, confused about a complicated situation like skin tone.

Mam smiled and set aside her work. She held her wiry, emotional child, and Diny melted into her lap. "Oh, *Gerardina*, I wish I could tell you. I wish I could offer a simple answer about heritage and people." Mam sighed. "But life is not simple, my darling girl, not easy. Things here in The Indies are not the same as in the Netherlands. Most people first see the outside of a person: skin color, eye shape, hair style, type of clothing. But I try to see people as God sees them — their character."

Diny nodded slowly, trying to understand.

Her mother continued, "Friendship does not see color or heritage, but gives and loves and serves. It offers a bond from mutual experiences and connection of emotions."

"I have many friends of different skin colors, Mam," Diny told her, "and they are all *mooi* — so lovely! We play together, sing, and paint pictures. But they do not go to my school. Why?"

Mam nodded, and considered the neighborhood friends. She stroked Diny's cheek. "Yes, your school is only for European children. Others have created those unfair rules. I am so proud of your love for all people, *Grietje.*"

Diny frowned, "Some of the Dutch children are horrible to islanders. Just terribly mean! I wish my dark-skinned friends were loved by all Europeans. At least they feel my love, Mam."

"Diny, look at me." She gazed into her daughter's eyes. "All people are loved by God, and that is what I know, what Dad and I believe. We try our best to live in that way, and we pray we are making a difference." She continued, "I am certain you are making a difference too. Keep loving everyone in your life, even those who act unlovable, who hold an unfair way of treating others. The older you become, the more complicated it will be to love others, especially those who are outright hateful."

Diny realized, *Mam is not afraid of my silly questions or challenges*, and relaxed her body into the comfort of her mother's embrace. Mam's heart swelled at the depth of love Diny exhibited to those around her.

Cornelia did not divulge details of the great divide felt by those groups born mixed-race, the negative slang others used to denigrate them, the social exclusion they experienced. Just as the Dutch East Indies was ruled by white men wearing suits, the contradictions of their time steamed over decades. The Dekkers' picture albums were filled with idyllic images, but beneath the surface they all struggled with race relations. Those incongruities were not easily explained.

Over the years, Diny watched Mam entertain friends of every race, loving all people, sewing clothing for those in need, or helping at a local event cooking with other women. Mam's friendships were connections of one soul drawn to another, without notice of skin coloring.

Her friendships were suited to each other sometimes despite a lack of similar activities. Instead they shared an ability to sit on the veranda with hot tea and cookies, discussing their great admiration for books or music. They talked about pertinent issues while sharing their love for the island of Java. Every encounter was intermixed with laughter, some resulting tears, always encircled by a deeply innate desire to live and love well.

However, the social groups surrounding the Dekker family were sometimes mean-spirited and outright racist. Mixed-blood friends shared heartbreaking stories of being called inappropriate names, of having property stolen or damaged, being unable to find employment, excluded from social circles and events. The Dekkers knew brilliant islanders with fantastic ideas and incredible leadership skills, who only found employment in low-ranks of a career. They were never permitted to lead a company or serve as manager or owner. Yet the local population also had names for pureblood Dutch settlers, calling them "*took*" and other slang words.

"There is no way to change the mentality of hatred," Mam told her children, "unless we first show those people how to love. Some people in our world do not know what real love looks like. And we learn how to love by first accepting God's unconditional love in our lives."

Well then, Diny considered, just what color is love?

Semarang, July 1933

Now Diny was twelve, and her level of social interactions became more complicated, but she always enjoyed time spent with *Kokki*, the Dekker family's cook. Kokki engaged Diny in lively Malay conversation in the kitchen as Diny helped prepare evening dishes or fruit desserts to learn important skills just as Mam had learned. This became a weekly ritual with Kokki mentoring a young, eager student.

"*Tab*, Diny, hello. Thank you for coming to assist me today."

Diny kissed Kokki on the cheek then stepped to the side, watching Kokki work, settling down on her haunches.

"Not today, love. Off your *djonkok*, Dien, and on the stool. Mrs. Dekker asked me to train you." Kokki encouraged Diny, pulling her onto a stool.

Diny sat on a wooden stool, inspecting each glass jar of spices lining the counter: cinnamon, mace, ginger, nutmeg, cumin, coriander. Kokki told her stories from centuries ago, of animals and their adventures, true stories about children living in shanty villages along the Ciliwung River, in patched-together huts and shack homes.

"Where do their parents work?" Diny inquired.

Kokki placed rice into a serving bowl, and said, "Some work for foreigners, like the Dutch or British people, and others work at the docks unloading cargo ships or driving *becaks*. You know, pedaled taxis driven by men on bicycles?"

"Yes, Mam and I have ridden a becak before. Those men riding the bikes are skinny." Diny grimaced.

Kokki laid her spoon in the rest and sighed at Diny. "They pedal becaks for Europeans, and work hard for their families, *Meisje,* just like your father does." Kokki covered the bowl with a towel to keep it warm. Then she ground an array of spices in her heavy stone bowl. The chicken cooked and sizzled, and Kokki sprinkled the spices on top, tossing and swirling the meat into a fragrant mixture.

"But do you live in a patch-hut with your children, Kokki?" Diny asked.

Kokki smiled, shaking her head, reminding Diny, "*Grietje*, you are kind to us, and I am thankful. Your father also cares for us and shows it. He pays a generous wage. Please do not worry about *Kokki*, sweet Dien, nor be concerned for my children. We are well." She chuckled and reminded Diny to wash up for tea.

Diny felt badly for those children living in poverty. When Diny and her parents floated on the Ciliwung River, they watched herds of women tending shacks, cleaning their clothes in murky water after long hours working for other prosperous families. She supposed the effort required to labor all day, then return home exhausted to spend little time each night with family while trying to remain optimistic.

The river proved a waterway and a great divide — the gap of society — a deafening space between them. There was little possibility for change without the genuine efforts of those who afforded their own life and could extend aid toward the destitute. They were caught in a current, unable to paddle upstream or circle back.

Pieter's police role of Adjunct-Chief Commissioner/Superintendent of Semarang's Police involved intense training. He had been promoted to adjunct-technical-leader of the field police in the Semarang residences of

Japara-Rembang. His role included the enforcement of "moral policing" of communities, an important assignment of police. He traveled for work, and was involved in fundraisers, dinners, and galas.

His career held Diny's appeal, a sense of mystery and importance, and during this prelude he became increasingly quiet and reserved about the nature of his work, burdened by troubles, by the general challenge of policing and his desire to remain confidential about serious issues. If the police state had expanded, growing with reputation and size of force, they must be considered "modern." The upper leadership surmised that modern police officers proved the islands were "civilized." In response, recently-graduated recruits from the Soekaboemi Police Academy conveyed their thoughts to Pieter concerning new methods of policing and how they were using the police manual to inform their work.

Johan Hendrik Smith arrived for dinner to join in hearty conversation and delicious eating. Diny remembered Mr. Smith was the co-author of the police training manual and often hosted him for dinner when they lived in the mountains. Mr. Smith was Semerang's newly appointed Deputy Superintendent of Police. They ate dinner together and then watched darkness descend upon the veranda.

Cora studied Smith's neatly pressed white suit, and asked, "How has Pieter kept you busy this last year, Mr. Smith? Are you quite overloaded with work?"

He chuckled and slapped Pieter on the back. "My old colleague here appointed me the Chief of Intelligence. I think my role is just grand! I spend most of my time sorting out all the criminals and trying to manage the opium investigation." He waved his cloth napkin in the air, and continued, "These islands are a gem, Cornelia, but they produce vices far more damaging than just nutmeg." His laughter echoed into the gardens.

Cora warily glanced at her children, who paid little attention to the conversation. *Djongos* cleared the dinner dishes, then lit the veranda torches to keep away mosquitoes and bugs. He returned balancing flaming plates of bananas, *Pisang Goring*, much to the delight of the children.

"Magnificent and *lekker*, dear Cora! You have really succeeded with this one!"

Pieter piped up about the value of moderation in life, now being disrupted with a luxury like a dinner treat, but Cora lightly waved him back, spouting off about "the value of friendship and generosity."

Diny savored warm banana slices melting into her mouth, with vanilla, nutmeg, and cinnamon swirling into creamy goodness and sweet reward. She anticipated this moment all day, and smiled at her father's friend, who raised his fork to her in salute.

"Little Diny, worry not: I oversee Semerang port and will make sure not all our bananas are exported! We must save some for you so *Djongos* can flambé them to your delight."

Diny beamed with each bite. Smith continued on about his idealistic view of the country, of a future Indie well within their lifetimes. His irresistible zeal for people, for good purposes, and toward educating the police force inspired Pieter, in better spirits that night than in months. Their time together spurred him toward cheer.

Pieter leaned against the railing of the veranda and covered his face, then flashed the flack of his lighter and ignited a cigarette.

Mam tucked her children into bed and the evening continued on the veranda, with Smith and Dad talking about possibilities and plans. Over the next two years stationed in Semarang, Mr. J.H. Smith became a regular guest on their veranda each month for dinner, and always requested flaming plates of bananas.

Medan, Sumatra, Dutch East Indies, 1935

Diny eagerly anticipated their mail delivery. Depending upon where they lived, they might only receive mail once a week. When living in a more populated area, they received mail nearly each day. She found a letter addressed to her and tore open the envelope from the Netherlands and removed the thick pages of writing. Tante Sietske, farmer's wife to Oom Cor, faithfully wrote letters, and Diny was thankful for a Godly woman to mentor her through some challenges.

Late in the school break of 1935, Pieter Dekker was placed in Medan as the Adjunct-Head Commissioner and Technical Leader of the Field Police. The Dekkers moved from Semarang onto a new island of Sumatra when Diny was nearly fourteen, Nelly was nine, and Jan was six. They knew every 3-4 years Dad would transfer to a different place — sometimes a different island — but each of those important transfers provided Pieter a promotion.

After they left Semarang, Pieter was moved into a new role in Medan, the capital of the island of Sumatra, which would be their home for several years. Medan blossomed into an enterprising city after Dutchman Jacob Nienhuys, the

Sultan of Deli, authorized the cultivation of tobacco in the rich, volcanic soil. The area transformed from pristine rainforests prior to 1860 into a promising endeavor of profit as the landscape and economy shifted. The discovery of oil in the 1880s, the founding of the Royal Dutch Society for the Exploitation of Petroleum (forerunner of Royal Dutch Shell), and other important exports fueled growth, including rubber, palm oil, and tea, providing wealth for many families in Medan.

Pieter's new role was the Adjunct-Chief Commissioner, Superintendent of Police. After a few months, in September 1935, he was again promoted, to Chief Superintendent of Medan Police, the head of all of Medan Police, overseeing all of Sumatra. His successes with each location provided the reward of promotions in Medan.

His promotion was noted in the newspaper as the surrender of the leadership of Mr. Halkema and the establishment of Mr. Dekker, which happened through the resigning of the Chief Superintendent of Police Mr. Halkema. As noted in their local newspaper:

In attendance of the promotion ceremony was the Deputy Resident of the Governor of the East Coast of Sumatra, Mr. Allaart, along with local Medan Deputy Resident Mr. Bruggeman, and other representatives of Deli and Serdang. The gentleman Halkema commented that his departure stemmed from difficulties and disagreements at the office of Chief Superintendent of police and with strict maintenance of discipline in a large corps. He thanked the present police civil servants for their understanding and cooperation. Ultimately, the gentleman Halkema determined his successor, Pieter Dekker, would better serve as the Chief Superintendent of Police to make the East Coast a name for itself.

The Adjunct-Chief Superintendent of Police Dekker then spoke and established that he accepted, in accordance with the oral orders of the Governor of the East Coast of Sumatra, the management of the Field Police, the Provincial Investigation Department, and the Cities Police of Medan. He thanked Mr. Allaart and Mr. Bruggeman for their presence. Then he mentioned he would accomplish and fulfill the arduous tasks before him, he would set forth to secure the help and cooperation of all, and to jointly strive toward a first-rate police force. Thereupon, on behalf of the Governor, Mr. Allaar led Dekker's oath of office, which they prepared with a written declaration, on which by him the office of chief superintendent was fulfilled.

Finally, the gentleman Bruggman spoke of the tremendous value of devotion and work, noting the well wishes of the resigning official Halkema, and declared thanks for his pleasant cooperation, and for the cooperation of all those present during the transition. With this, Dekker was deemed the Official, and a group photograph was taken.

* * *

Participating in cultural activities proved vital for Pieter's career, including the 40th Anniversary of the Medical Circle, an event in which leaders assembled in the capital. At these events, floral arrangements filled the hotel halls and reception rooms, and walls displayed the extensive and interesting accolades and awards of the physicians, some of whom had received the Dutch Orange highest honors. Of note was the presence of Dr. B.M. van Driel. The collection included Dutch and other European doctors.

In another newspaper article, an art exhibit was noted:

In January 1936, an important Chinese exposition came through Medan, entitled, "Painting is Poetry; Poetry is Painting." The gentleman Chen Ten Siaw, manager of the Kunst Museum in Hankow, toured through Europe, exhibiting in Paris, Rome, and Geneva. Now, on his trip home to China, his exhibition opened in Singapore and Pinang just prior to Medan. The opening of the exhibition at the Su Tung Middle Hid at the Sportlaan drew crowds of people, including various European Societies. Attendants included Lady Van Suchtelen, the Sultan of Deli, the Deputy Resident Mr. J. Allaart, and Medan's Chief Superintendent of Police, the gentleman P. Dekker. Many authorities had been accompanied by their ladies. The Chinese consulate, the gentleman Tienmai C. Huang, loved the opening, and introduced the gentleman Chen Ten Siaw with a few words on the depth of China's age-old culture and painting. Chen Ten Siaw argued that the source of the world's civilization has been from China, the Realm of the Middle. The ups and downs of the written Chinese characters followed the ups and downs of everyday life. He then painted a demonstration with the brush and with his fingers — especially the pinky finger — which offered an interesting result. And after the speeches and opening, guests could admire the artwork and tour the five halls of the exposition.

The Dekker family's life in Medan was like Batavia, Soekaboemi, and Semarang with the magnitude of Pieter's work, which brought new depth to their lives. Time flowed across her parents' faces, aging them, as their lifestyle from one destination to the other was quite similar, participating in the same culture between islands, establishing work and home structures, spending happy evenings on the veranda.

Some evenings entailed letter writing to family, or spending time discussing Pieter's younger brothers' latest events back home in the Netherlands, as well as Jan Wolter's promotion and Cornelis' farming challenges. Each month Pieter wired money to Nicolaas to help with monthly expenses in Amsterdam while finishing school. Now Nicolaas found a permanent job and moved into his own flat in Amsterdam with his partner, a man he committed to for life. When Nicolaas called on the telephone to discuss the delicate issue, Pieter listened and thanked Nicolaas for entrusting him with such important personal information. As the eldest son, Pieter held the mantle for the family. He found it difficult living thousands of miles from his younger brothers, as he could not adequately guide and encourage them from afar.

Likewise, Cornelia corresponded with her family via letters and occasional telephone calls, and relished news from home and from the vibrant lives of extended family. Yet Cornelia received the dreadful news of her father Huibert van den Bout's death on the 8th of February 1936. The frigid Dutch winter of 1936 was even more icy than ever for Cornelia's mother Pieternella, now a widow. Cornelia seemed to settle into pain and fear, distraught that she was unable to attend her father's funeral in the Netherlands.

"He was only 68! So young and alive!" Mam groaned, as though she ignored Huibert's wavering strength and lack of vibrancy as of late, his infrequent letters halting completely. Their telephone often rang for Cora, but her migraines intensified, and she remained in her bed unmoved. Thousands of miles away in the Netherlands, Mam's brother Rokus settled their father's dealings, and settled the home in Hilversum. He resided in Amsterdam, with a room for Oma van den Bout in his home, and the comfort and ability to provide for her.

While they were saddened by the loss of Opa van den Bout, Pieter reminded his children that Opa lived a full life. Pieter seemed sensible about such matters but grieved in his own way. Diny's parents were her rock, her strength, leading her to God, the Ultimate Rock. Later, Diny considered that the loss of her Dad would devastate the entire Dekker family, as they all benefited from his capable way of loving others completely and unreservedly. The depth of richness her parents experienced together, their lovely marriage, and balance of personalities and perspectives, would instantly shatter.

Certain places varied throughout the islands, like the boat-shaped mountain homes outside Medan, but the generosity of the people remained similar, including the offering and scope of shopping markets, educational opportunities for their children, and social interactions like church friendships and professional connections.

The area surrounding Medan was lined with tobacco, tea, rubber, and timber plantations. The city was formerly named *Deli* by the Dutch enterprising the original tobacco plantations. The Dekkers lived near the shoreline, on the borders of nearby jungles, close enough to walk to swimming pools.

On this part of northern Sumatra, orangutans enjoyed a natural habitat amidst jungle trees, high above the ground. The creaking overhead canopy stretched broadly across miles, providing them a thriving forest home. Orangutans were brilliantly colored burnt orange, brown, and crimson. These spectacular apes of the rainforest dominated the jungle in compelling ways, their aerial acrobatics like ballet in the trees, and Jan looked for orangutans every time they hiked through the jungles.

Diny's depth of love for her parents soared, and she thanked the Lord for their love, for their steady example, and for their dedication to God. She settled comfortably into family patterns within their home, yet ventured out to bicycle or swim with friends, exploring some independence.

Swimming with friends over the summer provided a routine to keep her social circles adequate, exerting energy in activity, finding an outlet for her outgoing personality and enthusiasm. Her first splash into the water exhilarated her, and she emerged from the aqua wave chilled. Diny felt invigorated. She always held a fondness for sports, and built friendships through tennis, badminton, and table tennis, which extended into daily life. On holiday, they traveled to mountains, stayed in bungalows, and hiked dormant volcanoes. Their lush paradise surprised them at every turn.

Monsoon rains flowed water runoff into a river, gushing down streets. Even with foliage absorbing the rain, the amount of water pouring down had little avenue, and raced along the street like a river. Local children swam in the monsoon waters, but the Dekker children were never allowed in those rain rivers. Mam was afraid her children might fall and be swept away, and diseases were transmitted from river water. The Dekkers watched from windows while those other children splashed freely.

Some Saturdays Dad took the family to the Sumatran shore, where waves provided a respite, a certain energizing, and left a balmy murmur echoing in

Diny's ears. Pieter's laughter resonated across the shoreline, mingling with the wild noises of jungles, birds, and orangutans. His confidence and brightness contained a sense of buoyancy both hopeful and peaceful. Pieter's influence as a great optimist offered a wonderful lesson to teach his children, instilling in them a sense of possibility.

"To laugh at myself and look at the positive side of life always brightens a situation," he boomed. Pieter could be serious, but usually concerning "serious" things, like his love for God, family, or work.

With busy and fruitful years and a burgeoning police department under Pieter's able leadership, their children matured. Her father's colleagues often visited, and all became closely acquainted with the police force families. During school breaks, Diny went swimming and played tennis with neighborhood companions. While their two years in Medan were enjoyable, fulfilling years, the children were still growing and excelling in their own ways.

Batavia, Java, Dutch East Indies, June 1936

The thick, intertwined branches of the winding banyan tree enveloped the backyard of their Batavian home, and seven-year-old Jan attempted to climb the vine-like branches, sometimes successfully, to reach the roof of their home. He remained determined despite being petite for his age. Diny advised him of the considerable distance from their roof to the grass below, but he hushed her.

Banyan trees commonly housed birds which build nests in the hardy wood. Mam said the local birds — even parrots! — ate the tree's figs. No wonder those parrots were so colorful! The thick web of spindly branches attached upon other trees, building an almost maze of vines from the ground up to the tops of the host trees, with the crisscross of tentacle-like branches appearing like steps up the original tree. Some banyan trees appeared as a curtain of long spindles, almost an array of parallel walking sticks extending from the tops. Diny hid inside the base of some wider banyan, or *ficus,* as Kokki called them, inside a cave of her own design.

The Dekker family had just settled into their home after relocating again to Batavia, island of Java. Their return offered an ecstatic reunion with Diny's best friends Lenny ter Haar, Anneke Hennink, and Johanna Meijer. Diny also enjoyed meeting fifteen-year-old school classmates, especially the social, fashionable girls who dressed in high-waisted skirts, with button-down collared shirts and white canvas shoes. While Diny was now required to wear glasses, at least, she decided, she could wear more stylish frames. She and Lenny sported matching haircuts: bobs with a curl on the end, swooped across her forehead, sometimes pinned.

In their move, Pieter received a generous promotion, from Police Chief in Medan, on the island of Sumatra, to Chief Superintendent of Police (*Hoofdcommissaris van Politie*), in Batavia, on the island of Java. Pieter advanced into the apex of his career: the role of Head of Police for the entire country, headquartered at the country's capital city of Batavia. They would live in the Tjideng, a residential area for affluent Dutch. While the Dekkers were not wealthy, the Governor wanted them living in a safe place.

Their home seemed more vast than houses on side streets, for on Laan Trivelli homes boasted large living spaces, a living room, three bedrooms, a kitchen, a study, and front veranda. Economic downturns still gripped much of the world, and the financial crises reduced Dutch governmental policing expenses, but all remained "rust en orde" (law and order) and "zaman normal" (normal times) in Pieter Dekker's world.

Pieter did not look directly at the camera in the photograph which appeared in their newspaper. Three other monumental leaders posed with him on 9 June 1936, the day prior to starting his role as new Chief Superintendent of Police. Meanwhile, Maseland, Latour, and Van Ginkel stood solemnly next to Pieter. They wore starched white ceremonial uniforms with badges and awards honoring rank and length of service. All soberly stared down the camera, as though contemplating the gravity of the future. Pieter looked down, away, as though suddenly shy or unwilling to be recognized for his honors, unfamiliar with the attention a position necessitates.

Pieter became Chief Commissioner of Batavia as the Police Chief of the capital of the island of Java, and as Batavia was also the capital of the entire Dutch East Indies, he was Head of Police over the entire country of Dutch East Indies. Later, in a different ceremony, vice Adjunct-Chief Commissioner of Police, Louis Dekker, was named to his post as Pieter's assistant. They previously worked together as colleagues, creating the Police Academy on the Soekaboemi, found a solid affinity in their efforts, and were eager to continue as collaborators.

Pieter collected a few souvenirs over the years, including rare stamps, amassing into books a collection he felt was worthy of display. He kept them on his office shelves. Likewise, he gathered articles written about him or written highlighting notable efforts of the police force. A clipping from *Eerste Bataviaasch Nieuwsblad*, dated Monday, 9 June 1936, depicted him as *The New Chief Superintendent of Police* over Batavia, with his accession into the circle of absolute police-authorities. The article loosely read:

Tomorrow the new Chief Superintendent of Police, the gentleman Pieter Dekker, begins his role. He arrived on Sunday from Medan and accepted his official position in the presence of the Resident of Batavia, Mr. H. Fievez de Malines van Ginkel; the Head of the Provincial Inspection, the gentleman F. Latour; and many members of the higher personnel of the Batavian police body. The Resident gave a word of welcome and wished luck to the new Chief Superintendent. Tuesday Dekker begins his appointment, in which he is set to prove to the trusting public that the leadership of Indies and her largest cities — Indie's largest police force — is in his good hands.

His task is difficult, and he stands beside the troubled current state of the police body, which is not as strong as it previously was; yet, as the Resident surmised, "We can only row with the oars we have, and we row quite well." That expression conveys the hope Batavia's new working environment will be conducive to Dekker's work, and as a gentleman, he will extend his efforts until he is satisfied with his result. The Resident ended with the promise the new Chief Superintendent can always count on the police staff for complete support and cooperation.

After The Resident spoke, the adjunct Chief Superintendent PHJM Maseland extended Dekker a welcome on behalf of the entire Batavia police body. In response, Mr. Dekker responded to the greetings. Regarding the ups and downs of the role, the gentleman Dekker stated the verity that he was an heir to the police department and felt a certain sense of an historical moment while stepping into this new role, as he was prepared. It would be the first time a graduate from the Soekaboemi Police Academy would be called to serve as the Chief Superintendent of Police to Batavia.

Dekker gave all in attendance his personal guarantee he will do everything in his power to establish the strongest police department in the Indies. There was a self-aware efficiency in his attempting to convey that the tasks which he seeks to accomplish are heavy, but he mentioned others working in joint efforts with him will together strive to accomplish the target. He called on all his coworkers to fulfill this just calling in unity. "With all his inner strength and energy, it is surely achievable." With all the police force's power and energy, he considered the goals certainly reachable. Ultimately Dekker assured the group he runs a strict police force, and his practice is to begin with a strength and hardness concerning the law; he would also work under strict integrity. Dekker ended with the expression of the hope none would be ashamed for placing their trust in him. The final speech marked the official welcoming and swearing-in ceremony, and afterwards, all the present authorities remained at a reception, to speak with and converse with the new Chief Superintendent together.

Pieter's new job encompassed overseeing various departments: Criminal Investigations (*Misdaadrecherche*), Economic Investigations (*Economische recherche*), Identification and Photography (*Dactyloscopic en Fotografie*), Traffic (*Verkeerspolitie*), Police Vice Squad (*Zedenpolitie*), Firearms Equipment (*Afdeling vuurwapens*), and Administration (*Administratie*).

As Police Chief, Pieter and his family lived in a home provided by the police force, and *Djongos, Baboe, Kokki* and *Kebon* were assigned to them as helpers. Since the newspaper announced his arrival, they welcomed many visitors. Pieter and Cornelia also attended numerous induction ceremonies and events, and Pieter mused that if the newspaper published his photograph, those in the city would know him, even though he might not know them. This was a challenge surrounding the public role, of constant scrutiny, being watched when in public at the market or cafe, knowing those around were witness to his life for better or worse, and the reminder that a life of integrity was worthwhile.

Diny recognized from an early age her Dad held an extremely prominent position, as the third-highest ruler in the entire country of the Dutch East Indies. Tjarda van Starkenborgh Stachouwer became Governor-General on 16 September 1936, and was a man of strength and lineage, aristocracy now complete as the absolute highest Dutch official in Indie. The Resident of Batavia, second in command, was a mysterious man of Dutch social nobility, named Henri Fievez de Malines Van Ginkel, often nervous and uncertain. Third in command held the title of the Head of Police, Pieter Dekker, who happened to be her Dad.

Pieter emerged as the epitome of diplomacy and decisiveness. His tall, commanding frame hovered jovially but steadily, and Diny always sensed his admirable love for her. Over the years, he labored skillfully and rightfully earned promotions. Diny marveled at the news that her father was the first Police Academy graduate in the Dutch East Indies to hold the title of Head of Police.

Moreover, she beamed when Dad wore his crisp white uniform, with the regality of his epaulets on his shoulders, the sash crossed his chest, and his sharp metal sword securely placed in its encasement and fastened tightly upon his side, ready for battle. He had one white uniform and another black uniform for different ceremonies, with golden buttons and ironed clean lines on his uniforms. The symbol of the Police Chief Commissioner was signified by a gold crown with two crossed swords and oak leaf beneath.

Pieter and Cornelia were humble, although living in a circle of influential people, simply because of Dad's work and prominent position. The Dekkers acknowledged God as the giver of all and gave him glory and thanked him for the possibilities he gave Dad to develop his gifts and knowledge. Mam's skills as a great cook involved her planning wonderful meals with Kokki. She sewed the most beautiful clothes and loved to embroider. Over the years she taught Diny to cherish the art of sewing and embroidery too.

Because Cornelia accompanied Pieter to official parties, she was dressed nicely for occasions and designed elegant dresses. They hired an Indie seamstress just prior to a major event, who arrived at their home each day, sewing all morning and afternoon, taking an initial fitting of the garment, then returned the following day, laboring until finished with her original creation. Cora was stunned to have her own personal seamstress!

And for the duration of those social interactions, because of the social status present at notable functions, women were not permitted to attend a social event twice in the same dress, but required to wear specially designed clothing, specific for each gala or function. Cornelia was always bothered by the financial waste, judgment, and comparisons from the ladies in the "high society" and from their social club, sometimes sharing her hesitation to attend receptions.

"Why must we present ourselves so formally — and with the pressure of a new dress? How can we afford luxuries when our priorities are not for those indulgences?" Cornelia sighed after dinnertime, while still on the veranda. Their children were in bed, but Diny heard her parents' echoing voices, listened from her window.

Pieter folded his newspaper and tapped it on the coffee table beside Cornelia, frowning before responding, "We both know and realize maintaining appearances keeps our government happy." He smiled. "I am thankful for this job and for the blessings and rewards it provides us," he continued, then walked toward her. "But I join your disfavor for the falseness of spectacle, the disingenuous way of appearing… perfect."

"Well, you surely understand, then! But why do they all insist on shallow rivalries?" Cornelia grumbled, leaning into his arms.

"Trivial matters are important to some people; not to us. We sometimes forget God's love too, even though we know God has saved us by grace, and we are forgiven. But every day we must remember and remind ourselves of His enduring love."

Cornelia never sought to be part of the gossip, comparisons, or empty discussions of socialites. Because of Pieter's job and the society they lived in, they were required to attend fancy receptions and lavish parties. Pieter might present a speech or develop an interpersonal connection, sometimes with foreign leaders and diplomats, so they must look presentable.

A rivalry festered among the ladies, with groups of women whispering about other women. Cornelia remained quiet among chattering groups of women. Sometimes she spoke to the ladies who spread gossip, asking them to remember their manners, or departed the conversation. Besides, Pieter possessed a quiet sort of success concerning his role; only she knew of his humanness.

When the newspaper published reports of Pieter's achievements or of new police advancement, he read the journalist's perspective of their interview and chuckled about the situation. Later, Cornelia found the paper and cut out the article to save in her scrapbook. He never asked her to save those articles but appreciated her decision to do so. She never looked forward to social events but felt rewarded by Pieter's Godly influence on the police force.

At times, Cornelia either suffered a debilitating migraine seeking to be dismissed from Pieter's work activities and formal gatherings, the scent of Tosca 4711 permeating their home. In moments of chaos and crowds, she became introverted. Diny tried to decipher her Mam's condition. Her parents had a general medical book for guidance on simple medical issues, and she read the pages, hoping to glean important knowledge to someday become a nurse.

In the meanwhile, her dad needed a companion for his work outing, and sometimes Diny attended these functions, which further fueled her love for social gatherings. Diny assumed Mam stayed home to rest, and after tenderly tucking in the younger children at night, she might settle into playing Mozart records, while cross-stitching a new creation.

As part of his role as third-in-command over the country, Dad received a chauffeur to drive him around in his business car, with the number plate

B2, which stood for Batavia Car #2. The Resident had a car with plate B1, Batavia Car #1, and Diny assumed the Governor-General just took a horse and buggy everywhere. When Dad brought Diny with him in the car on some minor business necessity or to a social outing, Diny felt like a princess. Their time together was precious, and Pieter only utilized the chauffeured car for business work, but also spent precious time with his children, alone, to build into them character traits through specialized, individual outings.

Sometimes Diny and Pieter bicycled to the *Tanjung Priok*, Batavia's western harbor, near the bustling area formerly known as Sunda Kelapa docks. They pedaled their bicycles past palm groves, green rice fields, and coconut trees, along the coast, to the central hub of chaos around the docks.

Diny grabbed her dad's hand for comfort amidst the general roar of noise surrounding the import-export structure of the docks. The general lack of orderliness disturbed Diny, as men scrambled everywhere, catching outgoing boats, or assisting their team in tethering an incoming vessel. Strong, able-bodied men paraded up and down long ramps, into ships and out again with items. Diny and Dad rested on a bench to watch the action.

Diny observed men on the watchtower, positioned at the outermost area of the dock system, armed with guns, as though protecting a kingdom or a fortress. In a sense, they were, and stood stoically, peering out at the endless inky sea, for any approaching danger. If they added a lantern to their tower, they would become a lighthouse.

"Are those guns real, Dad?" Diny cried.

He glanced at the men in the tower, then stifled a laugh. "Yes, those are real guns. My staff inspected and issued them." He pointed at the guards. "They are watchmen, to safeguard our city, *Dien*, to fortify the port," he told her. "Their mission is to protect Batavia from harm."

"What if we are attacked, then?" Diny's face paled.

"Oh, darling, we are strong Dutchmen! Nothing can defeat us. We have a solid defense and our enemies are few. The army is small but powerful and will never see war. Rest easy in this security, *Grietje*."

He slipped his strong arm around his daughter and pulled her close. Dad's chest smelled like musky woods from soap, and sweat from the bicycle ride. Even after her father chased them in their palm-covered garden, his sweaty scent became somehow familiar and reassuring. His thick dark mustache tickled like a caterpillar when he kissed her forehead, changing her worried disposition into one of comfort and security.

They passed a length of time while watching ships maneuver through the water and guessed at their intended destinations. Ships ambled to stake a claim on a slip of port, hurriedly unveil their treasures, and deliver goods they carried. Diny considered the crates, their destination, and contents. She examined the Indo men with able hands who heartily scrambled around. She watched for a long while, deciding the chaos contained order, as a round of men used pulleys and cranes to unload two-masted sailing ships — *pinisis* — which had been full of timber from another Indie island. Then, another group loaded the vessel with heavy bags of rice hurled over their broad shoulders, or they hoisted massive wooden crates, presumably with spices, for another voyage west.

The entire wharf was occupied with animated, colorful Sulawesi ships as though anticipating the arrival of an armada. Distant lands echoed romantically in Diny's mind and beckoned her adventurous spirit. She longed to visit Bali or Guinea, as she heard of those islands and their unconventional dispositions and landscapes. Cinnamon procured from these islands would be delivered to Oma's wooden baking rack in Amsterdam, and pepper harvested here rested in a crystal pepper shaker on her Tante's mahogany dining room table.

She remembered maps of ancient cities, artist's renditions of naval ships with *Batavia-Werf Lelystad* emblazoned in orange, with a scroll unrolled revealing a flaming lion in battle, holding raised sword in right hand and three scrolls in left hand, a background of criss crossed anchors. The official crest for all ships in the Royal Netherlands Navy consisted of a crown on top, with four panels revealing a silver sword cross on red, a warrior lifting his sword atop his raised steed, a seven-masted ship in full sail, and cannon. Crests bore the name "de Ruyter," the great Dutchman of shipping legend.

Those wooden ships settling into Batavia's port were like those she studied, with royal carvings on the back of multi-masted *pinisis*, carved artistry of fierce red lions standing on two legs, with golden manes, holding ornate shields of lion and birds. Above them was a descriptive gold-jeweled crown alongside scrollwork. In other sections of the back of the ship, the stern boasted rows of mermaids, and protective angels sat atop with lanterns and swans. Ornate luxuries for a ship seemed frivolous and more appropriate in a church than on a fallible ship, yet what an impression to leave on those who saw the ship sailing away!

Diny and Dad walked toward their bicycles to journey home again, and she glanced around for the market where *Djongos* and *Kokki* selected freshly-caught fish for dinner. She longed to join in those early morning voyages, the scent of the sea beckoning her. They cycled home via the wharf, where Diny and Mam had browsed through the market, examining colorful materials, marveling at the ornate intricacies of fabric patterns and hand-carved household items in tiny shops. Just once a year they gather in Koningsplein to celebrate Queen Wilhelmina's birthday at the end of August and beginning of September, also called *Pasar Gambir*, or Gambir Market.

The Gambir Market featured hundreds of Asian-styled buildings containing kiosks selling food, artwork, and other items. It featured dances and movie showings, singing competitions, and artistic performances. Skilled Indos performed nightly *wayang* (shadow-puppet theater) performances which were especially popular, accompanied by gamelan music of metallophones and *kendhang* (percussion) keeping the rhythm. Locals enjoyed the cinema under bamboo tents. The regular market returned shortly after the annual *Pasar Gambir*, and was equally charming.

Dad took Diny home, then bicycled to *Hotel des Indes* on Molenvliet and prepared for the arrival of a Dutch diplomat, evident in the breezy, clean look of the Hotel that day, complete with smoothly polished marble columns and special banners welcoming a VIP. He situated his bicycle near the banyan tree offering shade, and sat under fraying palms, sipping a drink of paradise while watching dignitaries filter through and enter for the special event.

Chapter Six
Batavia, Late 1937

The carambola fruit bloomed in their neighborhood of Batavia, exploding fragrantly and hanging heavily from tree branches, as though the juicy goodness would leap off bright orange star-shaped fruit. Drips of overflowing juice streamed down one clumping bunch of fruit, and ants licked up the excess. Hidden luminescent starfruit cascaded down from underneath the expansive canopy. Sixteen-year-old Diny laughed, noting the waxy starfruit certainly deserved its name. Not until directly underneath the tree, looking straight up through the dappled sunlight, could she find a poetic moment of peace. Stars reminded her of an embellishment atop a Christmas tree and evoked festive family gatherings.

Earlier in the season, the carambola tree appeared as merely decorative and ornamental greenery, with bright red floral stems stretching out delicate pink and magenta petals. Monsoons fed blooms, pouring each day in the rainy season and halting at 5 o'clock in time for tea, the air resfreshed. Eventually, red and pink blooms transformed into orange-yellow stars, as though God was not satisfied with only a handful of blushing colors and wanted star fruit to dazzle.

Other lush and fertile landscapes also beckoned Diny. Green vines surrounded a large mahogany tree, banana tree fronds interlocked and banyan wooded foliage, thick like a canopy of grace, swayed overhead. Diny lounged on her back on the wet ground under the expansive carambola tree during a sweltering afternoon, trees dripping, intermingling with sweat and saturated soil. She dug her fingers into the ground, pulling up two fists of grass and fertile soil, clumps in hand, grime embedded into nails, as she whispered her promise to remain in Indie forever.

Butterflies flocked to various bushes and trees sodden with fruit and bloom, fluttering around, silently sipping nectar from stems. Any glimpse of a yellow butterfly reminded her of gentle brother Huib and his deep love for nature. His affection for small creatures, husky voice, and peace remained with her. With Huib buried in Bandung, now tied to this land, he would remain here, as Diny would remain here on Java. She was saturated by atmosphere, and vowed to remain, to grow old and raise her children in Indie.

Diny's brown eyes filled with tears, overflowing in the depth of the oath. A lofty pledge was like vowing her life to this country, and a sense of overwhelming urgency surged through her arms and legs. *Nothing will ever force me to leave this magnificent homeland*, she thought with certainty.

Diny heard Mam's call for her afternoon tin-bucket bath, and Diny lingered in a moment of reflection. After several minutes, she sprang up from the soil, released the clumps of grass, and ran.

On her way back into the house, she called for Nelly, who wandered in the gardens and waved, acknowledging Diny's call. Diny searched for Jan, who climbed through the mahogany tree branches. His eight-year-old frame remained small but wiry, full of mischief.

"Why are you crying, Diny? What happened?" Jan asked, dropping to the ground.

She shook her head and wiped her face. "I am sweaty. Time for the afternoon bucket bath. Grab the *gajong* and splash quickly. Then go inside." She tousled his blonde curly hair.

He seemed unaffected, shook his head, and called out, "Only if I can chase you there!" His cheery voice echoed in the trees as they headed toward the house.

That night as the carambola fruit blossomed, dripping juice along yellow ridges of starfruit, two men visited the Dekker's home as the family finished evening tea on the veranda.

Pieter remained in his chair as a clunky old car arrived at the front of their estate. His posture straightened, his breathing quickened, and he casually — yet sternly — asked Cornelia to take their children inside. He only spoke in a formal way when talking about his job as Police Chief and she immediately understood his polite mannerisms. These men were not friends from church, whom they had over to their home for an afternoon of coffee. *These men must be other police officers*, Diny considered.

As the car's motor halted, Pieter joined the men, affably speaking Dutch. Diny objected to her dad's orders, as she stared at the taller man's mustache, much like her dad's "thick caterpillar," as she called it. The shorter man's blond hair and limping walk seemed familiar.

Mam placed her hand over Diny's open mouth and shushed her, reminding her with a whisper, "This is Papa's business, *Meisje*, and not yours!" She looped her other arm around her darling Diny and escorted her away from her dad's conference, assuring her, "He will be fine, my dear girl. Do not worry about him."

Inside, the house grew darker. Diny prepared for bedtime and poured a warm pitcher of water into her rose-colored basin on the small nightstand in her room, the water swirling in the basin until it filled halfway up the sides. She splashed her face, then opened her small jar of rosewater, which offered a refreshing scent. Diny placed a dot of scent behind her ears and along her collarbone, and opened her lavender cream, churning the soft white fragrance on her hands before placing the lids back on the jars and setting them next to her basin. She brushed her teeth and tidied her room. The wind outside increased and Diny walked to her back-bedroom window, looking out to where her father and his associates had meandered in order to obtain some privacy on Dad's estate.

She watched the three men huddled in a triangle, each passionately expressing something, all of which seemed so… *important*. They smoked while standing together, shielding cigarettes from the wind, approaching three views, it seemed from their body language. The tall dark man swayed. The shorter, blonde man limped around a bit as though he was uncomfortable. Pieter stood solid, firm, his legs apart and arms staid, his body unmoved.

This meeting inflamed Dad's anger, and he shook his head, then broke his frozen stance and waved his hands, squeezing his cigarette between two fingers as though he would extinguish the smoke with just his fingers. His bellowing voice echoed in the gardens, lifted in the gusts surrounding them.

Pieter tossed his cigarette on the ground, smashed it with his boot, and motioned for the men to leave. The triad broke, the standing men scattered, and Pieter paced among the foliage, behind bushes, speaking passionately to nobody. She sighed. Diny creeped in nearing darkness to the front of their home and watched through the veranda as their car chugged and rumbled away from the Dekker home.

Diny raced back to bed and leapt into comfort, and in her evening prayers shared with God the troubles of her day, especially her fears surrounding her dad's encounter. Mam arrived and noted Diny's compliance for staying in bed, and slotted shut her bamboo window shades, then tucked her children into bed amidst Nelly's requests for a drink of water and Jan's desire to go outside to climb his tree. Mam quieted the children and softly assured them of their father's love, then prayed with them. She sat at the edge of Diny's bed and sang to them, then requested they remain inside to sleep.

As Diny rested, she tried to sleep while light faded outside. She attempted to settle into the onset of coolness of the imminent evening. Those familiar sounds of *tjitjaks* scurried on walls, while frogs echoed sounds from the nearby pond. The local *saté* man resounded outside, dragging his cart down neighborhood streets, and familiar scents settled into their home.

As the sky grew darker and the sun turned pink and amber, she had not heard Dad return home, so Diny checked on him. She could see from her window he remained in his special walking spot, pacing a footpath into the soil. Moments later, Diny's mother found him in the backyard.

"Cora! My sweet!" he exclaimed, then nestled his face into her hair.

Pieter affectionately called her *Cora,* and she was quite fond of his sweet name for her, which Diny rarely heard. She thought her dad only used the name when alone with Mam.

Cornelia had pulled her long wavy hair out of the upswept caramel bun, allowing her long tresses to glow in the light, hair flowing down her back, a hairstyle she reserved for bedtime, for the intimacy of the evening. Cornelia rested her face into Pieter's neck, as though breathing in his skin, and they remained together, holding each other while Diny barely perceived their mouths moving as though talking. Their swaying turned into dancing in the breezy evening.

Relief flooded Diny's body, swelling through her heart and stomach, reaching her arms and creating exhaustion. She nestled in bed and gazed out the window. The sky became black, and lingering streaks of red remained, as though a volcano's fury unleashed from the stars.

For weeks after, Diny longed to ask Dad about his backyard business conversation, but she knew better than to anger him or interrupt his Bible reading in the quiet early mornings. In the evenings, he was preoccupied with work. He spoke of general life challenges and difficulties each person faced, often within a thematic lesson.

Pieter often reminded them, "Well, my children, in many cases in life, we are required to go through hardships and disappointments to reach our goals — and there is no other way."

He now devoted more time at the main headquarters of the Police, and brought home notebooks to write in at night, beside a lantern, often remaining awake after the home grew hushed and serene. Their family time never suffered, yet worked late at night. Their veranda evenings together continued just as sweetly as before, if only for the addition of Dad's narrowed blue eyes gazing into the distance. His sparkle undiminished seemed displaced.

In prior years, in other roles, he spoke about his roles: creating the Police Academy, training new police recruits, or writing the academy manual, his face beamed with happiness and confidence. When they moved to Semarang, and later, to Medan, he glazed over details like names and events, as though experience brought increased restraint. Diny was uncertain of the reason behind the sudden, complete secrecy. With more power also came more responsibility.

Within weeks of the two mysterious visitors, Pieter and Cornelia were invited to another social event: a fundraiser for a police force philanthropic organization. He urged Cornelia to join him, and she reluctantly hired a professional seamstress to prepare an outfit. An Indie woman arrived the next morning to measure and sew Cornelia's dress, stayed until late afternoon, and arrived early the next morning to complete her project, incorporating an additional fitting and hemming. This type of expected requirement for each social regalia became exhausting to Pieter and Cornelia. Even so, they could hardly complain about the opportunities in his new role as Police Chief.

All through the years, Diny knew her dad as a hard worker, and learned from Mam how to run a home. Cornelia paid special attention to Pieter, especially during busy seasons. Dad assumed the head of the house, but Mam stood behind him — beside him, really — and together they made necessary decisions. The children understood when Dad was away, they were required to uphold the same rules he had established, and respect Mam as they respected Dad, completely.

They rarely witnessed their parents express love for each other in physical manifestations, like hugging and kissing, with the children as their audience. If Pieter placed his arms around Cornelia and kissed her, whispering, "Cora," dramatically into her ear, she exclaimed, "Pieter, the children!" and blushed against his affection, while returning the gesture of love. Their respected love, expressed in smiles, spoken gratitude, doubled as a simple look, smile, or nod between spouses, an expression of love without the need for words. Their children knew they adored each other and were a solid match of personalities.

A beautiful harmony resonated between them, as though their marriage sashayed a delightful dance. As they held hands, Pieter stepped forward, and Cornelia stepped backwards in response. If he twirled her in one spinning direction, she joined him in whirling around, and took notice of the scenery, discovering a reason to laugh along the way. Diny also noted her parents never quarreled in front of the children. Those discussions happened in the privacy of their bedroom, or outside in the far-reaches of the backyard garden, away from tiny ears.

Her parents raised them in a loving, strict, yet fair home. They were examples of Jesus' love, even through her shortcomings, disobedience, and rebellion. Mam urged her to look to Jesus, instilling a great trust and deep love for Him. She taught Diny to embroider and sew and trained her — by example — in God's model for a Godly wife and mother.

Mam became angry when Diny disobeyed or stubbornly talked back, or when Diny escaped out her window during nap time to swim with friends. Diny claimed a sixteen-year-old was ready to make her own choices, which indicated she was swayed by the influences of her friends, who also decided to sneak out of their homes.

Although most of her rebellion seemed innocent, behind her parents' rules and regulations were love and the assertion they knew more than she, as they were older and had witnessed great tragedy and disappointment. They did not want to lose her because of some foolish teenage mistake.

She asserted herself, crying, "The world is a safe place, Paps! Especially here in the middle of the jungles! What can happen here apart from a curious monkey chasing me for food? Are you afraid I may encounter a ferocious tiger?"

Yet they prevented her from reading newspapers, and rarely listened to radio news reports with children present, so unless her parents mentioned notable tragedies, Diny remained unaware of rumblings and rumors in the world, of local skirmishes, or natural disasters. This was meant to protect her from mature situations.

Instead, she deliberately disobeyed her parents during nap time, which she claimed she was too old for. The window unlatched quietly, and she climbed silently, slipping off the frame and over the bush below. Other times, she simply wandered through the house to leave out the front door.

One afternoon as Diny escaped to go swimming, she jogged along the cool marble floors and forgot *Djongos'* daily task of mopping the marble floors during naptime, slipped on the wet floor, and fell into a heap of a crash. She smacked her face on the hard marble floor and three teeth pushed through her lip and broke her skin, resulting in tears and blood. The floors had always dried by the time the Dekker family awoke, but Diny skipped napping to meet her friends and experienced a bloody lip and a bruised ego. Moreover, a stern discussion emerged as Mam and Dad were awakened from their restful naps.

With Sundays reserved for church services, Pieter included himself as part of a rotation of men who enjoyed reading the Bible and discussing their insights and perceptions from the front of the church. This group of men served as a leadership team and took turns offering a sermon. Only once per year a visiting pastor arrived to deliver the message. When her dad preached a sermon, Diny and her family settled in the first row and she smiled widely, her heart full of enthusiasm and pride for Dad's accomplishments. She would not always understand the topic of discussion, but Diny hoped his efforts helped encourage people to know God. Pieter's father, the Reverend Jan Dekker, preached inspiring messages for those in his congregation in the Netherlands so many years before, and he would have been proud of his son's preaching ability and Diny's matured ability to sit on the front pew and listen.

At night, as evening sounds descended, Diny surmised she had been afforded a wonderful childhood being raised in the tropics. Nelly, Jan, and Diny grew up in Indie as normal kids, attended Dutch-speaking schools, relished holidays in mountain bungalows, and enjoyed life. Their lives were marked by commonplace occurrences, like frequent earthquakes which moved palm trees to bend from one side to the other, while rumbling volcanoes simmered. The Dekker family enjoyed leisurely vacations, surrounded by palms which lined the coast, swaying palm fronds fluttering in the air, thriving precariously at water's edge: never quite in the water, and never completely suited for the land.

Batavia, Java, Dutch East Indies, 1938

Their childhoods progressed easily, with few immediate troubles. The general merry nature of Furloughs kept Cornelia afloat and buoyed full anticipation within her spirit, and friendships grounded them into a sturdy life in Indie, with connections via Pieter's vocation, compassionate friendships transcending place or similarities.

By the time she turned seventeen, Diny realized apart from her own rebellions, she experienced a wonderful childhood, and she was surrounded by much love. Diny's best friend Lenny often visited after school, and they read the school material together and studied for tests. Lenny's bright wit and eagerness to learn, coupled with a solid memory base, allowed her to almost instantly know and understand the work, and her exemplary work was evident. Diny tried to remember as much as possible, yet toiled relentlessly to make decent grades, requiring much effort and arduous study sessions.

After primary school, Diny graduated to the academic high school, HBS (*Hogere Burger School*). For students excelling in math (*Mulo B*) or language (*Mulo A*), there was also the Mulo (*Middelboar Uitgebreid Lager Onderwys*). HBS school subjects were difficult and diverse: sciences, geography and history, complex mathematics, classic literature, and drama, among others. When required to learn different languages, her mind reeled with the complexities of other vocabularies besides Dutch: French, and German, with some English. The final examination (*eindexamen*) endured before graduation included challenging, lengthy essays and multiple-choice tests which confused her and complicated matters. *If I spoke with the teachers, telling them verbally what I know*, Diny thought, *I could complete HBS and be closer to my dream of becoming a nurse.*

Long familiar with the varied Dutch heroes who shaped the world before her, Diny found interest in the Dutch explorers they concentrated on in social studies classes, men like Willem Schouten, who discovered a passage around the southern tip of Chile in 1616, and seemed to keep exploring, or Henry Hudson and his northern river adventures in 1609 America. Men like Adriaen Block were less familiar though still intriguing, as his navigations brought depth to the American landscape.

In science, they investigated Dutch men like Copernaeus and Galileo, men who sought exploration in the array of galaxies and stars, of the immeasurable expanse of space and heavens. They beheld beauty in the skies, as Van Gogh, Vermeer, and Hals sought in painting daily life, depicting simple scenes, still frames, arranging color within light and shadow to portray the textured everyday existence of milkmaids and women composing letters; of blue expanses in the fertile Dutch fields; of fruit bowls; and of rich Aristocrats prominently displayed in Rembrandt's masterpiece, *The Night Watch*.

Explorers and painters traversed the field of science, astronomy, and art, and perhaps their own accomplishments enlightened souls who found beauty in their work. They transcended daily life, for the masses to understand, grapple with, and love.

Diny continued to reach out in friendship to her sister Nelly, who withdrew from social interactions in a peculiar way. As Diny pursued, Nelly retracted. Opportunities seemed missed, and Diny longed for a close sisterly relationship with Nelly. As younger girls, Diny climbed into Nelly's bed for morning giggles. But Nelly shoved her out, rolled over, and continued sleeping. She never pursued Diny and seemed to live in her own world, apart from family, apart from relationships. When they were in the yard together, Nelly wandered away to the far reaches, with her doll, jacks game, or book.

Now Nelly was twelve, and Mam voiced challenges in drawing Nelly out of her defenses, claiming small victories over the years toward lowering Nelly's protective shield. At age nine, Jan marveled at Diny's excitement and followed her, eager to join in her adventures. His light humor charmed Diny, and she read him books on the veranda. Jan practiced reading to Diny, who challenged him with difficult books.

She held his hand when walking down the lane to the swimming pool or on a family outing through street markets, and Diny proudly pointed out animals, antique treasures, or carved wooden boxes to hold trains, books, or balls. Jan's curiosity expanded, with his interest in creating new things. Dad reserved pieces of old clocks or bicycle parts in a spare shed outside, and let Jan explore his desire to create a new machine or tinker through an idea from the spare parts, fueling his interests as an inventor.

Diny's exuberant friend Willem De Vries was also seventeen and of Dutch heritage; his father worked for the Dutch government in foreign enterprises, yet he admitted an aloofness and confusion concerning what position his father held.

However, Diny felt certain about one aspect: an interest in the energetic Willem and his shiny blond hair, bright green eyes, and broad frame. She knew nothing of his character but his impeccable attire drew her attention, as his clothing was designed and stitched by a well-known seamstress, Djahit, who created his family's clothing. The allure of his financial steadiness appealed to Diny.

Willem surrounded himself with numerous friends, especially teenage girls, who seemed to angle for Willem's friendship as he engaged their acquaintances with zealous stories of travels in the Spice Islands. Willem's stories always sounded farfetched. At the end of a school day their teacher waved them goodbye and students began to walk home.

Willem gathered his textbooks and asked Diny if she was an islander or of pure Dutch ethnicity.

She scowled at him. "Why does it matter?"

He whispered, "Could you just indulge my curiosity?"

"Of what importance is heritage? All people are created equal in the sight of God. Man is the one who destroyed that legitimate truth."

He cleared his throat. "Sounds grand in theory, Diny, but it remains a fairy tale."

Diny shrugged.

Willem continued, "So you have one islander grandmother? Let me guess — are you Dutch-Javan?"

She fumbled her books and growled.

He picked up her history book and handed it to her.

"You might as well ask about my weight or to see my unmentionables drawer! I am as Dutch as you are, Willem. But you have blond hair, blue eyes, and fancy outfits you hire someone to make. I have none of those."

Willem's eyes widened as the volume of her voice raised and classmates turned to watch them.

She continued, "I am a Dutch person born here, living here, and maybe my blood runs thick with spices!"

Willem blushed, "Try to not overreact."

Her eyes glared. "Then speak with a measure of tact! The Dutch have long been recognized as open, tolerant people. If you seek a life of peacekeeping and government work, while still concerned with ethnicity, then maybe talking to me is forbidden too?"

His mouth dropped, and he again surveyed her skin, hair, and eyes.

Diny raced out of the classroom and sobbed all the way home.

Later, after family tea time together, Diny walked to Lenny's house to play cards and found Willem also walking along the way. She crossed to the other side of the street behind palm trees.

He jogged over to her, his face reddened. "Sorry, Diny. Those questions were so inappropriate. I will not ask anything of you again." His right hand covered his heart and then extended to her.

"I never shake hands," Diny replied, "upon my mother's assertion of the vulgarities of the practice. But on this occasion, I will accept your apology with a nod." She nodded once and then crossed her arms.

He chuckled.

She glared at him and said, "Willem, take a more diplomatic stance on issues of ethnicity and culture. You know I tan quite easily, right? And have you seen my father's dark hair? Why does it matter if my ancestors are Asian? How is that offensive to you?"

He shook his head.

"Because you would not befriend me unless I was Dutch?" Diny stepped back into the street to cross to the other side.

He sighed.

"Well then," she said and continued walking, "Dutch people are not as identical as you might suspect. We are as varied as any other culture, and our variance provides diversity in thought and ideals. These are positive traits, Willem, remember this."

"You are right," he admitted. "I am still learning about these majestic islands. My desire for a friendship can only result in my embarrassment and the laying bare of some prejudice."

"Well, the next time you speak to me, consider greater substance." She ran for Lenny's house, not daring to turn around to see Willem's reaction.

They bicycled as a group of friends after school or joined in swimming parties when term was finished, and Diny perceived Willem as the center of attention for their gatherings. She felt wounded at his ignorance, then later decided to use caution in her interactions with him.

Willem's career ambitions included becoming Governor-General of Dutch East Indies or Prime Minister for the Netherlands. After HBS, he would seek a political degree in the Netherlands. Willem's family also took Furlough every six years and transferred to and from Batavia several times over the years, including the month Pieter became Police Chief.

Late in the second term, 1938, their collective group journeyed to the Tanjung Priok, Batavia's western harbor, to walk along the docks at dusk. This sun-splashed wandering reminded Diny of her outings with Dad to the Priok, when she rushed ahead to the coast line, eager to feel the familiar sensation of water tickling her feet and sand encasing her toes. Willem walked near her, finding a shield from the breezy air. Her floral dress fluttered, knees showing in the wind. Mam advised her against wearing fancy dresses apart from special occasions, so Diny hesitated to act on her impulse of splashing into the water, especially with the tide.

As she considered slipping off her shoes to feel the adrenaline spiral through her stomach, she guessed at Willem's thoughts if she acted spontaneously. Perhaps she should stop worrying and ask Willem to hold her shoes as she danced in the surf. The sun slipped past the horizon and pink-hued cotton clouds thinned toward the clearing. Remnants of air swirled around, and for a moment the clouds wisped and obscured the rising amber moon like a swirling mustache on a blank face.

Diny generally acted on impulse, but with growing maturity decided to think about her actions. She observed others in her group: her best friend Lenny in her polka dot dress was walking with Willem's friend Calvin. Their two other girlfriends, Anneke Visser and Johanna Meijer, wore fluttering blue and green blouses and black flouncy skirts, always had groomed hair, and conservative arm movements. Ann walked beside Simon, another of Willem's friends, with Jo alongside Frederik, Willem's cousin. Diny's girlfriends seemed compelled into maturity and adulthood more quickly. She felt responsible at home, challenging her younger siblings in their studies, yet her own mind still drifted into daydreams.

Perhaps four years ago, among female companions, her friends may have suggested a splashing game while wading into the water, emerging soaked from the sea. Yet during her Semarang days, Diny was not permitted to travel alone with female friends unless chaperoned by adults, and Dad claimed Medan too populated to let down one's guard about safety. Even an unchaperoned journey to venture to the coast at almost eighteen years old did not bode comfortably for Diny's Mam. However, with Dad away on a neighboring island for business meetings that month, and his work all-consuming, her venture went unnoticed.

No matter the situation, Diny considered, *since Dad's work does not interfere with my life.* Instead, his role as Police Chief offered them opportunities they might not otherwise imagine, with the comfort and privilege of their home, daily helpers, and Dad's chauffeured car. Now, with Dad away, absorbed with urgent issues, Mam became overwhelmed with managing their home and family. A request for a journey to the coast was not what Mam had envisioned in a day off from school, yet her weak voice beckoned Diny to remain safe, and Diny called out to her mother as she was leaving, promising to return home that evening.

Diny and Willem walked behind their group of friends. The churning water sprayed against boats docked along their path, and she watched as his eyes scanned the water. She also stared into the expanse, hoping to spot birds, vessels, or sea creatures.

"Diny, I should tell you something." Willem stopped and allowed their friends a moment to pace ahead, then spoke softly. He reached out to hold her hands, and recognized her startled retraction and wide, fearful eyes as she pulled away.

"Now that my Father is working in Batavia, I think he will live here forever. I plan to go to the Netherlands for trade school and then return to live here on the islands. Plus, I am excited about the prospects of our growing friendship. Maybe you feel more for me than just a friendship?"

Her throat dried and she could not speak. At nearly every encounter he found a way to offend her.

Willem frowned. "Sorry to overwhelm you. I always speak my mind." He sighed into the distance. "Look! Where does that ship sail? Sumatra, maybe?" He pointed toward a ship sailing away from them.

"Or maybe to Holland," Diny suggested.

Willem commented on his father's work and frequent absences. Despite all appearances, perhaps the home was not as cheery as Diny imagined.

"I would rather have Father here at home, instead of the money his work affords us," Willem said. "He is traveling among the islands now. I wish he played tennis or badminton with me! I barely even know him, Diny."

"I am sorry, Willem. I cannot imagine how hard it is for your family. How does your mother handle everything alone?"

"She has more hired people at our home than family members," he said. "She even hired a *Baboe* to tend to us when we were small. Our caretaker still helps my younger siblings but is no longer welcome in my room."

Diny always imagined all the parents here took care of their own children, as her Mam and Dad did. She could not fathom Willem's pain, the disappointment of obtaining worldly wealth and opportunity, but being emotionally bankrupt and relationally distant from his parents.

She asked, "Can you share your thoughts and feelings with your dad? Or tell your Mam how you want to spend time with her? My parents encourage respectful honesty."

"I tried before, but he says his career helps me, too. He calls his work 'golden handcuffs,' because he is offered finances and opportunities, but feels bound to the job. He said I should be thankful for all it has afforded." Willem sighed.

"Then I will pray for you, Willem," Diny promised, "and I will ask God to offer you direction and insight. I hope our friendship can be an encouragement."

He looked uncomfortable and crossed his arms. After a minute, he frowned, and mumbled he was glad she was thinking of him. As they continued walking, fog and darkness covered their view of the seas. The group hiked up narrow wooden stairs from the beach toward the market street, leaning against each other to offer room for other couples who descended the steps in happy merriment, perhaps starting a bonfire on the shoreline.

Diny's group wandered the market square and meandered stalls lit for *Pasar Malam*, the vibrant and busy night market. They sorted through colorful fabric, handbags, scarfs, and jewelry, and marveled at hand-carved wooden accessories, furniture, intricately woven rugs, dried spices, and foods.

After searching through treasures, Jo and Ann purchased some items. Then they lined up behind *becaks*, the pedaled taxis, where men served saté and other meals from their vendor carts, and the air was fragrant with spicy chicken with peanut sauce. Lenny and Diny shared a saté plate while Simon and Frederik ate *Nasi Lemak*, a banana leaf filled with coconut rice, roasted peanuts, cucumber, hard-boiled egg, and *ikan bilis* (dried anchovy), topped with the spicy *sambal* (chili) sauce. Soon they all needed to return home. Their laughter echoed as the group paired off to ride a *becak* home. Two of the *becaks* lurched forward and sped away with their friends, while two other *becaks* awaited them.

Willem offered Diny his hand as she stepped into a *becak*, and sat next to her, then spoke Malay instructions to the driver. He whispered in Diny's ear and they both laughed lightly. Her heart raced, surprised by the familiarity of his presence. The becak pitched in movement along the street.

Lenny sprinted over to them. "Diny, I am late and Mother is bound to send out a search party. Can we share a *becak* together?" Her eyes were wild. "Calvin seems intent on staying for a while to enjoy saté and shop on further streets, and I most certainly would not walk alone...."

Willem frowned but promised Diny a ride at another time. He spoke directions to the driver, paid him in advance, and helped Lenny into the *becak*.

"This was *heel mooi,* so *prachtig* — a fun and beautiful evening, my friends," Willem sighed. He tapped the side of the *becak* and gleamed at Diny, as the *becak* lurched forward and began to cycle away. Diny squeezed Lenny's hand, and they both rode home silently, grinning broadly about their evening at the coast.

Batavia, December 1938

Just two days after Christmas, their class field trip to a volcano arrived. They would journey to Mount Gede Pangrango National Park to hike along twin volcanoes Mount Gede and Mount Pangrango. Pieter walked Diny to school Tuesday evening, after the family meal on the veranda. Dad sternly reminded her to remain on the train, and with her teacher for the entire hike, especially as the trip was at night and vicious beasts like tigers could be lurking in the shadows of their volcano or in moments where their train slowed at stations.

"Be assured if those instances happened before, Diny, they can certainly happen again," he forcefully reminded her. Diny pulled a sweater around her tightly, blushing in the evening darkness, glad her father could not see her eyes.

If only he knew about the becak ride, she thought. She was anxious to spend time with Willem, yet he had not called on her, nor telephoned over the last few weeks. Diny still felt haunted by Willem's vacant, blank eyes after she spoke of praying for him. She preoccupied herself with Willem's ideas and blond hair instead of concerning herself with Dad's rules. After her class assembled at school, Dad walked home, leaving Diny to remember his expectations.

Diny searched the room to spot her group of companions. Anneke and Johanna dashed over to her, and linked arms. Lenny arrived just as the group departed to the train station, and rushed up beside Diny, eager to visit on their train ride. They chuckled at their teacher's assertion they must sleep on the train, but soon fell asleep. When they awoke at Mount Gede Pangrango National Park, they began the hike to the top of the volcano in darkness, except for the full yellow moon, serving as a shining light to guide their steps in the dazzling moon.

From the height of the ominous volcano Mount Gede, brisk air filling her lungs, Diny felt eager to conquer the rocky landscape. Their classmates chatted noisily, and Diny heard the musical outpouring of Willem's laughter ahead of them, further up the slope, his chuckles echoing. Diny and Lenny pulled each other along to complete the final ascent of the hike, and at last they had scaled the mountain.

The teacher talked about the volcano: eruption dates, the composition of the rock at their feet, and other important data, all of which they discussed in class the previous few days, but Diny's mind soared with imagining the view of the sunrise. The stillness and clarity of the air in the valley below and horizon beyond provided an almost serene canvas for those sunrise colors.

The last moments of darkness before the first light of day felt the coldest, especially in the mountain air. She tried pulling on her sweater but could not find the sleeve. Even with the bright moon, she could not distinguish her friends amidst huddling, giggling teenagers and the uproar of the wind. Diny felt Willem's arm assisting her into her sweater. She pulled her sweater cozily around her and turned to thank him.

Willem's eyes glistened in the full moonlight as he mumbled something, but the wind continued to hasten, as though it were ushering in the dawn.

"The sunrise has started!" he shouted, offering a sideways glance at her, and turned toward the arc of light emerging on the horizon. She nodded and he shuffled rocks under his feet.

"You smell like a jasmine flower, *Dien*," Willem said, and lifted his hand to swirl a piece of her long wavy hair through his fingers.

Diny thought of the white glossy flowers in her family's garden. She clipped jasmine from the garden and placed stems in her hair. By now, the wind had dislodged the jasmine. She thanked Willem but did not believe his assertion. They stood together, in awe of the majestic splendor. The light was rising higher with each minute, streaks of orange expanded toward the grasslands and jungles far below, shining over the canopy of trees interlaced in a shelter, light like a window opening to the sunshine beyond the sky. As orange hues faded into the golden moment of the daybreak, Diny determined to treasure this moment, to fully face the dawn, her eyes on the eastern horizon.

Willem again leaned over to Diny and asked, "May I call on you this evening, after tea time? There is something I would like to ask your father."

She nodded.

He smiled with relief, then rejoined Calvin, Frederik, and Simon.

Diny returned to her group of friends. Their class descended next to Javanese Edelweiss. The Edelweiss was an alpine flower she had long-ago associated with Huib, as he happily picked bunches of flowers during their mountain holiday just weeks before his death. Though the flowers matured and bloomed months ago, a few selected blooms remained, lingering. And near the train station, among other stalls of goods, a man in a booth sold garlands of flowers. Diny purchased a small dried bundle of orange, pink, and yellow Edelweiss blooms for Mam and joined her class for the train ride home.

When she arrived home Wednesday morning, just as the family awakened to the day, she entered the house with a renewed vitality resulting from her windswept journey. However, Diny sensed an atmospheric alteration. The vigor she still experienced from her volcano expedition, along with the conviviality and certainty of their lives in Batavia, suddenly seemed distant, as though a frigid winter surrounded their tropical and rational senses. Diny handed Mam the flowers and Mam weakly smiled her thanks.

She sighed, "I have not seen Javanese Edelweiss in years, *Grietje,* since our Selabintanah holiday more than a dozen years ago and dearly appreciate your thinking of me. Not since Huib's Edelweiss…" Mam's eyes glazed. She sat on the veranda, and Diny — feeling her mother's momentary aloofness — crept back inside, allowing Mam a moment alone.

With each turn in their home, Diny sensed a quiet pervading their haven. Her parents spoke outside, in hushed tones, with arms crossed, and Mam occasionally in tears, covering her face with a lacy handkerchief. She darted between rooms with reddened eyes and a mottled face. Diny assumed her perceptions were mired by lack of sleep, so she went to her room and fell soundly asleep in her bed until early afternoon. When she awoke, her siblings exited their own states of rest, yet the frigid atmosphere remained.

Diny stared at sister Nelly, who calmly read a book in the sitting room. Diny wondered if Nelly held memories of their beloved lost brother Huib or a misplaced emptiness in his absence. Surely a large chair seemed ample space for nine-year-old Jan, not content sitting for long moments or snuggling unless he was ill. But Jan played outside in the yard, digging holes or building huts.

Perhaps at that age Huib would no longer sit with his teenage sisters, instead preferring drawing portraits, painting watercolors on canvas, or convening with nature. She would never know. His talents had not yet matured at age four, at his death, not yet emerged forward, pressing into a confidence or a profession. Huib's photos had been tucked away long ago, into those tidy piles in the corner of a bureau, or Mam's memory book about him, and he was never mentioned.

Perhaps those who pass on can grow even more dear in the mind through recollections shared by family, photographs, and written stories, Diny considered. Since her parents no longer spoke of Huib, Diny resolved to share with Nelly about their darling brother from memories, which faded in the last decade. But Nelly refused, pulled her book away, and retreated to her room, leaving the large chair empty and Diny evicted from her emotions.

Diny remembered Willem's visit that evening and freshened up to cover any symptom of worry from her face. She wore a favorite blue dress, tan sandals, and a shell necklace, a memento from a coastal holiday. When their four o'clock veranda time arrived, her parents presented themselves from their backyard conference with a satisfied disposition even, amid their wrinkled clothing.

Dad had planned a feast for their meal, including a pig roasted on a fire. As the Dekker family ate dinner, and sipped tea while listening to Vivaldi, Pieter's smile returned, and conversation mellowed into humming, a rhythmic narrative keeping time with Vivaldi, and later Chopin. As Djongos bought a crispy and sweet banana dessert, Diny's mouth watered. She casually mentioned Willem's imminent visit and Dad's smile faded into a stern, disapproving look. His blue eyes were icy and distant but Mam reassured Diny her friends were always welcome to join them.

Djongos lit six torches around the perimeter to repel against pesky bugs, and as a light for evening activities. Diny tried to not allow Dad's concern to persuade her emotions, and when Willem arrived, she noted his blond wavy hair groomed neatly. Willem wore crisp tan trousers and a cream-colored linen shirt cuffed at the sleeves, and carried a blue sport jacket, as though he were attending an afternoon garden wedding. His tidy appearance was accompanied by a garland of jasmine wrapped in paper and tied with a yellow ribbon.

"These jasmine blooms are from my parent's garden," Willem said as he handed Cornelia a bouquet which Diny assumed was intended for her. He said, "My favorite flowers are jasmine. Now I see you have a fine assortment in your own garden."

She blushed and he continued sharing, "They may seem like the simplest of flowers, being mostly white, but their scent remains all day long." His brow was damp with sweat. "While the *jasminum sambac* is a gentle flower with sweet fragrance, the Dutch East Indies considers it sacred and symbolic. The white color symbolizes purity."

Out of the corner of her eye, Diny caught her dad conveniently leaning his head back, drinking the last few sips of his drink in one giant gulp, his eyes rolled back in the moment. Cornelia invited Willem to sit down, and Nelly and Jan suddenly finished dessert and were excused.

Willem glanced around the extensive front garden, unrelenting in his sincere compliments to Pieter on his expertise at botany and graceful floral aesthetics. Pieter stood at the corner of the veranda. Diny hoped he would not dart away unnoticed. But he did not.

Pieter finally spoke, replying, "Well, Willem, we have hired a *Kebon*, as I assume your father also has the budget for, so our gardens are impeccably maintained, at little exertion on my behalf and entirely upon our hired help. I appreciate your compliment, as I enjoy wandering our garden estate, which extends into the back."

Djongos cleared the dinner dishes. Willem spoke of his interests and job aspirations, yet when the conversation turned to Pieter's police work, Pieter's pacing halted, and he froze, his face like stone. He set down his glass and walked away. Diny frowned as she examined her father, and his pained expressions. *I should have warned poor Willem to avoid my family today.*

Willem did not seem to notice and smiled, perhaps lost in his own momentary lunacy. He was oblivious to their stern assertions and asked to speak privately to Pieter. For the first moment in their meeting, Willem's eyes carried hesitancy and doubt. Pieter lit his evening pipe and stood at the edge, teetering toward the garden. Diny sighed inside.

Pieter motioned with his pipe for Willem to join him in the garden. Willem jumped from his seat and clanked dishes, while nodding his thanks, apologized, and profusely thanked Cornelia for tea and cake before joining Pieter.

Mam looked at Diny tentatively. "He certainly has a way about him. Willem needs to convince your father of his intentions toward you. We know nothing of his character and I have no time for frivolities." Mam retreated into the house and Diny remained on the veranda, surprised by her mother's sudden departure.

The descending sun dropped behind the mangrove trees and light glowed across the yard until fading.

When Dad and Willem had not returned one hour later, Diny grabbed her cross-stitch pattern to keep her preoccupied. As she stitched, using the light of the torches, she heard a rustling in the mangrove next to the veranda and caught Jan jumping from a height to the ground.

"Willem is so *leuk*, a funny guy, Diny, and so peculiar," Jan laughed. "He kept talking about our garden! Who cares, right *Dien?* From up in my tree, I can see him pacing in the backyard, like he is following Dad."

Diny's eyes widened and she tossed the cross-stitch on the table, then whispered, "Leave them alone, Jan! This is an important discussion!" She chased her brother into the house, but Jan's blond hair bobbed up and down as he jogged faster than she could catch him.

A few moments later, Willem emerged alone, and mumbled his need to return home, considering the late hour and his previous absence with the field trip the night before. With Cornelia retired into the house, Diny sat alone with her cross-stitch, trying to visualize each hole in the pattern, breathing away tears. She realized his dialogue with Dad had not been favorable.

"What happened, Willem?" Diny abandoned her work and joined him.

He stepped down the driveway, his hands up in resignation. "Excuse me, Diny. I highly regard you, yet I must leave." He sprinted and reached the street before he turned back, calling out, "I will see you at school tomorrow!"

But she ran toward him, unwilling to let him go that night in confusion. "Willem!" she called into the darkness, and turned to the street, stumbling on a scratchy bush.

Willem pointed a finger at her, guarding his space. "Your father said no." He looked deflated. "I may not court you right now, Diny. He rejected all my ideas. We can remain friends until you are eighteen, and afterwards, chaperoned visits here until he decides otherwise."

She crossed her arms, defending herself from the cooling air. "I am sorry, Willem. I knew what a state my parents were in today and should have advised you to postpone your visit." She hoped he did not feel rejected.

He straightened his jacket. "Waiting one day never changes the outcome."

"Who really believes that, Willem? But we leave for Furlough soon, anyway."

"We are also taking Furlough, and my dad thinks immediately afterwards he will be transferred to Australia. You know how the Dutch government likes to keep us mobile, especially after nearly a year away."

Uncertainty brought knots to her stomach. To think she finally transferred her friendship into a possible affection, and suddenly they might catapult into other lives, away in other continents. Willem promised to see her at school and raced off into darkness. She considered following him but lingered on the street, transfixed.

One weekend afternoon soon after the climate changed in their home, at lunchtime when Diny looked worried and escaped to her bedroom to lie on her bed, Mam followed her, and sat at the edge of Diny's cozy bed. Diny cried and held her fuzzy brown teddy bear, and she was again four years old, holding the precious bear now thinning with a rubbed-off nose. As a young child, the teddy bear provided joy and laughter. But as she grew older and less disposed to playing with toys, it was tucked away for instances where she needed tangible cuddles and encouragement.

"Diny, why are you crying?" Mam searched her daughter's darkened eyes.

Diny's throat surged with a knot of emotion, her pillow soaked, and she wiped tears from her face. Mam stroked Diny's head, pulling the hair into a bun, allowing the heat to escape from her head and neck.

Mam reminded her, "You have always been a truly passionate girl, darling, and I feel sad when you do not aptly express yourself. I do not think this is healthy, running off from lunch and retreating to your room."

Diny nodded and replied, "Mam, when I express myself, I get into trouble…"

Mam stifled laughter and replied, "The goal is to speak respectfully, my darling *schatje*." Mam leaned over and kissed Diny's forehead, then grabbed Diny's hands gently. "What bothers my eldest *Miesje* today?"

New tears formed in Diny's eyes as she swallowed at the persistent throat knot. She whispered, "What is wrong with Dad? I see you talking outside in the garden and you both look hurt. Are you and Dad angry at each other?"

Mam's green eyes widened. "*Dien,* this is not about our marriage or family. Dad and I love each other tremendously and are committed to each other. But we prefer to discuss delicate police work matters in the privacy of the backyard, and there is nothing you can contribute to those conversations." Mam smiled radiantly.

"What of my friendship with Willem, then? Why did Dad reject Willem's offer at a courtship?" Diny glared at her.

"We hesitate because of Willem's character and his false personality. Dad needs to become more acquainted with your friend before making such a decision. The only goal in that relationship would be marriage, of course." Mam reminded Diny of the importance of honesty, Dad's approval, and humility through the process. Diny's eyes pleaded for a more suitable answer, as Mam's response was not enough.

Mam continued, "Diny, your father has a stressful and significant role at work. He is the Police Chief of the entire country, the third in command for the Dutch East Indies. This is a tremendous task! While his job is more than just a place to work — but a meaningful career — he recently encountered some terrible difficulties."

Diny knew those difficulties were outside her scope of understanding. The atmosphere shifted within their once-peaceful veranda in the evenings, with Cornelia's down-cast eyes and Pieter's once-light demeanor brooding. Both emitted a silence like stone.

"Why do you talk to Dad outside, at night, far from the house?" Diny knew what her mother's response would be, but her curious nature seemed to always ask the probing questions.

Mam blushed. "Diny, what if God told you all the hidden and unacknowledged struggles in the world? What if God shared everything, from poverty to sickness, financial ruin to moral bankruptcy? Would you become worried, feeling anxious He was unable to bring hope and peace? Perhaps you think you can handle those heavy issues. Or perhaps not. You might wither in pain from the burden of the world. But He can handle all our needs."

Diny's breathing evened, and she sighed, her throat knot residing.

"God knows all of those things, and delights to hear our prayers and provide for our needs," Mam said. "So now your earthly father faces monumental challenges. Trials so weighty, I weep to think upon them. If you knew of the particulars, you would be extremely disappointed. I believe our Governor-General tries the best he can to lead, but I think he is trying to appease the Dutch government in the Netherlands." Mam sighed.

Diny lay in her bed, astounded. *What issues were of importance?*

Mam cleared her throat and stood, smiling. "Another thing too, Diny, God has called me to help Dad, talk about issues, and encourage him. Everything he shares is confidential. Now, remember, these are heavy burdens which you might face someday with your own husband. Someday, but not soon for you. For now, you do not need to know all the complicated details of these challenges."

Mam walked to the doorframe and turned back, her eyes and face softening. "Diny, do not make yourself ill by worrying about Dad. Keep trusting the Lord for his strength. Dad is a strong man of sound faith and will weather this challenge fine."

Chapter Seven
Batavia, January 1939

Pieter paced in his tidy, efficient office, sturdy boots clomping on waxed marble floors. Three years of police work in Batavia had been excruciating and exhausting, and he felt weariness and age in his gait, along his back, in his legs, and within his boot-laced feet. He anticipated the promise of a new year and their season for Furlough just six months away, especially as this furlough, delayed for more than six months already, was extended due to the rigors of their police investigation.

Pieter rescheduled furlough for August, for a spectacular autumn in the Netherlands. He stopped pacing near his office window and habitually flattened his thick mustache. "*A dark caterpillar,*" his children called the mustache, which always brought a smile. Late morning sun beamed through the translucent glass, and as he pondered the details of a new enterprise, Pieter gazed into the active square adjacent to the building.

Governor-General Tjarda van Starkenborgh Stachouwer caught Pieter mid-step and entered his office without knocking. He shook around a stack of papers in his hand, waving them in Pieter's face.

"May I wish you a very Happy New Year, Stachouwer," Pieter began, tentatively.

The Governor-General ignored the welcome and furrowed his brow, his face turning crimson, and looked aghast. He spouted, "What happened with my report, Dekker? This was to be completed weeks ago and intended to be conclusive! Yet I only have a half-finished project. Where are the arrests? When can I read those searing newspaper articles splashing the apprehended faces of evil on the front pages, dignified men cast down, arrested with your capable hands?"

Pieter shook his head as Stachouwer continued, "Only a few hundred men have been captured? I frequently read about cleansing processes, but police officers other than you are doing all the arresting!" Governor-General Stachouwer puckered his lips together tightly, his face dappled with anger.

Pieter's quietly responded, "Yes, sir; I understand your directive. And I respect the orders you gave me, even though the instructions sounded dangerous for my men." He scratched his head. "Many arrests have occurred, and we are pursuing leads about high-society Europeans — people of good standing. Precaution should be taken before disrupting the lives of noble men, and moderation in all avenues seems a most respectable course of action."

Stachouwer recoiled, still visibly agitated. "Let me remind you of your duty, Dekker. In the most basic way, the colonial state and the police are commanded to serve and protect the community. In this case, you are more enthralled in your own causes: sheltering women and children against prostitution and trafficking. My mandate is Article 292 of the Indies Criminal Law translated as this: 'cleansing pedophilia from our colonial state, protecting underage young men from the advances of other men.' If you think investigating the situation beyond this directive is unnecessary or dangerous, then rethink your role. No man is above the law, even those who are supposedly of consenting age or nobility." He sighed.

Pieter stepped away for a moment to the office window where palm fronds billowed silently in the sunny breeze. His face revealed confusion as he turned back toward Stachouwer and replied with conviction, "I remember you urging me to take action and I listened to your guidance. Yet this is most certainly not a 'witch hunt' to uncover a scandal greater than we can handle, or some hidden plot, buried beneath the façade of trafficking. Trafficking is a crime, obvious and punishable. But the personal acts of consenting adults are not."

Stachouwer opened his mouth to reply.

Pieter held up his hand to offer a refrain, as he continued, "You reminded us to maintain the proper relationship with this country's local population as we carry out our business and duty. I accomplish everything you command me to do, including providing safe houses for women caught in unorthodox lifestyles, and places of protection for children suffering in grim situations. We offer resources for escaping, offer alternative employment options, and training on making better choices."

"Marvelous, Dekker, but I asked you to do more." Stachouwer looked stern.

Pieter continued, "I do not think it mandatory or judicious to continue to uncover more than what is presented, to engage in a new type of detective work, which I leave in the hands of the *gewestelijke recherche* division, as the Regional Investigation Department has more time and resources. The newspaper *Bataviaasch Nieuwsblad* has splashed about our actions, for certain."

Stachouwer seemed surprised at Pieter's bluntness and bravery, yet in the next breath continued his intended discussion. "Indeed, Dekker. I applaud your efforts and thank you for striving to protect women and children. But what about the actions of men? Your directive was to gather all those men — Dutch or local islander or native, or whatever you want to call them — adult men engaged in physical relationships with underage boys. This is no supposed 'homosexual witch hunt' by any means but the mere enforcement of the colonial law in which we must protect minors!"

Stachouwer inhaled the cigarette he carried like an accessory, which Pieter had not noticed, but smelled as Stachouwer exhaled the smoke toward him. Their commanding frames were situated in the same room, with similar uniforms and united purpose, yet felt kilometers apart, distanced, and Pieter's noticeable height could be used as an advantage, but he refrained from any act of disrespect. He shuffled away from the bright window toward the opposite wall, safeguarding additional room between them. Pieter stood behind his mahogany desk.

While he did not fear Stachouwer's repercussions, he remained concerned at the agitation and outrage Stachouwer displayed about this issue over the last several months, growing from frustration to livid display, as though his legacy hinged on arrests. Pieter could not decipher whether the Governor tried to appease wealthy men who had suppositions or theories, or whether the Dutch government in the Netherlands supplied unnecessary pressure, or if his directive based itself on the certainty of local tips from those seeking financial gain.

Pieter found great difficulty in simply standing before his superior official and receiving the negative diatribe directed at him as Stachouwer proceeded to speak in great depth about the contents of the reports in his hand as he waved them around. Pieter refused to receive those angry outrages as personal condemnation yet stood distraught at the length of disparaging remarks. Stachouwer's stories consisted of vitriolic letters and nebulous reports from various police officers in the field, describing underage liaisons, underground gambling rings, deceit and increased violence, and ultimately, whispers of rumors of corruption within his upper leadership.

Stachouwer continued pacing while talking, narrating the episodes described therein, flipping through pages of Dutch police officers' reports of witnessed illegal liaisons and activities, with each report explaining sickening details.

Pieter lowered his forehead in his right hand, and placed his left palm in the air, signaling for Stachouwer to halt his discourse. "*Genoeg*! Enough, please," Pieter implored, exhorting Stachouwer to halt. "I will read these reports, but to openly speak of them is nauseating."

"So now you finally understand my purpose! This is a priority, Dekker!" Stachouwer growled, "And your role as Police Chief hangs on the thin line of resignation or termination with my command! Success in this matter is your only hope in retaining your job as Chief." He slammed the reports on Pieter's desk, sending other papers and desk accessories flying.

Stachouwer paused at the door, and reminded Pieter, "Our police advisors in the Netherlands have already discussed a reality. We may need to reorganize the force, decentralize in Batavia in favor of local or regional control throughout the Indies. More power at the city level already transpired within the last several years. Our *veldpolitie* are skilled Field Police, proven as mobile and well-armed, but hired mainly in rural areas for security supervision. This type of decentralization will only continue, especially as the Indien elite access higher ranks these days. As you know, I will always stand as the ultimate power with my role as Governor General."

He thundered out of the office, leaving a wake of stale smoke behind, his cigarette smoldering on top of Pieter's previously tidy mahogany desk. Pieter stood up to usher Stachouwer from his office, but the Governor never looked back for a handshake or salute.

"Happy New Year, indeed," Pieter mumbled. "Not happy for the police or anyone involved in this mess." He used an envelope to sweep the cigarette into his ashtray, then reluctantly reached for the stack of typed police report papers Stachouwer tossed to him. As Pieter flipped through preliminary reports, he considered their call to be men of courage, strength, and cleanliness, with composed, dignified power.

Pieter read one statement after another from Dutch policemen, and wondered, "Only the Dutch policemen. Where were Indie reports?" In those testimonies, Dutch officers patrolled slums and dark corners of Batavia, providing valuable information about the troublesome activities of men they had arrested.

Other major port cities around the world also faced prostitution, and Pieter's mind reeled with the devastation those lifestyles produced. He attempted to clean up those practices, yet never procured Stachouwer's complete support or respect on the matter, and as soon as crime slowed in one area, it sprang up in another location, creating new lines of poverty.

Reports used code words, hidden police language, and described horrific, lewd acts of assault on underage men. Some accused were local police officers or prominent Dutch men, who recently relocated from the Netherlands to Java to take pleasure in worldly obsessions, from temperate weather to exotic opportunities. Others coexisted in the same social setting circles as the Dekker family, always hovering on the outside of a friendship, nervously speaking to Pieter briefly before retreating from his gaze. Pieter's confidence inspired some and frightened others, as though his blue eyes inspected the contents of their soul.

After reading through many police reports, Pieter was horrified to realize those young, impressionable men who were victims of assaults and "supposed-consensual liaisons" were locals, or *islanders* as they were sometimes referred. Ultimately, few reports listed those underage men as white or willing partners, and the evidence was clear.

The offending men deserved to be arrested, Pieter realized, if only to preserve the safety and dignity of all citizens. He sighed, "What was this civilized state? And why does the police force insist on asserting power through fear, control, and this urge to *civilize* this country?" Their Police Academy functioned smoothly, raising first-rate men of integrity to serve on the Force, resulting in highly-qualified men throughout the islands. Within those ranks some were ruined by corruption, intrigued perhaps by the allure of recognition while living an alternative lifestyle. In addition, local islanders were among the ranks of the moral and upstanding, and their numbers far outsized the highest leadership of all-white men. Even amid inequalities, Pieter felt generally certain their country was being governed with a sense of decency and distinction. This was his goal, his aim, at fair and unbiased service.

Now, with global issues pressing upon them, Pieter wondered if the Governor-General pursued an argument or some type of round-up to secure a legacy of honor? Or perhaps he sought to maintain the control of his kingdom? Had he suspected something generally devious about this directive? Pieter's hands trembled, and he shook his head. He lowered his head, overcome with emotion and unrelenting fatigue. *How can we proceed with this, while still honoring God?*

Pieter's youngest brother Nicolaas participated in an alternate lifestyle and Pieter held compassion for the homosexual community, despite his commanding officer Stachouwer's directive to gather homosexuals and place them in jail. *What shall they do with those men? Try them in court? Imprison them indefinitely? Deport them?* Pieter's youngest brother Nicolaas lived in Amsterdam with his partner, and Pieter genuinely cared for Nicolaas while simultaneously understanding the cultural ramifications surrounding that lifestyle. Nicolaas' care and friendship were separate from his sexuality, but as the upper-level government decided to target homosexuals, Pieter felt cornered, hovering between his roles as dutiful Police Chief and dutiful brother.

He paced to his office window and noticed the sun had shifted position over the last several hours. He lost track of the time and forgot to return home for twelve o'clock lunch with the family. His stomach rumbled out of pain and anxiety. Pieter remembered many times he was challenged by unexpected difficulties. He frequently visited these offices while a 2nd class lieutenant, and later, as a 1st class commissioner serving on the city's police investigations department, when even his busiest of days paled in comparison to the trials he now faced. Yet those smaller previous trials provided ample opportunity toward forming his leadership style and maturing his character, and he marveled at the Lord's hand of grace and timing for each new role.

As Pieter prayed aloud in his echoing office, he reminded himself of the vision he originally carved for his new role, and his desire to lead with genuine integrity, connect with trustworthy peers, and respectfully serve God and the country with the best possible methods. He searched his heart to eliminate selfish disrespect or dishonest motives, especially concerning the Governor-General's directive. Pieter laughed for a moment and whispered, "My job will not rise, or fall based on one simple event! This is just a difficult circumstance, stemming from destructive liaisons of selfish men. They must be held responsible for their actions, and I enforce those consequences."

He was determined to not let any challenge create friction with his family at home. He would leave this drudgery in the office, physically, and emotionally. Perhaps after he returned home and rested, he could figure out this mess. Pieter knew when the newspapers in Batavia and Amsterdam caught wind of this, they might pin him as the perpetrator. As Police Chief his aim was to protect and serve the people of his country, and uphold consequences for illegal behavior. For doing his job, he faced condemnation, which itself seemed intolerant, biased, and bigoted. Yet even the Netherlands viewed homosexuality as a disease or perversion. He only felt sorrow and pain for those involved in this entire situation, wishing the issue was not so polarizing and abstract.

Why did Christians seem to forget God's greatest commands? *Love God, and love others.* If Christians were to strive toward loving God and others, they might remain too busy caring and serving instead of judging. Love could soften a heart, cheer a discouragement, and bring hope to all.

Again, he peered out the window and watched small birds hop about the stony square outside, and envied their carefree, simple ways. They nibbled on crumbs, bugs, or worms, then lifted their heads and bounced around again. At length, they flew to the nearest tree. At times, birds gathered in unison, formed a wind in their synchronized movements, or swirled in chaos, each setting course for their supposed need or instinct. Some were perched on tree branches, others lined together, huddled on a branch. A flick of his finger would signal a chain reaction, all falling together, scattered. Even in the mild breeze, birds continued to float, hovering in the air, sailing into the atmosphere. Pieter continued to pray, seeking wisdom, speaking words aloud while watching and waiting.

On the tree closest to Pieter's window sat a colorful *budgerigar*, perhaps a pet escapee from someone's home. The bird's brightly colored feathers shone red, intermixed with yellows and blues, silky and smooth. This vibrancy rarely emerged in this busting city neighborhood. The bird's head cocked from one side to the other, as though listening to Pieter's words through the glass window. As curious as the bird seemed, he contentedly basked in the sunshine. Certainly, this *budgerigar* did not know where his next meal would come from, or where he might find shelter at night.

Yet Pieter was certain, and relieved to remember, if God provides for the birds, then God would most definitely provide for Pieter and his family. He would offer Pieter a way, a direction — in the morning, perhaps — but in the right moment when His words were most vital. His spirits lifted, Pieter slid the stack of reports into a large envelope, then placed the envelope in the top drawer of his desk. He locked his office and returned home.

Over the next two weeks, as Pieter cautiously carried out the Governor-General's directive, he felt enmeshed in the details and consequences. Second in command was the Resident of Batavia, Henri Fievez de Malines Van Ginkel, Pieter's direct report and mentor. Van Ginkel stood as a slight man with a limp handshake and small rounded spectacles. He seemed quiet and tentative, almost intemperate in his mannerisms, his dark hair groomed slickly against his scalp, his thin and delicate frame almost frail. Weekly, Pieter met with Resident Van Ginkel concerning issues involving crime and during this strained and important moment of time, met twice weekly regarding the Governor-General's directive: how to cautiously proceed, while sustaining the spirits of the officers.

Resident Van Ginkel seemed dismayed over the trafficking and prostitution of women and children, calling the homosexual clean-up "a lunatic witch hunt," and sniffing a nervous chuckle when they talked about the accused men, who usually cruised for younger boys. The Resident's voice strained, face reddened, as he fidgeted and cleared his throat. Pieter realized the pressure of this investigation must be great, and perhaps the Resident should not be encumbered with explicit details and problems as this one, best left to the Batavia city police to handle.

With each passing meeting, Van Ginkel grew increasingly aloof and distant, requesting shorter meetings, keeping distance in the hallways, or generally absent from work. Pieter asked Van Ginkel to propose an additional action plan but The Resident admitted his occupation with other crucial issues. Afterward, they no longer met concerning the Governor-General's directive, so Pieter operated alone. For weeks following, he rarely noticed Resident Van Ginkel's presence in their building. If he failed this mission, Pieter felt certain to receive the blame.

Pieter remained at work all day and saw his children less frequently than usual. Evenings were spent reading papers under a study lamp, or called away to covert operations, resulting in arrests and next-day newspapers calling for investigation of the "witch hunt." Dutch newspapers pointed to the slippery, deceptive, and assuming word: *Scandal.*

A letter collected during a raid revealed an influential, esteemed European man with an extensive network of relationships stretching from Indie to the Netherlands. Names listed within correspondence led to more arrests. Those caught in the scandal included financial leaders, physicians, teachers, and a head police officer in Bandung.

The young Indie boys ensnared in scandal were sent to a youth educational institution. Each morning, as Pieter scanned the papers, still achy and bones feeble from the beyond-midnight-hour arrests the night before, he shook his head in disbelief at the lies, mistruths, and misunderstandings the newspaper printed. Reporters rarely requested an official interview, and in the beginning, he called newspapers with his general insight into the ongoing investigation, while asking them to refrain from gossip. Even speaking "off the record" seemed useless now.

But those Truths he offered were just that — honesty, integrity, morals — and he never provided a juicy tale, a morsel of scandal, or names of those arrested. Those men were promised a fair trial in Batavia, and he felt trials were worthy to happen locally, with sensible judges and wisdom within the local ranks, not transported to the Netherlands, where people were eager to immediately render blame.

One late January evening Pieter sat in his wicker chair as Diny, Nelly, and Jan huddled closely to him on the veranda, a rare occasion of their three wiry bodies needing additional comfort before their nearing bedtime.

If each child experienced a similar joy in response to their mother's love, the parallel lines of grace and felicity extending before them, some ailments and faults intersected at an angle, sideswiping them into stark reminders of their mother's humanity. For the battles Cora faced, of sacrificial living coupled with selfish outbursts, all her mistakes seemed forgotten and forgiven by Pieter's presence.

While Pieter felt content with warmth and togetherness, he told them fairy tales, and when finally relaxed with Cornelia on the veranda, the front gate rattled, and he could not visibly see who was present at their driveway. He thought Baboe, Kokki, or Djongos had returned for some reason, and excused himself to the gate. Their children groaned, bursting into tears for more time with Daddy. He urged Cornelia to place their children into their beds.

The children knew he would be called back to work, but his naïve and sheltered children could not foresee the events which loomed before him. The man with the limp and wiry mustache leaned into their front gate, knocking adamantly, calling for Pieter's immediate presence. They spoke for a moment and Pieter turned to Cornelia, who had just settled into her chair on the veranda. She frowned, "Go, Pieter," she told him, "You are needed out there."

Pieter's blue eyes met hers, and he blinked a message of love. He thought of those moments he urged his family to remember, "Well, my children, in many cases in life, we are required to go through hardships and disappointments to reach our goals — and there is no other way." He knew this was a moment of sacrifice, raced to his office, grabbed his gun and bullets from locked cabinets, along with a lantern and overcoat, then joined the man in his car. The man briefly described his discovery, along with another on their force, who could vouch for the validity of the claims. Pieter's face paled, then he nodded his approval and motioned with his hand for the man to drive. His breath felt extinguished.

Several minutes later, they arrived at the man's home and went inside. The man's jolly wife prepared food for them to take, and wrapped together meats and cheeses, with containers of water, and a stack of thin blankets in case the night grew cold. The man carried an extra rucksack with other items. She wished them well, although seemed oblivious to their mission, which Pieter felt was prudent and wise, if not unintentional. They thanked her and scurried off to the car, then continued toward the Ciliwung River.

The car hobbled as violently as they rumbled down bumpy roads for a length of time as darkness obstructed their vision. Holes and debris were prevalent, and the man skillfully navigated back alleyways near patchwork shanty villages. To his right, Pieter mentioned the burned-out hollow of a sugar cane factory. Eventually, beside the river inlet, they parked in obscurity, under a thicket of mangrove trees. And they waited in darkness, each remained stoically in his seat in the rusted car, unmoved. The man stared straight ahead and whispered their location as one of complete distinction, because other similar police units lingered on other side streets, attempting their own inconspicuous patience surrounding this area, to capture the act which would soon be underway.

Pieter trembled, slightly, still surprised at the upcoming heist, his right hand tightly gripping the barrel of his gun, his left hand feeling around in his overcoat pocket, mentally counting the bullets tumbling around, tapping each other. He hoped the bullets would not click into the barrel of his gun to be pointed at a familiar face.

The night tarried, with a full golden moon offering light in the inky sky to observe their shadowed surroundings. Their car teetered too close to the mangrove trees, he thought, trees rooted halfway on the side of the embankment and the other half in the stench of the stagnant Ciliwung River. After a length of time, as darkness and clouds obscured the moon, eyes weary of constant watching and supposing, they saw a shadow walking beside the river and toward the house.

A slight, frail man walked quickly among bushes, a shadow of energy who took no notice of their presence but entered the shanty home. Pieter and the driver then exited the car and lit lanterns. They silently loaded their guns in unison and allowed a few moments to pass, to remain certain the intended liaison had time to begin.

At once, several units descended on this unveiling, with men in combat uniforms waving hand signals and gestures to Pieter and the man. Within moments, the combat team wrestled a familiar man out of the shanty home and onto the dirt outside. Under the glow of Pieter's lantern was the man who abused an underage islander boy.

The shadow man in the filth, face-down in the stench of dirt, was the Resident of Batavia, the sniffing, sobbing Van Ginkel. The same man in charge of this "witch-hunt," and ultimately supervising Pieter, was in fact one they inadvertently hunted. Van Ginkel was a repugnant deception surrounded by men of integrity, and lay prostrate in the mire and mud of the scandal.

They were shocked by Van Ginkel's dishonor, but local newspapers did not accompany them to record the scandal at its height of misery. One officer admitted he and a few others knew Van Ginkel frequently visited "The Avenue," where Indie boys congregated, but felt if Van Ginkel remained discreet about his personal lifestyle, they could keep peace and order. Officers lit cigarettes and everyone joined in a collective sigh.

Pieter handcuffed Van Ginkel and transported him back to the Police Headquarters and into a holding cell. Hours after a period of debriefing with strong coffee, Pieter telephoned Governor-General Stachouwer's house as daybreak illuminated their bustling city. Stachouwer responded that Pieter should visit in person to describe the story. He was known as an early-riser, and Pieter notified the armed men at the gate that urgent police business would have to interrupt the Governor-General's breakfast.

Pieter stood in a stately dining room, and Stachouwer sat serenely in his crisp white suit while Pieter explained the previous night's affairs. However, Stachouwer did not feign surprise at Van Ginkel's indiscretions or lack of integrity. He shook out his starched napkin and told Pieter that Van Ginkel could not remain The Resident, or even a Batavian citizen. Moreover, Stachouwer asserted, they would discipline those leaders aware of Van Ginkel's personal habits, who deceitfully turned away from the situation. Because they knew Van Ginkel lived on the outskirts, obscure and private in his actions, they wrongly supposed his personal life would remain separate from his professional role. Stachouwer sent Pieter to police headquarters until a later briefing.

After much discussion with his leadership team that morning, the Governor-General allowed for Fievez de Malines Van Ginkel's resignation from the Police Force and from his role as Resident of Batavia. Until a trial for his crimes, they would file paperwork, clean up the devastation, and figure out where to send these underage boys. Within three months' time of entering police custody, during his imprisonment, Van Ginkel's hair turned completely white, as the stress seemed to create a severe level of anxiety. They scheduled Van Ginkel for an April 1939 trial, yet the Attorney-General allowed the humiliated man to sail West to America, into a new life. Pieter was devastated at the cover-up. A lack of integrity would not forge a long-lasting government, and their Governor General remained at the helm, to absorb the responsibility and fallout of those tragedies.

In August of 1939, the Dekker family prepared for another Furlough in the Netherlands, already several months delayed due to the challenges within police leadership. Pieter prepared a *Memorie van Overgave* (Memorandum of Leaving Office) for his assistant superintendent, Louis, who would serve as temporary Head of Police while Pieter and his family went on Furlough. In this *Memorie*, Pieter provided "a clear description of the organization, hierarchy, responsibilities and tasks of the different elements of the police and the relations between them, among which he also pointed out the specific political movements which had to be watched in Batavia."

He also evaluated in detail the qualities of the members of the different departments of policing. He was leaving the entire operation in Louis' hands for seven months: anticipating the control, organization and practice of the city police and its many departments, the "*gewestelijke recherche*" and the "*veldpolitie*," and highly functioning police units. Pieter expected to return to the same level of quality within each division of the police, from field police to investigators, within the highest levels of leadership.

Diny had just turned eighteen with a party alongside all her friends and felt she finally matured into adulthood. In anticipation of their upcoming Furlough, she cherished afternoons swimming with Lenny and friends. In addition, she felt keenly for Willem, who Dad promised could court her when she turned eighteen. As Diny's affections for Willem increased, he sulked, overwhelmingly busy the last few months, preparing for education beyond their HBS, as their careers took diverse paths and schooling.

Additionally, Willem continued to offer excuses for his hectic lifestyle. Sailing was extremely important to him, and he hoped to qualify for the national team. He took great pains to appear groomed and pressed for every occasion, including church services, where his family sat in front. Willem's extreme interest in Pieter's social galas appeared as an enthralled enchantment in who attended, what they wore, and what social importance those situations held for their changing country. Willem's involvement in prestigious events like sailing, golf clubs, the Dutch social club *SOOS,* and other esteemed gatherings, increased his reputation and status, all which were honors in his opinion. He favored pleasing others and appearing high in status before them.

Diny held a few moments alone with Willem after Pieter allowed for the courtship, as though Willem's ego had suffered initially at the disappointment of courting Diny earlier, his self-image bruised and subsequently mended. Now, his pursuit of Diny lacked adrenaline as he finally triumphed as a welcome addition to the Dekker family. The idea of the unobtainable had deflated into normalcy. They both noted the swift upheaval of the complete momentum of relationship they achieved during the school year, once their studies concluded. They were apart for two full months before her July birthday. Perhaps the thrilling chase of attaining a relationship with Diny was no longer something to fight for, to hunt toward.

Their times together were alternated by visiting at his family's home with his artificial parents and silly sisters, or accompanying the family to picnics in the park, with more freedom along shady park paths, yet those moments alone were dotted by sudden visits from Calvin, Frederik, or Simon, causing her to pause and consider their supposed relationship. Those unexpected meetings seemed too contrived and planned to remain a coincidence. Willem cooled into untroubled lenience, and as monsoon season had dwindled in its intensity into the dryer months of July through November, Diny realized Willem may have mentally moved into another direction in life. Their fragile interactions staled into stagnation, with novelty fading into indifference and aloofness. At this point in their friendship, she hoped they might progress into a closer relationship. Yet this course was not natural, and the sparkle flattened.

After a painfully icy and boring evening with his parents in the sitting room, he asked to escort Diny home. She wondered aloud if this was an opportunity for their *becak* ride, the one they had to delay, but his distant demeanor increased. Their walk to her house was brisk and quiet, even though they would not be in each other's presence for more than seven months. They hugged briefly. Then, as Willem rubbed his brow and looked down, his face solemn and stone, they unceremoniously decided to correspond in letters during Furlough, and upon her return to Batavia, would decide if they should continue their courtship.

Pieter smoked in the shadows of the veranda and invited Willem for a chat.

Willem said, "I can only stay for a moment, as Mother has a schedule for me at home."

They spoke about the upcoming Furlough season, and Willem consistently complimented Pieter on his role as Police Chief, along with their move in the direction of "decentralization," as he called it, which baffled Diny — who viewed her dad as wonderful, certainly proud of his accomplishments, yet realizing the devastating troubles a prideful spirit would incur.

Pieter lit a new cigarette and sighed, reminding Willem, "I do the best I can, each day, and try to seek the Lord for guidance and insight."

Diny watched the conversation from a high-backed chair and sank into the orange fabric as Willem babbled. Instead of puffing her dad up unnecessarily, she wished Willem would seek a genuine friendship. She never felt he attempted to offer more, yet only aimlessly poured out compliments. *Just who is Willem pursuing, anyhow?* Diny pondered. Pieter smiled weakly at first, and after a few minutes, just blankly looked at Willem and nodded his thanks, then mentioned the late hour. Willem jumped up and bowed, thanking them, before darting off, and Pieter glanced at Diny before extinguishing his cigarette.

He settled back into his own wicker chair and draped a blanket over himself, before hoisting his feet up on another cushioned chair and leaning his head back in exhaustion. Diny recognized new wrinkles on her father's face, around his tired eyes, and his mouth drooped, without a smile or hearty laughter. *The atmospheric alteration must have some connection to his work*, she reasoned. Everywhere he turned, he seemed haunted and found little respite. Within a few minutes Mam joined them outside and gathered Pieter to deliver him to bed.

Daytime hours after work, Mam encouraged him to remain outdoors as much as possible, and instructed Baboe to remove the telephone from the extension, and only make a call in a moment of emergency, not answering any messages for Mr. Dekker.

"The air is invigorating, Pieter!" Cornelia urged him, gently pulling on his arm and shuffling him outdoors the next week, after their Saturday morning breakfast together. She called to her children, "My dears, please allow your father enough space to wander, alone, and do not interrupt his peace."

They nodded and escaped to their bedrooms, yet Diny remained in the shadows, staring at his altered countenance. And then Cornelia soothingly led Pieter outdoors, humorously chiding him, "Off you go, and please stay outside to enjoy this glorious weather!"

He waved his compliance and shook his head, responding, "*Schatje*! Thank you, my darling Cora," then wandered in their backyard gardens for hours, finding shade under banyan, mangrove, or rambutan, only pausing to prune or contemplate with his pipe. If his children peeked into his retreat, Pieter nodded kindly at them, raising his pipe in acknowledgement. Diny scrutinized Dad as he stood between the house and the garden, transfixed. He seemed at a crossroads requiring decision.

"These gardens are my sanctuary," Dad reminded them, as he had for many years, "and my gardens are a truly holy place to meet God." The outer reaches of their verdant estate held a revitalizing escape for their father: a place of refuge and haven within his own yard. His greatest moments of inventiveness, along with an invigorating rest, he told them, were found amidst the swaying flamboya trees with red blossoms, bougainvillea sparkling with violet blooms, or florals saturated with crimson or cobalt.

Banyan trees spread farther in scope, russet roots knobby and branches reaching heights stretched out toward the heavens, as though they were praising their Creator. Rubber trees swayed nearby, branches creaking whispers to the passer-by, stretchy and bouncy in the temperate breeze, awaiting harvest. Bamboo shoots, banana trees, thriving orchids, sturdy teakwood, sandalwood, and ebony all lined the outlying forests, the ancient landscapes lining beyond their backyard. A diverse arrangement greeted them, blooming about their yard and world with remarkable enthusiasm, and Pieter interred in the sanctuary he discovered, both in his gardens and on the veranda.

On Saturday, long after she sent him into the yard for a walkabout, when nap time approached, Cornelia found him sitting uncomfortably on a craggy stone, his face in his hands. She tenderly clutched his hand, and again led him to their front veranda, sitting him down into an orange-cushioned lounging chair, then pulled up the ottoman for his feet, and covered him up to the neck with a knitted blanket. He immediately appeared relaxed and smelled the blanket.

"Lavender, Cora. My favorite, you know. You always know." She bounded over to him and gently stroked his thick black hair, sat on the arm of the lounging chair, and gazed into his sparkling eyes.

"You are going to be just fine, Mr. Dekker. God still has control of this — and every situation, despite how horrible it feels. We both need to trust, and not worry. Easier to say than to live, I know!"

He nodded, his eyes gazing distant, unfocused. She kissed his forehead, then walked into their yard and closed their front gate, which the *Kebon* allowed to grow overhead with floral blooms and vines.

"Time for a nap," Cornelia urged, as he had recently neglected afternoon rest times.

Later, she quietly stepped out and placed a few artbooks on his side table, containing the works of Rembrandt and Van Gogh, hoping the deep inky atmosphere and golden swirls of ambiance in Van Gogh's "Starry Night" could infuse peace into Pieter's countenance. He slept on the front veranda every afternoon for weeks, escaping the house there, children hushed away from his presence during those moments, those painting books serving as a reminder of the humanity available to him if he mustered the energy to read. His diversion on the veranda incorporated a small hidden world away from reports, demands, and needs. His Furlough started early.

PART TWO

Chapter Eight
Batavia, Java, Dutch East Indies, 1939

The time arrived to depart for Furlough, and Diny felt the moment of exodus appropriately timed every six years; Dad's exhaustion was contagious and depleted their humor, energy, and perspective. Diny feared he had some illness or other difficulty, which he never discussed. By the time their four o'clock tea time arrived, Pieter perked up, folded the blanket, then asked Cora and their children about their day. Mam sent them off to the swimming pool with friends, or to a classmate's home to play for a few hours. Of course, they were all eager to step into the new season of change.

As the children packed their important toys and books into sturdy trunks, along with clothing and personal items, Cornelia organized her home, efficiently settling things into proper places for their six-month absence, chuckling at how she would not long for the humidity. She always felt satisfied to bring a trunk filled with family photographs and gifts for the family, and receive scarves, hats, mittens, and blankets her own mother had knitted in anticipation for their wintertime abroad and set away everything else for their return. Those daily life essentials would remain when they arrived back from the Netherlands, and their household helpers received a well-merited holiday, and would be ready to return to their efforts when the family arrived home. Pieter and Cornelia provided paid time off for their servants and wished them well in their time with family. They beamed happily as they lined up at the dock to wave the Dekker family into the expanse of the next three seasons.

As soon as the ship departed the Tanjung Priok from Batavia's western harbor, and their friends were far away and seemed like tiny dots, Diny felt the invigorating freshness of their sea voyage return. She looked back at their beloved port, and the busyness surrounding the massive ships coming and going until she could no longer see Batavia. She held the railing, watching the boat glide through the harbor water, and closed her eyes. Suddenly she was fifteen again, leaning into her father's shoulder as they sat together on a bench in the harbor, watching for a long while. She smelled the heavy scent of wood and spices intermingled with stagnant, brackish water, seasonings of street vendors mixed with mangrove forests and banyan trees.

As they exited into a broader expanse of waterways, the captain ordered all the passengers inside, as beside them the furious volcano Mount Krakatau was still erupting and from their ship, they witnessed the bubbling burning and bright reddish orange glow of lava as it emptied into the ocean, thick smoke unfurling into the air as the magma collided with frigid ocean water.

The captain warned inhaling the air would damage their lungs and required passengers to remain inside until the open seas. Krakatau had been erupting since July of 1938. The air suspended above them, ashy and thick, as though a fog or mist lingered in the atmosphere, which several islanders called an unlucky omen. The flame seemed to light the way for their ship, until they moved northwest, away from smoke, away from danger.

Hilversum, The Netherlands, summer 1939

Together they traveled along seas and rivers for three weeks aboard a familiar yet exhilarating boat, complete with games on deck for children, a large dining hall, and other delights before they arrived in late summer to the Netherlands, ready to enjoy six months of family time. The season and climate altered from their tropical humidity into a mild summer enthusiasm, and they were accustomed to the acclimation periods.

At this moment, the Dekker family eagerly embraced change after an especially busy season, ready to rest and recover from their tropical lives. Diny perceived her father had aged over the last few years of work, and a general exhaustion overwhelmed him at times. He rarely spoke of career struggles yet seemed to concentrate on the blessings of his work, with caring people and opportunity to reach others, to build a stronger and safer framework for life in the Dutch East Indies.

Pieter always required a measure of time to adjust to the changes in season, schedules and temperaments during Furloughs, especially concerning cold winters in the Netherlands, with frosty chills instead of an always-balmy, humid existence. He always felt so vibrant and lively in the tropics, he told them.

During the first week of Furlough, Dad planned a holiday-within-their-holiday, and mentioned a relaxing adventure, suggesting a family escape to Switzerland. They were elated to hike the rugged alpine tundra of the Swiss Alps, view the white capped majestic mountains of the Matterhorn and other prominent peaks, and experience the new customs, foods, and language of another country. Mam described the serenity they would find in their secluded chalet, lush green hills leading up to brilliant Swiss mountain peaks. They knew the German language, and Dad felt comfortable in their journey there.

Dad and Mam rented a traditional bungalow in Switzerland for a few weeks in August 1939 and they looked forward to the adventure; Diny imagined the traditional Swiss Chalets her Oma Dekker had talked about, with steep peaks, rocky and sheer cliffs jutting into the sky with precipitous crags, and foreboding heights. They would splash in streams and hike peaceful, verdant forests, eat schnitzel, pretzels, and fondue dinners, drink spiced beverages in tiny village restaurants, and her dad would order a rare splurge — a frothy beer in a big glass. Diny pondered the loveliness of bell-clanging cows grazing on grassy, dewy, meadowy pastures, surrounded by crystal lakes and snowy glaciers and winding roads leading up near heaven, it seemed.

But they never went to Switzerland, because the Dutch government recognized the eminence of war as a reality sooner than they imagined, so a military mobilization came, with soldiers recruited and prepared for battle, training and shining boots, sharpening their wits. All personal holiday travel was canceled. The Dutch had prepared poorly for any battle, should it arrive, because the country's last major war was the Seven Years War in the mid-1700s. Dad speculated that over the last two hundred years, with trickles of the Golden Age still reminiscent and echoing in their family histories, perhaps the Netherlands softened their defenses to war, and were numbed to the idea any conflict would occur in their lifetime.

While listening to the news on their radio, they learned German Chancellor Adolph Hitler had invaded Poland and there was a genuine, increased fear of another world war. The Great War in 1914 was a far-away memory for Pieter and Cornelia, yet one which never permeated their lives. They were not acquainted with soldiers who had lost their lives fighting in the battle yet recalled the devastation and challenges Europe in general faced, even as the Netherlands remained neutral throughout those four years of battle and served as a passageway for trade and commerce for both sides of the war, the Allies and the Central Powers.

The general world-wide Depression after the war was astute and profoundly felt, even in the Dutch East Indies. And with another world war on the horizon, the quaint and idyllic bungalow in Switzerland seemed a distant dream, and the Dekker family was disappointed to miss an opportunity for beauty, rest, and jolly entertainment. Yet who frivolously pursued a holiday with the possibility of a war looming overhead?

When they initially arrived in the Netherlands for Furlough, Dad rented a three-story gabled home on Ruysdaellaan in Hilversum — a charming home displaying age and wear. Some simple color tones kept the appearance unadorned and clean, with cream outer walls, and tan or charcoal accents and shutters. Inside the furnished rented home, efficiency reigned, practically serving the Dekker family with little clutter and still plenty of enchantment to serve their needs.

While the structure of the outside of their home was decorated in an uncomplicated manner, the inside became their own, each family member exuding an expression of their own tastes and style, a signature of their cozy and welcoming nature. The Dekker family consistently extended a loving hand of hospitality to others, and enjoyed hosting friends and family, with a grace which seemed at once effortless and carefully planned.

Cornelia made enormous efforts to establish their family within a greater community in Hilversum with each Furlough, enjoying the six month stretches as though their family transplanted permanently back into the Netherlands. Perhaps Cora's desire was to create a safe place of respite for Pieter, a haven away from the desperation of the preceding year. In their home, Mam provided a comfort zone from the inimitable difficulties plaguing them in Batavia. Pieter was rarely pestered by extended family members to speak about his job, and even then, only commented on general, obscure, vague terms, as though speaking to a newspaper about scandalous events, for his extended family had not realized the magnitude of the role he encompassed in Batavia as Police Chief of the entire country.

And as a result, Pieter refrained from speaking about his job amidst a general discourse with a family member or even out of any sense of obligation. Maybe they read nonsense in the local Dutch newspapers, plenty of falsehoods and distortions. Perhaps as they visited with Pieter, they sensed his presence of strength and resolve, or his solemn disposition the first few weeks returning into a Furlough, with his great difficulty at resting and stepping out of a working environment to encompass a forced rest, a mandatory step away from the circles of Batavia, the jungles of accusation and misinterpretation.

Certainly, he did not solicit interrogation from family as he already had encountered those devices in Batavia. Pieter's misgivings surrounded his passion for his work and complete investment into the lives of the Dutch East Indies residents, from the local islanders to Dutch transplants. He exhausted himself in his efforts, operating at the maximum level possible for integrity and idealism, including confidentiality and discretion. Incapable of becoming enraptured in the gossip of any circle, Pieter maintained a refusal to divulge any information about any cases — even internationally-known, "scandals" of the system — so he realized their conversations would become a nothingness of looping questions, pauses, and silences, with grim faces. The family knew to refrain from asking, and he seemed relieved for an exclusion. He instead preferred exploring the outdoors.

The topography surrounding Hilversum was lined with meadows and lakes, leading to heathland, at the edge of woods. Other smaller villages bordered Hilversum as well, circling the city with inhabitants who visited Hilversum for markets, employment, and socializing. The landscapes enticed Diny, who longed for an invigorating adventure. Part of Diny's daily routine included an early morning rejuvenating walk in her neighborhood or a bicycle ride to explore the outlying areas. Dad warned her to not wander too far away, so she usually brought Nelly or Jan along, and sometimes Dad and Mam found opportunity to join them, especially if walking in town near the cafés and shops. Those market stalls were just awakening to the day and always alluring, Mam reminded her, with the scent of pastries, breads, chocolates and cheeses tickling the senses, so one had better keep a bright mind about purchases and *needs* instead of *wants*.

So much warning and danger looming in every turn in Dutch cities, Diny pondered glumly. When I start school again in a few weeks, would Dad continue to offer his hesitation? Perhaps his thoughts would linger toward my finishing school, increasing domestic skills, and stretching my aptitude toward marriage.

The brisk autumn air was a welcome change from the summertime humidity and heat. As Diny journeyed around on her bicycle with Nelly and Jan, she enjoyed the flatness of the Dutch topography. Straight, smooth, cow-filled pastures bordered fields with hay ready for harvest, for bundling together in rolls or bales, in preparation for filling the barn and feeding the livestock through winter. Farmers were always steps ahead in filling their silos and in operating systems of preparation for the next season.

Those early mornings in late summer, as Diny prepared to attend Dutch school, she sensed a shift in the air, as the immediate heat eased for several days, until bright mornings required the use of a sweater. Amidst those Hilversum bicycle rides through the neighboring purple lavender-like heath and near the dark shadowed wooded outliers, she felt as though she were entering a dreamland. The air was thick with fog as if one awakens in a hazy state from an absorbing dream or senses the dream has enraptured them, as though one is pulled toward slumber in a careful, hypnotic way. Hands of cool clouds fluttered over Diny's face and eyes, as though summertime had waned overnight.

Other bicycle journeys required early morning rising, traveling with her dad, who covered up in a large-brimmed hat and overcoat to the village center and to the market to collect a morning's prize fish for evening supper. After Pieter selected the right fish and they bicycled home, he placed it in their icebox for preparation later, and invited her to venture out again on bicycle.

They cycled along quiet alleyways and behind-businesses streets near their home, to a quaint bakery. Once inside, the breakfast items unfurled the glorious scents of buttery, flaky pastries baking, delicate layers of baked delights, intermingled with chocolate, caramel and nuts, along with coffee and tea infused in tones of comfort, soothing scents of memory ignited, and pathways altered. This was their special spot, he told her, and together over coffee and a pastry, they talked as Pieter became momentarily transparent.

Each conversation at home thereafter, they began conversing as adults, instead of stern father and rebellious daughter. She hoped to someday discover a friendship like this with a young man, someone with whom to build a home and a future. Perhaps Willem was that man, and perhaps not. But her time with Dad stretched her beyond her own interests and reached into the realm of man, establishing the idealism of conversing with a man, helping her develop confidence as well.

Soon, the summer holiday completed, the children prepared to return to Hilversum's school. Diny returned to the company of familiarity, friendships forged through writing to her friends, over the kilometers and the years. *Six years can change anyone,* she pondered, *and I was nearly-eleven during our last Furlough.* Diny stepped into the school year, open to rekindled connections, with opportunities for exploration.

One of those new friendships brought a great surprise. Diny's friend Bert was an acquaintance six years ago during a partial school year in the

Netherlands while on Furlough, and he now seemed intent on spending time with her. Bert shared his feelings with Diny, his significant fondness of her, although reality took a month for her to realize, and she became reserved in her actions and emotions around Bert.

Bert eagerly spent time with her, escorting her to and from school. At times he walked slowly, deliberately, to investigate life ideas or inquire about life overseas. Bert frequently popped over to the house and talked with Mam, Diny, and her siblings. Dad was unavailable for conversations, which proved a relief to Diny, as she feared Bert might engage Dad in a courtship discussion. She appreciated Bert's efforts, but did not desire to know him on a deeper level. New neighbors thought Bert was her cousin, and not a potential suitor, and Diny refused to correct them. While she and Bert had agreeable interactions, Diny quickly realized she only felt friendship for him. She sensitively shared those platonic thoughts with him. And while she was friends with Bert and spent time with him, she made every effort to include her dark-haired, dark-eyed friend Marieke Rosenthal or other school friends when she realized he desired a romantic relationship. She faced great difficulty in telling him the truth.

Their friendship seemed to dwindle afterwards, and he hesitated when Diny only saw their time together as a friendship. Her friendship with Bert cooled, and Diny received a brief letter from Willem, detailing his family's permanent move to Australia, with his complete devotion to medical school, and his sorrow that they would not continue a courtship when she returned to Batavia. Indeed, a courtship composed over a series of letters, stretching years and kilometers between lagging islands, and in differing continents, would never survive, he contended.

They never took that pedaled taxi *becak* ride together, and Diny tossed his letter on her desk. The last few years involved only a crush, nurtured by his vibrant personality, charming disposition, and frivolous conversations. *Have I blinded myself to his empty intentions?* She pondered his true objectives.

Diny also realized the pragmatic reality of Willem's father moving the family for his governmental role was a massive convenience for Willem, an opportunity to cut something which bored him, yet offered dignity in leaving their relationship as just a pleasant friendship. Another possibility turned sour, into another "frothy, untroubled friendship." She keenly felt the pang of rejection, and at the same moment realized her behavior toward Bert seemed unpleasant, no doubt providing a bitter taste of jealousy when he realized Diny was intended for another.

Yet all complications were finished now, both with Willem and Bert, and for a length of time, even before Willem wrote his farewell letter, she felt great satisfaction with singleness, learning from God how to best serve Him, to tread into independence in this country. Her optimism was deflated momentarily, but she possessed tenacity to rebound quickly from discouragements. After all, her fluttering for Willem remained a juvenile fantasy, a shallow and limited interlude amidst the whole of the magnificent opus. He was just another treble clef, or better yet: a pause-in-between, the breath and exhale of intermission, the interval from the tumultuous Act One to the glorious and increasingly adventurous Act Two.

* * *

The Netherlands corners the North Sea with a general provoking, constantly reclaiming soggy land under layers of roaring salt water, innovatively constructing a surrounding wall to tame the sea, pumping away swampy underlying areas to create a new coastal expanse, as an almost mockery of the sea and her power. Those who journeyed her seashore borders enjoyed pleasant scenery while traveling the expanse of the country, with greenery and seasonal fog alongside fields of colorful flowers and bicycle paths.

Extended seasons of sunlight in summer were tempting and beguiling, with the Netherlands situated as an ultimately northern and western coastal country in Europe, far north of the equator, away from consistent warmth and humidity as Indies. Sunlight was visible until the 10 o'clock hour, affording them more time for exploration. Bordering the sea brought comfort and maritime margins to extremes in atmosphere and temperatures throughout the year, as a polarity for transplanted Dutch citizens acclimated to the hot, balmy, year-round disposition of the Dutch East Indies.

A regulated, predictable disposition as Indie was easily managed, with the ability to plan, for each day was nearly the same. Save the July through November dry season, they expected rain and heat, planning accordingly. Yet if Indie was predictable, the Netherlands was diverse in climate and growing in culture. However, the approaching weather in the Netherlands was not easily foreseeable, but the temperament of the landscape offered light, bright days during summer, long hours of sunshine and time for sailing along the shoreline, or traversing the countryside with little regard to time or boundary constraints.

Yet Diny knew from their previous Furlough six years prior that following a brief interlude of autumn, winter appeared as a tiresome succession of snowy mornings and morose afternoons, with tedious travel and a generally dreary climate following them home. They carried it on heavy shoulders inside their homes, with enclosed spaces, creaking floors, and closed shades of silence, in darkness. With fewer hours of sunlight during the winters, and a nearly constant gray sky, they feared the repetitive and monotonous progression of days, and sought to fully seize the intensity and sunshine of the countryside if it was afforded.

Autumn in the Netherlands emerged graceful with cherished days of bright mornings, mild afternoons, and later, sometimes a thunderstorm or breezy entrance into evening, requiring sweaters and water-resistant jackets. The most glorious autumn surrounded them with crisp morning air and bright blue skies, warm afternoons with a gold hue, and broad, colorful sunsets. Twilight cast exceptionally yellow rays and subsequent shadows onto trees, stony paths, late-summer flowers, or bicycling riders traveling through the billowing wind, along lingering wildflowers in the heath and beside the wooded trails.

Small children walking with their parents laughed at their tall, clunky shadows in the sun's late rays. The children chased their lengthening shadows ahead on the path, away from the splendor of the sun, into the approaching dimness, unable to successfully reach the tips of their shadows, exhausting themselves in the pursuit.

As the sun dropped behind the horizon, spilling into the North Sea, the air ensconced with a hue unlike any other, as though one could grasp the light, clutching a handful of the ambiance. No photograph fully captured the glory of those sunset moments, which lasted mere minutes, entirely missed if one were not paying close attention. Those golden moments passed quickly, and the precise nature of pink hues in the clouds, or the bright open fading blue sky, never again repeated in the exact same style.

In their Hilversum townhome, Diny savored those dusk experiences and leaned against the wall of the porch — their Dutch veranda — her breath shallow, voice silent, eyes wide with amazement, and mind in awe and wonderment of God's artistry, His landscapes of nature. Weekend outings with Dad were especially meaningful, as the family enjoyed his restful demeanor, escaping their classrooms. During the months of August and September, Pieter appeared to be grieving some loss from leaving Batavia, like Diny healing from personal grieving, of leaving behind friendships and courtship with Willem, the closing of those wounds especially challenging.

Wandering the creaky old Hilversum woods, she spotted the heath, and rolling pastures, with deer and birds populating those lands. If thicket woods housed the hiddenness of their world, she was content to escape, to fly through meadows into the thickness of the woodland. Forgiveness, from a distance, required immense imagination, and she scribbled angry notes to Willem about his stony heart which was crowded by his earthly, material desires. Later she bundled the letters together as though to send them to Batavia but tossed them into the sitting room fireplace. He was finally a completed interval, and she bravely stepped into the season of hope.

Pieter relished his compassionate confidant in Cornelia, and during Furlough continued their secrecy surrounding his discouragement just prior to Furlough. No longer able to escape to the lush carpets of his garden or the security of his veranda, Pieter found the necessity of relinquishing the past. It was behind him, without any reservation of the Governor-General's mandates. He felt aged by a decade over the last two years, and moments of restoration and respite had been a salve.

In those first few months back in Hilversum, Pieter hardly socialized or kept appointments, but he traveled with the family for an early-September outing to Boombergpark in Hilversum, for a picnic lunch, and later bicycled in the nearby heath. Deer frolicked together, the moorland changed into lavender, and crisp crimson and gold leaves crunched underfoot and hung from trees like billowing canopies. They bicycled throughout the park, exhausted by the time they arrived back home for dinner.

Autumn breezes yielded to frosty winter, with white snow coating grassy expanses and muffling cobblestoned streets, the demeanor even more withdrawn, pulling a coat over relationships, a dividing line within the confines of their closed doors in the small Hilversum townhome, with a roaring fireplace drawing family members together to gaze deeply at the flames, huddled around the heat and energy of the moment, yet not always sharing in the community of togetherness.

October and then November arrived, and with cooler weather, Pieter longed for another outdoor exhibition, again ready for an outing. He took significant efforts to visit his youngest brother Nicolaas in Amsterdam several times. Diny anticipated Dad's relationship with Oom Nicolaas provided some sense of insight and perspective into his role as Police Chief, notions the rest of her family could not offer, along with the ability to lead and guide his younger brother in a positive way.

One especially unseasonably balmy Sunday afternoon in November, Pieter suggested they escape to a Hilversum park for a family picnic. Cornelia gathered items together in a picnic basket filled with meats, cheeses, and crackers, along with a few baguettes Pieter picked up at the bakery down the street, with biscuit-like cookies, stroopwaffels, fruit, and pastries. Mam passed around floppy hats to shade from the sun and filled canteens with juice and tea. Jan brought along badminton and a kite, and began playing games, while Nelly carried a large blanket, spreading it under shady trees. The afternoon stretched gently before them, with children frolicking along the meadows, and evening darkness arrived far too early for their tastes. Weather became reserved and nearly aloof, as though the personality of the landscape again was altered.

Hilversum, December 1939

Family togetherness increased over the season with nostalgia of previous holiday moments together, both in the Netherlands and Indie over the years. Diny sensed a time of swelling uncertainty on Sinterklaas Day 1939. Togetherness with Dad was a sweet time. Their next Sinterklaas Day in 1940 would be in Batavia, again in their old life. Diny observed a change in her father since their arrival, discerning he had finally settled down, relaxing into Hilversum. He was disconnected with Batavia, healing from pain and trauma he experienced during the season of atmospheric alteration.

Their time together brought a *gezellig* coziness which emitted from the festive encounter. On the 5th of December, Dutch tradition held for small "gag" or comical, witty presents, with an attached poem relating to the present. The poems involved humorous passive-aggressive Dutch directness. Laughter accompanied festive evenings. Before bedtime, the children set out their wooden shoes for Sinterklaas, along with carrots for his horse, then awoke on 6th December to an array of goodies and gifts inside their wooden shoes.

After Sinterklaas Day, they prepared to celebrate Christ's birth on Christmas Day, Diny found an evergreen bough outside and formed it into a jolly round wreath, bound the ends together with red ribbon, and placed it on their front door, hanging from another plush strand of red ribbon. The house smelled like cinnamon, nutmeg, and cloves as Mam prepared holiday baking and cooking. They arranged small white candles on the fresh-cut pine tree and lit them as darkness arrived. On 25th December, Dad read the Biblical account of the birth of Jesus from Luke 2 and offered a prayer of thanksgiving, and then they walked to church together to celebrate Christ's birth, the ultimate Gift.

The family customarily ate Indie food, yet in the Netherlands prepared a seasonal, traditional supper of Dutch foods: fish, potatoes, seasoned vegetables, and breads. All these long-established meals were unavailable in the tropics of Batavia but craved in their Dutch life. Now in this other Dutch life, Diny craved those aromatic Asian rice dishes.

Mam and Diny made *oliebollen* to celebrate on New Year's Eve, to usher in 1940, as the round cake donuts with raisins and powdered sugar were a treat for the family.

After the New Year arrived, they turned their hopes toward the *Elfstedentocht,* "eleven cities tour," the 200-km ice skating race event, which loomed on the horizon. Northern rivers and canals froze deep, and exuberant skaters sped on those frozen rivers, through all eleven quaint villages and thriving cities in Friesland, finishing before midnight to receive a medal. The local newspapers discussed the excitement surrounding the event, along with Fries frontrunners as possible notable skaters. Diny hoped her family could attend the race, if able to travel on short notice to watch. She pondered the chilly race and temperatures skaters tolerated, denoting an especially frigid winter, cold enough for the rivers to freeze over to sustain the weight of many skaters, those attending the competition cheering on the skaters also extremely cold.

CHAPTER NINE
HILVERSUM, JANUARY 1940

When Diny's friend Jacob Sluis invited her over after school one winter's day, Diny considered visiting him. She sat next to eighteen-year-old Jacob in mathematics class at the HBS (*Hogere Burger School*) since the first day. He seemed like a nice young man with his slick dark hair neatly arranged and a happy smile. His large eyes were framed by thick glasses. Jacob was quite sociable and pleasant to everyone in class, a quiet leader. Upon learning her friend Marieke would also attend Jacob's small gathering, Diny decided to join them. It was a brisk early January, late in the afternoon, and the New Year seemed full of promise. Diny felt a spring in her step, even though winter was long from concluded. New friendships felt rare. When they arrived at Jacob's quaint gabled home in Hilversum, he introduced Diny and Marieke to his family, including his older sister Stien, who was tall and slender with long dark hair and a broad smile. Diny appreciated Stien's warmth and connected with her instantly, enjoying the easygoing, jovial way she carried herself.

"As the eldest of eight," Stien started with a wry grin, "I have to assert myself."

Diny nodded, "I am the eldest of three, but I can understand!"

After a few minutes of conversation with Stien and Marieke, Diny noticed their entire math class arrived, so she was not Jacob's only guest. She shrank onto the couch, feeling slightly overdressed and vaguely dejected.

Jacob was all kindness and hospitality, cheerfully buoyant, as always, thoughtful and welcoming. Their conversations were encouraging and light, but throughout the course of the evening, she viewed him less as marriage material, as she lacked a passion or interest in him, as though he were suddenly boring to watch. She was relieved and decided to enjoy the remainder of the evening in the best way possible.

Smoothing her bright blue dress and wavy hair and crossing her feet at the ankles, Diny settled into the couch and attempted to portray the elegance and charm she felt inside. No longer bitter or disappointed thinking about the Willem episode in her life, she instead recognized the maturity she had gleaned from his friendship, and later to Bert, and further, with Jacob.

Now, at Jacob's New Year's party, memories swirled through Diny's mind and she pieced together long-forgotten amusements. She surveyed the room and noticed one young handsome man with tousled wavy hair and steel blue eyes. He lounged alone, quietly and casually, in the darkened corner in a solitary red antique chair, the fireplace nearby glowing an amber to warm the room and illuminating his face.

His arms were poised, and his legs crossed, and he judiciously watched Diny as he slowly, methodically smoked a cigarette. It was as though he did not inhale but puckered his lips to tolerate the moment. Wisps of smoke twisted and curled around him, rising in ribbons of gray.

He smoldered.

She gasped, caught in his grandeur, as though his coolness simmered. Diny detected no wedding ring on either hand of this mysterious charmer and smiled in relief. He seemed confident and focused, in a composed posture, even blinking his eyes between deep puffs. When he briefly spoke, his calm, even words were soothing, lyrical, and rhythmic, and others leaned forward to hear his words. His hand teetered the cigarette like a party accessory between two long, thin fingers. This young man's gaze continued to fall on Diny, scanning her round face, caramel hair, chocolate eyes, and creamy skin. He perceived the size and slight of her body.

Even from a sitting position, Diny sensed his extended height and lean build. She was drawn to his tall, lanky frame and broad, expressive hands, and stared at him. He stroked his elongated face and prominent chin, then ran his long fingers through his thick brown hair, which curled up near his ears. As he turned to laugh with friends, his hair proved tousled in the back. While he watched her in an almost brooding fashion, his blue eyes narrowed, and she imagined he was commenting inwardly on her snarled stockings, or snug, scuffed shoes.

She pulled her feet underneath the coffee table. Diny was surprised he did not introduce himself, although she heard Jacob's other cousin Henk calling him *Nico*. Diny also remembered Jacob mentioning his charming cousin Nico. She recalled Jacob speaking of Nico's prowess on the field hockey team. His speed and quick skills advanced their team in winning local tournaments. At the time, she thought Jacob was showing off, drawing attention to himself, although Diny played hockey too at the HBS and yawned at the idea of that sport being a novelty, especially in the Netherlands.

Why did I ignore Jacob's thoughts or opinions on Nico?

She decided to escape her friends and the couch to offer Nico a chance to follow her and begin a conversation. Diny wandered the house, poured hot tea into her cup, and ate a cookie. Then she wandered again and returned to the couch. Later, she slowly shuffled to the restroom, looking at pictures in the hallway, offering Nico ample opportunities for conversation alone. She glanced at him to gain his attention, but he seemed entranced in other talks, ignoring her completely. He remained in quiet contemplation and contentment, satisfied with watching her when she breezed in or out of the room.

He was certainly different from Willem's bubbly, outgoing characteristics, or Bert's overly dramatic abilities to listen too intently. If Willem were here, he might loudly engage the party in another story or tale. And if Bert were here, he would undoubtedly deliver her drinks and food all night amidst her indifference.

Over time, she anticipated Nico would excuse himself for a beverage or another cigarette. But one of Diny's female acquaintances provided him with steaming coffee with *oliebollen* New Year's donuts, then hot tea with cookies. *Perhaps she tries to allure his affections by offering him food,* Diny marveled, surprised. *Or perhaps they are courting, and I have been mistaken.* Yet he seemed unmoved, apathetic to a female's obvious exertion.

This *Nico was intrigued,* appearing to observe the company surrounding him. In one span of time, as Diny refilled her tea cup, he swirled around completely, closed off to any lingering conversation, instead absorbed in one of Jacob's books from the shelf near the antique chair, the commotion of the party insignificant. The glow of the fireplace seemed to warm him and even in the shadows he gleamed.

At last, as darkness settled and temperatures dropped, the party began to disperse. Diny expected to return home for family dinner and prepared to depart with Marieke. Diny thanked Jacob, Stien and their parents for their generous hospitality and gathered her coat. Marieke lingered inside to say her goodbyes, waving Diny along, Marieke's dark hair framing her olive face, asking for a moment to help Jacob wash dishes, much to his disapproval and Stien's laughter. The air thickened with fog as Jacob's party scattered.

Classmates shuffled out of the house and echoed merrily into the village square, while darkness quietly encapsulated them.

Diny stepped outside for her walk home and pulled on her heavy wool coat and green wool hat her mother had knitted for her. She startled at Nico, situated on Jacob's front porch rail, smoking yet another cigarette, lounging with only his long-sleeved buttoned shirt, without a coat. He leaned against the railing on the porch, directly in Diny's path, as though he had marched ahead to deliberately occupy the porch.

"Hallo! Jacob has a coat if you need to warm up," Diny began.

Nico smiled as though whimsically amused, his bright blue eyes dazzling and alluring, his height more commanding than his frame suggested while seated. His smile scintillated, his sloped, sturdy nose happily turned up a bit at the end, and his face was welcoming, pleasant, and somehow familiar.

He cleared his throat. "I stepped out for a moment as I wanted to properly meet you."

Nico's smirk was both goofy and straight. He spoke in a genuine and straightforward way and slid his cigarette to the side of his mouth, stuck out his lanky arm to firmly shake her hand, and introduced himself.

"Nico Pouwels, originally from Amsterdam and also the Dutch East Indies, until a handful of years ago, when I returned to Hilversum...." He trailed off. His eyes sparkled when he laughed, adding to his endearing look.

Diny's heart raced as he mentioned her beloved country of birth and she leaned toward him, replying, "I was born there — *Batavia* — and have lived in the Indies for my whole life!" She swooned, her caramel hair swishing forward as she smiled widely, revealing dimples. "And I am Diny Dekker, by the way. Gerardina is my given first name, but I prefer to be called Diny."

Nico turned away and crouched, extinguishing his cigarette into an ashtray on the porch floor.

She stepped back, thinking she had overwhelmed him.

But he grinned as he stood and turned toward her, his head tilted, eyes narrowing. "I have never met a person named *'Diny'* before, Gerardina. We have much to talk about, I think. Our Indie islands are truly an enchanting place to live. I anticipate returning there someday to build a business, and a life."

He spoke fondly of humid jungles, *Tempo Doeloe* old times, and the promising prospect of returning to the tropics. Even within the frosty Dutch evening, his words warmed her, especially to hear of his affection for Indie.

White flutters of snow sifted down in the night sky, icy flakes illuminated by street lamps. Diny felt frigid in the winter air, cocooned in her thick coat, and pulled the collar up, shielding her neck from the bitter cold. She wished she had remembered her scarf.

Although it was winter, she felt warmly affectionate in spirit, and sensed an ease in conversation with Nico. What a familiar name, as her father's youngest brother was named Nicolaas, and yet the name fit this new *Nico,* who would turn 23 years old at the end of the month, he casually mentioned. Diny turned the conversation toward family and interests, his eyes alighting to her mention of her father's police profession. She inquired about his connections, education abroad, and hobbies, while composing her galloping mind.

"I hear you are a star field hockey player," Diny said. He looked down, embarrassed, shifting snow into fluffy little piles and stepping on them, crunching them down into squeaky flattened steps.

"Jacob is generous with his words, and is an equally advanced field hockey player," Nico quietly told her. "Field hockey is a team sport, and cousins are loyal, you know. Especially cousins who are also kind and humble friends." He looked up at her, directly into her eyes. "We make a great pair."

Energy and chemistry hummed between them, their communication natural and intentional, yet she sensed he cautiously balanced, not allowing her to feel entirely overwhelmed by his intensity, by the unruffled sureness he expressed.

She laughed, "Field hockey seems like a cold sport for the winter."

Nico nodded. "Have you played field hockey only in Batavia? Here in the Netherlands, we play indoors during the winter, just practicing for springtime tournaments." He chuckled, shaking his head. His smile was irresistible, sweet, and serene, his frame composed.

He stared at her long chestnut hair as pieces of snow clung to her hat while more flurries swirled under the tiny covered porch. He frequently brushed snow from his thick hair, nervously smoothing it down in the back, where it curled against his collar, and reached out to catch a snowflake before it fell into her hair.

She again wondered about his state of mind for shivering on a porch in January, in the raw icy air of a Dutch winter, although her intrigue grew as they discussed field hockey in one breath and then in another, the tumultuous situation in Germany, the recent military mobilization, and the inevitability of another war.

"There is no reason to worry about what *might* happen in a war, especially a war which has not even started," he reminded her, sounding like her dad in his dismissal of *possibilities*. "We just have to wait and see what happens, Diny. Perhaps the Netherlands will remain neutral again." He shrugged.

She did not dismiss the worry. "I cannot feel so easily about this possible war, as the last one did not turn out favorably for us, even while neutral."

He recognized her heavy sigh and turned toward her. "We can pray about it. In the meanwhile, to keep you occupied, maybe you can watch one of our field hockey games."

Diny recognized Nico's remark on prayer, which comforted her. Then her head swirled with this introduction, and suddenly tired, she gently thanked him for the conversation. "A pleasure to know you, Nico," Diny gushed, extending her mitten hand to shake Nico's expansive hand.

He seemed surprised at the end of their time together, and his hand lingered, holding hers. "Oh, the pleasure is mine! Can I offer my arm as a support to escort you home?" he solicited cautiously, sliding her hand through his arm, as he cheerfully pretended to walk her home. She giggled and admired his undaunted candor.

"Or perhaps a ride on my bicycle?" He dramatically gestured to a lone bicycle in Jacob's alleyway, burdened by several inches of snow. *How can he bicycle in the snow?* She again wondered if he was crazy or merely childlike.

Marieke emerged from Jacob's home, brimming with red coloring, warmth, and laughter, flushed, her raven hair pulled up. Jacob appeared equally content, and Diny insisted on shuffling off into the evening, eager to hear of her evening activities. Nico was captivated with Diny's sparkling, vivacious persona. His cousin's gathering seemed dull after her exit, as few remained and a certain quiet pervaded the room.

Indeed, as Nico stared at her the entire afternoon, Diny charmed each person in discussion, her kindness permeating the engagement. As the party concluded, Nico felt like the only man at the party as they conversed on the front porch, captivated by her sincerity, enthralled in her gentleness, insulated from the world on Jacob's porch. He continued the evening alone, barely surfacing from his trance for light tea with Jacob's parents, his Oom Sluis and Tante Rie, and the other seven cousins, but instead pondered over that day: smoking and brooding, attending an awkward party, not certain of his own desire or aptitude to remain at Jacob's party, and jolted into a prodigious reality in meeting effervescent Diny. His perspective shifted, and he no longer felt lonely, yet inspired, and he remained the night at Jacob's house.

Both Nico and Diny felt eager to continue their dynamic encounter. They were drawn toward each other by some undeniable force, and Nico finished his afternoon appointments quickly to meet Jacob after school two days later, to casually visit again with Diny. She feigned surprise at seeing him outside the school, and Nico leaned closely to Diny, speaking softly as they meandered along tree-lined streets.

"I cannot stop thinking of our meeting the other night," Nico mused, "remembering the questions I never had a chance to ask you because Annika had to hurry you home."

Diny chuckled and blushed. "Oh, *Annika*? Her name is *Marieke*, but you are correct, she keeps me busy. She is even more outgoing than I am!" Diny smiled at him.

Nico wondered, "Are you overheated?" He looked at her knitted green hat, hoping she would remove it to display her soft caramel hair.

"No…I just blush sometimes, especially when I am embarrassed or nervous." She noticed him staring at her hat and removed it, then shoved the thick green knit into her bookbag. Nico jumped back, dramatically surprised at the beauty of her hair, and then jokingly shuffled his feet into an improvised dance.

"So! I embarrass you?" He stared intently into her hazel eyes, keeping a straight face.

"Well, yes. I mean, no. I feel flustered, seeing you again. But I have thought about you, hoping we would meet. Maybe you can meet my father." Nico stared at Diny while dancing, noting her dark brown eyes. His feet halted their awkward hopping, and his gaze lingered on her face. Her hair bounced and puffed on her dark coat as she walked, as though her gait enlivened when she was around Nico.

"I am glad to see you again, Diny," he told her, his dazzling blue eyes sparkling with animation and mischief. Nico was certain if he were to begin a friendship with her family, he could further fascinate her. Beside his desire to enthrall her with his charming sentiments, Nico sought to treat her — and her family — appropriately. As they walked, they discussed life in Batavia.

"I fully intend to return to Indie," Nico confided, "and I plan to raise a family there in the balmy, tropical climate. Maybe my Father Pouwels will develop a close friendship with my children, like he connected with me, while playing games and having adventures."

Diny was confused, and she whispered, "Well, how old are your children, then, Nico?" she began. "You forgot to mention them the other night."

He looked shocked, "Oh, of course! I meant to say, '*Someday in the future, when I have children,*' because I do not have children. But I hope I become a father someday. I should stop confiding in you about all my future ideas or I will scare you away."

She laughed and reminded him, "We spoke of this on Jacob's front porch, Nico. I remember, you shivered so badly, how could you remember much of our first meeting?"

"I do, *Dien*. Or shall I call you *Meisje*?" He began to shuffle along quickly on the snowy sidewalk near her home, as though ice skating. She pointed to her gabled townhome, and asked him to wait outside for a moment, and Diny tossed her green knit hat to him. "In case you get cold!" she exclaimed. Meeting Diny's father was an absolute necessity.

As Diny approached her front door, Nico realized a sudden and unsolicited visit might not be appropriate, so at the Dekker's front steps, they decided on a suitable afternoon to visit with her family, and she entered the home alone to discuss the matter with her parents. A few minutes later Diny returned, inviting Nico to the following Sunday's *koffietijd*, mid-afternoon. She grinned and waved, eager for their upcoming coffee-and-tea-break together. He agreed, then tossed the green cap back to her before sprinting to the train station.

It was the beginning of 1940, and amidst the changes stirring in their souls and political hemisphere, with rapid succession Nico and Diny became a real couple, dating each other. After a few preliminary visits at their home, Pieter offered Nico an equally firm handshake and the blessing of the courtship, marveling at Nico's characteristics and tender, steady spirit, a careful balance for Diny's zeal for nearly every topic in life.

"He certainly is a settled, confident fellow," Dad told her after their initial introduction, inspecting the jar of marmalade jam which Nico brought as a gift. "And, he is unquestionably solid, unlike Willem's constant fluttering and flailing about to offer a halfhearted compliment, his rebuff of your friendship. Even Nico's gift is unique!" Dad held the jar up and grinned. Mam nodded in agreement, joyful and content.

Diny was thankful Dad commented positively on Nico's maturity and humility, and when he pointed out Willem lacked discretion and insight, Diny ignored a mention of Willem and would not be deflated. Yet later, she mentally compared Willem with Nico, and felt convinced of Nico's charming yet authentic personality, his cool and tranquil contentment. He was unlike Willem and did not require an audience, nor did he seem intent on playing a role. Willem's personality was self-centered, while Nico's gentle persuasion seemed bent on kindness and selflessness. Only more time together could reveal Nico's true character.

Nico enfolded into the Dekker family and the distinctive togetherness they created. Their home was indeed small but ample, and truly *gezellig*, emitting a "warm, cozy togetherness," a welcoming spirit providing a sense of peace. Encounters with Nico were authentic and familiar, like a deep-rooted, spirited friend. Mam played records, serving as a background to their activities. Afternoons were spent in conversation surrounded by melodies, symphonies of hope. Their favorite tunes numbered the dozens, and music felt like a faithful friend, joining the family in their adventures and daily routines.

Nico shared dinners at the kitchen table, socializing about the activities of their day — or in Nico's case, the expanse of nearly two weeks' time — as he was on leave from the East when meeting Diny, he was soon to return to the normal rigors of his job, only able to visit every-other weekend. Their home was an oasis, an example of a balanced marriage, with a sense of normalcy.

In the brisk morning, as their home heated to a friendlier air while Dad added wood to their living room heat stove, Diny warmed her hands around a cup of steaming tea. She gazed out the kitchen window at the wooden fence, which sparkled with the previous night's flurries of snow dust attached to the surface, as though someone had tossed handfuls of glitter in the air, and yet the chilled icy wall would soon melt in the full sunshine of the day, evaporating the shimmer.

Diny thrived in a town like Hilversum, relished extended time with family, within cafes, bakeries, and cinemas, and strolling parks for Saturday afternoon picnics. Over the years they lived in the Dutch East Indies, the Dekker family corresponded with family and friends through letters which traveled thousands of kilometers on great ships, over many seas and throughout seasons. Those friendships and Sunday afternoon coffee events at homes, which often lasted through dinnertime and into late evening, were equally important during Furlough months. It was rewarding to place those friendships into the timeline of their years of raising families together.

On 25 January, along with Jacob, Stien, Henk, and Marieke, the Dekker family celebrated Nico's twenty-third birthday with ice skating followed by cake, pie, hot tea, and coffee. On 30 January, the entire country gathered to cheer on more than 3,000 competitors of the *Elfstedentocht* through Friesland with an early 5 a.m. start, and frigid temperatures, even along the sidelines, with the winners crossing the finish line at 4:34 p.m., just a dozen kilometers from Pieter Dekker's hometown of Kollum. The marvelous event dominated the front pages of Dutch newspapers the next day.

One afternoon soon thereafter, Dad lined up his family on the couch in the sitting room and discussed the reality of returning to the Dutch East Indies after the Furlough ended the following month. Diny dreamed of remaining in the Netherlands, unable to differentiate her love for both countries for differing reasons. Within the country of the Netherlands, her roots and bloodline emerged, and surrounded her dreams with Nico and their future. The Dutch countryside was a magical enticement for adventure. Although she missed the balmy climate of Indie and her friendships there, she felt certain she could remain in Holland permanently.

"In just a few weeks, we are scheduled to leave for Batavia," Dad reminded the family as they gathered in the sitting room, "and when our ship leaves, we must set aside all we built here and return to our lives there."

All three children looked at him with panicked eyes. Diny's feelings for Nico had blossomed, and she contemplated the logistics of staying in Hilversum to remain near to him. She shook her head at her father.

"We have done this before," Pieter reminded them with a chuckle, "and while this move will not be easy, we will adjust to our old life. I am certain. You will see!"

Diny sank lower into the couch, and then acquired some courage to speak her thoughts. "Dad," Diny mused, "what if I stay here for nursing school? I can receive my training quicker here, live with Tante and Oom, and rent a room from them."

Pieter looked sternly at Diny and crossed his arms.

Yet before he could say anything, Cornelia looked up from her knitting and nodded, sustaining the momentum of Diny's idea. She murmured, "Diny is right."

Pieter swirled around to glare at Cornelia. "Not you, too," he growled, his head lowering.

"I just do not know how we can leave now." Cornelia set aside her knitting and stared at her hands. "The Indie humid climate is so tiring for me, with my migraines," she continued. "Perhaps I could remain here with our children? The Hilversum schools are wonderful, and Diny is nearly finished with HBS. Nelly has finally deciphered how to succeed in school, while Jan has surrounded himself with wonderful friends. Our three children feel connected to their lives here… and to special friends." She glanced at Diny, who blushed.

Pieter uncrossed his arms and sighed, but looked lovingly at Cornelia and softened. He paced the length of the room, which was not difficult due to his long legs. He did not have the luxury of a year-round outdoor office in the Netherlands, in which to pace and think and pray, which his garden spaces in Indie afforded.

"Cora, *schatje*, my darling," Pieter began, "Look, I have to ponder this turn of events." He offered Cornelia his hand, which she took, and they walked together to the back of the house and closed a door. Their children heard muffled whispers but could not interpret any words as they awaited their parents.

A few minutes later Pieter returned alone, and declared, "Your Mam is tired and going to bed. We will settle this matter shortly. Do not be alarmed, my *lievelingens*. I will pray about God's plan for this next year, my darlings."

Diny considered, *perhaps I can go to school to become a nurse!* If she lived with Tante and Oom, she might remain in the Netherlands and near Nico. It was a good plan. She felt the Intermission of her life was over, and Act Two would soon begin.

Amidst their Dutch winter on Furlough, February arrived, and Pieter drove them to a popular greenhouse, *Pinetum Blijdenstein*, a local Hilversum charm, to enjoy the thriving tropical ecosystem inside, a world of its own. Within the warm greenhouse they discovered earthy scents of home, beloved plants and flowers from Indie. These floral wonders were also transplants, taken from a tropical landscape and redistributed into a new culture. Their afternoon included a tour of the tropical conservatory which captured the humid climate she adored. The owner took great lengths to coax a fickle seed or reserved bulb toward maturity. There were groupings of cycads, palms, ephedra, Tasmanian flora, and rhododendrons. Diny felt a fondness for the papaya tree, and Jan was astounded at the magic of the cacao trees. Mam found a species of burnt orange parrot tulips.

The vermillion, orchid, and water lilies they all marveled over would not thrive in inhospitable and frigid landscapes as a Dutch winter. The enclosed structure of the greenhouse coupled with the heat of the sun magnified the windows and created a pressure cooker of opportunity for growth. Certainly, trials may feel painful in the moment, with the heat of intense challenges, but Diny was sure God would sustain them through difficulties, allowing them to thrive in this environment, if only they allowed Him freedom to work in their lives.

Courting Nico proved difficult while living far from Diny, who lived in a quaint yet growing suburban area of Hilversum, a place of importance in the northwestern part of the Netherlands. Nico was employed in Elst (between Nijmegen and Arnhem), in the southeast part of the Netherlands, near Germany, and visited his mother in Hilversum every other weekend. During the week, he worked for jam manufacturing company *Taminiau Jam Fabrieken*, selling their jams. Taminiau Overbetuwe Elst (TEO) was one of the largest jam factories in western Europe. Nico held long hours as a salesman and the job was more than an hour away via train; moreover, he sought to support Mother Pouwels, so time outside those responsibilities was limited.

Nico and Diny visited together every other weekend, as he worked until lunchtime on Friday, took the train West to stopover with Mother, sometimes stayed overnight at Jacob's house, shared most meals during the weekend with Diny, and lingered until the last train East on Sunday evening. Diny's parents accepted Nico as their own son, and Dad was as a father to Nico, whose own Father Pouwels lived half-way around the world in the Dutch East Indies. In the meanwhile, between visits, they wrote letters, her rolling cursive smooth and wavy, and his miniature print a neat and exact style, precise. Their letters were expressions of their true selves on paper.

Over long afternoons in the sitting room, the Dekker family learned more about Nico's background, as he shared openly, telling of his family, upbringing, and life situation. He played with the stirring spoon, twirling it through his coffee. It was his only expression of nervousness. As Nico spoke, he stared at Diny, before realizing his intense scrutiny might intimidate her father. He soon relaxed, able to allow his gaze to scan the welcoming faces of her family.

He was the youngest of five children, born to Klasina and Pieter, who had married on 7 August 1902, at twenty-one years of age. Nico's Mother Klasina moved through life as a sweet, delightful, and tender lady. She loved the Lord dearly, and she also possessed a deep, unswerving affection for her five children: eldest daughter Stien (born in 1903), daughter Jopie (1905), firstborn son Pieter (1910), daughter Iekje (1915), and youngest son Nico (1917).

Nico Pieter Pouwels was born on 25 January 1917, during The Great

War, amidst a Dutch neutrality and a mild winter. Two days after his first birthday, he was fortunate to experience his first winter of the *Elfstedentocht,* the eleven-city ice skating race. His mother Klasina Aaltje Van de Wetering, affectionately called Mother Pouwels, raised him with kindness and a gentle spirit.

After all their children were born, they moved to Batavia in the Dutch East Indies, building a solid home there together, or so they imagined. Mother could not settle into the lifestyle of the tropics. Pieter flourished in a successful accounting business, and his younger brother Hendrik settled there with his family. Likewise, two of Klasina's brothers also moved to the Indies for prosperous work, and it was a sought-after place for opportunities not found in the Netherlands. Nico supposed they were happy in those early years, although his mother never could accustom herself to a life in the tropics.

Although Father Pouwels' career as an accountant soared, their marriage dissolved, and in August 1924 she and their children retreated to the Netherlands for several years as Nico attended primary school in Hilversum. They lived on Sumatralaan, while older sister Jopie stayed in Batavia with Father. On 26 October 1926, Nico's older sister Stien married Wim Geuken and eventually settled in Den Haag.

Mother returned to the Dutch East Indies in early 1929. Yet, even after many years of marriage and five children together, Pieter and Klasina's marital foundation was not solid, and unraveled, leading to divorce, which was official on 4 October 1930. One source of concern was the difference in spiritual depth and faith. Mother Pouwels was a devoted Christian, and practiced her beliefs in all aspects of life, while Father Pouwels was a steadfast Atheist, as he did not believe in God or any divine involvement in the world. Their love for each other was not enough to sustain marriage, and their love for their children could never nourish or grow a faulty union. At the time of the divorce, Mother Pouwels found refuge in the comfort of Hilversum with four of her children. She remained a steadfast member of the Dutch Reformed Church.

At the time their marriage ended, Mother Pouwels departed permanently for the Netherlands, and settled on Javalaan in Hilversum. The divorce caused incredible pain for the entire family, particularly for Nico, the youngest of the five children, and the only one to remain Merten in Indie. The three eldest children were established in life in the Netherlands as young adults. Mother took fifteen-year-old daughter Iekje along with her to Holland; Iekje became a nurse in Ede in 1939. Nico remained in the Indies to be raised by Father Pouwels.

Although his mother was no longer a daily influence for his teenage years, Nico considered his needs were cared for and he was safe. Mother had been the spiritual leader, raising children with solid morals and values, and Nico remained true to all he learned. He possessed an unshakable faith in the Lord and belief in Jesus, although quietly managed that portion of life.

Father Pouwels was interested in Nico's daily school program and his education, and frequently enjoyed participating in games together, soccer in open fields, flying kites on breezy days, or marble games on the veranda during the monsoon season. This was the beginning of Nico's love for playing games. They went to the movies together and discussed the themes of the films, lingering at the cinema. Father Pouwels was always surrounded by a lot of children, as he loved them with a father's love. Neighbor children gathered to fly kites, battling to send their craft into the air as the highest or achieve complicated spinning tricks.

As Nico shared with the Dekker family, he showed them pictures of Father Pouwels, in which he seemed stern, strict, and serious about his work. Yet in everyday life, he was a kind, sociable, and compassionate man, caring for those around him. Nico's enjoyment and intrigue with games flourished when Father played with him in Indie. Perhaps the difficulties surrounding divorce, Nico thought, coupled with the harsh decision to raise Nico alone, spurred Father toward investing in his youngest son, who seemed and felt like an only child. Going to the movies offered a cool respite from the tropics and an entertaining escape from reality. Most importantly, time together allowed Father to know his son, as they often sat together until sunset, conversing about school and life.

Truly, Father Pouwels missed his older four children as well, and the blessings, humors, and complications surrounding raising a large brood. As a mark of dedication, he continued sending money to his family in The Netherlands, as a support to them, especially for Mother Pouwels' daily life and for raising their daughter Iekje. But it was impossible to live there now. They played in the tropics, enjoyed seasonal respites from school and from his laborious work as an accountant. Nico would meekly enter the accounting office and patiently wait for his father to complete his work.

As a matter of principle, Pieter Pouwels remained groomed and trimmed, his mustache thin and neat, his hair curling up only at the humidity, but short enough to require frequent barber visits. At Pieter's sturdy wooden desk, a large map was displayed behind him on the wall, a date-stamp in front of him, a pen in his right hand. He wore a white button-down jacket and kept a crisp and polished appearance, with a triangular handkerchief tucked into his left chest pocket and a watch fob in the middle of his jacket. His thin round spectacles were fastened securely to his nose. He often chuckled on those rare moments his son arrived at his office, and postured to return to work before realizing the time, then tidied up the desk to join Nico for the evening.

Flying kites as father and son challenged their scientific senses, field hockey offered exhilaration and intense exercise, and walks through jungles engaged conversation and unity in action and purpose. Father's brow glowed in perspiration over a shared activity, and laughter flourished in those days.

In Hilversum, Mother Pouwels continued her close relationship with her children, providing a loving, Godly home for them; a number of Van de Wetering relatives lived nearby. Klasina's compassion provided stability despite the lack of a Godly Fatherly role model inside their home. Their eldest Stien already was married, Jopie was out living on her own, and Piet was working, but all three still returned on occasion for meals together. Iekje had completed her studies and was more independent as well. When Nico turned eighteen, Father sent him back to the Netherlands to further his education and finish his studies at HBS.

Mother Pouwels received a small income, which made it rough for her financially. Tante Rie Sluis (her sister-in-law, and Jacob's mother) helped her a lot. Mother was always welcome at Tanta Rie's house for meals and visits, amidst Rie's bustling household with eight children (Stien, Jacob, Herman, Rietje, Joost, Pieter, Bep, and Brom), which felt like a boarding school at times more than a quaint home. Tante Rie was also a towering persona with dark curly hair, and a strong frame, powerful enough to carry the burden of raising so many children, yet soft enough for sweet conversation and *koffietijd*. She was Father Pouwels' sister, but she remained closely connected to Mother Pouwels even after the divorce, and the Sluis family extended God's love and grace to her during her time of need.

Father Pouwels stayed in Indie, and eventually re-married there. Nico and Father Pouwels frequently exchanged letters, sharing about their lives.

As Nico finished sharing about his early years, he was relieved by the smiles and kind glow of the Dekker family surrounding him. His memories of games with Father Pouwels glimmered brightly in his heart.

"One afternoon," he told them, "just before I moved back to the

Netherlands, Father took me to our favorite park where we frequently visited over the years." The day was glorious, full of sunshine, with gentle breezes.

"Together, we launched carved wooden boats off into the lake, and the boats were fashioned with three sticks to hold two colorful sails, planked into the base of the boat."

They encountered challenges in setting boats across the lake as some toppled and sank into the murky depths. That one magnificent afternoon their boats reached the opposite shore, vibrantly skimming across rippling water. Just a few weeks later, Nico found himself traveling across the seas to the Netherlands, his own colorful Indie story etched across his heart, his father's steady hand raised in farewell, until the fog hazed over, through steam and tears, and away from security, into the next life phase.

Nico also admitted to worrying about the consequences of his parents' devastating divorce, and assured Pieter he would alter his heritage, dismissing divorce for a marriage of blessing and promise, based on the foundation of God. Nico insisted, "When I marry one day, divorce will not be a topic we discuss. My upbringing will not determine my course of actions. I am determined to set an example for future generations, and marry only once, remaining married until death." The Dekkers embraced him, welcoming him as their own, inviting him into their sitting room and into their lives.

Evenings including Nico's visits were lively with conversations. After dinner, Jan and Nelly read upstairs, while others settled into conversation. Sometimes Pieter and Nico played chess games, their competitive natures on full display. Nico's easygoing and considerate personality became engaged in a combating rivalry. His ability to dominate water polo or field hockey further highlighted his love for sports. And with Pieter, Nico's conversations flowed freely over a chess game, or while playing ping pong, or tennis, much like moments with Father Pouwels in his days living in the Indies. Nico found a new confidant in Pieter, as enjoying a game or activity unlocked their pretenses, allowing for deeper discussions about life, side-by-side.

At the Dekker home sitting room, Mam played a radio show or gramophone, and allowed the cheery songs of the 1930s to permeate into the corners of their household. Mam embroidered or mended clothing, or read a novel. Diny and Nelly baked together and Diny marveled at Nelly's ability for deeper conversation while working on something with her hands, as though the undertaking distracted her, whether a baking task or sewing project. Nico peeked into the kitchen as Diny and Nelly prepared the dough and baked their treats, lovingly admiring Diny's cheery profile and her laughter as she bashfully turned away, sending him away from the kitchen with flour-covered hands.

The next weekend, Pieter and Cornelia left for a social outing, and Jan visited a friend's home while Nelly tucked away upstairs working on projects. Diny and Nico found themselves alone in the sitting room of the Dekker's townhome. The evening stretched before them with conversation and laughter, each settled into their own plush chairs, then dancing. Diny brewed tea and coffee with cookies. With Mozart on the gramophone player, Nico stood and offered his hand, and they sashayed around the room.

The following evening, her parents away at a church event and snow piled on the Dekker's front porch steps, Diny played some 1920s jazz songs. She rested beside Nico on the couch, tea cups in hand, talking in the low-light of the sitting room, curtains open to watch the snow fall outside in the early evening. Although she met him only one month prior, Diny could not imagine her life apart from Nico.

Nico shared about vines of jasmine which engulfed the front fence of his Indie home, and the bougainvillea reached beyond the sidewalk, where hibiscus plunged their heads. A sprint down to the seaside brought refreshment, and the landscape gleamed with yellow and mauve fragrant blossoms. From a distance during a summertime hiding game, his older sister Iekje's voice would echo along the bay and he would lay on his back in the grass, motionless among the quietest trees and hold his breath until she passed. The canopy of banyan tree branches would reach out with craggy arms but never catch him. He would leap up from the ground and chase his sister through ferns and along the road until they reached the shoreline. Memories would remain in his heart, he considered, for the shores and inlets would have surely changed by the time he returned.

After sharing a few memories of his upbringing, he decided to dance. He placed his cup and saucer aside, and reached into his coat pocket, retrieving something. Nico whispered softly in Diny's ear, singing along with the music, creating his own lyrics, and slipped a note into Diny's dress pocket. She opened the papers, examining his miniature writing assembled in tidy stanzas, and eagerly began to read his thoughts.

Nico grabbed her hand. "No, *Dien,* save this for later," Nico insisted, "and only read this after I go home, so you know how happy I feel." Her face looked worried, but he beamed reassuringly. "This letter is good, Diny. Savor the meaning, and refrain from rushing through my poems."

She delighted in their unexpected moment of togetherness.

Later, when the evening was growing late, and he returned to Mother Pouwels' home, Diny played jazz music and admired the bouquet of her beloved's words. Nico enjoyed writing in a small font. He filled several pages with petite handwriting, and she loved to read his tiny, precise words. The poems composed in the note lyrically expressed rich friendship blossoming into a deeper aroma, an unexpressed flavor, and vibrant reality. He perfectly articulated emotions, surrounded by descriptions of seasons and his hope for their future. He halted his prose before using the actual word *love*, but the intention was clear. She sparkled at his words.

Chapter Ten
Hilversum, late February 1940

By now, the end of Dad's six-month Furlough neared, as in February Pieter was required to return to his role as Head of Police in the Dutch East Indies. He only required one more year of service before retirement, to receive the maximum retirement pension. The Dekkers arrived in the late summer on Furlough, and now prepared to leave their Dutch lives behind and return with him in February. Diny feared disrupting the momentum of her relationship with Nico. Mam also voiced her disappointment at returning, especially unsettling recent world events. She imagined a complicated sea voyage and possible troubles in the Indies, but reminded her family she honored Pieter's decisions, so she began to prepare to return to Batavia beside him.

Pieter sought God at length in prayer, and felt he must go alone, to fully concentrate his efforts on those delicate work matters he left behind in Batavia. Besides, the thought of uprooting their family for one year seemed like nonsense, especially as the boat rides from one country to another lasted at least three weeks. In this tentative world, with country borders closing for mobilization, who knew how long the journey would take? Several months at sea? Pieter reasoned one year is merely a moment in time. Taking the family along would disrupt Diny's courtship with Nico, unsettle Nelly and Jan's studies, and damage Cornelia's health. Pieter grew extremely fond of Nico in a short span of two months, and felt thankful they could rely on Nico's strong, steady presence and emotional support during Pieter's absence. Pieter and Cornelia gathered their children into the front sitting room. One look at Mam's blissful face, and Diny knew Dad allowed them to stay.

"Everything is settled, then," Dad told them. "And after one year in the Indies, I will return here. Do not worry for me, sweet *Grietjes,* as I am certain this year will quickly gallop past us"

As Dad prepared to leave alone, Jan turned eleven, and started to shift in his own changes and restlessness. Pieter requested Nico look after Jan and spend time with him, as men, to introduce him to the ways of the world within a Christian framework. Just as Nico lost his Mother's daily influence at age thirteen, Jan was now losing his dad's presence at a tender age. Again, he reminded them of those important lessons which required character development. "Remember, my children, in many cases in life, we are required to go through hardships and disappointments to reach our goals — and there is no other way."

The morning of his departure, Cora cooked Pieter his favorite breakfast. "You will only be gone to Batavia for a year, Pieter," she assured him as she untied her apron, then placed it on the kitchen hook. She chuckled. "Why are we swooning over such a brief season?" Cora wondered aloud at his travels and the safety of a sea voyage at a precarious time.

Pieter bellowed, "Why, we each steamed over to Indie on our own! Not a problem. My, that seems like a long time ago." He folded his newspaper and placed it face-down on the kitchen table, then covered the headlines with his coffee mug. "Nothing worth reading now, my love. Not to worry, Cora!"

"Yes, Pieter. You are right. We will trust the Lord, as we always do. And we embarked on that path in the Indies before children. We hardly knew each other then."

"It only took a few weeks to remedy that," Pieter winked. "And long before those heavy policing responsibilities arrived. Life was like a snake, slithering along, suddenly threatening. How could I know it would nearly strangle us?" He pulled at his white collar, which stood tall and covered half his neck.

"Over-starched, it seems," she grimaced, and twisted his tight collar into place. Her fingers burned and she clenched her stinging hands. Pieter reached for Cora's hands and held them together, against his chest.

"As long as we are apart, my love," he whispered, "I have to work extra hard to remind you how much I need you. How dearly I care for you!" His eyes were bright and blue in the sun.

"I know, Pieter! Tell me in your letters home and promise to write that you are safe."

"I will send you money, as much as I can, as I liquidate our estate." Cora stared at him and recognized how much he had changed over the last year.

She stroked Pieter's head. "Your hair is flat in this February chill, and will puff into a curl as soon as you arrive in the tropics."

"This is true. Then, when I return, we will holiday in Switzerland, just like we planned," he assured her. Nico tapped on the front door. Pieter's ship would depart from Rotterdam and arrive three weeks later into Batavia's main harbor. The swamps and mangroves would welcome him back to the Indies. As she watched Pieter leave, Cora's face was illuminated by the sun. She held up her hand and offered a smile.

Before Dad left, he expressed concern about Mam's frail health, migraine headaches, and wellbeing. The week prior to departure, he daily reiterated his reminder to Diny, "Zorg goed voor je Moeder."

She would, she promised.

"Take good care of your mother." His words echoed in her head, his blue eyes serious. Pieter offered Diny a heavy responsibility, but only because he sought to protect his Cora, who would rely on Diny as the eldest. They all knew with his return in one year, Dad would reclaim the role of leader in their home.

This next year will be difficult, Diny reasoned, *yet our Heavenly Father, who knows what we need, will provide for us.* Off her dad went in late February 1940, with Nico and Diny delivering him to the bustling Rotterdam docks. Pieter's tall, commanding figure waved so-long. Before his boat was out of sight, she already missed her dear father and the steady, optimistic role he played in her life.

Diny was thankful for Nico's presence, for his compassion and pleased his companionship would cheer them all in Pieter's absence. As they departed for her Hilversum home, the winter air stung her throat and chill picked at her skin. White landscapes were always muffled and silent. From the train station to her house, the sky darkened, threatening another snow. The bitter air pierced, stinging their eyes with tears.

Later, in March, the springtime glory of tulip fields extended farther, as beyond Tante Sietske and Oom Cor's property in the far northern district of Groningen, the walking trail looped a neighbor's yard, around a rich, fertile soil. As Diny strolled in tempo with her breath and heartbeat, she listened to the steady crunching and sloshing beneath her feet. The heathlands, woods, and meadows m were invigorating and offered a respite to her weary wonderings. Diny lifted her gaze to the blue sky, with bright possibility. She leapt at the chance to spend a brisk week with her farm family, again amused by a chestnut horse.

Stepping beyond the stone wall into fields felt like striding into a magical dream world. The woods were lined with tall leafy trees, a peaceful sanctuary. Green meadow grass offered the darling horse a place to gallop. "*Schatje!*" she cooed to him. At age eighteen, the entire world stretched before her, supple and fertile. Possibilities were achievable, and she dreamed of a future with Nico.

Windmills paired rivers and tulip fields up north, when the breaking of the frost crackled the solid soil and began to melt into verdant yield. Diny and her family bundled in knitted sweaters, thick trousers, rubber boots, and chunky scarves to again slosh through bountiful fields of vibrant and varied colors. Her cousins, now fully grown, renewed their friendship as happy companions.

As they reveled in refreshment and chased butterflies through pastures, she imagined her father working long hours alone, returning in the evening for a simple meal in his hotel room, spending his journeys in solitude and silence, save his conversations with other hotel patrons. Dad now resided at Hotel Schutte Raaff, room 1, Koningsplein Oost nr. 12 in Batavia, Dutch East Indies. He had liquidated the house and sold most of their belongings. Pieter wrote letters frequently, and added silly and joyful personal notes for Diny, Nelly, and Jan, and all three children squealed with delight, to each have a special note from Dad. Mam hid her letters away, which Diny felt had something to do with the tenacious world unrest and uncertainty.

Memories of Batavia were like distant reminiscences, Diny's uncomplicated, pampered life suddenly thorny and convoluted. She further imagined Nico would love to join them in these fertile fields, but his business kept him on the Eastern borders of their country, working in trade, establishing his reputation, picking up various translation jobs. As her family wandered the farm, they observed freshly-born lambs and calves, stumbling through fields on unstable legs, never wandering too far from their mothers, yet wobbling into the freedom of discovery in muddy pastures. Those new animals exhibited immense possibility, as life commences unsullied and promising.

The Dekker family received a lengthy letter from Dad at the end of April, and Mam scanned through the letter, page after page, then scurried closer to the sitting room for privacy, masking her expressions. Her face was grim in one minute and beaming in the next. Dad enclosed a generous sum of money and promised additional finances over the next year as he closed out their former home, sending some of their valuables along to the Netherlands and packing many items into trunks for his return trip. While she knew Dad would return to the Netherlands permanently within the year, Mam would not disclose what he wrote, page after page excruciating and raw for her to read.

Over the next few months, the Dekker family welcomed Nico as much as possible, becoming acquainted with his calm serenity, kindness, and strength of presence. Sunday afternoons, after church service, Oma van den Bout welcomed visitors for coffee, tea, and desserts. After sufficiently visiting with her grandmother, Diny met with Nico, visiting parks where tulips, daisies, daffodils, delphiniums, and chrysanthemums bloomed.

Bicycling on Saturday afternoons, Diny's long auburn hair floated behind her, freely uninhibited, her legs stretched while pedaling, browning in the sunshine. During long rides, they talked of people in their lives, of the commonplace sameness of one week to the next, savoring time with each other. Nico listened more than he spoke.

She jumped off her bicycle to browse a book store, and her allure remained in the array of adventures found just beyond their doorsteps. Her optimism and laughter never dimmed. She claimed her positive outlook and hard working ethic would sustain them through challenges. Nico grabbed her hand to hold as they rode, clamoring over cobbled streets. The assurance of spring burst forth gloriously — a pink tulip pushed up through the snow, melting runoff beyond daffodils. Upon spring's arrival, their love may begin in full bloom.

Narrow lanes wound and meandered, with city goers on bicycles zooming throughout every nook. Together with Nico, Diny seemed determined to explore every corner of the country. Sunday afternoons, reading together with Nico on a picnic blanket near the river remained a cherished routine. Diny found questions to challenge and inspire Nico and they felt insulated in their own cozy cocoon. If they reserved two hours together, both would rather settle into a booth with tea than waste hours in a darkened cinema.

They boarded the train from Hilversum and watched a blur of pastures out their window as the train paced quickly to Amsterdam, their landscape scenery as though a painter dipped into a bright lime green palate and brushed horizontal strokes of paints on the colorful countryside, an impressionism masterpiece.

After exiting the clacking train, they meandered from Amsterdam's Centraal Train Station beside one looming church overlooking St. Nicolaaskerk.

The church was built of brown stone with a large octagonal tower, baroque dome and lantern, and crowned by a cross upon the center of the cathedral, flanked by two silver turrets. They sat along a canal as clouds furrowed behind the church, layers of white fog like ripped paper pasted onto a dazzling azure sky. Levels of mist permeated the air, providing the Church an ethereal quality. They wandered the city for hours and the church rang out six times before they returned to the train. In Hilversum he delivered her home, bidding her farewell until twelve days later. The time between meetings was passed with letters and contemplation.

Some days they observed men surveying villages and fields in military clothing. That became a more frequent occurrence, until they were unable to venture anywhere without stern looks from uniformed men, as rumors continued swirling about a Dutch mobilization. In April, Nico was called away with other men in the Dutch Army to stand-by for battle, unable to leave his military post for any time off. The air of uncertainty once again pervaded their lives in their small country, with the real threat of Germany's strength now imminent.

On 10th of May 1940, war broke out. Germany invaded the Netherlands, and Luftwaffe bombers attacked Hilversum's military base. The Dekkers huddled in their basement, uncertain whether they would survive the attacks, while Nico crouched on the front lines as a soldier, traveling to the far western reaches of their land as a fortress from sea invasion.

They listened to radio news reports: fighting lasted for three days, as the Dutch held limited resources against invasion. At the climax of the altercation, Queen Wilhelmina wanted to lead the Dutch government to Zeeland to meet with the German army. Instead, she was forced to escape to London or face death. Her beloved country had surrendered. Then, Germans bombed Rotterdam in southern Holland, even after the capitulation, even after their surrender. Nico was gone, missing, absent from Diny's life, from their weekend togetherness, unsure where they stationed him or whether he might return. She became overwhelmed and irritated yet managed to busy herself with daily necessities at home.

Hilversum, June 1940

After weeks of uncertainty, Nico knocked on their door one warm June afternoon, alive, yet haggard, holding a handful of carnations for their lapels.

Diny embraced him, drawing him into their home to hear of his travels, shrieking, "Nico! You returned to us!" He sighed into her arms.

"Ahh, yes, I survived!" His hug lingered, his arm around her, looking down at her bright brown eyes, her cheery face. "I do thank the Lord for his mercy, and won our skirmish, yet we lost the battle. Germany invaded, *Dien*. What a failure!" His face looked older and weathered, his body thinner than usual.

Diny led Nico to their front sitting room and gazed at him fondly, remembering his blue eyes and lanky disposition, his calm serenity and charm, and recollected all she had forgotten during their time apart: his smile, humor, and unruffled way of living.

She encouraged him. "Nico, you fought bravely with your Army of soldiers. We heard the *Radio Oranje* updates." Mam brought them coffee, cookies, and yogurt.

Nico described, "My fellow countrymen and I valiantly fought at the Afsluitdijk! Mrs. Dekker, you might remember that area lies between Northern Netherlands and Friesland over the Ijsselmeer, a section of land recently reclaimed from the sea through polder draining."

Cora nodded and motioned for Nico to continue.

"We protected the Kornwerderzand Fortress, and the Dutch defense there was strong. But the Germans invaded, with Nijmegen in the east the first city to fall. What a shame! After an unsuccessful peace agreement, we knew real war was certain." The sun beamed into the windows and cast shadows in front of them.

Nico continued, "On the 14th of May, Dutch forces surrendered, because Germany bombed Rotterdam. It was flattened, hopes for neutrality were deflated, and the city burned for days. Many lost their lives and now we go to war." Nico described the fires, homes ablaze and destroyed, shards of concrete, brick, and glass. The smoke billowed, and hopes faded. Germany attacked quickly, decisively, and without hesitation.

Mam cried, "What a shame, Nico, since our leaders promised peace." He turned to speak, but she continued, "Well, no need to worry. Maybe neutrality is possible, and we shall hear from Pieter soon with an optimistic plan."

Nico looked at her kindly, but solemnly, and shook his head. "Neutrality is a fallacy, Mrs. Dekker. Hitler's power has grown too influential. There were initial reports which testified the Netherlands promised surrender or neutrality before the Rotterdam bombing, a forceful example of their power of invasion."

Mam looked weak. Nico assured her, "Captain Christiaan Boers assured my unit we fought '*like lions, like real, strong Dutchmen!*' and we successfully held the Afsluitdijk for the Dutch! But we were forced to surrender to spare additional cities from bombing." Nico's eyes blazed with disappointment. "Had Captain Boer been General of the entire military, perhaps every unit could have held their ground. But our country has not faced war for two hundred years, and we are not prepared. Resilient men are needed now!"

Mam concentrated on his frightened eyes. She said, "We were a neutral country in the Great War, which seemed like apathy at the time. Pieter felt action against Germany in 1914 would subvert any retribution in the future. He was only twenty-one years old but saw the possibility of another war. Many Dutch supported keeping their men alive by not engaging in the war." She leaned back against her chair and sighed.

Diny considered her father's wisdom and missed the man she loved across many miles.

Nico replied, "This is just as we supposed, right Dien?" He pointed his spoon at Diny, who vaguely remembered a war conversation on Jacob's porch just five months prior.

Mam softened. "And long before our generation, the Netherlands found great pride in navigating the seas and securing a shipping monopoly. Remember the Dutch Golden Age? Our commerce strengthened, yet with money placed in the VOC, our military became vulnerable. An unguarded and unprotected defense allows an enemy to invade."

"Well, Mrs. Dekker," Nico said, "the reason Captain Boers is so highly decorated is because of his bravery. I would follow him anywhere, as his leadership was so direct, precise, and humbly confident, and his encouragement of our troops so esteeming." Captain Boers was seemingly a hero in Nico's view of things, and they were the only Dutch Army unit to defeat German troops in their area. They spoke longer of possibilities: rations, prisoners, and an ungoverned season of life, before discussing Nico's family, and work. Diny shuddered at all which might transpire.

After several hours of conversing and later taking a stroll in their peaceful neighborhood, Nico was again hungry. Jan and Nelly returned from their afternoon activities to join them, indifferent to recent events, as if they remained unaware of the impact of a war. Cora prepared roasted rosemary beef, scalloped potatoes, and carrots for supper and they remained settled in their own warmth.

Diny mentioned an outing to Rembrandtplein and Amsterdam's city center. "We will visit the movie theater, *Pathé Tuschinski*, an exquisite cinema!" Diny gushed. "Our school attended a film there last month and we were stunned at the size of that building!"

Nico looked up from his plate. "Now is the best time to visit, before Germany secures that cinema for their own films."

Diny nodded glumly, yet squeezed her cloth napkin tightly underneath the table. *Will the Germans squelch the Dutch way of life?* She silenced fear and instead pondered the elegance of the theater. *Pathé Tuschinski* boasted warm orange undertones, red fabric chairs and carpeting, and yellow ambient lighting. The entrance was spectacular and the theater stage grand and elegant, with intricately archways, and two levels of balcony seating. Diny especially loved the ability to step away from the confines of each day and into another world. The light was contrasted by dark wood details, and as her teacher suggested, combined Art Deco and Art Nouveau styles. "Perhaps you might accompany us, Niek?" she offered.

"Certainly. I will return to Hilversum in twelve days and we shall plan for it."

Mam lit candles for the table as darkness approached, while Nelly cleared empty dinner dishes and Jan gathered firewood for the stove. Diny returned from the kitchen with fragrant banana fritters, a reminder of their memorable Pisang Goreng desserts in Indie. Mam started her gramophone, aligning the needle on the beginning of Tchaikovsky's *Swan Lake* record. She felt certain a bright musical tone would lift Nico's demeanor.

In the weeks following Rotterdam's bombing, nothing changed, and all seemed to remain eerily normal, except the attempt to clear rubble. After Germany's initial occupation, not much changed in the Netherlands, so the Dekkers optimistically believed a war would be short-lived. The only immediate alteration for the Dutch was the requirement to cover every window with blackout paper, so not a ray of light passed through at night. Inspections were held, and the rule enforced, but few Dutch considered the depth of darkness that a long winter behind blackout paper might just entail.

Apart from frequent *Radio Oranje* news updates, the Dekker family's existence was unmoved, with schools and businesses functioning as before, trains kept a normal schedule, and Amsterdam offered diversions of new movies, plays, and musical events. Diny was fascinated by Nico's tranquility, even after more than several weeks apart, on the cusp of war, with spring afternoons full of remarkable sunshine and vibrancy amidst emotional uncertainty.

She prayed for his safe return, then leapt into his arms after 12 days apart. She had forgotten his calm demeanor, lanky gait, casual gestures as he spoke, and musky scent, the aroma of life which lingered in the air. They quickly reconnected with cheer, even with the dark, inevitable reality of war. His unflustered character offset her blustery bewilderment. They shared passions and goals, including family dreams and relocating to Indie. They felt insulated from the war, hidden from reality and the growing momentum surrounding them.

Diny watched as Nico played field hockey on splashy fields at Hilversum's Laapersveld Park, amidst spring showers. Her hat and umbrella could not keep her warm or dry from brisk spring rainstorms. Nico played field hockey so well, she soon realized, because of his speed! On his long legs, he sprinted from one end of the field to the other with force and hustle, and the ball sailed into the goal. After hockey games, they joined his teammates for a meal. Later, they bicycled the quiet neighborhoods of Hilversum, down narrow side streets, looping to her home.

Their discussions picked up from the last and ended before they desired, always continuing, as though their entire relationship consisted of one long conversation, bantering through their day with a sparkling chemistry she had never experienced. Conversation found interruption at the end of the evening, into the exchange of farewells of the night, when each retired to their own respective homes. But dialogue progressed and developed into maturity and hinted at a future, where hours could stretch before them like happy gifts, offering the most cherished prizes of marriage, of hands and hearts clasped for life.

Their minds and hearts felt joined, their togetherness *gezellig*, enigmatically connected. They sometimes found a small cafe open into late evening hours, with the large clock chiming many times and the swinging pendulum dancing to the music of the cheery piano player. After each song, the pianist swirled around on his bench, stood, smiled, and bowed, then sat to begin the next song. With each turn his ambiance changed and altered into a new, different song, each with its own unique composer, tone, and variation.

With a light atmosphere, quaint booths, and smooth coffee, Nico and Diny found themselves isolated for hours, emerging as the restaurant closed for the night. He escorted her to the front porch and tried not to linger in the disappointment of a good-bye, so a warm embrace must satisfy until their next meeting.

"So-long," Diny cried. "I never say '*good-bye*,' but prefer '*so-long*' until next time. And in this way, we are not apart for very long."

Nico agreed, and embraced her again before walking to the train station, his scent still sultry from field hockey, sweat intermingled with spice.

At home, as Diny read Dad's recent letter which expressed his stern caution about staying outside beyond sunset, yet she could not fully comprehend the abstract fear of impending terror from Germany. She imagined dad writing from the Hotel Schutte Raaff and recalled the hotel as a place of majesty: clean white marble floors, ornate furnishings, open lobbies, detailed Sumatran wood scrollwork, and lavish gold candelabras. The rooms were adorned with decorative paintings of the VOC heroes: explorers, ship captains, industrialists, and entrepreneurs, men who changed the pathway of the Netherlands in a remote island country in Asia. Would Pieter Dekker's painting ever appear on those walls?

The Dekkers heard on nightly *Radio Oranje* reports that Dutch Prime Minister de Geer in London advocated a peace treaty with Germany. If he had hope for harmony, they had nothing to fear. Germany did not seem aggressive, at least in Hilversum. She remained largely unaware of all that was transpiring in the world.

Chapter Eleven
Hilversum, Summer 1940

The summer of 1940 was filled with swimming in the community pool, tennis near Jacob's house, and dancing at the social club, wandering through Laapersveld Park. Other moments, they escaped to Amsterdam, sitting together on the same side of the train, watching homes and fields spin past the window along the way. While on the train, Nico pursued her thoughts. His steel blue eyes gazed intently at her, and she drew a breath, retreating backwards. Her eyes tempered, and she stared out the window as the train rambled along the tracks.

He continued, What distinguishes Diny from other girls? I know the answer: your sparkling personality and cheerful countenance. But I want to hear what you think."

Diny laughed, then clutched his face with both hands and looked into his eyes. Both breathed deeply, entranced in the other's expression. Finally, Diny replied, "I am as human as you are, Niek. Although, you are near perfection, apart from the dreadful smoking,"

He gasped.

"I also have dreams and desires of my own but fear they might fail to see completion. And my passion? Well, you know my strong will, as you have experienced it. I am entirely flawed." She released his face and again turned her gaze toward the countryside flashing past them, the train horn resounding.

He seemed flustered by her direct physical contact and stroked his jaw. "Flawed? How so? Perfection is fruitless. But your type of passion is rare, and when combined with meaning and purpose, is dynamic and exceptional! You should never apologize for the zeal which drives you." He grinned and settled back into his seat. He continued, "However, stubbornness borne out of selfishness is weakness, and egotistical. Nothing good can emerge from those thoughts. I have yet to observe this in you, though."

"Just wait, Nico, and you will see, like others before. It will be *genoeg is genoeg* — 'enough is enough' and you will bore of my charms."

Nico slid a cigarette out of the box and slipped it between his lips. She scrutinized his mouth, upturned lips, and gleaming eyes, noting his easy countenance. He leaned toward her, fragrant of tobacco and mints, and covered his face with his hand as he flicked his lighter. Nico stared at her. The spark flicked but did not ignite.

Diny tilted her head. "And you, Nico; what power motivates you? How are you all at ease in moments of despair? Are you so unworldly you have all you need?"

He rolled his cigarette between his thumb and forefinger and stared at it while answering, "Simplicity. This world grows increasingly dark, but I can be a light, a beacon for those in pain or doubt." He held up his lighter symbolically. "I intend to live well and love well. When we marry one day, you will see and experience that faith and trust, my absolute commitment to care and provide for you."

She blushed.

"A light, Diny, can be unfussy and austere, but it remains necessary, bringing warmth. And light has no shadow." He flicked his lighter, and held his hand beneath the flame, which cast a shadow of his hand on the table.

She could not break his gaze.

"I run toward disaster, seeking to assist others. But I know who I am and express it unashamedly. Simplicity — just that straightforward." He flicked the lighter and watched the cigarette ignite, glow and ash forming, then inhaled away and sighed, smoke shooting from his nostrils, before looking sideways at her.

She found her voice. "How certain of you, Nico, and undistorted. You are quite certain of many things." She whispered, "I deeply admire this quality in you, although it borders on being arrogant and prideful, if you ask me. And you do not seek fame or riches, I would guess?"

He shook his head, flicking embers into the ashtray. Smoke swirled higher and animated, whirling along with his fingers pinched around his cigarette, his eyes ablaze behind the vapor. They spoke of dreams, of ideas yet to discover together. When Diny asked Nico questions, she gazed confidently at him, her brown eyes analyzing his blue eyes. She decided not to reveal all which still seemed unknown.

Nico thundered, "You have already deciphered my character, and yet I will require a lifetime to ascertain yours. Well done, Diny!" Their train flashed beside homes and arrived in Amsterdam.

They explored parks, bistros, and village markets, a slower venture through familiar streets. After reading in the shade at VondelPark, they enjoyed a herring or *kroketten* (a meat ragout roll, coated in breadcrumbs) at the food stall, followed by a canal boat tour, which transported them back in time, history around each corner and recess in the canals. They ventured past the House of Oranje, Golden Age spice warehouses, shipping locations, and homes of artists. She considered Nico's idealism, his desire for simplicity and love, and remained silent during the canal ride, contemplating. Amsterdam flourished with the promise only summer can deliver. Later they returned by train to Hilversum and Nico continued on to Elst.

Twelve days later Nico returned to Diny's heart and her arms. A relaxed afternoon with Jacob and Marieke delighted them, and all four joined Jacob's other cousin Henk Mulder and his girlfriend Janneke Bosch. The six of them visited together at their favorite restaurant under a terrace, on a tree-lined street with cobblestones, bicycles lined up in neat rows. Marieke's laughter and Jacob's hypnotic smile were a memorable interlude. Henk offered everyone cigarettes, and Janneke had baked cookies.

Idyllic scenery for Germany's occupation, Diny thought.

Nico's Tante Sluis invited them for dinner, her warm embrace encapsulating Nico, and her welcome extended in a generous way. The Sluis family front gardens reminded Diny of Batavian verandas stretching around their home, with layered blooms of crimson, emerald, or sapphire, above smaller ruby and yellow flowers, all fenced in by a black iron gate. Vines intermingled with sunshine yielding overgrowth, creeping up the side of their townhome.

With her life now in the Netherlands, she no longer observed flamboya or banyan trees, and the scents of teakwood and sandalwood no longer ebbed on a trade wind. Instead, tulips and other springtime delights bloomed forth. A berry colored tulip patch lining a stony path provided bright, stunning scenery, with field after field of various tulips of every kind, the brightest colors of reds in contrast to oranges, yellows and purples, and so forth, for great distances. A group of butterflies chasing the approaching evening shadows danced about the air, fluttering to bright music Tante Rie played on her piano. Tante's curly hair bounced with the rhythm, her merry dark eyes glimmering with memory. Butterflies provoked a fleeting, yet happy memory of Huib, before

Diny dismissed the somber past for the cheery present moment. Tante Rie's meals were always hearty and encompassing, leaving them full of goodness.

After their fill, she invited them to unwind under her back-porch veranda, which surrounded community gardens and personal estate spaces. Ivory and gray stone statues interspersed among the gardens, as though they were relishing the elegant grounds. The leaves would turn a fiery burnt orange in the autumn, like a blazing tree in flames.

Other late afternoons, following field hockey games when they encountered time alone, Nico's eyes glistened bright blue in the sunlight. These were carefree days, but untroubled moments would not linger, with soldiers convening, forming organized units, marching closer to Hilversum's center square. Diny's long hair billowed behind her as she bicycled, whipping around in the breeze, dancing in time to the sounds of their wheels whirring. She enchanted Nico, who momentarily forgot the bleak prospects for their country. They bicycled to Nico's mother for dinner.

Mother Pouwels' home welcomed them into ornate luxuries, and they settled on upholstered couches in her sitting room. She warmly visited with them, sitting in her own separate chair, the entire house quiet and austere. Crystal plates were filled with boiled eggs, savory cheeses, and smoked meats — salmon, herring, and eel — along with salads and imported tropical fruits. Dinner concluded with coffee and sugar cookies. They ate the unexpected bounty, sharing about their lives over the last six months. The pendulum clock chimed, and Nico and Diny sat outside in the cool evening air and she marveled at the close proximity to a church.

"What a grandiose church," Diny said. The lowering sun gleamed through stained-glass windows and shined bright.

Nico agreed. "Just like in Java," he mused. "Father and I played catch on our favorite patch of green in a little local park next to a church. It was rare to see a Christian church building in Indie! The stained-glass windows were massive, and streamed light inside in a holy, solemn manner. Father Pouwels felt uncomfortable, as though God watched him. Sometimes, on my way home from school, I stopped into the church, sat in the light of the stained-glass windows, and prayed for my Heavenly Father to change my earthly father's heart, for Father Pouwels to accept the saving Grace of Jesus."

She nodded.

He continued. "I was convinced playing in the park with him might transform him. But sadly, it was not possible. I was too young to know better.

And just walking into church a few times is not enough to transform a man, unless he hears the message of the Gospel as well."

Diny reassured him. "You were younger then, Nico. How could you know what path your father would take, or what might transpire?"

His face was flushed with emotion.

"Nor could you change him, Nico."

When darkness completely settled in, they waved so-long to Mother Pouwels and walked to the train station by the light of the moon and stars. The depth and breadth of The Milky Way was enough to silence them in the abundant majesty of the moment.

If they became slowly occupied as a country, they found it surprising, or perhaps unavoidable. There was a slow transition, small losses of privileges, an aching pain of hunger, as food could scarcely remain on the shelves of their local markets. Diny felt hungry and wondered how long their troubles would continue.

This slow burn, this minimal invasion, and unhurried dawdling of complete governmental occupation was the most surprising aspect. Although Germany had invaded in May 1940, the country desired to remain neutral, much like their involvement in The Great War. They wanted both sides freedom through their land to utilize natural resources, and roads and waterway access for importing goods, while still growing their commerce with exports to America and Asia. However, when Rotterdam was bombed, complete occupation seemed inevitable. Yet this invasion had barely disrupted their lives. Their army continued to grow, to draft men of age, from ages eighteen to 49, if they were able. Nico's number had not yet been drawn, as his original involvement in the battle of Afsluitdijk offered him a deferment from service for a while.

After a few months of every-other-weekend togetherness with Nico and cheering in field hockey season and bicycle rides, the season changed, with summer humidity easing into a crisp, brisk autumn. Cornelia outfitted her children in wool sweaters she had knit all summer, a rich crimson for Diny and dark green for Nelly. She scrounged for five matching buttons for Jan, producing a handsome charcoal gray sweater for him, with blue buttons and a rolling collar.

Nelly spoke of her studies and her part-time floral work on weekends. Diny rarely found Nelly so attentive to conversation, but while they could engage her mind and hands at once, they found a beneficial and blossoming friendship. Nelly took some additional nurturing, patience, and space, which Diny would remember for the future.

Mam grinned at them during the conversation and knitted Nico three pairs of strong, thick mittens, for whatever use he might need.

"Three pairs?" Diny asked. "Do you think three is excessive?"

Mam shook her head. "Nico is meticulous, my dear, but he tends to misplace gloves and mittens, so I believe he needs three pairs."

It seemed ridiculous, thought Diny, to prepare for winter while summer lingered.

When afternoon thunderstorms rolled east, they opened windows to freshen the air, yet she did not fear the impending wintertime. She anticipated knitting sweaters with Mam, bundling under warm blankets, and watching gentle snowfall again with Nico. Each night, before dusk, Diny remembered to carefully return the blackout paper to each window so no light would shine through.

When she tired of knitting or embroidering pillows, or wall décor, Diny sewed dresses utilizing bold, colorful fabrics, from bright orange material honoring the Netherlands, to hand-dyed swirling cream and brown patterns of Indie batik pieces, or floral cobalt blues from Amsterdam's street markets.

Diny coaxed Nelly to stand straight as her dress model, gathering fabric to hold with a straight pin which she would later hem or tighten or edge.

Nelly groaned, "Must I pose as a model for you?"

Diny straightened the collar, cinched the waistline, adjusted loops and pleats, and lowered the dress several lengths to below Nelly's knee. She looked up at her sister with a wink, "I always stand taller than you, Nelly, and am more than four years older." She flattened the back of the dress against Nelly's shoulders, examining the alignment of the textured cotton material: a subtle blue-gray with rows of tiny red flowers.

"Just mind the button holes, will you?" Nelly pulled away. "I will be surprised if you can align this complicated fabric with your reckless sewing skills."

Diny scoffed as she tightened the waist.

Nelly sighed and reached up to secure her dark hair into a bun.

Diny's face flushed with concentration and precise measure. "You might be fourteen, Nell, but I must teach you how to sew, knit, cook, and clean. Dad and Mam expect it, and your future husband will thank me. All these important tasks remain ahead."

Nelly laughed, and said they had plenty of time to learn sewing.

"Besides," Diny said, "who knows when the Germans might demand my sewing machine?"

"How ridiculous!" Nelly laughed. "Did you think this war will change our lives? We have everything we need. Father will return in February, and my schooling continues, so what could alter? The Netherlands will remain neutral!" She trembled and offered a weak smile.

"Oh, Nell, at the very least, hold still, please!" Diny's face remained tense, and she aligned pins she pulled from a tiny pin pillow for quick access.

Nelly's breathing slowed, and grinned, "Is this a dress to wear with your beloved boy Nico?"

Beloved boy? Diny cared deeply for Nico, and perhaps started to glow outwardly from her feelings for him. If only Nelly would hush and hold still! Diny finished pinning and waved her sister away to change, then began preparing the sewing machine and table while Nelly slipped on her own old worn and faded dress.

Moments later, Nelly carefully handed over the pinned dress for Diny to stitch. Nelly had kept all the pins perfectly in place, the blue-gray color and rose patterns straight, all prepared for sewing. Diny's eyes filled with tears as she considered her sister's moment of kindness.

Nelly leaned over her and whispered, "I can stay with you for a while, Diny, to watch you sew."

Diny looked up at her and replied, "Okay, I will show you." Diny pulled a chair beside her. "This is how we begin...," and she motioned for Nelly to sit down.

Autumn 1940 surrounded Diny with new schoolwork. After Diny finished the HBS (*Hogere Burger School*) in May, wartime cutbacks prevented her entry into a nursing program, so Mam found it necessary for Diny to attend domestic school. Diny desired to attend as well, especially because she would soon marry, and had no intentions of studying more academics, but preferred a practical approach. Her program was called *Huishoudschool*, or the School of Domestic Economy. The domestic school provided classes in sewing, cooking, washing, ironing, hygiene, and sensible hostess etiquette.

Her growing connection to Nico was nurtured through bi-monthly visits and extensive letters. On his visits to Hilversum, long walks ventured through golden canopies of lush trees. Red and orange leaves served as a welcoming carpet for their strolls, hiking beside amber essence and the smoky scents of the thicket woods. She found comfort reading books beside Nico, each in their own armchair, cozy serenity by the wooden stove emitting heat and flame.

As they grew in zeal and delight and as summer faded into autumn, the danger of the world surrounding them also escalated. Goodness seeped into a chill, a frightened mass emerging. A menacing uncertainty marched toward them, with no end in sight except the shores of the North Sea.

And suddenly, the season arrived of air raid sirens, taking shelter in the deepest recesses of their lowest level, bombs blaring, RAF airplanes flying low and thundering overhead, lives shattering. It happened so swiftly, and yet so slowly. They failed to recognize the changes along the way except the moment of conflict had finally arrived. Homes were opened to the enemy, possessions were searched and confiscated. Weapons were yielded and utilized for the German advantage, and they awaited the day when the war would arrive with greater force in their homes.

However, domestic school continued. After the fall 1940 term at school, Diny received her first "*rapport*" (report card) from the "*huishoudschool*" (School of Domestic Economy). Although it was war-time, many local establishments tried to operate as normally as possible, especially factories and large businesses. Marieke also attended domestic school, and Diny and her friends had a marvelous time, largely unaware of the conflict around them. Although they learned very few practical ideas, they enjoyed going through those classes. They were not always ideal students.

Diny cooked sauerkraut in a big pot. She coarsely cut cabbage, placed it into a pot with heaps of salt, then a round piece of wood over the top, followed by a heavy rock. She let it stand for a long time, allowing fermentation and souring. Endive and beans could be preserved like that with salt, then rinsed and cooked, and chilled in their cellar. They could have vegetables all winter. Yet Diny preferred to feel entertained with her friends.

Their washing teacher presented her material in a boring, lackluster manner. They found out the teacher wore long underwear, which she brought to their class. She required the students to wash her undergarments! The class decided to put starch in the underwear. When the undergarments dried, the long underwear was completely stiff and unmovable, so much that they could set the underwear up on the table, standing straight up. The washing teacher did not think it was funny, but the class surely did.

Diny and her fellow classmates snuck out the classroom window to escape to the bakery on the corner to buy some substitute *"taartjes."* Butter was now rationed and unavailable. They knew the taartjes flavoring was not as delicious as original tarts or pastries, but at least they had a treat. They always loved cooking class, and could eat whatever they cooked, which was helpful for hungry stomachs. They used substitute items for cooking, for washing (as no soap was available), baking, and other tasks.

Diny cooked *gehaktbal* on the stove: a luxury when meat was so carefully rationed! At home, she simmered the meatballs in butter and water until fried and cooked through. As the meatballs cooled, the butter solidified into a fat which preserved the meatballs for next time. They only ate a few, preferring to ration their meat for another meal, another week.

After dinner, Diny carefully brought the pan with leftover meatballs down into the cellar, but stumbled on the dark stairs, and dropped into the meatballs as she fell onto the cold floor. Diny shrieked, covered in meatballs, juice, and grease, laying in the cellar.

"On the floor?" Cora moaned, glaring at her daughter. Diny stood and nodded, staring at the scattered meatballs. Cora decided the meatballs should be cleaned, and they would still eat them. They had no extra food or money to waste.

From 27 November 1940 onward, journalism and all culture in the Netherlands had to be in line with what the occupier wanted or tolerated. Germans declared all social groups and clubs were controlled by the NSB, (*Nationaal-Socialistische Beweging*).

This decision shocked the religious society of the country because of their decades of pillarization, allowing every religious group the opportunity to meet and create groups and institutions surrounding their beliefs (Catholics, Protestants, and Dutch Reformed Church). Diny's church condemned National Socialism, and her minister preached on the dangers of the group, urging resistance.

Now the NSB remained as the only group, and all others slowly disbanded or were unable to publicly gather. Nico grieved, since his friend Henk Mulder persisted, active in the NSB. Jacob tried to persuade Henk not to join, but he did not listen.

Nico wrote to Diny to be watchful concerning her political activities, and warned her concerning Henk's decision to align with the NSB. Even a visit to the cinema for a new Hollywood film could include German propaganda.

Diny could not afford entertainment like the movies, and remained home to enjoy other diversions like games or playing music.

For Sinterklaas evening on the 5th of December 1940, Nico joined her family gathering. With Dad away in the Dutch East Indies, she longed for his strong, yet calming presence, and Nico's leadership provided the comfort they all desired, along with the male companionship Jan was seeking. Mam and their neighbor Adriaan prepared traditional Dutch food, like *kroketten* (croquettes), *gehaktbal* (meatball), *erwtensoep* (split pea soup), with Jan Hagel almond cookies.

In prior years, they exchanged witty presents with poems. Dutch people traditionally gave comical, witty presents, with an attached poem relating to the present. The poems involved humorous passive-aggressive Dutch directness. Cora asked for Nico's help with the poems, since he easily wrote them. The poems he crafted were humorous and clever. Diny knew exactly which notes Nico wrote, due to his small, clean handwriting. His skill and elegance as a poet were obvious, as well as his wit and lighthearted style.

Diny escorted Nico to the front porch as he departed that night, and her smile gleamed with fallen snow. Snow sprinkled lightly on her caramel hair, the kind of dry dusting which glittered in the sunshine and glowed at dusk. Snowflakes alighted on her round face, and as she smiled, her eyes sparkled with hope.

As Nico left for his mother's house, Diny considered all which awaited them in Indie, including those tropical fruits she longed for while away which she ate whenever she wanted. The rambutan fruit, with a red spiky outer shell, felt round and with soft needles to the touch, as though the quills were merely a warning for predators. Inside the rambutan, the center contained sweetness surrounding a pit, and she could gorge herself on the rambutan and on time with Nico. She longed for extended, uninhibited time in her life.

Nico's family gathered at Mother Pouwels' house.

"My children have not always witnessed the best example of behavior, I realize," she told them, "with our divorce and messy personal lives. However, I raised my family to know God and abide by his commandments, no exceptions." Her faith in the Lord had not wavered.

They feasted on delicious foods Nico's older Piet brought — fish, chicken, potatoes with gravy, an array of vegetables, and buttered roll, coffee, heavy cream, and sugar. Mother Pouwels' cupboards were brimming with rich, filling foods.

As the youngest of five, Nico learned enough to keep afloat and became a determined salesman, as he had to consider ways to charm or speak quickly and efficiently to reach his audience, whether a busy older sibling or an interested customer. To adequately eat enough each day required quick hands at Mother's dinner table. As an adult, Nico effectively sold his trade, and being the youngest served him well.

Nico arrived during a snowfall and dusted off his coat before placing it on a hook near the door. Mother hugged him warmly. He joined his siblings and their families for an evening surrounding food, gifts, singing, and togetherness. They drank steaming spiced drinks, and ate a goose dinner with all the trimmings. Décor tattered and faded with time, but Mother Pouwels insisted on festive times, even in war, as a defiance to Germany, Nico supposed.

He stepped outside for a moment and leaned against the railing of Mother's veranda and observed the happenings in the gardens behind her home. The air was crisp and peaceful, and the dark sky full of twinkling stars.

Hilversum, 1941

In March 1940, Dad began mailing letters and money for their daily living. In his writing, Pieter always pointed Diny to Jesus and urged her to put all her trust in Him. After a while, all connection stopped, and Mam did not receive money anymore. They hoped he would return to them forever in March 1941, but with the war looming on every front, sailing the seas was not possible. Travel throughout Europe was dangerous and uncertain, and he felt safer amid his peaceful paradise than thrust into the center of the war.

Besides, he reasoned, the war remained in Europe, and would not stretch into the Asian theater. If he remained in Batavia as Police Chief, he may receive an extra pension, past retirement pay. Yet the family no longer received those precious letters, which shared about Dad's living, and they felt completely severed from any knowledge of him, whether he was struggling or in danger, or healthy and in positive spirits.

The war arrived at Hilversum, destroying many roads and lines of communication, but mail was still delivered if possible. She received occasional letters from Nico, whose work schedule and location prohibited his visits now, and mail correspondence would have to suffice for their growing relationship.

In 1941 the German army set up their ground troops headquarters in Hilversum, which greatly concerned the Dekker family. The soldiers were sturdy, groomed, and stern-looking, with rumbling trucks and artillery, and legs marching in neat row formations. They stomped in polished boots down Hilversum's quiet streets, held weapons across their chest, their thick woolen clothing securely fastened, a dark presence disrupting Dutch routine with units formed and streets cleared. The soldiers wore symbols on their shoulders and black helmets, buttons, and metals shining to gleam. Officers maneuvered methodically, with a plan and determination.

Mam commented, "Because the Germans convene here, in an important location, this will draw out more evil and darkness. Meanwhile, the Allies will try to bomb our city to dispose of the German headquarters. Either way, we are surrounded, with no way out." She wished their village was a tiny hamlet in an obscure place in the rolling countryside, but Diny knew even their farmer family Cor and Sietske and their five children in Friesland were not immune to danger and would need their food and livestock for survival.

The Dutch monarchy had escaped to exile in London in secrecy but produced a radio program on BBC. Dutch citizens daily listened to Queen Wilhemina and her calm confidence. *Radio Oranje* proved a daily highlight and they listened to their Queen's soothing voice and optimistic commentary on the war. De Geer was thrown out as Prime Minister and The Queen commissioned Gerbrandy as the new Prime Minister, offering renewed hope. Still, Diny wondered about her father's situation.

Diny continued to attend domestic school. After one snowstorm, with powder lining their streets, she went sledding, even though Mam needed her home immediately after school. But Diny wanted to sled with her friends and lingered in the snow. She called, "One last time!" and lunged down the hill and slammed her head — hard — on the sidewalk and got quite a nasty concussion. Marieke helped her home and Mam called a doctor. Diny learned her lesson: listen to Mam. The next several weeks of bedrest provided Diny ample measures of time to consider her life and the direction she sought to take.

From the beginning, the German language lumbered heavily in Diny's ears, striking sharply and less gently than the throaty, guttural Dutch language. Dutch could be described as a series of "hguh-and-yuh" sounds, interpreted as clearing-one's-throat, or echoing raspy, melodious tones. Yet German words stridently galumphed. The sound of a German officer commanding a conversation ensured feelings of panic. She was fluent in Malay, Dutch, German and French.

But the thick German, with its sharp staccato "t" sounds and grating escalations of "ine," "ish," "oon," and "zzz" at every turn were jarring and clacking, clamoring like marching troops. She considered no matter the language or culture of the invading country, Diny would probably detest them. In February 1941, transports of Dutch Jews were taken away, and the country rebelled against the injustice, resulting in more than a dozen executions. Amsterdam had been noted as the "Jerusalem of the West" for the density of Jewish families living there, and the Dutch were meticulous with record keeping, so it was easy to find and round up all Jews in Amsterdam. Nearly 80,000 of the country's 140,000 Jews resided in Amsterdam, and the initial welcome the country extended to those of differing beliefs and lifestyles stretched back four hundred years. Yet after transports began, everything shifted, and the social equalities shattered into distinct lines.

Marieke came to Diny's house soon after the first Jewish transport, flustered and concerned for her family, as several uncles had been rounded up and taken away. Until that moment, Diny had not realized Marieke was Jewish, and had not heard Marieke mention her religious beliefs. She was shocked at her friend's claims, except for the slight resemblance with dark hair and dark eyes and a decidedly Jewish last name, Rosenthal. Marieke feared for her safety and hugged Diny tightly. Mam insisted Marieke stay for dinner and urged her to escape into their home — and hide there, if needed. However, Marieke shared about her family's plan to escape to friends living in Sweden.

Soon after, the electricity was cut from their home save two hours daily until it was completely disconnected. Curfews were set at eight o'clock each evening and such regulations became more stringent. They encountered a mixture of emotions day by day, and tried to make the best of it, going through the days in a routine. Eventually, any feeling or emotion of possible elation for rescue, or depression for the state of their lives was dismissed to concentrate on the daily task of living.

Their primary goal was survival, working through pain and fear amidst daily tasks. Now she could not determine her dad's safe return, her marriage to Nico, or a nursing career. If they lost Dad or Nico, her heartbreak would be immense. Surviving this time would require a great deal of prayer.

"Nothing is impossible with God, my dear children!" Cornelia reminded them. Her bright optimism would surely vivify each dreary day ahead.

Nico's letters continued, and he scheduled a brief time together each month, but was not always able to make those dates for various reasons. The summer offered a longer length of sunlight, and they lingered in conversation, unwilling to say *so-long* for the night. They might sit in a public park for a few hours to escape the confines of the house, then continue discussing and walking. Their wanderings turned into journeys in the outer parts of town, beyond Hilversum in the heath, with auburn meadows leading to the thicket woods, walks which illuminated their friendship and their growing affection for each other. Nico reached for her hand and warmly clasped it closely as he spoke. Diny's hand softened until her arm blazed, and her whole body glowed with his gentle touch. She stood facing him, open to his ideas.

"*Dien*, I must tell you how I feel and where I see God leading our relationship. I hope to be your husband one day, and will propose marriage when we are ready for the commitment. I wish that time would happen sooner, yet war may delay us. I trust we will remain pure for each other, our thoughts and experiences for each other alone, for marriage." Nico's eyes glistened, and he promised his fidelity and a courtship preparing them for a future together.

She agreed, a feeling of true love commanding her being. The thicket woods provided a lovely backdrop to such a bold and hopeful promise. Lengthening shadows invaded their golden moment, with curfew and the eight o'clock hour soon approaching. They found their way back through cobbled streets into her neighborhood. He delivered her to her townhome, and both felt tightening throats when embracing until his next available time for a visit. In the meanwhile, each considered a longing and unfulfilled promise, an attempt to stay focused and pure.

Chapter Twelve
The Netherlands, Autumn 1941

Their daily lives changed drastically, allowing for a few dwindling privileges, as all valuables, weapons, metals, rubber, and other precious items were rounded up and collected. Radios and bicycles were banned and confiscated (an absolute outrage for a Flying Dutchman, who loved to bicycle daily!), and food was rationed. They each received a paper card for a daily food allowance, and no more. They were required to stand in long, winding food lines each day to receive half of a loaf of bread, or long lines three times per week to receive watery cabbage soup.

Monday was washday, utilizing surrogate soap, Diny facing the arduous task washing everything by hand, with heavy towels and sheets scrubbed on a washing board, without luxuries of washing machines or dryers, making it difficult to get everything clean. Washing remained a tiresome job, but Diny's youth provided vigor and she accomplished it all with flair. She arranged wet clothes on their backyard drying line, even in the frigid winter. Twice a week she found wood for the central wood stove on the main level of their home, as that stove served as their only heat distributor. Without real shampoo or soap, they were rarely able to bathe. Any water they could heat for a soak was more for momentary relaxation.

In order to collect firewood for their stove, Diny walked to the woods with a saw. Yet she could not simply carry a saw down the street, as Germans confiscated all weapons and tools. She wrapped the saw in a blanket, placed it into a baby carriage, and casually pushed the pram down the street and into the woods as though taking her baby for a stroll. When she arrived in the peace of those woods, Diny glanced around to see if she had been followed. Then she removed the saw and began her work.

Diny became skilled enough that within thirty minutes she could cut down three thin young trees, and saw the trees into smaller pieces, while darting her dark eyes around, looking for danger, listening intently for an intruder who might approach. Cutting forest wood was outlawed by the *Wehrmacht* German army, and the penalty of the offense was deportation or death.

Deep into the woods, the air was a verdant green, yielding an abundance of vines and moss. The landscape seemed serene and still, if only for a small applause of tree leaves clapping in the wind, or boughs of juniper and spruce whirring as wind blew through pine needles. It was a spirited wind, and heavy branches creaked. Birds chirped, bees hummed, and the air refreshed. She wished they could sneak away to the comforts of the forest and hide from the harsh realities of war, yet they would find little respite from the cold in severe, bleak winters, without food or shelter.

After she finished sawing down small trees, Diny piled logs into the carriage, followed by the saw, and then covered everything with the blanket for the return walk home. Going home with a buggy of chopped wood was dangerous. If a German soldier saw her, he would confiscate everything and send her away — somewhere she did not know.

Three times a week they brought a pan to an outside kitchen and after showing a coupon and standing in line for hours, the Germans gave them "chicken soup," or other days "cabbage soup." Mam joked the chicken and cabbage sat *next* to the soup pot, instead of *in* it. A few times in line Diny fainted, out of hunger and exhaustion.

She read her Bible each day, especially the Psalms, writing thoughts on the backs of yellowing pages, sometimes through open spaces in Dad's letters, words she read so frequently she eventually memorized. She reasoned journaling emotions helped her survive each day, navigating challenges and disappointments. Some days, all Diny could do was copy a Psalm. During mornings of exhaustion, she could only utter a small whisper of a prayer, she knew God listened.

"Zorg goed voor je Moeder. Take good care of your mother." Her father had urged her, his face solemn and his pale blue eyes icy with distress.

"I promise!" she had assured her father with an embrace. *Take good care of your mother.* She remembered Dad's insistence and repeated her answer aloud into the darkness. A burning thickness grew in her throat, the pain of dread in her heart, a foreshadowing of what might happen while he was away. The Lord heartened her in those small efforts of study and prayer, offering relief in a singing bird, a shining ray of sun, or the growth of her geranium plant, which flourished. If she was unable to dream, Diny maintained hope for her geranium. The little geranium plant — a gift from her father — grew in a pot on the kitchen windowsill, receiving light and tender care, water and prayers and songs.

Diny believed, *"If the plant lives, then Dad will live. He will come home to us in Hilversum and will return safely from the war."* Before her were glimmers of light, surrounding shadows, and impending darkness, like the appearance of a candle flickering brightly upon a wall, illuminating certain objects while obscuring others, unknown. Some days held little energy to decipher the truth, so she pressed forward with routine, relying on the rhythms of survival.

A simple note from Nico sadly announced his absence at Diny's holiday celebration. His presence was needed by Mother Pouwels. Diny could not understand his reasoning but trusted her steady man. When the 5th of December 1941 arrived, the Dekkers simplified their Sinterklaas Day celebration, although Diny longed to put aside the sorrow of war, at least for an afternoon, seeking the *gezellig* family togetherness which seemed all but absent. She layered warm clothing and took Jan and Nelly sledding until they could not feel their hands or feet, their woolen mittens and fraying boots soaked with snow. Nelly and Jan rolled mounds of snow into a snowman. They felt truly alive and exhilarated, even for a few moments.

Diny longed for those previous Hilversum Sinterklaas Day celebrations in the past, and later of Christmastime – a fragrant tree decorated in their front room, apple cider simmering, other fragrant spices in holiday baking and cooking. The reality of the poverty of their current situation, and their general lack of food remained profound.

Later in the evening, after eating watery cabbage soup and dry bread, Jan found a piece of chocolate in his desk, and Nelly had gathered a sprig of balsam from the forest for their table, so they each shared a nibble of the forgotten chocolate, and the scent of trees lingering, and retired to bed.

Diny dreamed of prior Christmas celebrations, cozy togetherness, traditional supper of Dutch foods: fish, potatoes, vegetables, crusty breads, spice cakes, pies, and special chocolate confections. After her dream, Diny could not sleep, and paced their quiet living room. On the mantle sat photographs of her father, spanning his career in the police force, family events, and loved ones long departed.

One photo was dated 1914, where Pieter was one of a dozen police officers, straight-backed in clean-pressed dark uniform, hat, buttons on the collars and lapels, and degrees of seniority. Pieter's height placed him in the back row of the photograph, and each face around him remained solemn, hands at the ready with leather gloves, the central officer holding a sword. A twinkle of mischief remained in Pieter's eyes, his mustache growing thickly, the world around him at age twenty-one yet unsullied to disappointment. His entire world remained ahead of him, hopeful.

Diny glanced at another photograph of her parents' wedding, a studio sitting; with Pieter sitting upon a bench in full uniform with a sword, as though he entered the marriage prepared to defend his wife. Cornelia stood next to him, her left hand lightly upon his back, prepared to support her husband. Pieter dressed completely in black, save his one gloved right hand which held his left glove. His bare left hand bore a simple wedding band. Cornelia's attire was entirely white — even gloves and stockings.

Diny caught her breath upon seeing a photograph of her brother Huibert, a grainy picture his final captured image of his life on earth. They were on holiday in April 1927, vacationing north of Soekaboemi for a month at Selabintanah Resort. The day her father spanned a suspension bridge and Nelly napped at the cottage, Cornelia, Diny, and Huib took a pony ride along the road to Wanasari, a shaded, stony path. She closed her eyes and remembered the rocks, the shade, the fern rustling in the breeze.

Three boys in crisp white linen with proper hats, somber dark eyes, and dark skin led them on winding peaceful jungle paths. The photograph revealed what she had long forgotten: Huib sat stiffly upon the pony and cried during that journey, the only moment an animal seemed to offer him a fright. Huib rarely cried or provided any fuss. Cora chuckled in the photograph, her face smooth with youth and joy, the solitary smile amidst somber faces. Perhaps Cora saved the photograph to recall a time of joyful innocence or happiness, the moment in time when her 3 children were alive, healthy, and fully human.

Diny remained awake until midnight, when Sinterklaas Day was no more, and the day after would be just another mundane day. She wrestled sleep, unable to appropriately direct her pain, the loss she felt in Dad's absence, and fear which loomed ahead of them.

Every day, their neighbor Adriaan visited with the latest war news, playing a brief update from the BBC for payment of one ration card per week. Diny supposed he fed his children with the extra ration card, as the provisions were meager and empty of calories. Some days they listened for a full 30 minutes before fearing interruption, and other days, BBC only crackled static, as though a line or wire went down, suspending news. Adriaan faced deportation for his bravery at keeping an illegal radio but did not seem worried. Just a few days after Sinterklaas Day, they heard the horror surrounding the Japanese attack on Pearl Harbor, with fires and tremendous loss of life. The next day, on 8 December 1941, the Dekkers realized their beloved Indies may also be at war.

Hilversum, January 1942

The line looped around the block, down the next street, and past three sets of German officers. One pair spoke, laughing, and consumed food in front of the awaiting Dutch; officers filled plates with German food, while starving civilians stood in three-hour lines. The Dutch were handed a dry half-loaf of bread, or watery stew the Germans called "soup," with no meat. Diny shifting her weight from one flat shoe to the other. Waiting on hard surfaces like cobblestoned streets, consumed more calories than they received in the meager food distribution.

If they rested during the food round up, pacing German soldiers wandered by, rousing them to stand. In summer's heat or winter's chill, a lone violinist played mournful tunes echoing the square, melodies of times forgotten, a sense of civility in war. Most songs were requested by German officers. The man could not always carry a clear tune, and his strings often strained, as his bow warped, and the violin's wooden sheen had faded. Diny surmised he was at least her father's age. After playing several songs, his arms shook, the tune warbled, and a German soldier delivered him bread and soup. Playing German tunes was his meal ticket. He nodded respectfully, looking down while receiving his food, staring at the combat boots of the soldier.

During the winter, the violinist lost half the bow hairs. The broken hairs flailed around, attached at one end, whirling underneath his chin as he played, like a beard caught in a spider's web. Over the weeks, the air grew coarse and grating. At food distribution day, the violin screeched miserably until a German officer paced toward him, drawing his pistol.

Diny shuttered, certain the man would be shot. He stopped playing, and looked directly into the officer's eyes. The officer seemed interested and placed his pistol back in its holster. He grabbed the violin bow, snapped it in half, and handed it back to the man. "Now see if you can play!"

The eyes of the Dutch were on the German, with expressions of rage, and on the violinist, with expressions of compassion. Using only half a bow, and with only a handful of horse hairs remaining, the old man mustered a pitiful, mournful Bavarian tune.

The officer stopped laughing and with a surprised expression on his face, smacked the man, the severe noise resounding in the silent square. He snatched the old man's bow, and shouted a foul German rant, then marched away.

The violinist looked bewildered for a few minutes, and peered in the direction of the German officer, awaiting his meal, his payment. Diny's line surged forward, away from the lone musician. As she rounded the corner away from him, she saw him shuffling away, near the northern thicket woods. His head was low. On her walk home from food distribution, she spotted a faded and frayed violin, cast aside.

Diny read Nico's latest enclosure of poems, and his miniature, precise handwriting seemed stoic. Some of his work had developed a darker turn with loss, pain, and devastation. She could not envision a life together while bombs fell, and to suppose optimism for the promise of peace in some distant *someday* seemed a hope too grandiose to verbalize. She dreaded speaking a dream which required a miracle to produce. Most days, emotions ushered exhaustion, with little food, warmth, or security, so routines were of more value, lasting and predictable.

She wavered in faith at times, but could trust a loving God, readily available to offer encouragement and peace. No matter what thorny road they navigated, she would rest under the shadow of his wings. She found Nico's poetic words expectant, under the surface, a slow burning flame, like a solitary candle, aware of his purpose, warm ambers illuminating darkness, casting light on the path before him, even as he stood alone.

Chapter Thirteen
Driel, The Netherlands, March 1942

Under a night sky lit only by a full moon, Nico sprinted North through barren fields with a package and sled stuffed under his arms. He was on the Eastern Front of the war. Frosted air burned his throat as the Rhine River churned nearby. Standard, unwavering instructions coursed through his mind and across his stiffening lips. He memorized the names, passwords, ideas eddying in his mind. Nico arrived at the appointed street and passed Driel's tiny darkened grocery market. His eyes darted hastily around, up, into the inky sky, for eyes, soldiers, stickers, window markings, candles, or other signals. Silence permeated the air in the tranquil village.

He pulled his wool hat lower over his ears, then checked his vaporous breath for names and signals, and recognized the tree with the blue ribbon beside the empty jewelry store. He quickly scurried over, huddled behind the tree, and covered his snowy tracks. Nico mumbled his cover under his breath as *Luchtbeschermingsdienst* (LBD, Air-Raid Defense). Nico's orange mittens failed to block the painful, deep chill and he kept his fingers moving. Cornelia knitted Nico three pairs of mittens and this final pair remained, now unraveling.

Yet who held time for mending? Their country could not mend relationships, resources, emotions, or people. For an icy spring, they hoped for rescue in the form of Allied soldiers. Or perhaps blizzards, Nico imagined, of a great southern wind from the Alps sweeping west to dissolve German troops into avalanches, the bowling ball of armies rolling, blowing into the North Sea, dusty flurries of powder left behind in a fantastic splash.

His numb mind beckoned sleep yet startled to reality hearing a squeaky-toy-sounding bird in the midnight sky. It was the Black-tailed godwit. His contact Joost arrived and huddled beside him; they exchanged passwords and opened their coats to trade brown paper packets. Their wrinkled envelopes matched with wax-stamped symbols, and Nico detected Joost's coat outfitted with numerous inner pockets, filled with other similar packets. Nico could only guess at the contents: *ration cards, fake identifications, or money?* They smiled briefly, and turned to leave in opposite directions, but Nico grabbed Joost's arm and pulled him down into the snow.

Joost doubled back, instinctively punching Nico squarely in his right cheek, pushing him backwards into the bushes with a great whirr. Joost grabbed Nico's arms to pull him back for another punch, but instead pointed a small pistol in Nico's face.

"What was that for? The punch, the holdup?" Nico whispered.

"Why are you grabbing me, pal?" Joost interjected.

"Trying to save your life, buddy." Nico scooped a handful of snow onto his aching jaw.

"Really? Impressive. I thought you would shoot me."

Nico shook his head. "Me? You hold the only gun, here, sport!"

Joost's bewildered face stared at the gun in his hand and he slipped it into his jacket pocket. "Okay. The pistol is packed away, so start over. How are you going to save me? From what?" Joost leaned close to Nico.

"Listen," Nico whispered to his comrade. "You see those lights moving in the distance?" He pointed north. After a minute of observation, Joost insisted they were stars or low-flying planets, and not approaching torches. "Remain here in the village for the night. I shudder at what dangers we may find out there."

Joost shook his head and motioned to leave. Nico's brow furrowed.

Joost replied, "No. We cannot linger. I may have been followed. Stick to your protocol." Joost's black hair feathered under a new layer of snow. In the northern distance, Nico detected faint flickers of yellow light, gathering together, growing brighter. Nico again urged Joost with a renewed sense of insistence.

Nico pointed. "Those golden flames are torches: flashlights or sticks ablaze. See how the lights flicker and dance? I have some instinctive thoughts, so you need to heed my warning."

Joost rebuffed, "No. I must move forward."

"Stay the night at my apartment. I live only six kilometers away." Nico pointed south.

Joost promised other homes awaited him. The enemy embarked upon risky liberties, and winter proved an ill excuse to postpone, but a cover of darkness proved useful.

"I must push north," Joost replied, "two kilometers to the next safe house near Doorwerth Castle, instead of lingering in the wolf's lair near Anhem's bridge." His eyes widened at his admission of the next moves of The Resistance. "Forget I mentioned this, please. For both our sakes."

Nico glared at him. "Then you can forget I live six kilometers from here."

Joost agreed.

Indeed, Arnhem remained close to the heavily-patrolled German stronghold. Another safe house seemed too far away, a resistance headquarters inside a greenhouse. If he found misfortune, Joost could try to hide from troops in De Hoge Veluwe National Park 10 kilometers north, but essentially Arnhem — and the Rhine River — came first. Nico pulled off his wool hat and offered it to Joost, who gladly accepted, along with the newest issue of *Het Parool*, a Dutch Resistance newspaper.

"Keep the newspaper only as long as necessary," Nico warned, "and then burn it."

Joost nodded.

As they parted ways, Nico traveled 6 kilometers south. He arrived at his apartment in Elst peacefully, and prayed Joost found no trouble navigating the Rhine crossing and two kilometers beyond. Those gathering yellow lights haunted his sleep that night as he wondered of their destination.

In times of peace, a man reading a newspaper would be commonplace, sitting on a patio, sipping coffee. In times of war, simple pleasures were not viewed as ordinary. Every action represented something deeper, hidden, or secret. Elements of trustworthiness were eliminated, as all could be suspicious.

Dutch resistance groups resourcefully outfitted dolls with hidden arm slots to hide valuables like jewelry, and then sewed up into the doll. Even pregnant, hobbling ladies may be suspected, transporting bulging packages of false identification cards, forged ration cards, or money. Spies served as double agents, as intelligence could be passed from one person to another, even ordinary citizens.

Dutchmen no longer found bicycles with rubber tires, but fashioned wooden tires, which whisked them away to obscurity. Hidden passages under stairs, wooden planks in floors, holes cut into walls behind well-positioned photographs on the wall; all could surpass appearances. A painting might indeed be just a mural or sketch, no more, or it could hide a safe in the wall.

Resistance groups sabotaged railways, distributed publications, created maps, and infiltrated factories.

Perhaps to conquer the enemy one must think how an ordinary person would proceed if living in a method of sheer survival. But with ready meals, warmer clothing, clean socks, and consistent shelter, how could a German soldier navigate the adrenaline of the hunted? When numb feet traveled, pedaled through darkness or fog, or groups journeyed to shelter, Nico prayed that God would still craft a dazzling future only He could see.

Hilversum, The Netherlands, April 1942

The mellow light of spring faded as dusk settled into the air, the glittering light fading. Their eight o'clock curfew remained several hours away, yet darkness arrived early in the northern Dutch atmosphere, a blanket of silence encroaching their lives, muffling crisp, icy air.

"Hello, Nico! Hallo, hallo!" Nico's friend Henk Mulder jogged over to him in an unlikely meeting, an exchange of glances on the Hilversum street outside a popular cafe near Diny's house. Henk seemed startled to see his friend alone in the West on a Sunday afternoon, and his face revealed the shock. He had just exited the cafe and smirked. Perhaps he had conducted important business inside.

Nico felt equally astonished to be seen upon an erroneous street at the improper time, enroute to Diny's house, and mentally reminded himself to avoid that cafe in the future.

Hilversum served as a growing bastion of German ground forces, *Wehrmacht*, who established themselves in the *Raadhuis*, or Town Hall. Nico was surprised by Henk's attire of a luxurious khaki-colored wool jacket, a shiny top hat, finely appointed glasses, and sturdy, solid constitution.

"Are you in good health, Nico?" Henk probed. "You look like a ghost!"

Nico paled as uniformed Germans exited the café. "I am well, my friend. I have not seen you since our work out East, in Driel."

"Ah, yes! Such a place like that, who knows what happens there now! But you are still selling jam, even during the war? What brings you to a little inconsequential village like Hilversum?" Henk appeared intrigued, his face alighting, eyebrows raised. Surely he knew Nico's Mother lived in Hilversum.

"Pardon? Why are you so robust as of late? Do you receive an extra ration card?" Nico stared at Henk's well-appointed build, and his own lanky frame felt more thin than ever. "Is this how you can afford to lavish your family with extravagant foods?"

Henk laughed, "Well now, join us, Nico, and starve no longer! Join the NSB, and our noble cause!"

Noble cause? The only noble cause is saving those who cannot speak for themselves and sparing those trapped in Hitler's snare. How can Henk so blatantly turn his face away from his family and support the Nazi-ruled NSB? And he could send me away, if he wanted...

Nico saddened for his friend. He shook his head, looking into Henk's narrowed eyes. "*All* clubs and social groups have been banned, remember? Is the NSB included?"

"All social groups but *one*. The Superior one remains." Henk lowered his head to light a cigarette, his fancy hat shielding his face from the wind.

Nico shuffled along the sidewalk while he paced, hands shoved into his pockets. He disagreed with Henk on issues in the past but always maintained civility about moral and spiritual differences, praying Henk would turn to God. Time faded hopes of true reconciliation, and their interactions were few and stilted. They used to work together, and travel together around Arnhem and Nijmegen, selling jam, but the war time challenged alliances.

Henk exhaled sharply, his cigarette smoke invading the space around them. Nico glanced around the street at shops, his gaze ascending to the rows of gabled homes above. In the approaching darkness, he saw nothing. Streetlights were no longer lit, so their encounter would soon become dark. The weariness of the war delivered Hilversum to an early bedtime, or perhaps those above listened in the shadows. He knew Hitler's henchmen arrived in varied forms.

After Henk quietly smoked, his voice stilted the silence as he asked, "What brings you here tonight, Nico?" A simple enough question, innocent and straightforward. Henk cocked his head, pinching his fingers around his smoldering cigarette, his eyebrows raising as though to demand an answer. Nico turned away, sheltered his mouth, and lit his own cigarette.

"You know those pretty little matches are in demand, Nico, to light real fires," Henk reminded him, as though the Germans found additional items to confiscate, as if there were anything of value remaining.

"These are false luxuries in war, I know." Nico's blue eyes danced, prepared to play the game. He was an expert at games, he reasoned, and how could this one prove different? Father Pouwels taught him well in all competitions.

"Now stop stalling, *Niek*. Where are you going?"

Nico inhaled, and his breath shuddered, as his face cloaked in shadow under a canopy. Then he exhaled, sinuous smoke surrounding them, shrouding both faces. "Tomorrow I will take the first train East to my job, selling jam. You know the job we both worked for years?" He hoped they would move to another topic.

Henk leaned forward and said, "I have been hearing rumors, Nico, about you and a friend of yours named… Gerrit, I believe… and your *subversive activities*."

Diny's uncle Gerrit Dekker participated in Underground resistance efforts, but what had Henk heard? Gerrit had children to protect. "Is selling jam a crime? I have nothing to say, nor anything to hide," Nico reiterated. "I serve God and my country."

"A door-to-door jam salesman, Nico?"

"Yes, a real job."

Henk turned to leave.

"So long, Pouwels."

"I am praying for you, Henk. Be safe."

Henk laughed. "Will your God save you when the Germans come knocking on your door one night?" His words echoed in the misty air as they departed.

Nico extinguished his cigarette and glanced around for German soldiers on the desolate street before sprinting. He dashed to the train station without looking behind him.

"God will vindicate Henk's life," Diny always told Nico.

Nico felt alarmingly nervous about their encounter but could not take the risk of being followed to Diny's. Henk had never visited Diny's home and Nico refused to jeopardize Diny's safety or wellbeing. As he reflected during his walk to Mother Pouwels' house, Nico wondered if Henk suspected any Resistance or Underground work. Nico prayed for Henk, for his salvation, a change of heart and lifestyle.

Chapter Fourteen
The Netherlands, April 1942

Afternoons in springtime were glorious, and the sun's warming rays illuminated their paths and brought warmth just in time for afternoon adventures. Small green stems pushed up through the snow, traversing desolate landscapes rattled by winter. Diny encouraged her family to venture outdoors to eliminate the stale, musty stench of indoors, explore the natural world, and recover the vigor daylight afforded before receding into darkness. They walked neighborhoods through dappled sunshine, with blue skies before rain encroached their idealism. If they ventured through the woods, their misery momentarily vanished, with clear air persuading them to linger longer.

On Sundays they attended a church service, and church hymns comforted them. At times sirens blared and airstrikes interrupted the service, so their small group raced to shelter in the cellar. Their small band of friends sang hymns like, "Oh God Our Help in Ages Past," and an ironic "Onward Christian Soldiers" along with steady standards, "Great is Thy Faithfulness," and "How Great Thou Art."

Diny found encouragement in bearing the encumbrances of life with others, remembering those prayers would be offered to God each day, with mutual sharing of the affliction of another through petitions to the Lord. Their burdens would become lighter and feel freer as they reached to others — and to God — with their needs and fears. Faith as small as a mustard seed could grow them up in him.

Diny dearly missed her strong and steady father, especially during their church visits. She frequently noticed a man who looked just like her father from behind: his tall disposition, dark hair, and sturdy build. Every Sunday, she caught herself staring at the man, as she felt unnerved by her Dad's likeness, when he was thousands of miles away, alone. One Sunday, Diny approached the man after service, and introduced herself. Over the next several months they got to know each other, and she bravely shared his resemblance to her father. He gave her and Cora a hug and said he would continue to pray for Pieter Dekker's safe return to them.

Later, they visited Oma van den Bout. Dear Oma seemed older now, in her seventies, the war tattering her spirit. She seemed frail, her gray hair thinning, and her energy often waning before the end of an afternoon. Yet Oma insisted they bake and spend long stretches of time with her, her optimism insulating them from the pain of the world (and lack of real sugar for baking). They enjoyed hearing stories from her younger days, with garden walks before nighttime curfew.

Hilversum, May 1942

Colorful tulips and green stems pressed up through landscapes like a brightly colored accolade. Petals wrinkled to resist the chill, and as sunshine warmed the land, the triangles of snow upon each tulip melted into the flower and into the sheath of waxy leaves. By mid-afternoon, the flowers — nourished and supple — relaxed and displayed full color, persuaded by the conviviality of daylight, as arms open to the offerings of the sky.

Their daily life felt as tenacious and tentative as Peter the Disciple walking on water, improbable and requiring immense faith. Diny knew if the apostle Peter walked faithfully in a storm, their father Pieter, another rock of faith, would weather his own tempests. Peter witnessed Jesus Christ's miracles, could embrace the glorious loveliness of His presence, and stretched his arms to a tangible, physical Savior. How much more faith was required for those who cannot see, and still believe? None have seen the transformative wind, but the results of the wind remain apparent in nature in adapting sceneries. The wind shapes landscapes, shuffles soils, uproots trees, and together with water carves river walls, creating caves, caverns and gorges.

"A life walking with God is a grand adventure," Mam reminded her children. "Be ready to go where He leads, because you never know where the next step will take you." And when they were loyal to trust God in a small manner, He offered renewed opportunities to demonstrate another step of belief. Diny knew trusting God and placing everything in his loving care, never guaranteed or promised safety or security. He was a faithful shelter from those winds.

By now, the Dekker family's faith stretched and defined them. Daily living became a slow, steady hunt for necessary items like food. When winter arrived, they had no heat, so several times a week Diny ventured into the woods to cut small trees to feed the stove. The Germans always declared the tasks as forbidden practices. If they caught her baby buggy with chopped wood hiding under a blanket, everything would be taken away, and they could be shot or deported to a camp. They knew nothing of such camps, only that those sent to them never returned.

Diny's blistered palms softened, infected, and healed, then scars turned into thick calluses. Her arms strengthened into defined muscles, more certain and fortified, even without proper nourishment. Her ability and capability to cut wood developed through practice and adrenaline. Hiding chopped wood in a baby buggy felt precarious, as how many routes could she take to and from the forest? And how many soldiers believed she walked a sleeping baby in a pram each week, chancing on the same journey through a wooded forest or wilderness? Stranger things, indeed, had been observed. She prayed the Lord blinded others to her actions, turning Germans' heads away from them, away from danger, which included listening to news reports on Adriaan's forbidden radio.

Later, after she returned from sawing wood in the forest, Jan delivered the buggy into the house before unloading the wood in the sitting room. They were surrounded by neighbors, and one could always hope, but not assume, those neighbors stayed on the Dutch side of the war. Most Dutch citizens carried a proud badge of tolerance for their diverse neighbors, but in war, one could not establish certainty of influences or deceptions.

Dutch Jews were forced to wear a yellow Star of David on their clothing, signifying their identity as *Jood*. Jews refusing the star were placed on trucks which never returned, supposedly transported to Germany for labor. One morning, Marieke did not arrive at domestic school, and Diny worried for her wellbeing, so she walked to Marieke's house and found it inhabited by a tall blond family. She checked the address and stood at the door, stunned, then inquired about Marieke Rosenthal.

The fair-skinned children alluded to a scuffle and truck which picked up the Rosenthals, but the adults remained quiet and stoic. The Germans assigned the tall blond family to this townhome, they said, because their previous apartment sat at an opportune intersection, where Germans established a base, evicting all the families nearby. Marieke's family belongings were piled on the front curb. Diny managed her disappointment and shuffled home, praying for Marike's safety. *Perhaps Marieke's family escaped to Sweden after all*, Diny considered. At night, Diny wept for her lovely lost friend.

Their radio was tuned to BBC during that time, and they once heard an announcement concerning Hilversum, publicized as the headquarters of the German ground forces, the *Wehrmacht*. The "defending, commanding, powerful force or might," as they titled their group, became a permanent presence in Hilversum. The Germans concealed the tall tower on their *Raadhuis*, or Town Hall, with more than 2,000 troops serving their Commander in Chief, occupying the whole Dutch village, overrunning the square and suppressing any sense of quaintness and security, along with any impression of freedom formerly felt in their lives. They stood ready for battle, poised in an opportune location. Dutch neutrality in The Great War now felt like a cloaked anecdote.

The idea of remaining neutral always bothered Diny. *Why not take a stand — and oppose all injustice?* Their country, long famed for tolerance, was now toppled and broken. It labored under the rule of Germans who not only moved into their quaint, cheerful village, but asserted themselves to occupy the Dutch in every way. None could escape the controlling power — but most citizens expected the country to remain neutral, as Switzerland claimed impartiality, assuming a detached objectivity.

Eventually, Mam hid their radio in the bread box, then wrapped the box in a small tablecloth, and lowered the entire piece into an empty hole under her bed, covering the hole with a loose floorboard. A year prior, German soldiers collected items of significance, including scrap metal, rubber, and all bicycles and radios, and continued to raid homes to secure hidden valuables. The radios were horrific to confiscate, with the Dutch tolerant but always aware, deeply interested in politics and world happenings. But the confiscation of their beloved bicycles became the greatest tragedy, the largest loss of independence and freedom.

Diny always carried a special love for her little brother, Jan. They understood each other, but over the war years, Jan became involved with corrupt friends and needed a father's guiding hand. Dad's absence placed a deeply wounding stamp on him. Months passed without letters or any word from Dad, with no way to mend the bond. Moreover, Nelly was often enmeshed in study even after neighborhood schools closed. Diny faithfully cleaned the house, cooked, mended, cared for Mam, and so forth. As the eldest, those were

Diny's heavy responsibilities. Subsequently, dreams were deferred: domestic school interrupted, nursing school lay vacant. Nelly and Diny's differences multiplied during the war, with varied temperaments under pressure, and despite their rare moments of connectivity, Diny developed resentment in her heart.

Diny prayed for those shipwrecked and destitute in their spiritual life, for those physically fed but emotionally starved. While interceding for Dad and Nico, she prayed for bravery and a sound mind for the strong men in her life daily battling the wars of their hearts and spirit.

The prayers lifted for Mam initiated the energy Diny required to manage Mam's needs. Prayers for Nelly allowed for renewed patience amidst Nelly's challenging emotional needs, while prayers for Jan's safety and protection from enlistment and poor social influences allowed her the opportunity to attempt a positive, loving example for him. Her outlook altered through kneeling in worship in her small room, her heart warmed by the generous grace of God.

Hilversum, Summer 1942

The Dekker family's fundamental supplies dwindled to where they could not find basic ingredients like flour, sugar, butter, or milk, as farmers utilized supplies for their own families or were forced to hand over their vegetable crop or eggs and milk to the Germans. Some farmers sold their harvest for outrageous asking prices: usually a family's antiques or heirlooms. But what good were old heirlooms like grandmother's brushed candlestick holders or a set of pure silver spoons if one hovered near starvation?

Baking and cooking seem like miserable impossibilities, Diny decided, inspecting her empty cupboard. Their neighbors suggested grinding tulip bulbs into a flour substitute, the BBC reported about this unconventional practice, which involved the drying, baking, and grinding of tulip bulbs, then pulverizing them into fine flour, although Diny hesitated to undertake a risky venture.

Centuries after the tulip bulb craze of the Golden Age, it seemed another immediate need was upon them. Those feverish days of rare tulip bulbs fetching the same money as prized homes once seemed ludicrous, but Diny soon realized desperate days required inventive courage. As she inspected her mother's frail posture and emaciated body, coupled with Jan's growing appetite and distant gaze, she needed to provide real nourishment for her loved ones, as the dry half-loaf of bread and watery broth rations would never sustain them.

Diny decided they would eat baked tulip bulbs, which she began gathering from paper bags in their garden shed and roasted over the wooden stove in the front room. After pear-shaped tulip bulbs cooked and cooled, she grated them into flour, crunching the crisp bulb within the grinding of stone to a fine flaky texture. They were pulverized and ready. She attempted to convince herself of their genuine flour-like flavor. If forbidden to enjoy the luxury of cheese, at least they could attempt baking. They used the tulip flour for all their needs, with sugar beets, producing sugar beet pulp, syrup, and so on, for the sweetness of cooking and baking.

When she ran out of flour, Diny scrounged through Dad's shed again, finding a few stray bulbs wedged between patio furniture or in hidden corners. Jan helped her procure tulip bulbs from the earth after they had bloomed in April. Some bulbs molded over, rotten, or appeared small, but she baked them anyway, hoping to utilize every scrap. No electricity powered their lives, because their country continued to fight for survival, and bombed villages meant their power lines fell, broken.

Even the sky and atmosphere seemed like a gray blanket of despair, the air smoky, containing a heavy, ominous haze from humidity, airplanes, and bombs, a smoldering glow of fires burning somewhere nearby, or the ash from far away. A smell of death juxtaposed glorious summer weather. The disposition of the people grew weary, fatigued, and disenchanted with the possibility of rescue. "Where does our help come from? How long will we remain in a war? Where is our rescue?" the Dutch begged the sky, without a verbal response.

Families read by lanterns or candles, huddling around a light source, seeking illumination, until candles burned down to wicks and lantern oil dried into the metal casing. Finding new candles was a scarce and futile search, as Germans confiscated any possessions of value. Smoky dark wisps signaled the end of a candle conveyed a solemn exodus, a gloomy ending. Mam saved every candle, scraped small bits of wax into a jar, collected it slowly, and bartered for a new wick, then melted the wax to create a new candle. This could go on for a while, she reasoned, and at least they reserved one candle to rely on for light, even one wick each time.

They surrendered to exhaustion in bed by eight o'clock every night because of mandatory curfew. There was no natural gas for the stove or electricity, and few candles; what amusement is obtained by stumbling around in darkness? According to the German commandos, who emphasized curfew every evening at 8:00 p.m., nobody would be allowed outside or they faced the possibility of being shot.

Also, for fear of being shot or bombed, the citizens must cover their windows at night. Not one small spot of light could illuminate or shine through their doors or windows; they meticulously covered each window with black paper, which also meant they were unable to stare at the moon or stars at night, nor allow a refreshing evening breeze to cool their house.

The nighttime black-outs enhanced the seclusion they felt. Germans argued they did not want Allies discovering where the cities were, and bomb them, so their emphasis on prevention would halt the advance of Allied power. The Dutch agreed with that in theory, not desiring their quaint villages and cobblestone squares to endure any more death or destruction or hardship.

If Allies bombed their city, nothing would be left standing at the end of the war: their homes, businesses, and lives. Yet the idea of the finale of their war felt as a speck of hope, a thought, and a fleeting prayer on some lonely days, the only consolation for the desolation they experienced in their circumstances. Especially as the headquarters for German ground troop forces, the survival of Hilversum was deemed necessary. They lived among the enemy in what was essentially a German stronghold.

Bikes, blankets and radios, long-ago turned over to the Germans as prized possessions, rarely appeared in town. While they could forage for wood to keep warm and share home-made radios or smuggled newspapers, the loss of their beloved bicycles seemed the greatest offense against the typical Dutchman, who sincerely loved the feeling of flying, of transporting along through the streets on wind, the exercise strengthening the body and freeing inhibitions. And in her heart, mind, and subconscious, Diny leveled with the reality in which they always sensed incredible, debilitating fear.

Throughout their day, no matter how cheery they remained or how buoyant in their attitude, fear of hearing a knock at the door and knowing their family could be led away to some unknown fate permeated each glimmer of hope. The dreadful tragedy of a war demonstrates that those within war lack perspective or outlook; they face an unknown, perpetual pain and fear. With a furrowed brow and tear-stained pillow — year after year — when would it end? Grief could make them despondent.

Diny felt weak, weary and exhausted. She bathed once a week during their two hours of daily electricity, and then, electricity depleted, even those two precious hours diminished. After 1941 all electricity was cut, so she compromised and bathed during daylight hours if she could boil enough hot water on the stove to make it worthwhile.

Morning sunlight illuminated the bathroom through the window. She peeled away blackout paper, to allow sunlight, a welcome relief. Through shadows, she stared at her slight frame in the mirror, surprised at her gaunt cheekbones and skinny appearance. She considered her dark eyes, decipherable as a recognizable stranger, one who seemed familiar but wandered away from her true self. She reminded herself of God's love, even on days when she could not feel his presence.

Diny dried off, dressed, and combed her hair, feeling refreshed from a bath, even if she had just soaked in warm water, with a little substitute soap. She climbed into bed with Mam, and stroked her graying hair, humming gently, and softly singing Indie songs, reminding her of the language which permeated their spirits with gladness, with a removed sense of peace.

Their *Baboe* had hummed and sang all day, songs which etched themselves into Diny's mind and memory. She hoped to bring relief to Mam's illness, to usher in the cool air through open windows, which at night were forced shut and papered over, darkened, enclosed away from the world. Mam's migraines persisted, and she spent a great deal of time in bed during severe episodes, the scent of Tosca 4711 wafting in the air, of jasmine, bergamot, and orange blossom. Some nights she remained next to Mam, listening to the comforting sounds of breathing.

Early the next morning after long nightmares — air raid sirens resounding, piercing silence and offering little sleep — the family might be interrupted by the enemy, who always appeared robust and rested, despite the trauma of the previous evening. It was as though the enemy realized Dutch families remained perpetually weary after air raids. German soldiers charged into the house without knocking or notification, speaking sharp, biting German words, stomping in combat boots, arms swinging wildly with self-assurance. Their crisp long coats trailed like parachutes in their wake, and their confident laughter echoed without invitation for rebuttal from the Dutch who were at their mercy.

A dark gray cloud settled in the sitting room as the German soldiers conducted an inspection raid. They appeared to inspect the home and searched for illegal items, like bicycles or radios, hidden Jews in the house, or boys 15 years and older, those of age to enter the *Arbeitseinsatz* and serve Germany as a laborer in fighting. They checked inner cupboards and if the family had secret spots, they were placed on a list and watched, and the raids on their home increased.

Sometimes an officer found an item of discretionary value and secured it for his own, stealing a fine possession. Thievery, in plain view of the family, proved especially difficult, considering their need to trade jewelry and other valuable items for food. But to speak out against thievery would result in being shot or deported, so Mam hid everything away. Life became practical repetition.

The calendar approached December. With new rules enforced for a year, Dutch people grumbled, amidst yawning children starving for food and longing for restful sleep. There were whispers and words tangled around corners and down long boulevards as citizens waited to receive half a loaf of dry bread or watery cabbage soup. Rumors were carried on breezes, in the beaks of birds fluttering around, masking as friends while serving the enemy. Still, Dutchmen churned, infuriated, because their freedom had been taken away.

In addition, they had to be mindful of public conversations, vigilant to remain neutral, as the wrong ears might overhear it and for a reward turn information over to a German Commandant. There might be dire consequences for one comment. Unwilling to offer leniency for freedom of any kind, including the freedom to speak openly, German soldiers demanded complete compliance, while holding weapons and exerting extreme force.

Deep hatred spilled over from the Dekker family's hearts, and their anger grew, festering like an infected wound, the disease of bitterness growing and spreading throughout the body. Hands and feet were reprogrammed to survive, to act in the best interests of one's family, to seek a distant retribution. A deep sadness permeated and remained concerning all the vicious and wanton things occurring around them, allowing for no explanation, rationale, or relief.

Diny read aloud from Psalm 139: "Where can I go from your presence? How can I flee from your spirit?" Diny sensed God's presence, soothing her feet as she stood in line for bread. She encountered His warmth as she waited for hours for watery soup to take home for her hungry family. She responded to his leading when warned of the dismal state of a street. Sometimes in a quick inhale, a sharp breath, a hesitation in her spirit which she interpreted as His guidance. Venturing down another street instead, she could only guess at what rebellion she escaped or avoided, to arrive home without misfortune.

On warm days, where the sun persuaded the clouds into a momentary retreat, she peeled back the blackout paper, basked in the gold of the warm rays, and felt — for the hour — fears escape her mind. Diny also lost her troubles as she read a novel, captivated by the dazzling imagery and sumptuous experiences of the heroine, someone in a distant land, slaying dragons.

Chapter Fifteen
Hilversum, December 1942

Nico's brief leave for Sinterklaas Day served as a temporary escape from the magnitude of the war, from daily, tiresome challenges. He celebrated a quiet Sinterklaas with Mother Pouwels and his siblings and their families, gathering for prayer and candles. Later in the day, Nico arrived at the Dekker household as Diny sat in the sunshine on their couch. Her stomach rumbled with hunger.

"What a lovely surprise today, Nico!" Diny exclaimed. "Are you well this Sinterklaas Day?" she asked with a dimpled smile, sparkling eyes expressive and eager. He nodded and reminded her of the brevity of this visit. Mam, boiled hot water over the wood stove for tea. Jan and Nelly joined them, and Mam tried to rally Nico's spirits with some singing and exchanging of handmade gifts, slowly drinking weak tea. He gratefully accepted gifts of Diny's soap and candle along with Mam's mittens, and silly poems accompanying each gift, his contentment appeasing Mam's desire for Nico to relax and feel safe.

Later, after Nelly and Jan retired to their own activities and Mam to knitting in another room, Diny investigated Nico's plight. He looked weary and she knew something troubled him. She sat closely to him on the couch, stroking his face.

Nico winced, then held her hand. "Joost was arrested," he whispered.

Her stomach turned to ice.

Nico continued. "He was my primary contact. And his real name… who knows… he was married with young children. For sure, he did not know my name. All his documents burned in the fireplace of the Driel safe house before he was arrested. It was as though he knew they were coming."

Diny's face paled.

"I know what you are thinking, but I warned him about using that safe house two kilometers north. He went to Doorwerth Castle instead. A spy arrived as Joost did, and when the spy chased him, Joost threw his entire jacket into the fire, including the contents of those envelopes. The family operating the safe house out of their farm was also arrested, and anyone connected to him cannot be protected."

"Nico, did he have anything to incriminate you?"

"No. My personal details are unknown to him."

"Will you stay away from Elst for a while?"

"Yes, I must be alert and avoid Driel as well, but only from those night assignments. And, no, Joost had not even a photo or my papers or anything, as we always connected on a whistle call and password. But still, I feel for him. I wish I did not know he had children. Perhaps if I asked my friend Henk Mulder what happened, he could find out the details…"

"Can Henk be trusted, though?" Diny crossed her arms. They discussed Nico's untimely encounter with Henk outside the cafe just eight months prior.

"Henk might betray me to the NSB for interrogation, or send me to prison," Nico admitted. "He would know I worked with the resistance, would look for you, and send you to a camp as well." He sighed, then walked to the window and continued his story, sharing further of other friends and their salesman work. He stared cautiously through the lacy curtains, as though frightened of something in the distance. Mam had peeled back the blackout paper for a sunny Sinterklaas Day but would paste it against the window at sunset.

"I am sorry for my gruff demeanor," he continued, unable to look at her. "This could be our final meeting for a while." Nico could not know where the battle zones would appear, nor where airplanes might bomb next. He embraced Diny, cheek to cheek.

"You are my pearl, Diny, and please do not forget about my love — or my promise for our future together," he whispered. Nico again hugged her tenderly, his scent like a familiar smoky woods.

"Were you in a clog factory today?" she teased. "Or in Harderwijk today?" Diny knew of a many generations-old smoker house and eel stall in the village on the Ijsselmeer.

Nico concealed his face from her view, her anxiety melting as she rested in his arms. She was mesmerized by his love. The mahogany grandfather clock chimed three o'clock and he looked up at Diny, his eyes wide. He kissed her briefly, his passion evident, their faces intermingled with tears. Nico raced away through the frigid afternoon, sliding on the slick stone streets as though he were ice skating on a frozen canal.

She lingered at the window, silently begging him to turn around and return. Diny wished to travel with him as his *wife*, after this mess was finished. She watched his lanky frame flee toward the train, the horrible, terrible train, to take him to the dreadful, angst-filled East. *Too close to the German border and captivity,* she thought, *but at least he has a job to provide a bit of income in these desperate times.* And perhaps a bit of cover for any other resistance activities, of which she was unaware.

"Help me, Diny!" Nico screamed, as the train dismantled around him. "Stay with me, my love!" She reached for him, but his body fell backwards, out the train window, and plunged onto the Dutch countryside, while the train continued to fly beyond the tracks. The train crumpled around her, and all became black.

Diny lurched out of a deep sleep, her body soaked with sweat, darkness pressing her aching temples as Nico's voice resonated in her ears, the shadow of a dream. All day, she could not shake the reality of that dream. She shuddered to think it might be true.

Three weeks later, Christmas Day arrived. Evergreen branches and silver ribbons were displayed over the large mantle. Velvety red bows were looped through staircase banisters, and an array of white candles were lit for the tree and dining table. The celebration felt simple but Mam wanted to make the most of their holidays, even during war times.

Diny received a letter in the mail. She ran to her room to read the letter alone. Diny's heart soared at Nico's formal promise for marriage and his official proposal. He said she was, *"Heel mooi, prachtig, een schat, mijn Lieverd!"* Nico believed she was *so beautiful, pretty, a treasure, and his sweetie,* and when she was in his presence, she felt that way.

As she read his letter, a simple, thin gold ring was enclosed in the envelope. Diny picked up the wedding band and gasped, rolling the ring between her fingers as she scanned the scrolling words on Nico's letter, wondering how he afforded a ring during a war. Absorbing the enormity of this engagement, Diny's sorrow permeated the joy, for Nico was not present to share in the engagement celebration.

She placed the ring on her left hand ring finger and would move the ring to her right hand after their wedding. Thus, Nico and Diny became engaged on

26 December 1942, via his letter of intention to her. Almost three years after their first meeting, he established their engagement. As soon as she read his promise of marriage, Diny's eyes spilled happy tears, and she wrote a quick telegraph accepting his proposal.

Then she paused, considering, *Why a letter*? Nico remained on the Eastern front, and wrote his intention of the letter arriving as a Christmas Day gift, sealing their relationship. He was dismayed at being unable to return for the next few months, but the hope of engagement consoled her. Diny then revisited the proposal letter, and again received his words expressing his love for her. Nico longed for a marriage which pleased and honored the Lord. She knew they would nurture their children as a solid, unified pair. They would fulfill their dreams and move to the Dutch East Indies just as soon as the war was over, when he secured employment in Indie.

"I am certain," Nico wrote, "that the ending of the war will unburden the world of much pain." Diny relished his letters, his hopeful optimism, and promise for providing a good, happy life. The following day, the newspaper read:

Verloofd (Engaged):
G.M. Dekker
en
N.P. Pouwels
Hilversum, 12 Dec. 1942.
Simon Stevijnweg 59.
Javalaan 35.

Hilversum, 1943

Diny realized it was an easy choice to hate German soldiers because they stood as a painted unit, a conglomerate of an army patched together like tin soldiers; stoic faces, zinging language, stern demeanor. How soon she might discover the contrary, remained uncertain, but knew eventually, her fabricated deceit would unravel. Perhaps witnessing the enemy's humanity, her theories might be swayed.

Diny's sorrow swelled for young boy soldiers, and often observed naïveté and fear. Jewish mothers also wept for missing sons, deported to an unknown malice. A generation of mothers all worried for their sons, and as Diny's brother Jan matured toward age 15, she could relate to the trepidation of potential loss. Even while at war with Germany, she felt certain those German women loved their children. Issues like love, family, faith, and loyalty all stretched beyond race or ethnicity.

When Diny's "one year of Dad being gone" became a "day-after-never" scenario, and three entire years passed without seeing him, and a great period without any knowledge if he remained alive, she refused to mourn her plight. Her hunger and fear were like a restless yawning, which permeated her being. If she assumed hunger, her mind transfixed upon food, unable to swerve from its course of need. Yet certain the ache was grief, a threat to joy, she could not discover any relief from pain or explanation for loss.

Her one true balm was the steady, warm love she felt from God in unexpected moments, including her forthcoming marriage to Nico. A sun-swept view of a peaceful field, bright, ecstatic tulips pushing determinedly through a spring snow, or birds singing to welcome the morning all gently hastened her heart. Small, daily encouragement could be discovered if she searched for that Truth.

Pieter was a valiant father and a noble policeman. How would he deal with persecution? The certainty of a siege loomed with evidence, the country laden with fear. Pieter commanded the Police Force, the array of islands as similar and varied as siblings with different stories and unique beauty. When encountering the enemy, would Pieter be offered judgment, or mercy? In front of brutal enemies, one's career or role played either insignificant (as all were treated the same), or utilized against, because of their responsibilities and knowledge prior to the war.

But the war broke out and Dad did not return to them after one year, as he originally expected. Mam had the responsibility to be their mother — and their father — overseeing the care of a young adult and two teenagers. Diny had been protected by many of life's disappointments, but she was not mature or streetwise at age eighteen, let alone now in her early twenties. Now with Mam's father gone and Mam's mother living in Amsterdam, Mam further suffered in her difficulties, loneliness, and frail health.

She often told Diny, "I have no idea what I would do without you, my darling *Grietje!*" Her words were a tremendous compliment. Yet Diny felt the weight of pressure, for Nico had promised they would relocate back to the Dutch East Indies after their wedding, with the hope to raise children on the islands. Diny faced a challenging struggle. Should she remain true to her original promise to her Dad to take care of Mam? Or would he grant her permission to embark on a new life as Nico's wife? She prayed her dad might miraculously return safely to them in Hilversum, giving the blessing to allow Diny to marry Nico and move to Indie.

Of course, Diny had already sacrificed other ideals and imaginings, slowly surrendering the career goals of her earlier years to focus on the daily task of surviving. She wanted to study nursing, and work in a hospital. Diny realized the beginnings of the dream during domestic school, and then Hilversum's hospital accepted her internship. This brought incredible joy, and she volunteered in different wards, caring for ill, or her favorite assignment: mothers and their newborns, tiny hands reaching to embrace the world for the first time. Diny loved the various rotations and felt accomplished in her brief season of work there, eagerly anticipating her profession as a nurse.

Then the war arrived, and Diny's father urged her to care for her mother and siblings, so she relinquished the nursing internship to care for Cora, Nelly, and Jan. She did not despise her decision, for it was a choice: a wisely calculated conclusion. Diny would utilize all her learning in caring for her family. By mid-year, Diny longed for a beach outing, to bicycle along the coast or splash in the undulating waves of the warming sea. German troops surrounded the coastal communities, with submarines and aircraft carriers, and lined the shore with heavy machinery, poised to stretch their advances across the English Channel and into Great Britain.

Adriaan's BBC report one evening cautioned civilians against any unnecessary travel in a precarious time, mentioning a preventative evacuation of the coastal village of Scheveningen due to invasion or bombing; Diny could barely hear what was happening. The town's name, "Scheveningen," was a word used to discern whether someone was truly Dutch, as native Germans could not pronounce the guttural sounds within the complicated city name.

Unable to concentrate on the BBC report, Diny considered the innocent residents of the little village, and hoped Germans spared the lighthouse from destruction, so the beacon could remain a vital protection for boats navigating the North Sea. Hilversum's situation amidst woods and meadows of heather provided a pastoral respite, with flowering scenery bestowing peace, unlike the trappings of Amsterdam, canals and waterways to the North Sea.

Each night, the eight o'clock curfew arrived, forcing them to remain enclosed in their home. Diny could not rest and prayed as Nelly slept peacefully in the bed near her. When she considered her dad's fate, Diny rolled feverishly in her bed, and imagined stair steps of waves, alternating, with one wave foaming, charging inland before settling into flat froth on the damp sand, then another underneath receding, pulled back into the expansive gray waters. An exhale of water followed by an inhale back to the center again. Each layer of wave would build on the previous one, until salty bubbles churned and intermixed, the sound a soothing lull of repetition.

Late afternoon at the shore would certainly be luminous, as morning fog burned into a misty vapor, disappearing in the full gaze of the sun. She might walk the shore without shoes, her feet caressing the sand and tickled by oncoming waves. White foam surfaced and remained, air bubbles popping as sea creatures stirred in wet lumps just under the thin terrain. She stomped bubbles, sending a frothy spray splashing around as she frolicked.

Longing for such a moment produced nothing, Diny realized, except additional yearning, a yawning ache like her stomach she could not fill, with incomplete memories of the evening lingering and unfulfilled in the next morning's dawn.

Some midnights, in an engrossed sense of dimmed eyesight, shadows sprawled in her mind and she perceived movement on walls as though *tjitjaks* scratched their presence while hunting for food. She heard the noisy chatter of the *saté man* calling out his selections, clanking his metal cart down the street. The smoky caramel sauce emitted a lulling scent, the aroma now powerless to lure her into sleep. She recalled the peace of ribbiting frogs vibrating through the airy, cozy veranda, beyond her parents, settling into Diny's tropical bedroom. Enamored childhood memories lingered.

During nights like this, unable to determine the line between dreaming and hallucinating, fatigue clattering her nerves, she wished to no longer dream about visions which were not an attainable, present reality. Her imagination persisted as church bells rang out with three chimes and were silenced, planes lumbered above, droning on in present life. Her mind implored her to eventual slumber.

She remembered her father, and wondered at his determination, his willpower for life. Years ago, when Pieter wrote the Police Manual at the Soekaboemi, he declared Diny was eight years old and needed to learn how to swim. Every day after four o'clock tea, she held Father's big, sturdy hand and they walked five minutes down a dirt road together, through lush green trees, arriving at the Prana swimming pool.

He jumped in, at once emerging to the surface, and then gently — but firmly — urged Diny to join him. She thought the water was cold. She knew the large inner tube around her waist would absorb some of the temperature, so she closed her eyes and jumped off the edge, splashing into her father's large arms. He trained her in basic swimming techniques, and at length, she became comfortable in the water while content to remain inside the inner tube. This routine continued for weeks, until one afternoon, her father forgot the inner tube at home.

When they arrived at the Prana swimming pool, Diny looked around in the pool area, thinking she dropped the inner tube on their walk to the pool. The mischievous look on her dad's face revealed he intentionally left the inner tube at home.

"Come into the water, Diny!" He hollered. "This is just practice. You can jump to me!"

She hesitated, emphatically shook her head, and claimed she needed the inner tube to swim. "Dad," she reminded him, "my tube is gone! I need it to swim!"

Pieter climbed out of the water and walked over to her. "Jump, Gerardina!" he urged her. "You will jump and so will I, *Grietje*. We will jump off together!"

She was her father's doll, but her eyes filled with tears.

"How will you learn unless you leap?" he invited her with a playful sparkle in his blue eyes. Father quickly and easily lifted his first-born, leaned over the edge of the swimming pool, and effortlessly tossed her into the water.

Diny went underwater and kicked her legs furiously, moved her arms around, and miraculously reached the side of the pool with only a small amount of water up her nose as a reminder to hold her breath when jumping in. She looked at her strong, tall father, who still stood at the edge of the water as he clapped and whistled his affirmation. She finally learned to swim!

For months after this important milestone, Dad and Diny continued to walk to the Prana swimming pool together, and Diny left the inner tube at home. While swimming and splashing around each afternoon, Diny created stories of fish and pretended to be a shark, tried to swim along the side of the pool as quietly as possible, not creating a single wave or sound, to sneak up on Dad and surprise him. Meanwhile, for more than an hour, Dad swam the entire length of the pool as though training for some swimming event, in methodical, rhythmic laps from one end to the next, and back again, as exercise and stress relief, he told her.

She imagined herself a spiraling, dramatic mermaid, attacked by an octopus, and beckoned Dad to save her. He quickly arrived at her side with a concerned look upon his brow, and when he realized her joke about peril, he cautioned her of foolish follies, of needlessly calling for help when she did not require rescuing.

From that point forward, Diny's adventures happened within her mind, in the spaces of imagination. She pretended to be a fish and looked for other fish. Some classmates also played as fish friends during swim times, but few returned to the swimming pool with frequency as Diny and Dad.

Eventually, when her exhaustion had finally surrendered to sleep, Diny's renewed peace jolted awake into the present by resounding air raid sirens, blaring loudly. They rushed down the spiraling staircase and huddled in tight balls on the bathroom floor, covering their heads with their arms. Their legs groaned and ached from the pain of being bent and drawn up under them while their townhome shook from bombs. They prayed bombs would not destroy them. The earth buckled, rippling, as the shaking continued, bombs falling over and again.

Between blasts, Mam interceded in short, hasty prayers and Jan gripped her hand, as Nelly sobbed. Diny's ears numbed into the rhythm of her pounding chest, pulsating in sync with heartbeats, the quickened pace of her panic. Her mouth tasted of blood and her head felt heavy. *What good is this, if we are to die anyway? We are better off sleeping peacefully in our beds, taken from the world while in the security of slumber, then sprawled on the floor like animals!* They were often awakened as airplanes whirred and hummed overhead, the droning low and harsh. Scores of planes flew together, in unison, in the cold, unforgiving sky.

In the years before the war, Diny spent Dutch Furloughs outside, enjoying late summer afternoons hiking under the broad blue sky. The majestic and enigmatic golden Dutch light illuminated everything, over tree-lined meadows beside woods. Birds swooped and soared, from exotic parrots in Batavia, to blue-chested birds in Hilversum. Dutch wrens bounced and hopped along a busy avenue, and lone eagles soared on brisk updrafts, white feathers smoothed in the wind, gliding through the air in looping patterns, wings expanded, proudly stretched to full length. As war invaded their humanity and they huddled for protection from air raids, Diny considered those long-ago days before innocence shattered.

Everything was divided, a boundary cut in stone and flesh, carving out their existence into a definitive beginning point, hurtling toward an ambiguous, never-ending completion, an unrelenting end game. Their existence detoured from ambitions and divided in half, from "before-war," to "now-war," from Dutch to Occupation, as this interminable war contained eternity, infinity, no dividing line, until its future end, or her end.

She longed for the simple days of youth, before the heaviness of family responsibility came barreling down and suffocated her, before the crisp golden Dutch air was invaded with cold, severe metal airplanes cutting the blue sky. The frigid spread of perfectly aligned enemy birds, in unison, without hesitation or regard, swept low, with roaring engines cackling evil laughter, resounding throughout the bodies of the sufferers.

Chapter Sixteen
Hilversum, Summer 1943

A fair summer afternoon beckoned Diny outside, and she covertly cut down trees in the woods to prepare for their frigid winter. Diny now ventured farther into the woods, as trees on outlying areas grew sparse from deforestation. Though uncertain what winter would bring, any opportunity to collect wood proved useful.

She quickly loaded the cut trees and saw into her baby carriage, covered it with a blanket, and extended the canopy over, disguising her efforts. An afternoon thunderstorm approached, and darkness swiftly covered her in the woodlands. She hurried toward home before the storm arrived, a wall of rain visibly approaching, pushed at her by a blustery wind.

On her race through empty cobblestone streets, blocks from home, German soldiers established a checkpoint. Usually the roads bustled with those about their business, and she blended into the crowd, families scurrying and couriers delivering packages. On this gloomy, brooding afternoon, two German soldiers on guard spoke to each other, and then noticed her in the empty, abandoned street. They pointed at her, motioning for her to come closer. She cautiously walked the carriage to the men, keeping the front of the buggy closed. All they would be able to see was the closed canopy, and nothing else.

The German soldiers demanded her identification papers, which she pulled from her coat and handed to them. She stood completely still and quiet, unwilling to offer them a reason to take her away or shoot her. She stared off blankly, looking not at the men, nor their boots or eyes, but away, into the distance. But she did not want to appear aloof or uncaring. She did not dare to look at the baby carriage, for fear they would request to see her baby, in some mood of interest. *But I do not have a baby! Only a saw and a pile of freshly-cut wood under the blanket!*

They made staccato inferences, beginning casually and escalating. Her heart pounded and she felt weak. She could not breathe, but prayed silently for God's protection, realizing any hesitation in answering the men might damage this innocent venture of fetching wood. Maybe they wanted to see the baby and if she requested they allow her baby to sleep, they may wonder how it breathed underneath a blanket.

Instead, the soldiers chatted to each other and smoked, looked at her papers and waved them around, then asked her a few plain questions about her day and the approaching weather, and handed back her identification papers. Neither man mentioned her baby carriage, nor did they look in the direction of the buggy, as though blinded to its existence.

The weather then unleashed its fury of rain openly on them, and the German soldiers swore, tossed their soggy cigarettes, then escaped inside a building as they motioned her onward.

She pushed the carriage and walked steadily but not quickly, confidently but not pridefully, and turned the corner to home, into the blowing wind and away from the shelter of the building protecting her. The wind pierced her skin with sharp pricks of rain and hail, blustering into the land behind her. The North Sea picked up in the air and fiercely torrented their village.

When she returned home with wood, she parked the buggy inside, her entire body drenched, unable to find relief from chattering teeth and shivering body. Diny peeled back the blanket, relieved the wood was completely dry! She unloaded the wood, then ran into her bedroom and stripped away her wet clothing, peeling it back while crying. She grabbed a towel and dried her body, sobbed into the towel, and wished away the pain of the moment, of what could have been had the German soldiers uncovered the blanket, and subsequently, the unspeakable feeling of being shot while running from an exposed carriage.

After a few minutes, her fears dissipated, and she could only speak gratitude to the Lord for his protection revealed in an invisible baby carriage and his rescue through the ingenious use of a rain storm. She was unable to imagine her fate had the men noticed the forbidden wood — and not a child — in her baby carriage.

Hilversum, late summer 1943

Nico stepped into the cafe, strong voice unwavering as he ordered coffee. Both hands quivered, however, frozen and clammy, shoved into his pockets. He spoke only to the coffee clerk, and scanned the room. His spoon swirled around a dozen times to incorporate sugar and milk substitutes into a weak brew. A man approached, sitting one place over and facing him. A few minutes passed before Nico allowed a glance over — and was shocked to lock eyes with Henk Mulder. Both faces fell with astonishment and Nico nodded cordially. Henk's newspaper was drawn to shelter their staccato words, they drew no notice of the others in the stuffy room. His tan hat remained firmly in place on his head. "I came to arrest… a certain resistance leader," Henk began.

"We suspected," Nico puffed, "but my contact will remain protected."

Henk glanced at Nico and said, "You place me in a precarious situation."

Nico sipped his coffee and responded, "I knew you favored this cafe, especially after our untimely meeting a year ago."

Henk removed his hat, sighing. Three uniformed men emerged from hidden corners and left the cafe, understanding Henk's signal. His hat rested on the table, brow sweat-laden, and he efficiently folded the newspaper together before placing it, folded in fourths, next to his hat.

Nico declared, "Now I know to eliminate further contact with my client."

Henk's face reddened, and he stared at his friend. "Has it been a year? You look health. My fortunate connections can only carry you for a while."

Nico knew Henk would need to claim responsibility at one time or another — whether now, or later after the war ended, when trials began. Henk slid the paper to Nico, a headline about Dutch East Indies in the column. "Be mindful of your wishes, Nico. I am aware of all your dreams."

Henk stood up to leave and swiped his hat from the table. His eyes were pained, his face mottled despite his robust appearance. Nico remained seated after Henk exited. Nico became more certain of the real devastation of Henk's life, his spiral into the enemy's grip.

The Dutch East Indies article spoke of harsh conditions in prisons and the transports of men to jungles to build railroads, and he contemplated his beloved Father Pouwels thousands of miles away, a noble man floundering, alone. Father Pouwels was older now, the war tattering his spirit. He might be frail, a gray beard masking his thin face, round spectacles resting firmly on his nose, wire frames tightly hooked around his ears. His seriousness would pervade in the war, but Nico hoped Father found friendships to buoy his spirit.

Nico watched through the front window as the three uniformed men left the outside of the cafe. They had been a readily visible presence, smoking and turning their heads to glance at Nico as he read his newspaper and sipped a cup of watery coffee. After the men left and the shadows of the sun shifted again, Nico ran to meet his train departing for the East.

Hilversum, Autumn 1943

"We cannot look back," Nico wrote to Diny in a letter, "and we must refrain from asking, *'What if the war had not come?'* because we cannot speculate or make any suppositions about the course of our relationship, had the war not knocked fervently on our doorstep. We cannot stand aside and allow others to die because of our fear, and must work tirelessly at helping others, and look ahead to the hope God promises us for those who believe."

The fierce fury of war resulted in relationships magnified through trial. As their relationship flourished, through letters and brief moments of meeting, Diny felt radiant with hope even on days their war outlook was grim. The four years of war had not hardened Diny, but toughened her into facing responsibilities previously unknown. She wished for those younger days when she was unaware of what burdens adults carried. She recalled those astonishing moments of youth: lying under a Batavian tree while romancing her life, dreaming of the future, and vowing to remain in Indie forever.

Diny wondered how she could persevere in the important task of caring for her family, an unlikely role thrust into her arms, a load too heavy to manage on her own. *Only by the grace of God*, she whispered, *might I carry on further.* Those evenings when her body ached with pain, loneliness, and fear, she had handled just enough for each moment, and set down the remainder of the affliction for the days ahead.

Silence permeated their home, and only the muffled ticking of the hidden mahogany grandfather clock continued, until Mam decided she could not bear the loss of another family heirloom. She reached into the framework and halted the swinging of the pendulum at 4 o'clock in the afternoon, the precise time when they assembled for their ritual of refreshing tin-bucket bath and tea on their Batavian veranda, when Pieter always returned home, prepared for an evening filled with family togetherness. Even after Mam stopped the clock's movements, Diny heard the ticking noise echoing in her mind, the staccato stomping which reverberated as predictable as marching German soldiers, yet which she swept from her thoughts.

In bed, long after the clock was halted, she faintly recalled the scuttling of small *tjitjaks*, whispering trees, relentless heavy monsoons, and echoing frogs in

Batavia. While outside her Hilversum window she perceived sounds of whistles, shooting, bells, airplanes, thunder, bombs, and wind. She imagined carefree veranda days, surrounded by peace, and steady layers of Java mountains, four layers of ranges, cascading at various levels with misty blue air between them. Those mountains remained, even if their land altered, even if her father was imprisoned somewhere amidst the paradoxical serenity of beauty.

Adriaan arrived after the eight-o'clock curfew with the radio ready for international news, and they listened to the BBC update. The *Radio Oranje* report from Queen Wilhelmina encouraged and inspired the country toward resistance efforts and standing strong and brave during war. She mentioned the plight of the Dutch East Indies, at which time Cornelia linked arms with Diny and grabbed Nelly's hand, holding her girls tightly.

Memories hastened Diny's breath, and kept her sane, reminding her of a time before their world went crazy, when her courtship with Nico began. Before days of rationing, lost valuables and lives, and doubts and deceptions around each corner. Diny remembered a spring Sunday evening early in the war, when she was to meet Nico, and reached the park on her bicycle before he arrived. She waited near a bench, watching couples and families enjoying the park. A solitary man caught her attention, precariously near oak trees, and flying an orange kite.

She finally recognized the man's hat and lanky frame, then ran to embrace Nico. "You found a kite to fly, my dear?" she exclaimed, giddy for his surprise.

He smiled from the side, and tipped his black hat, then handed the kite string off to her. They gazed at the bright blue sky and the orange kite. He commented on the stark contrasts of bold colors until the wind and sunlight changed, and the depth of the conversation astounded them both.

Nico counseled her, "We need to make a plan, Dien, in case we are separated and lose contact, if I am captured or something, if this war intensifies." His eyes softened, shaded under his hat. "I will send a friend to you, *Grietje*, someone to bring you food, someone who might know where I am, and how I am."

He looked up, the sun shining on his full face, and closed his eyes to receive the rays. "You can trust this friend," Nico continued, "since I would only send a kindhearted person. I pray we never come to terrible crossroads, but there it is, a bit of hope for you should we face this challenge."

She cleared her throat, the kite spinning in circle eights, as though the orange bird may come crashing down or ensnared in the oak trees. She dipped and looped the kite as Nico showed her. Her full intensity focused on the Flying Dutchman and not her Nico. The only opportunity for any control was this kite and in front of her stood Nico, his arms out and laughing, "Diny, settle down, and relax. All I shared is, 'What if?' and we need to have a plan. I do not plan to disappear!"

She nodded, her face contorted in emotion.

"Diny! Look at me! I am a healthy, vibrant, strapping young man. Where else would I go?" He began to dance, a distraction from the struggle. His smile faded into a serious gaze. "Diny, my sister Jopie exchanged letters with Father Pouwels. Did I tell you? But now we have not heard from Father in a few months. We fear his location has changed, imprisoned somewhere other than Java. I wish I could send your dad to look after my dear father, two stalwart Dutchmen in the Indies, sweating out the war in the tropics together. What hearty chats they would have, those gentlemen."

Diny's eyes filled, and she wiped away her tears. She handed Nico the kite and he grounded it and gathered the string. She pulled her sweater around her shoulders to protect from the chill of the impending sunset, the damp wool smelling of the shore. They again gazed into the sky together, spoke of their expansive freedoms, and for the day, she felt secure, unable to fathom how insecurity felt, much like the welcoming embrace of God's constant presence and the all-encompassing love he provided, no matter what circumstance. One could never comprehend the absence of God's presence, even in the depths of despair.

"Ready for home?" Nico asked, his eyes glistening and ears pink with the chill of the air. She chuckled and pulled his hat lower on his head.

Diny swung her leg around the bicycle and sat behind Nico, then looped her arms around his waist, while Nico's steady legs pumped the bicycle whirred and clanked along the paths toward her home. She held the kite loosely in her hands, and it fluttered as they rode over cobblestones and through church courtyards. Nico's back felt sturdy and able as she leaned into him, and his musky scent lingered. She wished home was far away, so they could ride longer.

When they arrived at her home, he mentioned the East-bound evening train, signaling the moment their weekend magic was replaced with reality. She wrapped her scarf around his neck and kissed him on the cheek before watching him ride away. Her dad had always surrounded her with security, happiness, safety, and Nico offered these attributes as well. In that early courtship moment, though, Nico's steady love sustained her. This happy evening memory brought joy to Diny's heart during war time, and she returned to memories on days she feared for Nico, on days she fought to remember his voice, his gaze, his light.

After several years of war, following a long expanse in which they no longer received Pieter Dekker's letters, his brothers abandoned the hope he was alive. They came over to the Dekker home in Hilversum to convince Mam and urged her to realistically accept Pieter was gone.

"Impossible, Cora, you must know, you are ridiculous to believe he remains alive," a sister-in-law howled, the lines in her ragged face showing the stress of her years, as Pieter's brother's face contorted with pain.

All their convincing, however, never swayed Cornelia, who shook her head. She sat down and scoffed, "Impossible? You truly believe a situation impossible for Pieter, or for God? How can you have so little faith?"

Cornelia looked at the family dejectedly, a sense of painful nostalgia for simpler times. She wished this pain was a nightmare, and desperately hoped she would awaken next to Pieter, safe, warm, secure.

When Pieter's brothers remained silent, she continued, "Losing my dear husband would be unbearable, but you fail to believe in God's power. Pieter is not gone. I know! I would feel the loss of my own husband!" Her face raged with a rare anger.

Unswerved, or unaware of Cornelia's true feeling, Pieter's brothers affirmed, "We have a friend who has a radio, and on the BBC *Oranje* Queen Wilhelmina informed us that the Japanese invaded the Indies in March 1942, more than eighteen months ago. They captured government leaders, and we all heard the Japanese are ruthless and merciless."

Cornelia nodded faintly, her eyes drooping in exhaustion. She looked outside at the sunshine radiating through their sitting room window.

Pieter's family continued, "We hear rumors of Japanese torturing innocent people. They are heartless, Cora, and indisputably cruel." And another more direct statement, "Pieter is gone. He will not return home. Truly, you must know and feel it!"

Mam lumbered over to the kitchen window and peered at the ledge, gazing at their growing geranium plant. Despite only water and ominous winters, this small plant continued to thrive, and Diny had faith Dad was still alive, too. Cornelia grabbed the geranium, then shook her head and dashed back to the still-clamoring family, bellowing loudly, "No! Do you hear?"

They all stopped talking and stared at her.

She continued. "I will never give up hope! If I get a telegram from the Red Cross and read it *black-on-white*, only then will I believe it. As this geranium still thrives, so does my husband. Now please stop exhausting me with this nonsense!" She sped past them, opened the front door, and pointed to the street to usher them out.

They glared at her and said they would return to console her when she received the inevitable news. If Pieter's own family deemed his survival *impossible,* then God rescuing him from certain death would be deemed an authentic miracle!

Later in the afternoon, Cornelia sat with her children as late-autumn daylight retreated, and they wept together. Diny shared her belief of Dad's survival, along with her covenant to God concerning their geranium plant, and they prayed for his safety and for encouragement amid whatever trial he might be facing.

Darkness descended and blackout paper secured to windows, and none were hungry for dinner, so Diny dug out their portable wind-up gramophone. She slid a round Mozart record out from its paper covering, placed it in their music player, then cautiously moved the arm onto the disc, aligning the needle. She kept the volume low to not cause a commotion outside and risk being caught.

As classical music started to play, Diny imagined her childhood in Batavia, and for a moment visualized those early days, with Mam clapping joyfully while Diny alternately danced around the front yard and ran to Mam for a hug. In her memory, Mam's wavy hair billowed long, the caramel coloring vivid, her body healthy, vibrant, and full of life, her form natural and spontaneous, the uninhibited moment she seemed entirely free. Back then, Mam waved her accordion fan, fluttering the pretty paper over her smooth round face, a respite from heat.

Now Mam's hair appeared thinning, brittle, and interspersed with gray wisps unseen before Dad left home. Diny attributed the weakness to a lack of vitamins, and those gray strands to difficult years of war. Mam seemed gaunt and delicate, like paper smoothed down on wet glass, her composure fragile, moments from breaking.

True joy and bliss had not eluded them as though they were incapable of gladness or amusement. Their family solidified into a unit, a sturdy, solid team. Some evenings, her mother longed for music by Dutch composer

Johannes Verhulst, and seemed pleased enough with his musical overtones, with similarities to more well-known German composers Franz Schubert and Robert Schumann. Diny adjusted the player, using the few records they could salvage, and aligned the needle to play the next record. Music ministered to them in ways words could not traverse.

And yet, through their challenges in this war, they were all precarious, walking a tightrope into nowhere, fog disguising footing and the ending to the harrowing journey, each of them on a different location on the tightrope, hovering dangerously over chasms of loss on one side and despair on the other, without harness or safety net, like the magical circus family, *The Flying Wallendas*. The famous circus family skillfully balanced on thin metal wires stretched across large crevasses and canyons. Their feet were steady and fixed as they floated across a cloudless sky.

As the Dekker family listened together, with Bach, Beethoven, and Vivaldi their musical company for the remainder of the evening, they balanced on an imaginary wire, gaining a steady pose, with enough vibrancy to carry them into the night, and all the uncertainty each night after would bring. The musical celebrations grieved along with them in serious tones with somber tenors, woodwinds resounding in a forlorn, subdued piece. Moments later they soared together in conquering sopranos and lively string instruments threading soothing notes.

Diny's spirits lifted as she rested her head back, dreaming of the sanctuary of freedom, an uninhibited ability to walk the tightrope to the other side without stumbling or succumbing to the abyss of distractions or hollowness of discouragement. Darkness surrounded them, but she felt no fear, only comfort and peace. In her imagination, Diny sprinted across the tightrope, emerging through the vaporous veneer to stand steady on the opposite side, victorious.

Chapter Seventeen
Hilversum, Sinterklaas Day 1943

The Dekkers celebrated a quiet Sinterklaas Day, exchanging light poems and knit creations of hats, mittens, and scarves. They dared not articulate the pain of Dad's absence, yet glances and tears revealed true feelings. In prayers they thanked God for his provision and safety, feeling grateful he allowed them to remain in their little home, and prayed for those who were unable to join them in somber celebration. Later, Diny escaped to her room and peeled back the blackout paper for natural light. As she held a letter from Nico, her hands shook, and her stomach churned with loneliness, and she sat upon her bed to read.

"During this uncertain season, with train track bombings and consistent air raids," he wrote, "my job requires my presence in the East, a sorrowful and unavoidable circumstance." Nico hoped to find a moment of leave to join her sometime in the spring.

She set the paper on her dresser and gazed out the window at the swirling snow lining the street. *Just as well,* she thought. *With train travel as dangerous as ever, he will be safer in Elst. If only he did not work so close to Germany!* Henk knew Nico assisted the Dutch Underground. He could easily inform the Germans about his friend, eliminating Nico's contacts. If that happened, Nico and his family would be sent away.

The fog and ice thickened, enveloping them in seclusion. Longer nights with little candlelight and few interactions with others provided the recipe for a melancholy time of year. Unless Diny waited in line for food or escaped to the woods to chop down trees, she might pass through several weeks without any genuine conversation with others, apart from Mam, Jan, Nelly, or Adriaan. No escape for bodies and minds withering, frayed clothing unraveling, temperaments fading, and bone-chill settling into spirits.

Hilversum, early 1944

Cornelia's hands ached to sink her fingers into the soil to garden, to plow the earth until it surrendered to her wishes. *At least one aspect might be within my control*, she considered. She layered clothing on her frail body to remain warm, with long garments, a sweater, shawl, coat, scarf, mittens, and hat as a bundling to wander outside in the garden on foggy mornings, the sky white and thick with humid atmosphere or impending snow storm.

Surely, spring would renew their outlook. Yet spring lingered months away, and the winter gloom stretched aimlessly, flowers and ambitions dormant. Cornelia began her morning prayers by pacing the stone-filled path, imagining roses, hydrangeas, or peonies in the frost and chill, now looking like brown stumps in the dry ground.

As she prayed for her beloved Pieter and his unknown fate, she knelt on the rock-lined path next to the flower bed and fluffed the dirt, cupping it into lumps, as though forming dough on her countertop. She reached deep inside the ground, seeking more tulip bulbs to bake and grind into flour, her hands numbed in the fossilized soil.

Perhaps Jan missed digging up bulbs from the garden bed? Certainly, he is as exhausted and starved as I am, unable to concentrate on a task! Yet teenaged Jan remained thorough in his efforts, intent on survival, even as his temperament matched the mood of the frigid weather. Cornelia's heart raced as she burrowed, her hand grazed an object, and she halted in the soil. Slowly, she lifted a frozen tulip bulb and held it, rubbing away earthy dirt to reveal dark skin, and slipped the pear-shaped bulb into her pocket, shaking her head at the marvel.

Every day, Cornelia roamed their garden, praying, leaning against the stone wall, envisioning Pieter and his daily strolls through their Batavian estate many years ago, through meandering paths, smiling with a nod, tipping his pipe in the air, a salute, a humble gesture. When they lived in those other lands before the war, his laughter resonated, echoing throughout the garden, while Diny chuckled jovially, revealing dimpled cheeks, her brown hair twirling in the breeze, dark eyes wild with excitement. In those early years of parenting, simplicity surrounded their lives. *Would Pieter be permitted to take those necessary walks if he was captured? Would he remain quiet?*

Pieter was more than fifty now, and perhaps beginning to gray around the edges due to the stress, like the former Batavian Resident, who grayed precipitously under pressure during the scandal just prior to their Furlough. But

Pieter was a man of courage and integrity and would have no reason to gray prematurely. Cornelia decided that when a man lost his will to live, malaise soon followed; he could not fight that inevitable path. She prayed her husband would not succumb to a fatal discouragement.

Cornelia considered her children: Diny was no longer a child, but an adult, and at nearly twenty-three, preparing for marriage; Nelly was eighteen and hoped to finish her studies; and Jan was fifteen and smaller in stature, which helped in avoiding military service. As of May 1943, all men ages 18-35 were required to report for forced labor in Germany. Had five years of daily terror altered her blissful memories? Did she visualize her previous life in the Dutch East Indies in a more romanticized way?

Perhaps these fanciful dreams and visions sustain us, Cornelia thought. Invariably, her hands were drawn to the garden, and every week she found new tulip bulbs. The realist in her mind argued, *Impossible! We checked the garden last week and already gathered all the tulip bulbs!*

Yet despite the improbable miracle, Cornelia only believed it when she dug and found bulbs in a barren garden. Again, the Lord provided for them in ways only He could offer, and they stepped forward in trust, even in places as ordinary as a garden. Those tulip bulbs were like flakes of manna from Heaven, blessed provision in the dry and thirsty desert. They were the sustenance offered as a rescue from famine.

If He made a way for the Israelites in the desert and forged streams in the wasteland, then surely God would remember her family. Cornelia thanked the Lord for his continuous offering of food and prayed fervently for the ultimate miracle: for their rescue, their own personal Exodus.

Hilversum, spring 1944

The trees had not fully blossomed, yet velvet buds formed in teardrop shapes, preparing to burst forth. A hot day promoted the sweep of sudden growth, an explosion of green, waxy leaves. Birds found a cushioned resting between each distinctive expressive bud. Diny could examine every flower in yards and parks. Nature knew no warfare and pressed along despite any efforts to stall or ignore her arrival. Each season passed with flourish and detail. Although war raged, the inner mind and heart of those captive by evil or pain could remain free.

With brisk morning air submitting to sultry afternoons, activity and exploration seemed to overtake any discouraging thought or lost hope. In the springtime, winter's dust of pessimism propelled away, brushed off, swept out, and replaced with gentle scents of ambition and renewal, tastes of possible opportunity. Each day she thanked God for the mercy he demonstrated in keeping them alive.

Mam and Diny shared a genuine concern about Dad. In the beginning of the war, Dad mailed letters and some money for their daily living. After a while, even his letters ceased. Diny longed to read his words of peace, to see through the letters and understand his intention, his heart. She wondered at his safety and location, as Mam alluded to using code words instead of writing directly. It was as though Dad was mysterious, or hesitant in his writing, yet Mam seemed to completely understand his words, phrases, and expressions.

Each letter had been screened before being mailed, with some words blacked or cut out entirely, so they knew Japanese authorities watched him. Diny carried forward, faith steady in God, who would provide strength for Dad, or healing for the Dekkers if Dad did not return.

In the years leading up to the war, Dad enjoyed various pursuits and passions, including one hobby of collecting stamps. He assembled a thick scrapbook containing his valuable finds with room to add to the collection over the years, and his assortment included extremely rare and quite expensive stamps. His hobby marched into a more lucrative practice, as an almost savings account for the family, a leverage to use in a time like war.

One day, not quite six months after his family last visited, sharing their certainty of Dad's peril, his younger brother visited Mam, begging her to allow him to sell some of those beloved stamps to purchase food. Dad's brother needed to feed his own growing, hungry children, he reminded them humbly, and arrived into a precarious situation where he was unable to provide for his family, having sold paintings, antique items, and heirlooms to purchase food. Certainly, the entire family struggled to sustain themselves for meals each week.

Mam agreed to allow Dad's brother to sell the entire rare and beautiful stamp collection. He promised to deliver the money after settling on a price and they discussed how to divide the money. His relieved face was enough to remind them of the importance of caring for family. Mam realized they needed to utilize possessions God bestowed to them so they could survive the war.

Chapter Eighteen
Hilversum, August 1944

Diny met him at the park near the city hall and wore a dark wool coat. They only had a few minutes because he needed to return to the East.

"I want to escort you home," Nico declared.

"I know, my love," she replied, but he wanted to protect her.

"I still want to marry you someday, when this dreadful war is over," he assured her.

His mention of Someday allured her, although Someday seemed like an unattainable memory, some distant promise, as though their survival served as a consolation. She smiled weakly, wanting to believe they would each survive the war, seeking to have faith the war would end, so their great and glorious Someday could become a tangible reality.

Nico again whispered, "Agree to meet somewhere else. In one hour."

Diny's eyes asked, *Where?*

"The place we met. Where our love began."

Jacob's house.

She arrived at Jacob's house nearly an hour later. Jacob's garden gate swayed, unlatched, a wobbly ladder leaned unhitched from the side of the fence, and inclined precariously toward the courtyard, caught within the thorny vines of a dilapidated rose garden overgrown wild in the springtime fever. The front door creaked slightly open, and she felt like an intruder, nearly unable to recognize the sparse sitting room.

In the entry hallway, on a wooden table, Nico had placed a letter to his *Darling,* his *"Meisje,"* explaining he would permanently live in the East, near Arnhem, close enough to a central train station for a swift departure if necessary. His company Taminiau Jam Fabrieken was going to Furlough, the factory seized by Germans for their own use, and he found work as a translator.

She shoved the crumpled letter into her left pocket, to read again privately at home before burning in her stove.

She looked outside and joined Nico in the garden courtyard. The entire yard shone brilliantly with green landscapes, although Nico made no mention of the springtime blooms.

His bright blue eyes glistened. "Can you trust me?"

She nodded, but he looked up toward the townhomes, to the neighbors, uncertain if open windows without blackout paper revealed an indiscretion, if listening ears were enemy ears. He held her closely, whispering into her ear, and she finally relaxed.

"Hush, my *Meisje*…and do not repeat what I have written, for your eyes alone. Burn the letter at home and speak nothing of this. Your family must believe I am still employed for the jam factory as a traveling salesman. Will you promise your silence? Will you wait for me?" His firm grip on her shoulders revealed his insistence.

She embraced him. He stared at her as though to remember, to carve her image into his mind: her caramel hair, soft smile, smooth glowing cheeks, always dazzling eyes.

He leaned in, to clutch her for one last moment, and she whispered in his ear, "Are you translating for the Dutch, or is this a cover for Underground work?"

This was her fiancé, after all, a man she would marry as soon as the war concluded. He did not answer but pulled back and tilted his head. He winked, then hugged again, her neck flushed from the heat of their expression.

"I will not be able to visit you any longer," he explained to her, "so please do not expect me. Travel between the North and South is becoming nearly impossible, and extremely unsafe."

She nodded.

They all feared a raid of soldiers which in the night would extract able men from their families (despite their papers swearing to their employment importance) and deposit them at the front lines of fighting, or to labor camps they heard of in rumors.

"Stay here a moment before going home, and do not follow me," Nico said sternly. He noticed her pale face and softened, "I love you so!"

"And I love you," she murmured. "So-long," she cried, refusing to say "Good-bye."

He kissed her softly and lingered, then turned away. She was again alone, surrounded by fluttering flowers stretching outward, the humming of bees scurrying about their work, and the wayward expanse of a once-tidy life.

In early September 1944, many of the Dutch believed the end of the war was near, with liberation an approaching certainty, so rumors abound about their imminent rescue. On *Dolle Dinsdag* or "Mad Tuesday," the 5th of September, scores of Dutch celebrated in the streets. They had rejoiced about the Allied troops landing on the shores of Normandy, France, that June, citizens surmising the war's finality, unaware at the mass destruction and death the troops faced during an invasion.

Unconvinced of rescue, Diny and the Dekker family prepared for another long, frigid winter. Diny received a telegram from Nico, who disclosed an opportunity to visit her in Hilversum on 17 September. Her delight soared, and she remembered their last embrace in Jacob's garden. Nico would finish his work near Arnhem and take a train to their home in the Northern part of the country, a journey of two hours.

After Diny shared the message with her family, Mam's face brightened, and she agreed Nico's visit would be a refreshing change in their day. All looked forward to seeing him. When the day arrived to welcome her beloved, Diny anticipated Nico's train journey from Elst to Arnhem to Hilversum and prayed for his safety. She imagined Nico standing outside the Elst train station, holding a travel bag, smiling up at the sunshine beaming down near the tracks.

The Dekker family busied themselves, sweeping away dust and ash from their central wood stove, baking a sugar beet loaf, and airing out their rugs and opening the windows to the autumn air around them. The sunshine was prevalent, and the last golden moments of summer were in the air. Despite their daily burdens of the war, the family felt giddy. Even their small woodpile was enough, and Mam and Diny prepared Jan's room. Diny stood in long lines, as she did each day, for their rations of dry bread and watery soup. Still, perhaps those meager portions would seem enough for that night.

By late afternoon, sheets finished drying on the backyard rope, into a crisp wave twirling in the changing air, the sky endless in its glorious expanse. Diny stepped outside to collect the laundry, and raised her face to envelope the moment, dreaming of another place. Sunshine beamed from behind approaching clouds, illuminating the rays of light, as though she viewed the presence of God glowing down to the land just beyond a rolling hill.

The sun's rays were only visible because of the presence of clouds, as though one experienced true joy and delight when surrounded with impending darkness. To understand the depths of an eternal night was to also encounter the eventual blazing joy. In moments like this, Diny pretended they were not at war, imagining their wedding, the garden for a cozy reception, with their beloved family and friends. Diny longed to rent a bungalow in the Alps of Switzerland for a honeymoon once the war finally concluded.

Diny gathered the dried laundry and returned inside before the rain unraveled her efforts. Diny's appetite diminished. Mam shuffled off to bed. Jan stoked the wood stove, and Nelly retreated to read beside the fading summer sunlight before securing all their blackout paper. They waited, but Nico never arrived. Evening arrived, with their neighbor Adriaan who tapped gently on their back window, and Diny hastened to the door. His radio hummed ready for continent news, and they listened to details of the horror and destruction of a train connecting the North and South of the Netherlands.

Adriaan flattened his map on the kitchen table to mark the places the news mentioned. Then came the current news of the day: Operation Market Garden, which Allies coordinated to advance the line of defense from Dutch-Belgian border across the Meuse, Waal, and Rhine rivers. The Battle at Arnhem raged, yet Allied troops could not secure the bridge over the Rhine in Arnhem. The German stronghold was too fortified, and many Allied casualties required an unfortunate retreat. Diny could not sleep, and remained on the couch, awaiting Nico.

Early the next morning, Jacob arrived.

"Jacob! Come inside!" Jacob's face was downcast and he removed his glasses and wiped his eyes.

"Diny, I have news. Nico's telegram indicated he would be on the train, but he never arrived. There were many skirmishes with Operation Market Garden." He held the crumpled telegram, which Diny quickly read. Jacob's eyes filled with tears, and his voice wavered. "There is no easy way to know where he is, especially due to the work of the Dutch Intelligence in the area. Some Dutch citizens carry false papers. He could be captured or perhaps he was killed."

Her mind swirled with possibilities of Nico's demise. *We disappear like a vapor, a mist which is only here today, and quickly vanishes,* remembering the Bible passage in James.

Jacob continued, "Nico was my cousin and my best friend. How will I go on without him?"

Diny embraced him and walked him home. How could they know

what would happen? Even Adriaan seemed stunned at the Operation Market Garden advance.

Diny did not hear from Nico. There were no telegrams or packages. She forced herself to remember he was gone. Each morning, her first thoughts centered on him, and her eagerness to marry him, followed by her stern discussion with God and a silent, mental reproach. *Nico died, and our dreams died along with him.* She held a small memorial service for him in Jacob's garden patio. The service was brief but meaningful, and she wished to telephone Nico's Mother, but Tante Sluis urged her to respect the family's privacy.

Diny's mind began tricking her, believing she saw Nico's lanky frame meandering along a canal or strolling in the village square. Or she caught a view of the back of his head, and sprinted toward the man and tapped his shoulder, convinced of her discovery. Yet she felt horrified and embarrassed to realize the man was not Nico, but only an equally bewildered foreigner. At one encounter, a benevolent man gently held her arm, his kind face encouraging her. "Do not lose hope, sweetheart. I am sure your soldier will come home soon. Godspeed." And with a smile and a tip of his hat, he continued again, disappearing as a dot in the crowd.

On her walk home, dejected, Diny noticed a tree encased in concrete, skeletal gray branches stretched to the skies like barbed wire: sharp, impassable. Only the warmth of a spring awakening could unfurl the softness of each leaf. For certainly each spring, small buds unfolded into the sun, then unraveled into full shape. Yet as mid-summer already arrived without the tree's essential radiance, and autumn shook forth its amber splendor, this tree still produced no leaves or fruit, and Diny could only assume the tree's ultimate death.

Her imagination searched for Nico, with every crowd of marching, mobilized soldiers, emaciated shadows in the street, lines of frail and weary people gathered into military trucks. She was haunted in her own city, and pondered death on cloudy days, as though the sky obscured sunlight, escorting an immediate darkness, a dreary covering, solemnity.

Those who were in Christ would only die once, to live anew in Heaven. But her mind was unable to capture Heaven, to comprehend the depth of eternity. In the realness of her day, haunted by memories in Hilversum with Nico, every street corner held some remembrance of their growing love, of innocent days before Dad's departure, unsullied moments of an unmatched closeness, a bond she never envisioned would be shattered by young death.

War hastened their closeness, the passion of which flourished and intensified during trial. The loss of freedom was sometimes interpreted as the loss of self, of the ability to engage in meaningful discourse. After losing Nico at age 27, she imagined a joyful reunion on Heaven's glassy seashores, along with those grandparents who passed away and dear brother Huib. But she realized her reunion would be with Jesus, which would be astonishing! She could not comprehend the depth and scope of Heaven, but she understood the "veil" of finite knowledge would be lifted when she saw Christ face to face.

Still, she could not accept the reality of his death. Diny tested her mother after dinner one evening, and asked, "How would you feel if you were alone, Mam? What if Dad never comes home?" Mam stared at her with an empty glance.

Nelly cried, "Watch your mouth, sister! Be careful how you speak of death! You are alone so keep Mam out of it."

Diny spoke through clenched teeth. "Nelly, enough. I can handle this. You know nothing of pain."

Jan sunk his head into his arms and agreed. "Diny, our sister is right — we are all Mam has right now. We need to give her grace and love." Their stomachs were not full, never satisfied during this autumn, and they spoke of trivial issues after dinner, to distract themselves from the reality of poverty, of the nothingness churning in their bodies.

Mam finally replied, "We should never lose hope for Dad. You are consumed with grief over losing Nico, you cannot function. Would he want you to act this way? So heartbroken you cannot keep one foot in front of the other?"

"No. He would tell me to live for myself now."

"Then there is your answer."

Diny's face was somber.

"We are unaware of Dad's fate, but I believe he truly is alive," Mam continued, "and remember, until I see the telegram, black writing on white paper, I will not believe he is gone! Either way, I still know God is good." Mam stood to leave the dinner table, hands shaking, body so thin and feeble she might topple with the intensity of her heated words.

Diny remained motionless, fused like stone to the table.

"No use ruminating on *Tempo Doeloe*, Diny," her Mam reminded her. "We are powerless to change the *past*. It was pristine and quite innocent for a time, full of promise and peace. Those 'olden days' are gone! But okay, remain here, in your grief, until you are forty years old and unmarried. But if you take my advice and step into the promise of tomorrow, what then? Nico might arrive home someday — if this war ever ends — and how would you feel then?"

Diny's mind jumbled, a clutter of confusion.

As Mam walked upstairs to bed, Nelly and Jan cleared the table, where Diny remained alone. Mam stopped on the stairs and called to Diny, who joined her. Sitting in the middle, she pulled Diny into her arms, reminding her, "I sound harsh, *Meisje,* but intend to remind you of Truth. God promised to take care of us, which is the only Truth I can contemplate. You alone decide your attitude about your circumstances and must ponder your next steps of life."

Diny sighed into her mother's arms.

"As the Bible reminds us, Diny, the Lord's love endures forever, and His faithfulness continues through all generations. God is the same yesterday, today, and forever; He will lead us each day." Mam remembered Scriptures her own *Moeder* trained her in all those years before. Certain the love of God rescued Mam, Diny decided to allow the Lord to stabilize them through these trials. Later, Nelly climbed into bed next to Diny and whispered her apologies in the darkness. They reconciled and embraced, and Nelly soon fell asleep.

Diny remained awake, considering her future. If Mam became a widow now, in her fifties and with more than twenty-five years of marriage and three young adult children, Diny assumed her mother's loss would be more manageable, or at least knowing they lived full lives and had raised children served as a balm to pain, to the sorrow of death and loss. Diny knew the painful loss of her younger brother many years ago. She considered, *how dare I compare our lives, or our sorrows? All loss is keenly felt.* Diny hoped to eventually find healing or closure in knowing her beloved one finally found healing, even through death.

Cornelia shared minimally with her children concerning the intricacies of marriage, yet agreeably about methods to encourage and support a husband, grow in the Lord, and raise children to know Jesus. Only through trials and determination could they bear witness to the beauty which emerged through ashes and pain. Their marriage contained arguments and difficulties, though settled in private conversations apart from children. Yet in the growth each displayed, as God brought them closer through misunderstandings, the chord of three strands strengthened. God, Pieter, Cornelia, together, woven tightly as a unit.

Even while Diny remembered her parents were a witness for others, she remained preoccupied with the details of Nico's death, of his last moments. Was he alone? Did he experience pain? Was his death quick, or did he linger for days in the hospital, some anonymous casualty, hovering between life and death?

Diny shivered and could not warm her body in the cold, lumpy bed. They might never receive details of Nico's demise. Consumed by grief and by the death of their future together, Diny could only recognize the torture of unmovable change. Nico casually, calmly, yet boldly expressed his love and devotion in an approach she had never experienced.

By the time he was gone, Diny realized Nico had offered her everything she could ever hope or need, as a selfless, gentle offering. She met him at the tender age of eighteen, and if she needed some space to discover her true talents or passions, their love deepened over four years of exchanging letters. His offer of kindness and humility were unmatched in her life.

Now as his light faded, she decided on a few striking truths: those dreams of a man "sweeping her off her feet," a "knight in shining armor," never resounded as magnificently as the surprising reality, which shimmered more brilliantly, vibrantly, and enduring than a dream. His love lasted beyond the interlude of romantic feelings, when initial energies faded into everyday life. Her stubbornness and unwavering drive motivated Nico to provide, to become the man he said he knew he could be.

With each year of war, life became increasingly complicated and difficult for the Dekker family. Mam's concern for Dad amplified, and she grieved the loss of Nico, who she also loved like a son. Meanwhile, Diny held the same concerns — her dad and Nico. There were times they did not know how to handle each other! Visiting friends in Hilversum became quite difficult when German soldiers could stop anyone and question them about their motives, demand identification papers, and send them to a line or to get on a truck. How could they continue taking risks with their lives and the freedoms of their loved ones? After Nico's train was bombed in September 1944, there was no more communication between North and South Netherlands, and information via radio and Underground connections grew dim as the frost of winter settled into the land.

Chapter Nineteen

In villages around larger cities, farmers lived and continued to sow seed in their fields, nurture growth, and harvest a crop. They filled storage units with the harvest yield, on a rotating basis, depending upon the season. Dairy farmers raised cows which produced milk for drinking, and made cream, butter, and cheese, while others tended chickens producing eggs and meat.

Before the war, Diny bicycled to purchase fruits, vegetables, eggs, and dairy from farmers, collecting food in her basket. Once the war began, obtaining those foods became difficult and costly. Few bicycles existed for any purpose, so many citizens relied on friends with illegal bicycles or the use of a car.

Eventually, some farmers refused money, demanding payment in the form of heirlooms, like fine linens, expensive jewelry, or valuable antiques. Charging a high price for food was like robbery, as farmers took advantage of the grim situation, realizing all citizens needed food. Many farmers became wealthy from years of deceptive actions, collecting antiques which were only valuable because of their price, not because of personal family value.

Hilversum, November 1944

In late 1944, the Dutch population experienced dwindling resources alongside a ravenous, treacherous winter. They called the perilous, nationwide starvation "The Hunger Winter." The German army began fraying, unraveling, unable to maintain pace with their occupation, as their army spread too far and thin. Truce negotiations with Germans proved precarious and should the Allies air-drop food to the starving Dutch, the Germans promised to bomb the barrier dikes and thus flood the Netherlands. The Dutch were locked within the battle of their lives.

The Dekkers continued walking by faith, their spiritual hunger satisfied, with plenty of encouragement along the way, but struggled to find physical food to fill their groaning stomachs. Real, wholesome food was scarce, especially for growing teenagers, and Mam concluded they must make an important decision. Diny was twenty-three years old, sister Nelly 18 years, and brother Jan age 15. At the age of sixteen, male Dutch citizens could be called up for military training. Due to his smaller stature, Jan had survived most of his fifteenth year unnoticed and would turn sixteen in February.

As of 1944, the laws were altered, and *"totale arbeidsinzet"* announced, where of-age men could be pulled off the street and shipped to Germany for work. Mam worried a German officer may stop Jan in the street, for any reason, survey his identification card, and enlist him into the German army. Jan's shorter frame proved favorable in this instance, as he remained more petite than some of his classmates. His entire generation stood shorter due to malnutrition from four hungry war years. Cora feared Jan would be sent to Germany for labor or the front lines of fighting.

In the meanwhile, once all the Dutch schools were shut down, Jan rapidly entered more dangerous, unhealthy friendships. Jan has been spending his daytime hours with friends sympathetic to Germany. He stole a necklace from Diny – her favorite gold necklace, which Mam and Pap gave to her – and used the money to buy guns, which he hid in the attic. His betrayal was a festering wound in the family, and Pap was not there to guide and discipline him. When Diny promised her father she would care for the family, she held full responsibility.

Mam attributed Jan's diminutive body to the lack of nutrition over four years, aged eleven to fifteen, and felt discouraged by the prospect he may remain severely undersized into adulthood. With only a brief amount of time to plan, the Dekker family proceeded swiftly. They must find a safe place for Jan for the remainder of the war. They previously visited Dad's brother in the Northern Groningen province of the Netherlands. During the Dekker family furloughs from Indie, Cor's picturesque Dutch farm served as a place of respite and refreshment. Diny learned to ride the glorious chestnut horse on previous visits, and the shiny, curious colt had transformed to a vibrant, intrepid stallion.

Tante and Oom operated their farm and possessed a large amount of land, freshly grown food and extra beds for guests, and in a letter to Mam they promised to care for and feed Jan, as they had enough food on their farm for a hungry teenager. They would care for Jan until after the war (whenever that would be!) and deliver him home to Hilversum. The Dekkers prepared to send Jan up to Groningen. At least, living with family at the farm, Jan would be protected from negative influences.

The flat landscapes of the Netherlands proved easily traversed by bicycle, with wide-open topography. Yet with a condensed and growing population, any illegal war activities proved difficult to conceal from German troops, including border crossings. People who needed to go into hiding had few places to disappear unnoticed. Moreover, the Netherlands was bordered by enemy-occupied land at all sides: Germany to the east, the North Sea to the north and west, and Belgium just south — all territory tightly controlled by Germany. There was no possible escape across borders, or via any boat over the sea. Allied and enemy airplanes roared overhead, using the Netherlands as a fly-over zone. The journey to deliver Jan to Groningen would prove a challenging task.

The wind howled as Diny prepared dinner and darkness already permeated the air. Their plan seemed more complex than envisioned. With the eight-o'clock curfew moments away, Jan seemed to wander outside limits, especially as the coolness settled upon the village near the heath and thicket woods. She heard a scrambling outside the front window and yelling, but her brother entered the back door and into the narrow-gabled house, clunking a bicycle into their home.

Jan's trousers were scraped and scuffed, and with muddy hands and wild blond hair, he exclaimed, "*Dien*, I discovered something wonderful. The perfect bicycle!"

She examined the straight wheels and spokes, and sturdy handlebar, but gasped, "No tires!" Rubber — long since confiscated and used for the elaborate German machine — was scarce and missing from the bike Jan brought home. Instead, wooden tires had been sensibly crafted to allow a rider passage. She was not convinced.

"How do you expect to ride a bicycle and avoid the Germans?"

He glared at her and parked the bicycle in the corner. "The cobblestone streets are quite bumpy," Jan admitted, "but our ride North will take us off the concrete and into the countryside."

"What countryside?" Diny's face looked blank.

"Through the fields to Groningen, Tante and Oom's farm," Jan laughed. "Look! I found this bicycle hidden in the purple heath —"

"The fields where we are forbidden to loiter?" Diny interrupted.

"How else could I retrieve the bike? Adriaan's friend made wooden tires, which will offer me freedom to ride at the farm," Jan concluded.

"Well, at least your evening was not wasted," Diny reasoned, recognizing the fear which lingered in Jan's eyes. She ruffled his messy blond hair, and reminded him, "We begin a long journey early in the morning. We need to finish."

They ate stew which was watered-down, with dry bread. Mam and Nelly retired to bed after complaining of headaches, leaving Diny to tend Jan. Diny cleaned dishes and swept the floor, while Jan prepared the wood stove for overnight heat. With a single lantern, and vigilant to not spill precious light past the curtained, black-papered window, they discussed post-war dreams. A danger existed to speak of hopeful ideals, and she often banished ambitions from becoming more than a fleeting thought. *Who knows what tomorrow holds?* she silently considered.

For now, she remained certain of what their real tomorrow held, and what necessity grew from the prior four years. Jan packed his belongings, and included several of Diny's favorite, worn books, read numerous times into near-memory.

That afternoon, Adriaan had delivered Jan's new identification listing an altered birthdate, making him only fourteen. "Keep this safe, Jan, as we only have one chance tomorrow." Diny paid Adriaan a steep price for the false identification, reluctantly yielding Mam's most prized gold with pearl necklace, but Jan required escape.

"Sweet dreams, little brother," she yawned enroute to her room.

"Little in size, but not miniature in wit," he bantered with a chuckle, bounding up the stairs past her, taking two at a time, his energy remaining into the evening. Despite his small frame, his youth and innocence had faded into maturity.

The journey North required a three-hour car ride or two-hour train passage in a season without war. However, any travel now challenged sensibilities and fortitude. After the tracks were bombed in September 1944, trains no longer ran, and supplies impossible to find. Rails remained rubble, and people could not rebuild. Without gasoline for cars, vehicles sat idly, or pieced away, stripped for metal and rubber. Their only transportation remained a bicycle, which featured wooden tires. When Adriaan discussed the plans with them, he advised them of a safer route, directions away from German encampments. He urged them to remain diligent when conversing with others, friendly while elusive. Then Adriaan demonstrated the method of refashioning the wood, should their tires unravel.

Strips of tree bark surrounded the tire frame, fitting into the narrow metal groove normally housing rubber. The bark was secured by metal screws, which could unscrew during their journey. If that were the case, they might have to walk the remainder of the trip. The bicycle itself cost another precious family heirloom — pearl earrings Mam received from Dad — but Jan would keep the bicycle at Oom's farm, for all to benefit.

They were running out of heirlooms to exchange. Soon their home would echo in emptiness, yet they could always purchase new jewelry and valuables. Mam, despondent at bidding her only son farewell, could not summon the energy to leave her bed the morning of their departure, so they set off alone before sunrise, heading North.

Diny and Jan alternated riding together or taking turns — one walking and the other riding — and the first morning they arrived at the Ijssel River. There was a strategic bridge they required crossing over to continue north and with no other safe crossing. To traverse the frigid waters beckoned certain death from freezing or being shot. Over the Ijssel bridge, Diny and Jan faced a challenge: a German checkpoint with mandatory proof of identity.

They stepped into line and feared the ramifications of bridge crossing conversations. German soldiers guarded the bridge, checking identification cards, speaking harshly to some and overturning the bags of others. Dogs paced, sniffed, and growled along for something suspicious. Germans looked for Jews, boys 15 years and older, and inconsistent stories. If they found any of these things, the person in question could be on the next transport to Germany. Fake papers were treason and they could be immediately shot.

Diny breathed heavily, and Jan grabbed her hand, his eyes calm and focused.

When they reached the front of the checkpoint, Diny and Jan handed off identification and stared at combat boots, nodding their answers, for they might laugh or cry amidst the deception if they spoke. Another group in the other line was crossing at the same time, and nearly all the soldiers began yelling at the other group and arresting two people.

The young, cigarette-smoking German soldier who stepped in to help scanned Jan's stoic face. He read the listed birthdate, smoke billowing around them, pointing at Jan while asking questions, before quickly returning the identification, and Diny and Jan crossed the broad bridge over the Ijssel River safely. The Lord heard their prayers and had his angels surrounding them, and the Germans did not notice Jan's false papers.

Prior to their departure, their minister in Hilversum provided three addresses of safe houses with the Dutch Underground to securely stay overnight. They rode through villages, walking whenever their bottoms ached from the strain of riding on rickety wooden tires, the air smelling of burning ash and death.

Each village held light and darkness; a promise of hope surrounded by despair, the heavy stench of fire and scorched buildings beside fields of vibrant wildflowers. With each stop for the night, farther north than before, they were graciously welcomed by the minister's friends. They marveled at the benevolence of strangers, the generosity and compassion extended. At each of the three stops, the families benevolently received them to their dinner table, sharing with kind and eager hearts, with stories of how the minister had been a true friend and brought peace to their hearts.

"If repaying the minister's love means giving food and lodging to God's children, then we are the ones who feel blessed and encouraged!" they humbly asserted.

"Write the Lord's blessings upon your hearts, and share the grace with others," one man told Diny and Jan, "so future generations will know and revel in God's goodness and faithfulness."

Some of the man's own beloved had been transported by trains to some distant land. Others had escaped in the early days of the war, safely fleeing to England. They did not discuss details or background of Jan and Diny's journey, but nodded knowingly, smiled kindly, and arranged comfortable beds for Jan and Diny.

The next morning, the families prepared a warm breakfast and a takeaway lunch for their journey forward. Each rest stop was a moment of relief and refreshment along the voyage, the togetherness of a love for God, and a time in which Jan and Diny felt a renewed sense of hope, a special sense of connection with these families, thankful for their goodness. As they traveled, they passed others on journeys. Germans riding in open-air Jeeps drove past them quickly. Jan seemed vaguely aware of the dangers surrounding them. Yet like many teenage boys, the allure and romance of war seemed to overshadow fear of death.

Diny's senses were enhanced while on lookout. They encountered streets with carts and men hauling bundled goods, all intermixed with Germans. Children sat near the street, eating out of tin cups. Old bearded men stared. Women with headscarves and turned-up collars scurried, heads down, wearing heels and nylons even in frigid cold. Homes of brick had shrapnel damage and bullet holes along the house, metal embedded into stone. Bodies were laid out into street gutters, or in piles along some obscure cemetery, awaiting proper burial. Bombed out villages and homes were evident, with crumbling walls, grasslands burned, and the permeating stench of death pursuing them.

After three days on wooden tires, and with much pain all over their bodies, they finally arrived at Tante and Oom Dekker's farm in Groningen. The trip from Hilversum to Groningen had taken them three stressful days, and they were delighted to arrive. The sun was retiring into the North Sea, tracing gray clouds with pink hues, sweeping blue skies into an embrace, as though a sunset should require a bright palette. They were delivered into the arms of loved ones, and relief encircled Diny, as they had arrived safely! Tante kindly enveloped her into their cozy home and Diny felt herself falling, exhaustion invading her mind.

Diny recalled the tenderness she experienced seven years ago. Back then, on Furlough, she thrived in light, bright afternoons illuminating the spacious farm sitting room. Their living was sparse there too, with antiques and heirlooms missing (either hidden or sold, she considered), but the general generosity of spirit remained present. For the first time in years, Diny and Jan devoured baked bread, with creamy butter slathered thickly on soft crusts, drank two glasses of milk and happily ate a fish and vegetable dinner before a long night of restful sleep. The next morning Diny ventured outside in the chill of the November air. A wall of stone divided the front from back fields, which always felt like stepping into a magical dream world. She breezed through the gate and into her past.

The back meadow was outlined with trees, serving as a peaceful sanctuary. Craggy branches reached out, the only sounds of rustling of leaves in the breeze, those crisp brazen leaves still clinging to the stems and branches. A smoky haze arose, and a tunnel of fog settled over the sunshine. She circled the barn, anticipating a whinny, yet detected nothing, and swiftly returned to the house.

Diny remained at Cor and Sietske's rustic farm for a week, and Sietske urged her to remain longer, perhaps for the duration of the war, as Diny's coloring had returned with nourishment and rest, and time outdoors was invigorating. They all treated Diny and Jan royally, and Diny stayed an entire week. She rested, ate well, and became better acquainted with cousins Jan Cornelis, Nicolaas, Pieter Jan Wolter, Sietske, and Gardina. But after the glorious week, she returned to Hilversum, to fulfill her promise to Dad.

"Zorg goed voor je Moeder." His eyes had sparkled as he sternly commanded. *Take good care of your mother.*

She would, she promised. Diny could hear his words and the deep, even tones of his expression.

Nelly and Mam were alone in Hilversum without any assistance. Nelly waited in long food lines and managed household duties yet lacked organization skills required for detailed tasks. Diny's call to care for her family felt noble and just, and Jan would fare well, especially with their uncle as a godly example. They all sorely missed Dad during the war years, but Jan suffered from the lack of a Godly man in his daily life. Upon her return to Hilversum, Diny could use Jan's ration card for extra soup.

For her journey home, Tante insisted Diny not travel alone. The countryside held too many dangers, with bombs, soldiers, unknown people on both sides of the fighting, a young woman alone during the war, so Oom contacted a Red Cross van (complete with a large red cross painted on the top and sides of the white van) and Diny received a seat in the van for the ride to Hilversum.

Tante handed Diny a large, heavy suitcase filled with special items of flour, rice, sugar, salt, tea, and coffee, and two packages of butter, and urged her to ration the food during the long winter ahead. She was determined the Germans would not steal her butter during checkpoints, so Diny wore long trousers and placed her two butter packets in her pants; the butter melted before long and dripped down her legs: another disappointing mess!

Diny said "so-long" to Jan, uncertain when she might again enjoy his jovial company. But watching him settle in so easily with Tante and Oom provided great comfort, even if their future was unknown.

"O zo!" her Tante shouted as Diny climbed into the van.

Diny beamed back at her Aunt and her use of the code expression to the Dutch, 'So there!' expression, and hollered, waving, "O zo!" She could not hold back the emotion as she left her loved ones, unsure of their fates, but trusting in God's provision to keep them safe.

"O zo," she sighed to herself, the 'So there!' meaning "Oranje zal overwinnen!" She was certain 'Orange will triumph!' And she trusted God in the darkness of her long, quiet journey home. In the Red Cross van, Dutch citizens traveled to all areas of the country. They packed tightly in the back, and after picking up Diny, fit even a few more people inside. They felt like sardines packed tightly in a metal can, surrounded by luggage and Red Cross supplies. Along the way they were stopped at inspection checks for them to hand over their papers and stand quietly on the side of the road while Germans paced around and dogs inspected the contents of the van, questioning the drivers about the necessity of medications and health items.

And during several frightening moments in their journey, the group pulled off the road to find cover in a ditch, because of soldiers shooting in the upcoming village, and later, a bombardment close by. Then, airplanes began swooping down toward them, bombing their Red Cross van. Diny prayed, her eyes closed, while the van rocked. Each time their van was attacked, the driver pulled to the side and commanded everyone outside. Diny sprinted from the van, and jumped into the ditch and huddled in a ball, begging for God's protection and rescue.

Airplanes swooped close to the ground, and Diny felt the zipping wind from the planes whooshing past them, the crescendo of war reaching a horrifying height. Smoke billowed and they smelled fires nearby. After a long while, the air shifted direction, and the bombing halted. The noisy drone of roaring airplanes overhead grew fainter and ceased, and they stood up from the protective covering and hustled back into the Red Cross van to continue their tedious journey.

The hazardous trip — which usually took 3 hours by car — took 36 hours. They were delayed due to bombed-out roads precarious to navigate, security checks, and bombings from airplanes. They stopped in one village and cruised into a farm barn, where they painted the van black, so they would not be so recognized from an airplane. The Red Cross pair alternating the task of driving realized they risked being bombed by Allies, too, but were unwilling to allow the Germans to get the best of them.

After 36 hours of travel and little sleep, Diny was mentally and physically exhausted, her restful week at the farm a distant memory. Along the way, she sat next to a pleasant Dutch man also traveling to Hilversum. They spoke little but he seemed friendly and calm. When they arrived in Hilversum at a drop-off point, Diny said goodbye, and began her laborious walk home with the heavy suitcase filled with precious food. When the pleasant man next to her noticed her heavy load, he offered to bring her suitcase home as a gesture of goodwill. He had a bike waiting, he assured her, and would deliver the items to her home later that day. Diny provided her address and thanked him much, and started her walk, returning home empty-handed.

She gently knocked on the door to her Hilversum townhome, and was overjoyed to see her mother at the door, with tears in her eyes. After two weeks of time away, Cora dearly missed her children, and she embraced her eldest daughter. They squealed at their sweet reunion.

"Two weeks felt like such a long time! I worried, my *Grietje*, wondering if you were safe? How was your visit with Tante and Oom?"

Diny smiled weakly. "All was well, Mam. God was with us, and I knew you and Nelly were praying for us."

Cora ushered Diny inside.

"I am tired, Mam. After a bath and a nap, we can discuss my trip." Diny walked up the stairs.

Cora called, "Certainly. You rest after such a journey. But where are those delicious goodies Tante and Oom promised us?"

Diny froze on the stairs, turned around, and explained what happened on her journey home. Cornelia was confused with her daughter's decision, wondering where Diny had left their suitcase of prized food, which cost much to obtain? Tante and Oom *promised* to provide for them, and Cornelia now questioned Jan's ability to stay at their farm.

Diny lowered her head and sighed, and reported a nice man from the Red Cross van would deliver the suitcase that afternoon. Mam began to pace in a furious fashion and cried.

"How can you act in this foolish, impulsive, gullible way? We will *never* see our suitcase again!" Her reddened face flushed, and she slumped into a chair beside her daughter. In reaction to that man's kindness, Diny forgot they were at war!

Mam continued, "Oom and Tante painstakingly saved their precious goods for us and you have ruined their food gift to us!" *Who knew such high hopes rested in a simple suitcase!* Diny could not imagine the cost.

Diny said, "The suitcase was extremely heavy, and he promised to help me, Mam! He was so kind! He assured me his bicycle was waiting for him!" Her mouth hung open, credulously.

Mam waved her hand at Diny, instructed her to clean up from her journey and rest in bed. She boiled water and filled the bathtub for her daughter's bath and scuffled off upstairs. Diny soaked in the water, embarrassed by her foolishness. She dressed in clean clothes, and wondered how Mam would languish over this matter, her delicate constitution already a concern.

After a while, there was a knock on the door, and on their front porch stood the pleasant stranger from the Red Cross van, with their promised suitcase! Mam welcomed him in with a shriek, and Diny briefly investigated the contents inside, astounded nothing was missing. Mam gushed with gratitude and hugged the man, thankful for his honesty, and then offered him a container of coffee as a reward for his honesty. He joined the family in their front sitting room for a visit, and a cup of coffee. Diny imagined he was an old friend of Dad's, and the war was only an abominable dream, an unfathomable way of becoming acquainted again with a friend. Later, after the man left, Mam stumbled around, dazed.

She cried, "Even during the war we find good, trustworthy people!"

If she listened fastidiously, Diny heard the earliest morning rustling of trees, of small birds chirping for breakfast, while mother birds scurried to collect and feed. Even in this hungry, famished war, birds found nourishment. If tiny animals found daily sustenance, she would trust God, who meticulously crafted her in his image. Surely, he would not forget them. He would provide food, just as he supplied them with their suitcase just in time.

"O zo!" (Oranje zal overwinnen!) their neighbors exclaimed when exchanging food or household items, with a wink. Indeed, Diny deeply trusted God that Orange would triumph. She knew the Lord remembered her family and her country.

Later in November, there was another bombing, this time coming from the north, with clunky thuds and rattling windows. They took shelter for hours, and the bombardment felt completely overhead the entire time. The BBC reports the following night stated more than 2,000 *Panzer* troops were stationed there north of them, along with Camp Crailo.

Diny wondered at the outcome of the bombardment, hoping the Americans were bombing German troops, if they may be aware of the location. And still, time trudged onward, and after safely delivering Jan up North and returning home, she felt a renewed sense of dread, unable to shake the pain and droning on of weeks filled with cloudy, gray expanses.

When Sinterklaas Day arrived, she wept for Nico. Days filled with routine necessary to keep them alive. With Jan's absence, strength and apt decision-making were more important than before. Without a male companion to offer protection, fears renewed within her heart. She stepped through her day in a stoic behavior, aware of that day's task, then wept as sharp pains of hunger and deep aches of sorrow persisted.

Diny long ago learned to balance her emotions before Mam, who was frail and no longer knitted or cross-stitched as happily as before, read and listened to Vivaldi and Mozart music on the hand-crank record player, until after a while, she concealed their music away to a hiding place.

Many evenings, after the BBC news report, Diny marveled at how Adriaan successfully kept an illegal radio throughout their occupation and sought for a payment of one ration card. They eventually gathered the nerve to ask him where the ration card went, and he mentioned he needed every spare card to help feed his Jewish stowaways! After they heard that, they started paying him two ration cards per week and outrightly surrendered Jan's unused card for Adriaan's efforts. He faced deportation for his bravery at keeping an illegal radio and for hiding Jewish people, but Adriaan never seemed concerned.

"What will be in my life — because of my actions — will be," he told them calmly. "Even if I am arrested, I refuse to change my actions. God has given me a home and the ability to help others. And in your way, you are doing the same!" There were plenty of traitors on both sides to turn him in, even for a reward of food, safety, or escape. Adriaan protected and channeled underground Jews to the proper location, allowing them shelter and respite, and those hidden were called *onderduikers,* supported by Dutch Underground.

In the evenings after those news reports, when their home settled, Diny again remembered her dad in his own battle, perhaps facing greater challenges than they envisioned. Pieter's considerable height carried him above crowds, thick hair swirling high on his head, sparkling blue eyes a contrast to his olive-colored skin. She hoped his leadership skills remained steadfast, as he provided hope and instilled peace in those around him. His thick, wide mustache sometimes hid his mouth's expression, or offered an additional disposition to his commanding rank and strength utilized in uncanny ways.

She wished Dad could whirl his way into the room again, a vortex of unbridled enthusiasm, and return to his beloved family. He was always eager to obtain details about their day, and came sweeping into the veranda, where he would embrace Cornelia's frame, muffling her giggle, whispering about children's watching eyes nearby. Life with a confident yet tender father was fading, and her old existence felt distant. Diny's mind returned to the bleak reality of their situation, and the grim dimness with which they existed. Yet glimmers of hope remained when she journeyed through their home and remembered God's providence and provision. The little geranium plant sat happily in the kitchen windowsill, receiving light during days she peeled back the blackout paper. She offered the plant tender treatment and songs and the plant thrived.

Diny and Mam were filled with hope, praying and believing, "If the plant lives, then Dad will live, and then he will return safely from the war." They survived more than five years without Dad, his strong presence, hearty laugh, and decisive charisma. This wish and promise were something tangible to sustain her until the war was over, when perhaps they might be reunited with him.

Chapter Twenty
Hilversum, The Netherlands, early 1945

Over the last five years, she awoke each morning and her stomach gnawed for food, her head throbbed in exhaustion. She thought of Dad, who seemed alive, uncertain if he was simply unable to communicate, or if he found healing through death. *An irony,* she considered, *of healing through God's mercy, to take away pain by allowing life to end, perhaps to prevent further evil or injustice.* As God promised, when they walked through fire, they would not be burned, although sometimes the fires of life would shape and refine or provide a testimony of a miracle.

She remembered reading in Psalm 116, "Precious in the sight of the Lord is the death of his saints." How impractical the phrase seemed at the time, to consider death as valued or prized in the eyes of the Lord. Those who loved Jesus and died would receive their reward of new, real life with Christ, face-to-face with him, completely restored. He was sparing those saints of all other earthly pain and sorrow, delivering them Home.

Perhaps she had been prepared for this moment through previous experiences. Over those many years of Dad's dangerous police work, she became aware of the fragile state of losing him in the line of duty, as some of his colleagues had paid the price of their lives, killed during a riot or amidst other policing hazards.

Pieter's absence brought exhaustion to Mam, and eroded her spirit. Mam appeared frail and suffered frequent headaches but possessed a strong character. Otherwise, she could never handle all the things she endured — war, separation from Dad, hunger, cold, and sending her son North to survive. So many variables seemed to age Mam, but they all remained strong and dedicated to their faith in God.

Liberated Hilversum, spring 1945

The winter of 1944–1945 had swept over them with extreme bitter cold, which led to "hunger journeys" to find family or acquaintances who could provide assistance, especially for growing boys and families with many children to feed. Severe malnutrition plagued the country, as they endured four winters and little provision for many years of stressful war. Diny heard of starvation, exhaustion, and disease, and eventually thousands succumbed to that fate.

This winter known as the *Hongerwinter* ("hunger winter"), or *Dutch famine of 1944*, arose following a railway strike ordered by the Dutch government-in-exile in expectation of German collapse near the end of 1944. Germans cut off food and fuel shipments to the 4 million people in the western provinces, a place which had no escape and little opportunity for assistance from Allied troops. By springtime, more than 18,000 people had died, and Hilversum suffered additionally from a 20 March 1945 RAF bombing of the German military center in Hilversum, which claimed the lives of nearly 200 Germans.

The city of Hilversum began to feel the rumblings of change in the wet springtime, but Mam shared apprehension believing the war could be ending, especially after rumors surfaced in September, only to cope with air raids, bombardments, and wintertime famine. The South had been liberated, including Rotterdam, but the North — including Amsterdam and their Hilversum — was forced to face the long winter.

Their salvation finally arrived in the form of 5th Canadian Armored Division troops, who bravely chased out the frazzled, unraveled German *Wehrmacht* Army, and genuine hope was realized on 12 April 1945 with the army's arrival. Their Queen announced the Bevrijdingsdag: victory and peace for the Dutch people, and claimed 5 May 1945 as their Victory Day, as papers were signed in Wageningen of a treaty the day before, with Germany's admitted defeat.

Hundreds of American B-17 bombers roared overhead during those weeks of change, and this shift was palpable: airplanes would no longer drop loads of bombs, but food and supplies, much to the relief of Dutch citizens. No longer would they need to eat sugar beets or tulip bulbs, but real food. The Netherlands was liberated, stalwart, strong and determined, with courage through adversity. On Liberation Day, bells across the country chimed again, and activities in each place came to a silent halt, as the bells rang an elegy and a shift in the tide of history, a moving and powerful end to the war. Diny wished Nico was alive to witness this glorious day of rescue.

And then unbelievable elation with singing, dancing, and music. For five years they labored under the oppression invaders, with no electricity and in darkness; waiting in long food lines, fainting many times in the heat, unspeakable pain, friends and family sent to camps, but they lived to see the liberation! Food drops on the 2nd of May provided relief for the starving Dutch citizens, with a white cross and green flares serving as drop-spots for British planes on the important mission of dropping 500 tons of food.

To aid the liberation of the Netherlands, the Dutch government requested each family house several Canadian soldiers, and the Dekkers happily complied, since they were so thankful and relieved to be alive, and for God's grace in sparing them. The soldiers shared Jan's room, as Jan remained in the countryside with Oom and Tante until they could deliver him. The two Canadian soldiers living with them post-liberation brought along gifts of chewing gum and chocolate for their new Dutch friends, and Diny slowly savored each bite of chocolate tasting sweet after years without sugar. Chewing gum tasted just as wonderful as ever, and she quickly allowed herself to recall little indulgences they lived without for four years.

Shipments of food arrived and care packages airplanes dropped included white bread, butter, and sardines. White bread tasted like cake after years of eating tulip bulbs! The United States also dropped Enriched Sunshine Crackers which saved many lives, as Dutch citizens were severely malnourished.

One Canadian soldier seemed especially fond of Diny, and blushed while in conversation. He helped her with cleaning, lifting, chopping wood, and so forth. He was a rightful hero in the minds of Dutch citizens and took certain liberties with his character and actions. She viewed him as thoughtful and helpful, fulfilling his duties as a soldier. Yet he was intensely interested in Diny and acted assertively in his affection. One evening, he handed her a small square packet, along with a bar of chocolate, presumably as gifts, and pointed up the stairs, smiling. She spoke little English and felt dumbfounded at his lack of communication.

He waved and gestured, then went upstairs. She shrugged and went about the tasks of her evening, before opening the small square packet to reveal a rubber tube of some sort, closed on one end; she remained naïve concerning the use of the item. When the soldier returned downstairs, Diny hovered above the sink, peeling potatoes, with the rubber tube on her finger, to protect her hand from the sharp peeler. She smiled and held up her hand, thanking him for the "potato peeler protector" to shield her hand from scrapes. His face reddened, and he laughed, and then ran outside.

Eventually, Diny learned other friends faced similar propositions, perhaps due to the nature of a long war which proved frightful on all sides and without real relationship, especially with soldiers on the front lines. Some European women who found victory also found a sudden relationship, whether forced into by situational poverty or mutual affection for those soldiers who saved them. Looting was another common occurrence practiced by soldiers, whether they desired to obtain the "spoils of war" for their family, or for personal gain, like securing a financial reward by selling the looted items once they arrived home.

After the liberation, excitement spread, permeating in dancing in the streets, and singing — happy times. After the final export of Germany, as discussion of war trials and criminals began to surface in the news, they discovered many sad stories. Some Europeans faced retribution for collaborating with Germans as an act of treason. Dutch women who had German soldiers as boyfriends or husbands were treated harshly by outraged fellow citizens, who shaved the women's heads and painted their bodies orange, while the women mourned, because they were traitors, aiding the enemy.

Some worked for the Dutch Underground and for the Germans as a spy, traitors cooperating with Germans. Those women were shot, the Law erupting independently, and violently as weary Dutch citizens believed the punishment was valid and legitimate outside of the courts. Those who betrayed their fellow citizens were identified as traitors and received a swift judgment after the conclusion.

Some Germans in Amsterdam would not leave quietly on Liberation Day, and machine-gunned crowds in Dam Square, shattering the liberation that dozens of people survived to see, only to die after surviving the war. Mam warned Diny and Nelly to remain at home with the paper coverings on their windows and doors locked and barred. Curfews and rations remained in place.

The Dekkers were fortunate to remain in their Hilversum home during the war and were never sent to a camp but suffered their own hard times. The Germans removed everything of value from their lives, replacing security with constant fear, without providing much food, all enduring frozen winters. Yes, they discussed their immense hatred and anger for the German soldiers spilling from their hearts, alongside a deep burden of sadness for the cruel events which occurred.

After the war, Diny brought those feelings before the Lord to ask for forgiveness and healing. She sought to reconcile, a way to move forward, away from hatred and bitterness. Post-war was an intense season of gratitude for being alive, shock the war had finally ended, and later, once those initial feelings subsided, incredible humility coupled with disbelief and sorrow for those who were lost. Friends were lost, entire lines of their families, candles of their own generation extinguished without memory or testimony. Grief seethed through their bones and festered concerning altered futures.

Chapter Twenty-One
The Netherlands, late spring 1945

When roads were safer and spring rains dried, rebuilding began. Food became more readily available, and Mam burned the blackout paper in the wood stove — a joyous day indeed, of sunshine spreading through open windows again, with no hindrances or darkness! And open windows at night, no matter the cold!

Then Jan returned home, and Oom Cor and Tante Sietske brought farm food to share with them, with stories and miracles of God's grace. They relayed experiences of distressed families visiting them, desperate for assistance, which they provided as they could. Gerrit and Etje had also fared well on the farm in Kollum, Friesland, which brought additional joy. They felt anxious to hear about Pieter. The geranium plant survived, still flowering bright blooms, leaves green and healthy, soil rich. In her heart, hope remained.

One evening, while cozily surrounded by neighbors, Adriaan shared the BBC update: tulip bulbs were poisonous and should have killed the citizens who consumed them! Diny felt more surprised by Adriaan's survival of the war, after boldly rescuing and housing Jews, and retaining a radio for daily news broadcasts. He was brave and unswerving in his gracious efforts, and she prayed God would reward him for those actions. The Lord kept them safe — whether from poisonous tulip bulbs or the enemy.

Over the years of war, with the postal service unable to navigate the disastrous roads and railways, Diny received sporadic letters from Nico (until the fateful day in September 1944), and Lenny ter Haar, her best friend from Batavian school days. Lenny remained in the Dutch East Indies and was eventually placed in a camp with her mother and sisters, facing an uncertain sense of severity in the war there, and the lack of supplies world-wide suffered many toward isolation and mere survival. After a few years, letters from Lenny faded, and Diny suspected the ter Haar family were probably rounded up and interned in a more confining camp which did not allow any outside interaction. Diny wondered if they were safe, as the war continued there, Japan unwilling to release the stronghold.

After the Netherlands found liberation, their lives tried to return to some normalcy, including radio programming. They all enjoyed commentator Henk van den Bout, who continued *Radio Oranje* during the war, and started the public broadcasting again, bringing hope and healing over the airwaves.

The end of the war provided the solution to numerous predicaments. In conversation one may wonder, what if a friendship was separated because of race, for being from the wrong country and living in a new country? A spirit of suspicion arose during those long years. Were actions justified, like a lie, deception, or false identification card worthwhile, because of the magnitude of evil surrounding them?

Could their actions be cleared before God, who called them to revere the Bible as their ultimate source of guidance? Creating ration cards and false papers may be viewed as survival, of outwitting the enemy at their own "game" (the most dangerous game), and survival meant creating falsities of their own. So much of those six years involved fear, despair, and lack of certainty. Their lives became necessarily insular, and basic. Hierarchy altered for survival. Everything emerged and changed.

Hilversum, June 1945

In June, when spring's fog evaporated, a figure appeared at the front door and knocked gently, three times, and in the glaring sunshine, Diny could not see who rapped at the door. At first, she thought the lanky figure through the glass might be Jacob, finally stopping over with Nico's correspondence, per noted in a telegram. She had not visited with Jacob or Tante Sluis in many months, since Nico's train was bombed in September 1944.

While she rejoiced in Jacob's safety, she sighed at the prospect of speaking to him, knowing their conversation would invoke emotions, since losing Nico remained a new trauma. For months, she refused to believe Nico was truly gone, that his train had altered the life they purposefully created. *So many tears shed for the living and the dead*, Diny thought. Diny never kept letters from Nico, even those simply addressed to his *Meisje*, as she feared those words would be used as leverage against her family. All letters burned in their wood stove, curling back into the flame; a bright flash, then ashes.

She opened the front door, and a man in his 30s turned to greet her. He was slight with black hair, sunken eyes, and dark complexion. She recognized his name as he spoke: Ro DeHaring. His embrace was willowy but sturdy, and his smile broad and welcoming.

"As one of Nico's jam salesman colleagues," Ro assured, his hand on his heart, "I promised Nico I would deliver something to you." Out of his worn rucksack he pulled a package and unwrapped bundles of sugar, salt, flour, and coffee, along with an Allied parachute.

Diny was baffled. How would Nico's friend Ro DeHaring come across this package — and the silk parachute?

"Nico wanted you to have this package, Diny," Ro explained. He looked at her quizzically and smiled. "You have not seen Nico in many months, I might guess?"

She shook her head and said, "We have not heard from him in nine months. He was to visit in September 1944, but his train was bombed. We know Nico is gone."

Diny theorized how Ro kept this package all these months, since before Nico's train bombing? She wished to see Nico, to ask about the parachute adventure.

"The North and South lost all contact after the September bombing, after Operation Market Garden," she reminded Ro. As the front porch whirled, her brain dizzy, and she cried about twisted metal, the stench of death, and the loss of their expectant future. All the emotions of the last six years culminated, and she fell in a heap, as she finally felt able to release the numbness.

Ro caught her as she fell, assuring, "Diny, let me help you sit down." He brought Diny into the sitting room and placed her on the couch, then brought a glass of water to her.

He closed the front door, slid the heavy brown paper package over near her feet, and sat next to her. "Diny, you must listen to me very carefully. Nico brought this package to me just two weeks ago. He was desperate for you to hear from him, since he was delayed in arriving all those months ago...." Ro trailed off.

She sat up quickly and gasped, "Could he possibly be alive? His train blew up. Planes bombed the tracks, *Ro*, and Nico's train derailed. The tracks were gone, people were gone. We never heard from him after that night!"

Ro repeated, "Nico knew you would ask about this! He feels terrible for any lack of communication. But he wanted you to know he exited the train just minutes before it was bombed. Diny, Nico is alive!"

Diny covered her face with her hands, weeping with joy and disbelief, with the pain of separation, of not completely knowing, and finally an answer in the sunshine of the late afternoon, a sparkle of a *Someday* together.

Ro allowed her a few moments to compose her thoughts and emotions, and to wipe her face with the handkerchief he offered her.

"Nico said he collected the parachute after his three days of hiding with one of our colleagues during Operation Market Garden, when Americans were parachuting into the Arnhem area. He had to hide in a bakery, or something. Did you hear news reports about parachuting soldiers?" His face was wild with relief.

She remembered the horrible night nine months ago when they grieved the loss of Nico. The radio crackled on into the evening, reporting hundreds of Allied soldiers successfully parachuted to Dutch countryside, unaware of all which lay in their path below, behind the enemy line into the Netherlands, safe havens of hay fields, barns, or trenches, to advance on securing the Rhine River. Their mission was to capture the bridge over the Rhine at Nijmegen, and deliver American and English armies into Germany, easily accessible from the river.

As the oldest city in the Netherlands, Nijmegen always trembled as a battleground, as Charlemagne built a castle there. Locals were hardy, accustomed to securing their location, yet became the first to fall into enemy hands. With only one way over the Rhine meant the Allied efforts had to work perfectly, yet the leadership provided minimal planning for this event. Meanwhile, many of the same planes which dropped soldiers took hits from the German ground troops, and crashed to the ground. The Allies named the attack *Operation Market Garden*, which the military called a big failure. But Diny remembered…a small glimmer of hope remained of the tide of war shifting.

That September evening, Diny recalled, Adriaan casually remarked, "They tried to drop all the men at once but were unable to successfully drop all the men at night, and the rest…well, their daytime advance was dangerous and foolish at best."

Ro de Haring leaned against the banister. "When they landed, they tried to blend into the countryside. Dozens of parachutes were discarded everywhere! I wonder how all those soldiers found each other! Those maps were a sorry mess."

Diny caught a glimmer of youth in Ro's eyes. And she pondered how strange an act might look, of a farmer out the next morning to milk his cows, finding a parachute in the field or soldiers falling out of his hayloft. But in times of war, nothing seemed improbable.

Of the 20,000 soldiers who successfully parachuted from airplanes (to later convene at Arnhem), more than 17,000 were killed, captured, or missing. Losing the Operation Market Garden campaign escalated the violence in the area, and Arnhem and Nijmegen remained an exclusive fighting area, as Germans held the rivers. The Dutch estimated an additional 1 million were killed through fighting, as a result of the Hunger Winter, and other causes, because the Allies were unable to conclude the war by Christmas 1944 as they hoped.

She touched the parachute's soft, durable fabric, crumpling the silk between her fingers, wondering at the *whoosh* sound the release must have made when a soldier deployed the ripcord, then wondering at the soldier's fate. When Ro told Mam the good news, she also shrieked with joy. They all thanked God for saving Nico. He was alive! Ro stayed for evening tea with her family, and they all ate with a lighter spirit, a renewed disposition. When Ro departed to spend the night with his own family in Amsterdam, Diny sewed a jacket out of the military parachute, so Nico could retain a positive war memento to wear, the steady sheath of a parachute transforming into rain protection.

As radio coverage increased, they learned more of Operation Market Garden and the subsequent results of that campaign. Henk van den Bout reported on the *Radio Orange* that because of the severed connection between North and South after September 1944, while parts of the South were freed during the winter (Nijmegen and North Brabant), they could begin to venture out and clean up the wreckage of the last five years.

Many Dutch found great difficulty returning to a normal existence. What was *normal* now? Where was a regular life when people lost loved ones, or simply never heard from them again? Did they dare move to another home, country, or life, in case their missing beloved returned to the family home, in some distant future? People attended church more frequently, and with renewed interest and tried to establish a new pace, find a house and a job. Schools had not yet returned to normal, and many companies were in financial — or literal — shambles. Rediscovering a new happy, positive way required flexibility and innovation — with as much grit as they demonstrated during the war.

Chapter Twenty-Two
Hilversum, July 1945

The next week Diny received a letter from Nico, addressed to, *"My Diny"* written in his precise print, and signed by his scrolled name, *Nico*. He explained everything, as he understood her deeply curious nature. When Nico disappeared in September 1944, Nico departed the train at Arnhem, a bustling station, to swap packages with another man working for the Dutch Underground, and spent too much time in the transfer, believing his train would linger before departing.

He dashed to board his original train, but in accordance with precise Dutch time keeping, his train had already departed the station. As Nico waited for the next train to arrive, he lit a cigarette, but the train never came. He could only wonder what happened.

The railroad line in the southern part of the Netherlands was disconnected, and as there were no resources to repair the tracks. Nico remained in Elst and his next assignment delivered him to Arnhem the week of 17 to 25 September 1944 during Operation Market Garden, where he witnessed Allied soldiers parachuting to gain the river stronghold against Germany. 11 miles north at Arnhem the British troops Red Devils were trapped, hemmed in behind enemy lines, facing slaughter.

At the Waal River, troops were ordered into a daylight raid with boats crossing the river. About 250 men started across, but 125 were dead in 20 minutes, as Germans spotted them crossing the river in daylight and shot them. Some aggressive paratroopers crossed successfully.

Four hours later, they all reached the bridge and heard tanks going north, but were uncertain if those tanks were Allies. The Germans failed to blow up the bridge, and British General Peter Carrington did not order Allied tanks across the bridge. He did not feel adequate supplies and reinforcements would follow and refused to lead his men into a slaughter. General Sosabowski's Polish unit, along with Americans, seemed more confident of their ability to hold the bridge, but the whole situation seemed as a way for each country to blame the others.

Nico wrote his memories for Diny to read, as though they were conversing in person. That Sunday of Operation Market Garden held beauty as a mild autumn day, and Nico heard a harmonious thunder coming from the west. There were airplanes flying low and covering the sky, heavy roaring and clanking noises in the air. Above, airborne soldiers lined the doorways of their planes, crouched, and prepared to jump. When a green light in the doorway flashed, soldiers jumped one after another from the plane, one every second, almost atop each other, into combat.

They freefell for a moment before deploying the woven nylon parachutes. Meanwhile, airplanes speckling the skies were intermixed with streaming parachuting men, and some parachutes entangled, men falling together, while other soldiers gracefully glided into fields. On the ground, they discarded their parachutes, then briskly advanced, bayonets fixed on their rifles, ready for combat.

Fires roared through fields, and in the frantic velocity of the moment, after gawking at the sight, Nico and his colleague sought to find shelter. They were jam salesmen and translators, completely surprised by men parachuting into the countryside. Without any cover or protection, and with distrustful farmers refusing to shelter them, Nico found an empty bakery and they hid there. At first, they hoped the owner of the bakery would not return during battle and turn on the oven in which they were hidden. But from the appearance of the bullet-ridden, rundown brick bakery, they realized it was abandoned.

They remained there, two jam salesmen sheltered inside the baker's oven in Elst, for three days during the heaviest fighting, to avoid being shot by either side of the fighting. They spoke Dutch, English, German, and French, yet could not trust an Allied soldier who had been trained to shoot. They were unable to chance coming across the wrong unit, or a group of soldiers unwilling to take prisoners before deciding one's nationality or loyalties.

Nico later learned his location was quite close to Brigadier General Sosabowski's Polish unit seeking to cross and secure the Rhine River, which was indeed "a bridge too far." But Nico humorously told Diny they never wanted bread to go with their jam! Additionally, one specific memory of Diny he focused on during the three days cocooned inside the baker's oven, as parachuting soldiers marched into the occupied countryside. To remain sane and quiet in the baker's oven, Nico retreated into his mind, to fortunate, blessed times, visiting a memory from the earliest days of their courtship.

He shared that memory with her in the letter:

Their Sunday afternoon ritual of saying "so-long" at the Hilversum train station was one of loveliness, just moments before he boarded the train to his return to work in Elst after a weekend getting to know her. In his memory, the springtime of 1940 warmed them, as their friendship became detailed, enhanced, important.

He noticed Diny's slender wristwatch, her lean frame, her dancing brown-eyes, the sweet dimples which framed her tranquil smile, the ease in which she wore a crisp red-and-pink floral summer dress with a blush sash tied on the side. Her caramel hair was light, her oval face was tan, and her dazzling pearl earrings danced on her ears. Diny's sparkling necklace boasted a single white pearl, the thin chain barely visible but mesmerizingly spiraling up and down, glimmering on her neck whenever she spoke and breathed, rolling up and down on her collarbone, iridescent.

There was an unmistakable agility and grace to Diny's entire being at the time, he recalled, her countenance both naïve and uncomplicated, before the burden of war. She laughed with a spirited lightness and they embraced, her luminous smile glittering, before he sauntered toward the train, reluctantly traveling east.

His neat writing looped in emotion at describing that memory, his wording widening as though he wrote at a quickened pace.

This moment in the train station was also the last time she purely saw him, he supposed, the last moment they connected in simple, untainted motives. It was the *before* time, *before* his mobilization and to fight in Captain Christiaan Boers' army in May 1940, the last time to observe their relationship unsullied from war or famine, without agendas or hidden counterintuitively.

While hiding in the oven, as Operation Market Garden clamored outside the bakery doors, Nico heard Diny's shimmering voice, rippling with laughter as though she were with him. Those final ephemeral moments his ears shrieked from pain and later went numb, his skin sweat clammy with streams of dread and fear, his eyes closed to the inevitable heat or bullet. It was all he heard: the pace of horse hooves on concrete, bayonets clashing, and his galloping heartbeat, but also Diny's vibrant laughter soothing him, before he simply concentrated on slowing his breathing, as he strained for air, for life.

Nico's letter overflowed with gratitude for God's grace, as his friend Henk Mulder never reported Nico and his Dutch Underground friends, and God's hand protected them from German retaliation. After the war, members of the NSB were arrested. After a trial, they received a punishment of execution or labor in camps.

Henk was arrested and accused of war crimes and faced his own court case and trial. The judge sentenced Henk to a camp for one year to serve as reparation for his crimes. Nico never learned of the complete extent to which his friend betrayed the Netherlands, the details regarding his arrest a shameful mystery. Yet Nico felt incredible pain surrounding their friendship. Still, Nico dreamed of reconciliation.

Nico was Diny's rock, and she only realized the truth after he disappeared. He bravely loved, even at the risk of his own personal harm or the loss of their future, their hopeful Someday together. After nearly losing him, Diny finally understood the treasure she cherished in her beloved Nico. And yet, Diny's emotions remained with her dad, and his unknown fate.

Nico updated Diny on the fate of his employment at Taminiau Jam Factory. When the Allied armies parachuted into the Arnhem countryside on 17 September 1944, the Taminiau Jam Factory plant was suddenly in the middle of great tumult, the war recklessly hurled upon their front steps without any intention of retreat.

The next day, a number of delivery trucks were blitzed with ammunition in the railway yard, which brought significant damage. By November 1944, those who remained at the factory had to evacuate, as they feared a flood of fighting from the Betuwe without escape. Mr. Taminiau decided to relocate the jam production to Oss, a Dutch city which had been liberated in the autumn. Meanwhile, the north remained in a steady state of war and would not find relief until May 1945.

The stock of jam was transferred to Oss via 654 car loads. The administration side moved south to already-liberated Nijmegen, and staff members returned to the factory in Elst as often as possible to restore it. After several months, the Elst factory could again be used for production purposes, but the raw materials — jam, sugar, packaging materials, and fuels — were lacking. Live mines littered the countryside and roads were not safe. The Elst factory hoped to resume its production in late August.

Hilversum, end of August 1945

On 15 August 1945, the war at last officially ended in the Pacific as the Japanese surrendered, the battles lingering months beyond the end of the European conclusion. The Dekker family prayed they would soon hear about their beloved family, and at length, weeks later, they finally received news. The Red Cross in Switzerland sent them a telegram, telling the family the fate of their dear, strong father Pieter.

Mam sat in her chair to read the news, *black-on-white*, tears mottling her face. The telegram reassured them: Pieter Dekker was still alive!

He required intense and immediate medical attention and was sent across the sea to Singapore. Pieter would require weeks of recovery before overseas travel, and would arrive on the *Nieuw Amsterdam* ship traveling from Singapore to Rotterdam in April 1946. Diny's emotions soared with the thought of Dad's survival. With their hero still alive, they turned their thoughts to their dear friends and servants who remained in Indie, and their beloved Batavian home, now in ashes. What was left behind in their previous home in Batavia? Their entire life was pillaged, all possessions lost. Would anything have remained?

Most European homes in the Indies were invaded by Japanese soldiers, ransacked, and stripped of valuables, which were sold on the black market. Then the home was occupied by a high-ranking Japanese official until the end of the war. Their servants were likely spared, able to remain in their homes. Any happy reunion with those Indie friends seemed implausible.

Mam recited that night from Matthew 6 in the Bible, tears on her face in truly absorbing the lesson. "Store up for yourselves treasures in Heaven, where moth and rust do not destroy, and where thieves do not break in and steal. For where your treasure is, there your heart will be also." Remnants of the war lay scattered everywhere.

On Diny's walks in the Hilversum countryside, she dared not wander from the paths which had been cleared of mines by the Dutch army. Weapons and machinery were still being discovered in homes and fields and collected by the Dutch army. Their lives could return to a semblance of normalcy, but the memories and pain would not soon fade.Diny walked past various pieces of shrapnel, bombed-out homes, and other items not yet discovered. Gathering remnants of the war seemed to unify the country, assisting those without homes or family. In compiling, they were connecting and healing.

Their discoveries were enormous — from elaborate and destructive plots uncovered in German journals to barns filled with vintage stashes of wine or halls of cellars layered with stolen paintings, the walls covered with Golden Age Dutch Masters like Rembrandt, Vermeer, van Oosterwyck, or Hals. It was as though one had stepped into the 1600s and into the effervescent light of place, the thick and golden air of remembrance, harkening back to an era when the Dutch East India Company was in its infancy and the entire enterprise of trade was still in the early years, the landscapes and optimistic capture of light unmatched.

The point in time recalled able seafarers and keen mapmakers touring the Emerald Girdle of the Dutch East Indies to establish the commercial enterprise launching the monopoly on Asian trade. Assembling a massive collection of paintings required the assistance of the enemy, food in exchange for family heirlooms, much like Diny and Jan had encountered on their journeys to assure his security and safety.

The grandest homes served as local German soldiers' headquarters during the war. Some salt mines hid treasures untold, corralled in there by Germans. Neuschwanstein Castle in Germany boasted the largest collection of stolen paintings, and the Allies sought to restore those to the rightful owners. Museum curators wept with gratitude when paintings were returned, so the masters could again be shared by all. Recovery continued in many forms along subsequent months, and they remained on food rations and other restrictions, slowly remembering what a normal existence resembled.

Hilversum, March 1946

One brisk spring afternoon, Nico telephoned to speak with Diny.

"Nico? Is this truly you?" Her elated squeal overpowered his engaging voice.

"Indeed, who else would I be?" Nico laughed, sounding deeper and more assured, maturity revealed in the depth of his intonation, of his twenty-nine years.

"You called to whisk me away and marry you, is that right?" Diny invited.

"True, although I am quite far away, and the roads to get to you are horrible," he joked. "In all seriousness, Diny, I desperately want to marry you, if you will still have me."

"I will. But I grieved for you, did you know, Nico?"

He cleared his throat. "What do you mean, my *Grietje*?"

"Every emotion, every thought I wished to tell you, a lifetime of regret and pain which lasted nine miserable months after your train was bombed. We thought you were gone, and I felt like a widow, even though we never married. And eventually, I lost track of all I needed to tell you, so I started writing it down, for later. Maybe for heaven. I rather wish to tell you in person, to see your eyes when I share with you—"

"My eyes, Diny?"

"They are quite lovely and expressive, Nico, and I discern your thoughts by looking at your clear blue eyes."

"Thank you. Your eyes are dark and mysterious, Dien, but I still fail to read your intentions."

"You called me to discuss our charms? Or hear my laughter?" She chuckled.

"So true. Your laughter sparkles! In fact, I have good news. I pursued employment in the Dutch East Indies and found a prosperous opportunity to begin working in New Guinea."

"New Guinea! I have never been."

"Well, now you shall live there, and very soon. The job is in a growing, flourishing profession as a salesman for import-export trading company *Jacobson Van den Berg.*"

"Marvelous and congratulations, dear Nico!" she rejoiced.

"Thank you, Diny," he replied. "But I also have very sad news, *Dien*." His voice trembled. "A telegram arrived from Indie, informing us that my Father Pouwels died —" his voice broke.

"*Niek*, how horrible! I am so sorry!" Diny cried.

"Father passed away in a prisoner camp near south Sumatra, on 9 December 1944. He was imprisoned at Muntok men's camp, on Bangka Island. Have you heard of this place?"

She gasped, whispering, " Tell me what happened, Nico."

"I have only pieces of information, but he went to a brutal place off the coast of Palembang, Sumatra, on the tip of remote Banka Island. Muntok was an internment camp for Dutch and Europeans, but it makes no sense. Father Pouwels was an accountant; he did not work for the police, like your dad. My father loved everyone, and was known as a cheerful, happy man."

"Yes. Why would the Japanese imprison him?"

"He was European, Diny. That is what the Dutch Government says, and what Mother believes. Europeans were rounded up and forced to live in horrid conditions with little food and forced labor. They were tortured, beaten, and humiliated. Only the lucky ones survived."

Diny gasped. "Lucky? We have not yet welcomed my dad home, and who knows what he will look like, but I would guess he does not feel *lucky* to live with those memories."

"Yes, Diny. Your dad will not soon forget his personal miracles! But this is so painful, still a wound, and my dear father is gone forever. If only you met him!"

"Again, Nico, I am sorry. I wish you and I met long before the war… to become acquainted with your father like you are acquainted with my dad."

"Indeed. We had not heard from my Father for several years. But still, we all hoped and prayed for his safety and wellbeing."

She insisted on more details about Muntok Camp, and he revealed what information he knew: It was a dozen hours' boat ride off the coast of Sumatra, secluded, inaccessible. Muntok Camp was not liberated by Dutch troops until 10 February 1946, long after nearly one third of the Camp's inhabitants had already lost their lives.

"All I can think is that when Father died, in December of '44, the Dutch south was already freed, while you had to endure the terrible *Hongerwinter*. Father's homeland was partially freed, but he was still imprisoned. Mother Pouwels remained isolated in her Hilversum home, also at war. If only he survived to see the Allied victory! What joy he would have felt!"

"That cannot take away the pain of your loss, I guess, nor at wondering of his soul."

"No, but I see the irony of freedom through death, and the Netherlands free after him, and I know he would appreciate that. But he is not here for me to share the irony! After I moved from Indie to Hilversum, I never saw him again, *Dien*, which I regret."

After Nico left the Dutch East Indies as a young man to return to the Netherlands, he could not afford to travel long distances back to Indie to see Father Pouwels. Then the war interrupted everything, all plans and lives and travel.

Nico continued. "Did I tell you my sister Jopie kept in contact with Father? Surely, I mentioned it, of their letters in the early days of war. After Father's arrest, he was first interred in a camp on Java, in overcrowded European housing, with high fencing and Japanese soldiers ensuring their incarceration.

But even then, his letters were full of hope, and he received food. Certain camps were homes surrounded by wires. The men in his camp showed great care for one another and courage despite the adversity, sickness, starvation, and death they all encountered. Then the letters stopped, just before that day we flew kites together. Do you remember?"

"Certainly, Nico, a frightening prospect!" Diny cried.

"Through those letters, Jopie discovered God's great blessing and promise, because Father Pouwels shared about his personal relationship with Jesus. He wrote about God's hope in his letters to Jopie. *God's hope*, Diny! Jopie discovered that Father Pouwels had accepted Jesus as his Savior! An atheist no longer!"

They both wept with gladness.

"Remember the grassy park next to a stained-glass church in Indie? Some days, I stopped at church after school, to rest in the light of the colored glass windows, begging my Heavenly Father to change my Earthly father's heart, for Father Pouwels to accept the saving Grace of Jesus."

"Yes, Nico," she replied. "God answered your prayers! Only He can bring someone to salvation. But the moral is: Father Pouwels accepted God's free gift!"

"*Dien*, I have an unspeakable joy and peace," Nico said, "because I know I will reunite with Father Pouwels again in Heaven!"

Nico considered visiting Muntok and his father's island grave, but would he discover peace? The Japanese transferred Father Pouwels from his camp in Java to Muntok in Sumatra in September 1943, as after that time, his letters stopped. As consistently as Germans documented every move, meticulously recording, photographing, and detailing their madness, the Japanese secretly moved prisoners to various camps to keep their location discreet. With less paperwork to track those prisoners, families might not find proof or trace their imprisoned loved ones. Father Pouwels was shuffled from Java to Palembang along with other men.

One of the nurses in the Palembang camp, Vivian Bullwinkel, was the sole survivor of the Bangka Island Massacre on 16 February 1942. She joined other women who formed a singing chorus under the direction of Margaret Dryburgh. The chorus rallied their spirits in the camp. Eighteen months later, in September 1943, all European men in Palembang were moved, serenaded harmoniously by the women as a gracious farewell, the men exiled to the breezy, remote Banka Island and treacherous Muntok

Camp. Prisoners squeezed tightly onto boats for 12 miserable hours to cross the teal-colored Bangka Strait, in choppy, headstrong waters surging against them, like an arm channeling the water in fury, warning them of peril on the island.

From September 1943 onward, Muntok camp (Muntok meaning "at the tip of," thus, at the tip of Bangka Island) east of Sumatra, served as an assembly location for all European men from Sumatran camps. They were annexed in the former Muntok prison, a short distance from the island's rugged, but glorious shoreline of black volcanic rocks and clean sand and clear sea, yet escape was futile. Residential camp leader, A. Oranje, was a former Police Resident of Palembang.

Muntok Men's Camp suffered under Japanese Army Officer Commandant Captain Saiki (Seki) Kazue, who treated prisoners poorly just for sport, his heavy hand an extremely harsh regime, especially regarding systematic starvation and withholding medical attention. One-third of the male occupants of Muntok would not survive to liberation. As an older man of 64 years old, Father Pouwels needed medications, care, and rest, and despite a sturdy constitution he remained susceptible to disease and malnutrition.

Infections like dysentery were common in close-quarter camps without proper hygiene. Prisoners suffered bouts of constant malaria sicknesses — or even "Bangka fever," a type of cerebral malaria — and beriberi (severe, deadly lack of vitamins and nutrients) and infections, pneumonia, starvation. But the notorious Captain Seki required excessive labor, literally working the men to their graves. His co-tormentor was Lieutenant Miyauchi (aka *Miachi*), whom the prisoners called "The Snake," spoke English and was meticulously groomed with a thin mustache and slick European haircut, as though to fit in with his prisoners.

Finally, after the Indie liberation and recovery process, the Red Cross informed Nico's family via telegram of Father Pouwels' death. Mother Pouwels faced her own "black-on-white" reality. Despite their divorce, they still loved each other and had raised five children together.

After the war, Dutch citizens who perished in Indie were buried in the Dutch War Grave Cemetery established for them, and Dutch military soldiers photographed graves for families, for some type of closure from their loved one's death. Pieter Pouwels' grave was in the military cemetery and contained a simple white cross with black lettering adorning his neatly arranged plot:

> P. Pouwels
> 5-9-80
> 9-12-44

P. Pouwels, born 5 September 1880 in Amsterdam, died 9 December 1944 in Muntok. Father Pouwels' cross and grave remained peacefully situated in a grassy plain, with green rolling hills behind, verdant landscapes with mango trees and palm plantations, and in the distance, the clear emerald sea.

Chapter Twenty-Three
Hilversum, April 1946

Insecurity no longer surrounded Diny as she strolled about their narrow home, tidying each book and candle, opening lace curtains, and washing the glass clear to invite bright sunshine. The previous six months were filled with recovery. She glanced out the front sitting room window again and closed her eyes. *Will dad remember me?* She recalled her father's tall frame and warm embrace. No doubt his sturdy constitution sustained him during years of war. She reminisced his laughter resounding over the echoes of their Batavian home, his energy and humor returning each furlough, as though rest and peace pervaded his spirit.

They survived five years without comfort from her father's engaging presence, years of uncertainty, bitter cold, and darkness. The geranium plant was nurtured and kept alive. She never hesitated in her belief. Again, she heard his voice and turned to the front door. Next to Mam stood a skeleton man, a head-shaved stranger. She recognized his gentle blue eyes — the same, yet gaunt and now haunted — and his weathered skin and embraced her father fiercely.

"Dad! What a miracle you have returned home!" she began, and recoiled as his skin was thin and fragile.

"Here I am!" his voice broke, crackling. "A bag of bones, I am… not much to welcome back, but thankful to be alive, all the same," Dad whispered. The embrace exhausted him. Dad showed his expression in his eyes, and he had lived strenuous years and war broke him.On returning home, Pieter slept for hours, all afternoon and into the evening.

Mam remained near him upstairs with rice, chicken, and broth, yet he could only manage chicken broth. He whispered, "Moderation in everything, Cora. This is crucial to a healthy and lengthy life," and then he slept again. After a week, he emerged from the haze to rejoin the family. Dad rested upstairs all day, reading and praying, then descending the stairs for tea and supper each night. He then retired upstairs, as though the dinner hour drained his vigor.

At night, the children heard his screams and Mam's hushed, soothing voice through her tears, along with her offer for a cup of tea to calm Dad's nightmares. This lasted for a few weeks, until he could remain with the family for evenings. He might not return to the robust presence they once knew, the man of joy and kindness.

"Pap," Diny asked one evening, "Have you heard of the miracle of our geranium?"

He shook his head and settled into his chair, his eyes alight with curiosity.

She brought over the plant, which still bloomed and grew.

He was delighted by the little geranium plant kept alive, and held it closely, inspecting its soil and smelling the earthy blooms, rubbing green leaves between his fingers. "A sturdy and exquisite geranium plant, Dien; I am impressed with your gardening skills. Well done!"

She beamed and shared her story: "I prayed to God, asking Him to keep you alive, and I proclaimed that as long as this geranium plant lived, you would stay alive. It was a pact with the Lord, something I begged him for, like a fleece on the grass. This promise kept me hopeful for six years!" Diny's eyes spilled tears and she hugged her father.

Pieter laughed, shaking his head, and held the plant in the air. Lifting his head, he thundered, "Thank you, God! What a miracle, *Dien*, of God's grace and faithfulness!" before handing it back to Diny. A sense of his sparkle had returned.

Upon his return to the Netherlands, Pieter refused to share personal stories or tragedies with his children, who each faced their own challenges post-war. "These trials remain close to my heart," he said, "and this is for your own protection."

Jan could not understand Dad's decision, especially as his formative teenage years without his father required adventure stories interlaced with that mystery. If he remained away for six years, he should provide tales of his voyage, of some kind of heroic journey.

"I was away from you, my dear family, whom I loved and prayed for day and night," Dad pondered. That was more horrible than anything the enemy could do. Being apart from you for six years was my greatest torture."

Mam carried a heavy burden, and some evenings the pain in her eyes returned, her hair tightly upswept each morning, by afternoon loosened to ease her head. Mam still suffered migraine headaches (despite her six-year absence from the humid tropical climate) and endured the knowledge of her husband's pain and suffering after learning of Pieter's experiences.

Surely, he cannot share everything with her, Diny considered, *for he knows of her frail health.* But she refrained from urging his discretion in speaking, realizing he remained the authority at their home. Diny sensed Dad's need for solitude, out of a way of grieving. Now, at her father's return, she could only assume the assorted dynamics of their home. She protected her heart against anger, for she knew Dad's brokenness and Jan and Nelly's pain from Dad's absence. She recognized their realized loss of humanity and cumulative deepest sorrow.

Pieter, once a man of vibrancy, returned a shell of his former self. He returned to their Hilversum home in April 1946 nearly as frail as Mam. Before the war, his larger frame and personality occupied a room, and as a sturdy, animated man of more than 91 kilos (200 pounds) of muscle, of capable strength. He returned to them after his six years of horror as a skeleton at 47 kilos (104 pounds). Pieter previously loved to laugh at games, and play with his children. After his return, however, he seemed haunted, his eyes vacant and occupied.

Pieter divulged to the entire family in terms of general, recounted stories, which they previously heard in the Netherlands on BBC or read in smuggled newspapers: the Dutch East Indies' highest commander, Governor-General Tjarda van Starkenborgh Stachouwer, with 100 local Dutch highly ranked government leaders (including Pieter Dekker), were taken captive by the Japanese on 9 March 1942, and placed into camps, beginning with Mulo School and Mei Ling Villa to assemble the official leaders, whose families were taken to other camps.

"Locations involved a community camp centered in wealthy European homes, including some leaders imprisoned in their own former, emptied home, much to their shock and dismay," Pieter said. "That once-vibrant, family neighborhood became a painful place for them." Fences with barbed wire, bamboo mats covering the outer walls, and guards established boundaries, to enforce a zone of a camp for those people, sometimes a dozen men to a single bedroom.

"Then came chaos, as they separated leaders and transferred them, our comrades removed from our presence. We woke up one morning and half of the leaders were gone, on to another place. We hoped to stay together during the war. In the middle of the night, early on, Stachouwer was taken away. We were already inside a camp, so where could he go? We all thought the worst."

The Japanese transferred Stachouwer and other KNIL military leaders to 10th Battalion's Encampment, which served as a processing unit before shipping overseas to other Asian locations. The primary governmental leadership was later separated to prevent communication or any capitulation plans.

Mam brought Dad a cup of tea for his throat. "Then they took me away. I was no longer in Batavia. We faced the monsoon rains, endured diseases, beatings, and labor, and felt constantly starved. Some military colleagues were shipped to Manchuria (China) or to Burma to work the Burma-Siam railroad built by those foreign hands, essentially thousands of prisoner slaves in Asian hands. Others were liberated in Thailand, the Philippines, or Formosa (Taiwan), and the rest, well, I cannot tell you their stories, for they carried their heroic tales to the grave...." He trailed off. Diny realized those friends did not return at all. Those poor families left behind!

Many of those heroic stories were never told, as they involved sacrifice — resulting in death — of true love pouring out, of glorious endings for honorable lives, and other men were spared because of a singular, sacrificial death. Those who were lost, who went on ahead, possessed stories never fully known, their storyline one component of an even greater narrative, just as the results of their efforts affected those whose lives were spared through those heroic actions.

Dad never fully divulged to his inquisitive, curious children the extensive anguish the Japanese inflicted upon him, nor could he state the measure of which he owed others his life. He remained on Java the prior six years, under the rule of harsh Japanese, in a state of horrific war, stripped of humanity, absent of most kindnesses. Only Mam knew details, intimacies, and pain. Dad witnessed and endured terrible things at the hands of the Japanese. And suddenly he returned to his family again, into a supposedly regular life, although his wife and children were recovering from their survival of the war.

"Regardless of all the pain," Dad considered, "God gave me immense joy upon my return to the Netherlands, because I discovered you were never taken away to a camp."

Mam nodded. "Yes. Despite our meager lives, we remained together at home."

Even the adjustment to comforts took a while, as Pieter laughed, "I am also thankful to sleep on a soft mattress in a bed again, instead of on a hard palm leaf mat on the dirt floor!"

Chapter Twenty-Four

In the deepest still of the evenings, their home quieted, in unreserved moments alone in cozy chairs before the blazing wooden stove, Pieter shared openly with Cora, his strength returning to attempt an intimate conversation. He piled wood into the stove and the air in their living room was warm and comforting. A singular lamp was lit between them, alighting their faces. Cora set a large pot of tea on the table nearby, with snacks. She poured a cup of tea for her husband.

Pieter relaxed into the comforts of his own home, the horrors behind him a bit more removed; his experiences seemed a faraway torture instead of a present fear. He invited Cora to hear his story, the narrative of his imprisonment. Her eyes widened as she nodded, then she stopped her cross stitch; he waved his hand at her, insisting she continue stitching.

"Well Cora, as you know, I lived at the Hotel Schutte Raaff during our year apart, and you received my letters detailing my work protecting women and children, setting the police force on a healthy course, and closing out our Batavia home, sending you money and letters."

She nodded.

"So, I will instead tell you about the changes, when my life there fell into war." He lit a match to ignite his pipe, the tobacco curling into the bowl, smoke rising slowly. "When the war began, I grieved at the disruption of Asian-European relations, since we made progress on relationships in Indie, providing education and infrastructure and leadership training. Let me start from an earlier time."

He inhaled from his pipe, then exhaled, smoldering. "When I arrived in Indie, I noticed the change in atmosphere. Something shifted, indiscernibly. I prayed, asking God to offer the way to reach others for Him. Then Pearl Harbor was bombed. At first the Dutch leadership panicked when we heard of Japan's attack on Pearl Harbor," he said, "and the sense of dread remained. I prayed the Lord would protect us.

"Looking back, while living in Hotel Schutte Raaff in 1941, I heard rumors from staff and had talked with world-traveling guests, and it was only a matter of time until Japan extended a forceful arm against other nations. Over the next few months, the Dutch leadership realized any plan of neutrality in the Islands would never prevail, especially in light of the Netherland's May 1939 declaration of war — of an advance — or at least a defense, and we knew Japan would invade Indie as well."

Bright orange lights flickered through the fire, and Cora removed her shawl from her shoulders, then continued her cross-stitch. She adjusted her glasses and gazed down to concentrate on her pattern but nodded for Pieter to continue.

He set his pipe aside. "On 21 February 1942, the Governor-General had a plan to step out and meet the enemy, instead of awaiting some unknown fate. He called for all high government officials to leave Batavia with him, and so we traveled in a caravan 200 kilometers to Bandung to prepare a truce and halt Japan from invasion."

Pieter held his blue and white teacup and stared at the rug beneath them, his large hands encompassing the delicate glass cup, the saucer rattling underneath.

"On 28 February 1942, Japanese began landing on Java, and a day later occupied Bandung's airfield. American-British-Dutch-Australian — ABDA — all fought hard to keep the Japanese off the islands, but they were quickly overwhelmed. 'We are the world's premier colony,' Stachouwer assured me. Then he asked, 'So why do we need a massive army when we command the respect of all we rule in our empire?' He could not envision the vastness of 17,000 islands and a miniature Dutch-Indie army, since he assumed the native Indies boys would always fight for us, as though their allegiances traversed culture or ethnicity!"

"Well, Pieter," Cora considered, "we all knew the Indie people always wanted freedom. You and I would fight for the same thing. No surprise the islanders supported a Japanese invasion. Everybody knew this except the Governor-General?"

Pieter took a sip of tea and nodded. "Yes, my love. This was always a point of contention between me and the police staff, of Stachouwer's posturing and assumptions regarding our general safety over the years, coupled with his disastrous scandal involving The Resident. He was naïve concerning the alliances of Indiens with other Asians. Despite my urging, Stachouwer never built the Dutch army to a fighting strength in numbers, as you saw here in the Netherlands, with the German invasion accomplished in a few days. That was a wretched embarrassment."

Cora narrowed her eyes. "Our dear Nico fought heroically at the Afsluitdijk over the Ijsselmeer, where the Dutch defense was strong, and Captain Boers was successful. They held the line, the only Dutchmen to do so! They were 'lions'! Yet the Germans threatened to bomb Rotterdam unless Dutch armies retreated, so they regrettably retreated. And you know, they bombed us anyway. Rotterdam was flattened in an instant."

Pieter leaned forward and slowed Cora's fast-stitching hands, looking into her eyes. "This will *never* make any sense, my dear, sweet *Grietje*. That was infuriating, one of many lies from the Germans. The whole war was horrific. We can never look back. We must forgive, thank God for his protection, and hasten forward."

The air began to cool, embers slowing in their descent, and Cora pulled her shawl tightly around her neck. Pieter calmed his rattling teacup on the side table, then sighed and stood to fuel the stove with additional wood to heat their home and conversation.

He returned to his seat and continued. "On the 5th of March, the Dutch surrendered to Japan. By the 9th of March, our whole Dutch government and military personnel, and all families — those still back in Batavia, too — were taken as prisoners, the men separated from the women and children. The Japanese commander told us we would be imprisoned by the Japanese military until there was peace, and that the Dutch East Indies would cease to exist because of this war. They took us to Glodok Prison and then we all were scattered to various camps."

The warmth in the room had adequately returned, and Cora handed Pieter her shawl. He held it tightly as he whispered, "Our first taste of horror was Soekamiskin (*Sukamiskin*), in Bandung, West-Java. At the Sukamiskin, notoriously rumored to employ the most horrendous torture, few survived to the end of occupation, encountering even greater casualties than the typical death of one-third of all imprisoned. Bu, thank God, I only stayed there briefly. After Sukamiskin, they transferred me to Kedoengbadak (near the rubber plantation) in Buitenzorg prison, housing us in bamboo huts. Then in February

1944 they sent me to another miserable place near Baros, west of Bandung, to a place called Tjimahi Battalion Camp 4.

"We were higher in the mountains there, and the mornings were calm and cool, reminiscent of our family holiday times there together. Yet, while in prison, there is no grace found in those morning mists. Only a dreadful anticipation of the daily beatings we would be forced to endure. We were told we had no homeland, that the Netherlands would shrivel into defeat, and that our Queen had abandoned us."

Cora nodded. "The Queen did escape to London in the early days of war."

Pieter continued, "In March 1944 in Camp Tjimahi 4, we were issued a number — a number! — to sew onto our clothing. I no longer answer to 'Pieter Dekker,' but rather 'Prisoner 28.377,' property of Japan. On 5 May 1945 — *Dutch Liberation Day!* — I was part of a transport of thirty distinguished men who were transferred to the VIP camp 6th Depot Battalion, also known as Tjimahi Baros 5.

"Upon arrival in Tjimahi 5, I noticed many prominent prisoners, including other high-ranking officials, professors, civil servants, and business leaders. We all suspected there was a reason for this, and then we received new "prominent prisoners" red triangles to sew onto our work clothes right next to our prisoner number. With Tjimahi Camp 5, none of us with a red triangle were permitted to leave the camp. They feared if we escaped, perhaps an uprising of some sorts might occur, with our leadership skills.

"The guards also watched a select group of intellectuals, including Rob Nieuwenhuys, Leo Vroman, and Tjalie Robinson. They printed a camp periodical called 'Kampkroniek' (Camp Chronicles) and a pamphlet named 'Onschendbaar Domein' (Inviolable Domain). They were eventually sent to another camp, however. Even the Chinese Mayor of Batavia, Mr. Khouw Kim An, was imprisoned in Tjimahi, and he sadly died a day before the Japanese surrendered."

"How tragic," Cora said. "What happened to the men who left the camp to work each day?"

"Several thousand men and boys were forced to work on the railroad outside Bandung, but I could not, due to my red triangle. My work remained inside the high white prison walls, underneath the red tile roofing, behind the barbed wire and *gedek,* the mats fashioned out of bamboo strips which kept us from seeing out the fencing, preventing hope. Not a single tree existed inside our camp. I longed for the shade of a tree, the breath of nature which

I so loved and where I always found God, a sanctuary. Each of the twenty-seven bamboo barracks had hard cement floors and were assembled around an empty quad where we lined up each day."

"So even though there were no trees in the camp, God spared you from working on the railroad," Cora said quietly. Her face was warm by the orange glow of the fire.

"Yes, that is truly a miracle! And even missionaries were given those red triangles, though they were a humble lot of prisoners. Their ministry and nurturing continued inside the camps. Eventually, the Japanese considered us 'unlucky VIPs,' but really, we were the 'wrongdoers,' or the *'djahats'* as they called us. Our Barracks, number 27, was in the Guard House and Police Center. They did not trust us, for certain, and kept their guards nearby to prevent any uprising."

Johan Henry Smith, with whom Pieter co-wrote the police training manual, also served in the police force. He returned to teach at the police academy at Soekaboemi in 1940, serving as the last Western director of that academy. The *Kempeitai* — Japanese secret police — tortured him dreadfully, yet he survived the war and returned to Amsterdam. Their journey side-by-side from one camp to the next remained one of Pieter's greatest comforts throughout internment. During moments of fear, they recited Psalm 23 to each other, a balm for the pain.

"Smith knew me before the war, Cora, and the kinship we experienced while writing together at the Soekaboemi before the war remained strong at all the camps in Buitenzorg and Tjimahi 4 and 5. He endured frequent, unwarranted torture, gone for days at a time, and we were not sure if he would survive, after his time in bamboo cages and God-knows what other beastly punishments. I, on the other hand, probably deserved all the beatings because I spoke up too often. I was accustomed to being in charge, I guess! I do thank the Lord that after the war, Smith was still alive, and he returned to the Netherlands with me."

Cora nodded and smiled through tears.

"Many prisoners, despite their status as POW or civilian, were relocated to other places, with expediency as though the Japanese chose chaotic methods to wear down and lose track of those prisoners due to excessive transfer paperwork. Family members might be unaware of the location of their loved ones. Moreover, the Japanese seemed stoic and reserved, considering surrender disgraceful and cowardly. They viewed our capture as a dishonor to our families. Perhaps they justified the bamboo stick beatings that way. But they wanted us to fight so they could keep lowering our spirits. If we fought back, we knew we would see the sharp end of their bayonet. It was humiliating."

Cora whispered, "Tell me about the conditions of the camp, Piet. You tell me where you went, but not what happened. What did you eat, and where did you sleep? Can you share those daily details?"

Pieter's eyes widened, and he gasped. "I suppose I can muster the courage. I am not sure you can handle those horrible things, Cora. It was as close to Hell as I will ever encounter. Each place seemed as ghastly as the previous, with no respite or liberation. What if I share and you have nightmares?" His face writhed in pain.

"Pieter, *schatje*! My darling!" Cora cooed, stroking his face, "I have raised three children, all of whom have faced incredible difficulties from illness to heartbreak. We survived our own war here, in our own suffering, so I am not immune to darkness. Please try. Perhaps in speaking of the horrors you can let go and heal."

Pieter nodded. "Labor camps were designed to terminate the prisoners. Imagine screaming, enraged men waving swords at you, yelling at you to hurry, striking you with a bamboo cane if you slowed. If the labor failed to mortally damage a person, there were diseases which easily took hold, like constant dysentery, bouts of malaria with subsequent sores and blisters, or *beriberi*, deadly lack of vitamins and nutrients due to the little they fed us; pneumonia, starvation, dengue, tropical ulcers, or even mental despair."

She held his hand.

"*Dat is alles*! That is all! No more, Cora. Nothing!"

"Set your heart free by relieving your mind of this pain," Cora urged.

He stared into the flames. "Every place is the same, from the beginning and lasting four years. Death…torture. Daily beatings or caning with a bamboo rod, Japanese chants, roll call before sunrise, calisthenics based on Buddhism which prisoners were forced to perform together. We stood in alignment in rows and columns for hours while hungry, bruised, bones broken, bleeding in body and soul.

"Then the daily work, for eighteen hours, of mostly meaningless tasks. If that did not finish a person, we faced solitary confinement for a simple slip, or a public beheading if we tried to escape. At the beginning, three men were lynched in the middle of the camp because they had escaped overnight to see their women and children at a nearby camp. Was that worth it? No! Surely, they regretted a foolish, hasty choice, which cost their life.

"If the commander did not like you, he might send you into isolation, days in the bamboo cage under the full sun, in a blistering heat. Do you know what happens to flesh under the sun for three days? Peeling skin off a live person, bit by bit. And then if you survived, you faced infection… and bugs that live off those infections and feed off their hosts at night."

He sighed. "If you want me to carry on, I can. But why? For what purpose? I keep the most torturous events quiet inside and ask God to banish them to the depths of the sea. But I tell you: by the end, we were lucky if there was a spoonful of rice or a slice of dry bread to eat or starch water to consume."

Cora remained pale, her mouth agape.

Pieter continued, "Maybe I was spared because of my VIP status? My work remained inside Tjimahi camp, and not out with the rest of the men. At times I felt guilty, but I trust God for that path. For sure, at this age, malnourished, building a railroad in Bandung would have led to my death."

She nodded and wiped away her tears. "And we praise the Lord for that Pieter, we do! I can only imagine the lack of hope — God's hope — that pervaded the camps. I believe the Lord spared you! A true miracle!"

She embraced him, and they remained in each other's arms, both sobbing. Cora handed Pieter her handkerchief and asked, "Now that you have bravely shared, can you tell me about what you heard from the outside world? Did you know of anything with the war ending in Europe? What could you hear about our troubles?"

Pieter's face softened as he wiped his face. "Throughout the years, the reports were sketchy. Someone in our VIP camp had an illegal radio and heard of bombings in Nagasaki and Hiroshima. For the first time in years expected liberation, that perhaps the Japanese Emperor would admit defeat. The Japanese finally surrendered our camp on 22 August, and we were freed — along with thousands of others — Dutch, Australian, British, French, and Americans. And the next day we held a church service to thank the Lord for his provision in keeping us alive! We sang and prayed and cried together. What a joyous day!"

"Did you find food, then, at liberation time?" Cora held the handkerchief to her chest.

"Yes, with the Japanese gone, we found warehouses piled full of stored, rotten food…unbelievable to us. But we were starved not only for food, but culture, for a sense of humanity and decency. Sometimes we were permitted to celebrate a Japanese holiday and the camp director allowed music or theater productions. They were meager and poorly acted, when men feared their pitiable performance might cost their lives. But for that hour, we were human, and for that moment, everyone sat before a stage, entertained and equal. These diversions were coping mechanisms. Those opportunities faded the next day, but music remained in my heart."

"What music?" Cora's eyes squinted.

"Famous Polish violinist Szymon Goldberg was a VIP in our camp, and his violin remained intact. Do you know, Szymon is a Polish Jew and was on tour in Asia when the war broke out? He left Europe, escaping the grip of the Germans, but the Japanese captured him."

Cora gasped.

"After liberation — which he survived to see — Szymon Goldberg invited the whole camp into his barracks and gave a violin concert, playing Mozart and Beethoven Sonatas, the loveliest of tunes ever delivered, and with gusto and emotion! Cora, I have never heard sweeter music at a tender time. And all I thought of was you, dear *Grietje*, to dance with you to Szymon's liberated violin, to the music which reminded us we were still alive."

She hummed, her voice straining, "Soon again we shall have our own music, my *lieve*."

He nodded. "Indeed. In due time."

Cora gestured to the gramophone. "Shall I, darling?"

He shook his head. "Szymon was a lucky one, with a special violin. The dear chap was clearly Jewish, and all the news reports show that Germany was determined to exterminate the Jews." Pieter stared at the carpet.

"What a blessing for Szymon, and for his family!" Cora exclaimed. "I do wish I could dance with you, to his violin playing or the gramophone."

Pieter shook his head and continued with his narrative. "Since we were all malnourished, everyone in camp was feeble and weak. And not all the artists survived. I need to tell you about the writers… the painters… Cora, the doctors, lawyers, and scientists, the inventors, accountants, so many brilliant men, gone. I cannot fathom how our world can carry forward without them."

Cora reached out for Pieter's hand, and he slipped his cold hand into hers.

"Despite all the beauty they tried to create with painting, writing, or music, many of their voices were forever lost. I looked at their faces as they withered and thought of how young they were, and each man had an entire lifetime ahead of him, and that creativity was exterminated."

Cora nodded.

"And then came the Bersiap uprising, the Indies people fought for their independence, and those who left the camp were rounded up again with curfews and gated off until the British secured our safe release. It was a big mess, for sure. Four months after the 15th August V-J Day and the end of my four years of Japanese internment, all the Western internees were finally emancipated from the Dutch East Indies. We were shipped to Singapore for transport just after Sinterklaas Day. Of course, as you know, I remained in Singapore, too ill and weak to travel, until I arrived home to you in April."

Cora cleared her throat and pulled at the fabric in her cross stitch. "And what became of Governor-General Stachouwer? Did he remain with you on Java as well?"

Pieter's eyes widened. "No, after various camps on Java, including the 10th Battalion in Batavia, in late 1942 the Japanese transferred him to the Manchurian camp at Hsien (now Liaoyuan), along with other prominent military prisoners, including American General Jonathan Wainwright, until his camp was liberated on 16 August 1945. Only military personnel were transferred outside Indie, which is how he ended up in China. Stachouwer was the military leader… and he survived the war."

She sighed. "Good news indeed. Perhaps he can move forward with his life as well."

"Well, yes. I praise God for that. But Cora, I could not bear to tell you at first —" He paused, his face foreign and contorted, his voice strained. "We were released on the singular condition to leave Indie permanently. I will never return to our beloved Dutch East Indies."

Cora gasped.

He continued. "The Japanese would only relinquish control under certain circumstances. They were determined to hand over power to the Indie people. They are not prepared for leadership and cannot grasp the full consequences of Japan's leadership over the course of four years, nor the way their trade and treaty would unravel."

"What then of your career? Pieter, you are the Head of Police in Indie! Your office is in downtown Batavia, in the government headquarters with the palm trees lining the square, with the red tile roof, and you — you are surrounded with an important task. You cannot abandon that post! What about your pension?"

He bellowed, "Yes, my perfectly aligned office in a stately building.

Think not of trivial pursuits. Our time there is finished! I served my year and intended to retire. And our desires matter little, now, Cora."

She covered her mouth.

He continued, his eyes wild with emotion as he kneeled before her, "I return to you a hollow man, a shell of my past, diseased and starved! What man is that? I cannot sleep or eat to fill the void! We lost all we formerly knew. There is nothing to return to there." He buried his head upon her lap.

Cora fumbled for the right words. "We can always hope, Pieter. Hope remains alive, as our children thrive, as we remain married. The world needs our message of hope! Maybe this was a temporary settlement. Of course, in war, commanders say strange things? Does Stachouwer know of this supposed decree?"

He lifted his head and nodded. "Stachouwer was liberated abroad with other famous prisoners and is negotiating his popularity here in the Netherlands, where he will receive honors and accolades. I do not desire frivolity. Moreover, there is no reason for him to return to Indie. His honorable retirement is imminent, and his lot is secured, so why should he trouble himself with my vocation?"

As part of his liberation, Pieter was forced to leave Indie, a country he loved, which became his home, a place he diligently served for almost three decades and nearly gave his life for, never to return. He arrived in the Netherlands after more than six years away, returning to a damaged country and depleted morale. He was a changed man, a thin hollow of his former self.

Pieter's voice was muffled, his throat raspy with emotion, and he wrapped his head in Cora's shawl. "This is all. I have nothing else for tonight, Cora," he moaned. "*Dat is alles… no more.*"

Cora set her completed stitch work on the side table and loaded more wood into the simmering stove, which would still be roaring when the household awoke. She turned off the lamp and recognized the first birds of dawn chirping, then shuffled Pieter upstairs.

Of course, he would never tell her some of the stories which haunted him, which disrupted sleep and would likely remain attached to those years away, ways he could never separate himself from that experience, nor find a measure of humanity within those cells. He remembered needless deaths each day in Tjimahi due to preventable diseases, malnutrition, and dysentery.

A women's camp only 10k away surely faced similar challenges. The

Red Cross was never allowed access to the camp prisoners, nor their conditions, but forced to speak only briefly to a camp leader. The valuable supplies the Red Cross delivered were never handed out but hoarded in warehouses and shacks for the duration of the war. Japanese guards withheld rations, and food supplies were meager. The Japanese leaders were often corrupt and recruited from substandard military ranks. They were arrogant, suspicious, and cruel, working the European camp directors against the prisoners. Japan promised more food, but the prisoners received less. Camp commandants would be transferred away, only to be replaced by an even harsher leader.

The camp breakfast came to them in a bowl of starch (like the kind for washing clothes) with brown sugar. Then, at lunchtime, they were fed bread, but that bread was created with yeast made from human urine, collected in large vats and assembled properly by a group of imprisoned chemists. And finally, dinner consisted of watery rice, only 100 grams per person, with some strings of radish swirling around. Not appetizing, nor filling. Men were lowered to accomplish meaningless tasks, lining up for roll call, spending hours in the heat of the day with the sun blazing on their heads and shoulders, required to stand still.

The unspeakable acts, the beatings, torture, men in bamboo cages in the square, under the heat, dying in pain, urine-filled bread and starch and famine all filling his mind when silence filled their home. He was stripped of clothing, belongings, and dignity. Perhaps to encounter those traumas now, the hope of returning to "normalcy" might provide Pieter with an opportunity for healing. Either way, he was permanently changed.

How much had Cora sacrificed for love? She fell in love with the man and not the adventure. Her roots had been established in the Netherlands and she longed for a life there. When she eventually received that wish, the war came and separated them for six years. Her eldest loved the Dutch East Indies, becoming attuned to the rhythms of that world. But Cora was an introvert and overwhelmed by social structures and formal interactions. The Lord provided her extra measures of patience and kindness to endure there. Surely her character was stretched and matured. And through the development of faith, Cora found deep and lasting joy. But sometimes her heart lingered on the sacrifice.

She recognized the irony surrounding her life, as their Furlough allowed Cora to return to the Netherlands, the homeland she dearly loved, but within the year, her darling husband was far away and in harm, in their familiar Dutch East Indies. Pieter, the epitome of certainty and decisiveness, always provided balance for Cora, who was rather swayed by emotion. During a long war, which stretched on for years, she needed his wisdom and guidance. The Lord provided evidence of love and provision as she navigated raising children in those lonely years.

Cora had prepared to marry a boat captain or farmer and instead married a police officer, navigating not ships or plows, but morality, honor, and ethical righteousness in Indie. She had been raised for a life of service and stewardship. And as a strong leader, an extrovert in the spotlight, Pieter drew attention to their family, much of which tended to overwhelm Cora and further suppress her abilities to mingle socially. Her migraines only exacerbated the challenges of an introverted life. As they settled back into a world of marriage and family, post conflict, Cora could only speculate how their altered lives would propel them into an uncertain future.

Chapter Twenty-Five

Pieter Dekker was forgetful, perhaps not remembering some of the six years away, mainly due to the malnourishment of his body. He was thin when he came back, just like a big bag of bones. Mam and the kids were required to adjust to having a man leading the household again, after years of Mam as the head of the house while Dad was gone. And she eagerly and willingly gave the role of head of the house back to Dad, glad and relieved to offer him the full responsibility.

The children were shy, as Dad had been gone so long, so much had happened, and they required tremendous time to become reacquainted. Even Jan's return took readjustment, from his life in the country and expansive space on the farm. He had changed, maturing into manhood at age seventeen, his gaining height and deepening voice and new command, while attempting to express his deepest sadness about Dad's absence during those important teenage years.

Frequently, they prodded Dad to share about what had happened in the camps, and Diny thought since she was twenty-five years old, he might reveal more, but Dad only shared the "nice" things. While eating supper one evening, he promised after they finished eating, he would indulge her in a memory.

"Okay, *Dien*, I have an anecdote for you tonight. Sit down to hear the entire story."

She settled into the straight-backed sofa and smiled eagerly. Jan and Nelly filled the spots beside her, eagerly anticipating their father's tale. They studied his weathered face. He held a book in his hand for emphasis, scrutinizing the cover.

Pieter's blue eyes narrowed, and his eyebrows were raised in anticipation. "One time…."

They all leaned forward, and he cleared his throat.

He began again. "One time, a Japanese guard gave me a piece of bread with jam."

Diny glared at him blankly. "Then what happened?"

Nelly sighed, her mouth open, and Jan fidgeted with his feet.

Dad stared back and chuckled. "The story is complete."

"A very short story, Dad," Jan mumbled, "and not charming enough to be a poem."

"Okay, you want more details, my dear children? Well, I relished every little crumb of that bread, and savored each sticky measure of that jam! In short, I ate the entire gift, and licked my fingers afterwards!"

"Grand story, Dad." Nelly yawned.

"Indeed, Nelly! That sweetness tasted like grace! It was an answer to prayer!"

Simple blessings like bread with jam were a lifeline and raised Dad's spirits, offering him hope for rescue. He remained free from bitterness, leaning into God's grace. But he was unswerving in his secrecy.

He exclaimed, "The past things which happened had a purpose. I am not sure I will ever know what every purpose was, but I trust God with each step. All I know is I am alive; I thank the Lord daily for his grace! I only want to look ahead!" Dad refused to linger in the past, in hate, which stunted growth and would not serve any productive purpose. This proverb of Dad became extremely important in Diny's life, to urge her to continue leaning forward, toward all the wonderful purpose God had in store, to journey with the Lord toward hope, reconciliation, and peace.

The war stripped away dignity, tearing at their souls. They could either choose to remain in a calloused place of horror and frustration, cycling around in fear and guilt, or live their best lives, demonstrating their courage to heal, to diminish the pain via joy and laughter. They must remedy the pain lurking in their hearts. Vitality and method coupled with discipline and honor always served him well for a police career. And yet his heart shredded as he unstitched four years, much like Mam ripped fabric as she unfurled thread, her embroidery piece needing a restart. This was his unraveling, and he would emerge from the swell, but he was first required to seek God's peace.

They went to Zandvoort to walk along the shoreline's lulling waves, and Dad traversed the fine sand edge between sea and soil, the line of wind forming a path to journey. Diny stared at the foaming remnants of waves, at the traces of swirling bubbles left behind on the damp sand, layers of lines washed smoothly into submission, layers enshrouded. Her Pap ventured up and down the shoreline, sorting out his emotions, much like he used to in their gardens or on other holidays, seeking God's voice and leading.

When they returned home from outings, a sense of simplicity emerged. Mam and Dad lingered in front of the wood stove at night, the whispers of Dad's war stories muffled, their togetherness much like their respite in sitting on the breezy veranda after Huib's death, holding hands, peace intermixed with pain slowly finding healing, a new bone reset and mending.

Pieter was not present during part of Diny's growing up years (February 1940 — April 1946) but faithfully mailed her letters during the beginning of the war. She vigilantly saved those letters, but soon, keeping the correspondence was not possible any more, as the thin paper tattered, and the ink faded into blank yellowed tear-smeared scraps. Her father was strict but loving in his discipline. He did not have to warn the children, often, because they knew he meant what he said. Dad was a rock. Diny admired him, loved him totally, and although he did not talk much about his love for the Lord, he certainly lived it. As a normal teenager, she rebelled against Dad's discipline, but he stood his ground and refused to give in to her crying and pleading. Now, as she had matured into young adulthood, she happily related to him as an adult.

Also, after the war, Mam was not looking forward to telling Dad about the episode where they had to sell his precious stamp collections to remain alive. When she finally gained enough courage, one morning over breakfast, Mam placed Dad's plate of food before him.

She then admitted, "Your stamp collection is gone, so please do not ask about the book. I know the stamps were precious to you. Their value was important... for your brothers and their survival, as well as ours, for money and false papers for Jan to go North to your brother's farm."

He glanced up from his newspaper, genuinely interested.

She fiddled with a napkin. "I apologize that I had to sell your stamp collection during the war, Pieter. At first just part of it, but later, we sold the complete collection, and for that I am deeply sorry. And ashamed."

He shrugged, then exclaimed, "It was just a hobby, Cora, a passing novelty — a sport, really, and a paper diversion at that. And I am so happy it saved your lives!"

She sighed, and they embraced.

He did not seem too surprised but understood. "I purchased and saved those stamps for many years as a delightful amusement, never realizing they would buy food and identification papers during war. It is only material stuff, Cora, and you needed to stay alive!"

She began cleaning breakfast pans at the kitchen sink.

He cleared his throat, then confessed, "And I suppose now is the best time to tell you… I had to sell my wedding ring to buy food in my camp."

"Oh? I wondered where we had hidden your ring, and here you had it all along!" She dropped the pan into the sink, ran to Pieter, and embraced him.

They both laughed and cried about God's provision found in material items, which previously held great sentimental value, yet possessions were tools for their survival.

As difficult as his years of internment in Indie had been, Pieter loved the country and deeply desired to return to assist with rebuilding the government and systems there. Yet he soon realized he could never again pick up where he left off. He discovered the sad truth in a disappointing way, for after he was liberated from his camp, the transforming government required him to promise to never again return to the islands. In exchange, he would receive his freedom and a one-way passage on a ship to return to the Netherlands.

At the time, he said, he considered a verbal treaty not a legal and binding agreement, but rather a scare tactic so those in Indie could begin the process of rebuilding without the Dutch, British, Australian, or any other non-native nationalities. He never imagined the idea would become a legal matter, so he eagerly pursued resuming his work there.

Pieter recovered at home in Hilversum, gaining strength, holding the hope of returning to Indie, until he reached the point where he felt prepared to work. That summer he contacted the police force. He was so enthusiastic to help set up the police again and regain the momentum established just before the war. Dual thoughts of his loving family and of his police work in Batavia often kept Pieter alive in the camps.

But when he called the police leadership, they just dismissed him flatly. "We do not need you anymore. In fact, they do not even need us either, as everything is in the hands of the Indie people now." The nationalist revolution began, and rebellions and uprisings simmering decades before the war, coupled with the disorder of the war years continued.

And the dreams Pieter had created, which had literally sustained him during the camp years, were shattered then and there in an instant.

He admitted to a sense of satisfaction only later, in realizing the Indie people desired peace and prosperity in their own way, on their independent terms. He eventually received a memorandum dated 28 August 1946, fully describing his immediate release from police duties. Pieter never imagined his own *black-on-white* reality. He eventually accepted it and did not fight it, recognizing the truth during an afternoon tea break on the backyard patio. Cora stitched, Diny knit, Jan sketched, Nelly napped, and Pieter read the newspaper, his face hidden.

He affirmed, "Cora, this transition was necessary for all of us, you see. The Indie people deserve a chance at ordering their own lives, at real independence… and this is the ideal time."

She wiped her cheeks with a handkerchief.

He nodded once, only his puffy hair visible, then folded his newspaper and set it to the side; his eyes were glossy and occupied, and he stared into the distance toward outlying Hilversum heath, where the delicate lavender-colored flowers and late-summer meadows gave way to woods.

Diny awaited his follow-up commentary, which she knew he believed, but perhaps this day he could not find the voice to state, as he had countless moments before in a bellowing and decisive voice, *"Well, my children, in many cases in life, we are required to go through hardships and disappointments to reach our goals — and there is no other way."*

Pieter looked at Diny, his eyes soft and glowing a magnificent blue through the tears, then stood, released a bicycle from its resting location by the wall and unlatched the gate, to ride alone into the darkening purple heath.

{4 Ministerial Decision of 28 August 1946, no. 10415 on the dismissal of the members of the commission, P. Dekker and P. Goeknegt, 1946}

CHAPTER TWENTY-SIX

Mam removed a record from the paper sleeve, dropped the record into place on the gramophone, and aligned the arm and needle for music.

"Cora, dear, I have little energy for merriments these days." His hand waved at her generally, and she stared back at him flatly.

"I desperately wish for music, Pieter," she cried.

"No Mozart or Beethoven — at least, not yet."

She clicked off the machine and sat in her chair with a book. Since Pieter's return, he could not bear extra noise, insisting on silence for recovery. Mam scoured the Hilversum bookshop for Dutch hymnals to replace the ones they lost in Batavia and hoped to procure a new collection of ancient European poetry. She felt especially lost without her Chesterton and Moody readings, consistently jotting down a list of a few items here or there which she felt saddened to lose and desired to replace.

Jan reminded him, "Dad, we do not need those dusty ancient books when there are new books being written of the ongoing revolution."

Dad looked up from his newspaper and said, "Because of the war, our beloved Indies were changed, and our life there is gone." He would not reveal what the Japanese probably did to their home and belongings in Batavia, but from Cora's expression, she knew those personal items were long gone, anything buried rotten or destroyed.

Their radio or gramophone hummed cheerily with music again when Dad took his daily walks, and when he returned, Cora raced to silence their music. Pieter gasped at newspaper reports stating 200,000 Dutch men and women died in the war, which meant the Netherlands had the highest per capita death rate of all Nazi-occupied countries in Western Europe, at 2.36%. Another somber report: more than 30,000 citizens died in the Dutch East Indies, either fighting the Japanese or interned in camps, including Nico's father, and many colleagues and friends.

Eighty percent of all people interned by the Japanese during the war were in the Dutch East Indies. The Dutch colony was #5 in the top ten countries with the most casualties during WWII (more than Japan, #6 on the list). During evenings in their courtyard, Pieter folded his paper, set it onto the table, and rode his bicycle into the heath until dark.

Eventually, Dutch public spaces like art museums reopened, and Cornelia sent Diny on errands to procure books filled with pictures of Rembrandt, Van Gogh, and Cezanne. As Pieter's energy slowly returned, he warmed to new experiences, and he was ready to listen to music, to allow melodies as background to their activities. Musicians like Schubert, Handel, Bach, and Mozart still felt like friends to Diny, although her father stated he may never feel the same concerning the German composers.

In the sitting room, Pieter wept during Wagner's operatic movements, huddled in his overstuffed chair, surrounded by a blanket Mam knitted one evening. He stared out the window during Beethoven's dramatic overtones, and escaped to the backyard during Vivaldi's cheerful melodies, to the late autumn splendor and the freedom found on bicycle, pedaling hard against the violins screaming *"L'autunno."* He returned after Vivaldi was silenced. The music could once again orchestrate their activities, even though their lives — and emotions — had become thoroughly complicated.

Jan remained especially distant and had grappled with a significantly trying adolescence while his father was gone. Returning to church services seemed especially important to Pieter, and he urged his children to prepare in a respectful fashion.

"Come here please, *Dien*," Pieter urged Diny one Sunday morning, minutes before their intended departure.

Diny shuffled over to Dad and scrutinized his eyes, which seemed tired just moments after waking, and she wished to remove the burdens he continued to carry.

"*Dien*," he repeated, "gaze outside at the weather, my *Meisje*."

She glanced outside at the steady rain showers down, gathering in pools in their yard. Their street turned into a river and gushed down toward the watch shop on the corner. She wondered why she had not noticed the roar of the water and wind against their home.

"Cora, look at Diny's *sepatoes*. Her shoes are unacceptable for monsoons." Pieter sighed.

Cora glanced at Diny's feet and nodded, her mouth upturned at his liberal mention of *monsoons*, considering their non-tropical location.

Diny shook her head and folded her arms, her face solemn and set.

Pieter continued. "I want you to change out of those silly shoes right now. Put on your galoshes for church."

Mam, Nelly, and Jan stood at the front door, with raincoats, hats, and galoshes on, prepared to leave. They all glared at Diny.

Diny refused, pointing at the suede slip-on shoes she wore. Weeks ago, a shop welcomed visitors by holding a grand-re-opening of sorts, with orange triangle flags stringed together to note the celebration. Inside, the store seemed reborn, shelves filled with goodies. There she found suede shoes.

Diny heard her father's opinion but looked lovingly at her shoes, their warm chocolate color matching her eyes and dress perfectly. Her shoes indeed looked striking, like a tiny luxury.

"Dad, I just bought these at the second-hand store. I am twenty-five years old, and this is my choice!"

He declared, "Change your shoes this instant! Diny, I am still your father! Though engaged to marry Nico, you are still a single woman under my direction. Moreover, you will ruin those shoes in this weather. They were a frivolous purchase!"

Dad's eyes reminded her, *I am the authority!* And she hustled to the closet and reluctantly changed into bulky rubber galoshes. They felt clunky and smelled like moldy car tires. The family sloshed to church and during the service, Diny stared at her feet, her head lowered, horrified at her galoshes.

Staring at the floor, she realized there were many lessons to still permeate her heart and ways to mature into womanhood, lessons of respect and submission. Instead of assisting her father, she found herself agitated, restless, and ready for adventure. She wished to hold her tongue from stubbornness and the struggle against compliance, both of which she viewed as weaknesses.

Later at home, Dad further explained, "We come from a very small country. The Dutch have learned to fight their own calamities and disasters — war on our territory, the constant fight against the sea, the broken dikes, and so forth. For ages, all these calamities have formed the people in this country. We learned never to give up. It has given us endurance and persistence. Remember those larger-scale issues when you decide to argue over your choice of shoes, Diny, for frivolities mean little in the grand scheme of life." She sobbed, and they embraced.

The sounds of local train whistles were once again heard through Diny's open window at night, and as she fumbled and twirled in her bed, the songs of the trains echoed in her mind. She awoke in the morning still hearing those echoes in her ears, intermixed with the present sounds of children playing before breakfast, bouncing rubber balls in the square. The sun rose delicately, spreading gold along the horizon and pinks along the roofs of houses, where taller tree branches swayed. Higher up, purple hues tucked in under clouds, shadows receding into full brightness. Birds fluttered, socially enmeshed in daily routines, babies chirping for sustenance.

When the Northern part of the Netherlands was freed on 5 May 1945, the Southern part had been freed already since April 1945. Nico and Diny had not heard from each other or seen each other since before the bombing of Nico's train in September 1944. As the war ended, Nico received a job offer in Indie, so he earned passage on a boat to England, and then via Australia to New Guinea (now Irian Jaya), to return to the Dutch East Indies for work and life. They often talked about seizing the opportunity to return to Indie, where Diny was born, and where Nico had lived happy years with his father. Nico and Diny were engaged on 26 December 1942, by letter, and their marriage would now finally commence when they would marry in September 1946.

Hilversum, September 1946

Diny sat at the edge of her tidy bed and affectionately stared at Nico's picture. A few photographs of him were all she held in her possession, and she pondered his warm and comforting voice, the pleasant contours of his face when he smiled, the affection of his embrace, and sense of reassurance when in his presence. Her wedding day had arrived, and Diny mourned Nico's absence. She also wished her best friend Lenny ter Haar could be there to support her. As the roads recovered, the postal service began again, and Diny received a letter from Lenny, sharing news about her happy marriage to an Australian soldier named Romeny, and her subsequent move to Australia. Diny planned to visit Lenny upon her return to Indie.

Nico managed all the necessary papers and arrangements, and Diny married Nico by proxy (like her own dear parents). For their 12 September 1946 by-proxy ceremony, Nico's cousin Jacob Sluis took Nico's place during the ceremony in the Hilversum *Raadhuis* (Town Hall), which only a few years prior served as the headquarters for Germany's *Wehrmacht*. Nico and Diny would later get married in a church in Indie. According to Dutch custom, they would marry before a judge in the City Hall first, and then later marry in church and speak their vows together before God.

After the City Hall ceremony with Jacob standing in for Nico, Diny's parents provided an elegant dinner for families and friends who attended the simple reception, and Nico's picture was framed, standing next to Diny's plate, because he certainly belonged at his own wedding! Pieter and Cora were present, with Nelly, Jan, and Oma van den Bout. On Nico's side, Mother Pouwels attended, along with Nico's sisters Stien, Jopie, and Iekje, and their families, and Tante Rie Sluis, with her children Jacob, and Stien.

The Lord had something beautiful in mind in allowing Diny the proper timing for her marriage. When Pieter came home to Hilversum in the beginning of April 1946, Diny was released from her promise to her dad to care for her mother and two siblings, because her Dad took care of Mam himself from then on as the head of the Dekker household again. Thus, Diny was free to marry Nico in September 1946.

On Sinterklaas Day in December 1946, Diny had supposed, *what if a miracle arrived and all the past would be forgiven?* The snarls of life unraveled like a ball of yarn unfurling clean and new. Broken frames and bones and paintings set right again, bicycles repaired with rubber tires. The cure for all malaise was Jesus Christ's birth, ministry, death, and resurrection. All foibles and failures were forgiven under his grace.

Yellow swirls of mist swelled from the humid field of stemmed autumnal flowers, while chirping sounds of a new morning escalated. These floral wonders with thick green stems held glory in springtime, when bright tulips lined fields, with vibrant hyacinth, crimson reds, and deep secretive purples, all sky brightening and stark, vivacious against the blue atmosphere. Those fields now lay dormant, without tulips. A humid air enveloped the purple lavender and russet heath. Thin brown stems reached skyward with quivering bristlecone tops and fields of amber wheat-like wavered beside the winding, glittering river.

Fog reached down above the river, as if captivated by icy water, and burned off the warming ground, rising like a vapor mist. As haze shrouded the cold patchwork mazes of colors and patterns each field offered, fleeting mornings were inviting. The river wandered beside an impressive spinning wooden windmill, a steady, practical building on farms hundreds of years prior to drain swampy fields.

The windmill stimulated a memory Diny had nearly overlooked. She remembered an outing early in their 1940 courtship, where Nico spoke of his Pouwels family's windmill, *De Bloem*, otherwise called *The Flower Mill*. The Westerkerkhof was built in 1866 on the Rijkeroord bulwark near De Bloem.

That spring, before the war broke out, they bicycled to Marnixstraat 285 in Amsterdam where Nico showed off a commemorative plaque on the stone wall where Marnix Street intersects with Bloemgracht to the east, depicting the original location of their windmill. They visited the windmill early in 1940, before deportations and railroad bombings, before separation and silence. Diny was fascinated by windmills, which seemed romantic and lovely in theory. Yet when visiting their friend's windmill as a younger girl, reality set in, as the owner proved the amount of strength, effort, and fortitude required to operate a large structure, sprinting up and down seven levels as he worked the mill each day, unable to simply sit at the window and gaze out into the fields.

Nico read the plaque to her. "From 1614 until 1878, *The Bloem* windmill stood on the banks of the Schans River by the Raampoort on the bulwark Rijkeroort, one of the bulwarks of the Buitensingelgracht, in the Bloemgracht, later renamed the 2nd Marnixplantsoen. *The Flower Mill* received its colorful name from the place where it originally stood. Namely the end of the *Bloemgracht*, and likewise, due to the windmill's earnest efforts to grind wheat *flour*. In 1877, the Mayor of Amsterdam decided the windmill — among other structures in the neighborhood — had to be demolished because of the extension of Marnix Street, developing the community into townhomes and businesses; the location of *The Bloem* sits opposite a park on Marnix Street. And now the canal is called Singelgracht."

Diny exclaimed, "This is truly fascinating, Nico! What happened to the mill?"

He pointed north, farther up the Singelgracht. "Through a miracle, it seemed, the mill was spared because Hendrik Pieter Pouwels (who in 1870 had previously sold the mill to the Western Church for 18,000 guilders) repurchased the windmill in 1877 for a mere 1,700 guilders. Then, Hendrik and his family purchased a parcel of land, 30 meters by 30 meters at Haarlemmerweg 465, Landlust, Amsterdam, just 3 kilometers northwest, on which *The Bloem* was relocated."

They bicycled 3 kilometers to the new location of *The Bloem*. Nico stopped at Haarlemmerweg 465 and they watched as the Pouwels' family windmill rotated peacefully. Underneath the windmill sat a houseboat, gently swaying on the Westelijk Markt Kanaal. Beside De Bloem to the east lay a cemetery, Begraafplaats Vredenhof. As the gentle De Bloem mill spun, its tall frame cast twirling light and shadow onto the streets near the cemetery, a reminder of the swift brevity of life.

Nico continued, "Following a rather complicated history of purchase and resale after a momentous time, the still strong and tall prize was finally purchased by the Dutch government in 1927. Afterwards, in 1931, the city leased the windmill to a caretaker family named Schuurman, who presumably maintains the windmill on Haarlemmerweg."

"Marvelous, Nico! What a treasure for Amsterdam!"

Nearly 70 years after *The Bloem* was relocated, Diny stared at a similar windmill, an ancient and necessary part of her history, like a lighthouse for the ocean, an emblem of purpose and a structure symbolic of strength and determination, a tall respite amidst the swaying grasses of the fertile Dutch fields. The inner workings of the windmill, with moving parts, accomplished works of great importance: pressing water away from the wet fields and into the nearby river, a waterway which emptied into the North Sea. Windmills enhanced the practice of salvaging land from the unpredictable sea to possess prolific soil. Constructing a retaining wall and a canal to provide a boundary, then draining and pumping away the water, brought opportunity for further farming and affordable housing.

Reclaiming the sea was a practice that seemed outlandish: to attempt to steal something sinuous and moving, which was never in their claim or possession, to demand land for a new purpose, to transfer something as fluid as water, as though it were golden coins or tangible currency. Land was the Golden Opportunity for progress and hope. If the North Sea lashed storms, swampy floods, and a persistent winter chill, the retribution was building additional canals, walls, and fortifications, pumping out water, and reclaiming their prize.

If one were lonely of others in this country landscape, the soaked fields gave way to tall thicket woods, the line separating farmers' property from the National Parkland, the forests of darkness. While fertile soil led to adventurous trails, in open meadows under the bright sky, thicket woods encompassed a cool sanctuary of creaking ancient trees, mysteries unresolved in the air whirl of clanging craggy branches and forgotten paths.

The landscape was familiar and haunting to her during the war, but now serene and still, if only for a small applause of tree leaves clapping in the wind, or boughs of juniper and spruce whirring as wind blew through pine needles. To lay on one's back in the woods and look up toward the endless expanse, watching dancing treetops sway in oscillating harmony, was to lounge under a blissful peace.

Diny could not quite fathom all God had done, how He had rescued them, or to what extent He spared their lives. Yet she remained certain of her expectant future with Nico. If she surrendered everything to God — all the pain, memories, and loss — then He could create beauty from those ashes of her former life.

PART THREE

Chapter Twenty-Seven
Leaving the Netherlands, February 1947

They had not seen each other for more than two years, since before the train bombing in September 1944 when Nico never arrived at Diny's Hilversum home. Then, he was unable to contact her until after the war, but quickly took the job abroad and could not see her in person before moving to Indie. His move would expedite her arrival, and she was only permitted to travel if they were married; thus, their by-proxy union was necessary.

Six months after her by-proxy wedding on 12 September 1946, until the end of February 1947, Diny remained with her parents and prepared to leave the Netherlands, sewing, packing, saying farewell to family and friends, and planned for married life. Dad warned her of the political ramifications of the war, as Indie had been transformed into an independent state, no longer ruled by the Dutch. With the evolution of fighting for freedom, riots and civil war would undoubtedly follow. She claimed Indie would be just as it was during her childhood, but Dad's uncertainty and hesitations haunted her. Now, she considered returning to the place which broke her father.

Her mind swirled in wonder with her Dad's strength, and in time, she pondered Nico's similar character and fortitude. He found Indie just as charming as they left it. *Would Nico remember me after all these years? And how long will our reacquaintance take?* Their first encounter was at Jacob's party seven years before in the New Year of 1940, when hope was alive, before war shattered preconceptions, when their instant connection and ease of conversation and laughter sparkled. At their last encounter in Jacob's garden, he held a job as a translator. Their final embrace seemed long ago, an almost three-year interlude which faded details of his face, the intonation of his laughter, the warmth of his voice, and his gestures.

How were his Dutch Resistance efforts successful? He was never arrested, but had his friend Henk — or God — protected him? Over the years she maintained a small diary, writing thoughts, answered prayers, and God's miracles which blessed and surprised them. She would relay her marvels to Nico, who no doubt assembled his own stories of the Lord's faithfulness.

During the time of transition into a "new normal" after the war, Nico began working in New Guinea in a growing, prosperous career as a salesman for import-export trading company *Jacobson Van den Berg*. Jacobson Van den Berg was part of the Big Five of the Dutch colonial merchant houses. They set up in 1860 in Semarang under the name of Jacobson & Co, and later changed in 1872 to Jacobson Van den Berg & Co. They established offices in Semarang, Batavia, Surabaya, and Cheribon, plus an office in Rotterdam, the Netherlands. The firm operated as a general import and export business, with interests in coffee and cinchona plantations. Quinine emerged from the cinchona bark for anti-malarial remedies.

Their 1919 Semarang exports included tobacco, kapok (cotton-like textiles for upholstery), maize, copra (dried coconut meat), tapioca roots, hides, woods, and so forth. Pearls, lobsters, and teakwood were shipped from the Molucca Islands. During World War II, Jacobson Van den Berg & Co were involved with the official organization of rationing fabrics for the *Rijksbureaus*, official Dutch agencies which controlled the distribution of industrial raw materials. Now that countries were rebuilding from the war, Jacobson Van den Berg quickly organized again and was poised to gain strength in the import and export business, increasing numbers of employment, and stepping forward in their industry. Nico sold upholstery materials, kapok, burlap, nails, food, fish hooks, knives, matches, and other tools. He found great delight in assembling order from chaos and could effectively provide an excellent reason for a customer to purchase his goods.

Nico traveled one week per month to visit smaller places on the island. Company policy moved him every two years. He would receive a promotion with each move to eventually manage a location, which was a feasible goal the longer he remained with Jacobson Van den Berg.

Diny would travel alone, across seas, each moment growing closer to the destination of her beloved. The realization was not any easier, even though she longed for adventure and relished opportunities for a change. Her first step in marriage must be an assertive independence to arrive in Indie, to join with Nico, each dependent upon each other and the Lord.

When late February 1947 arrived, with the Dutch winter still churning snowstorms and icy passage, Diny journeyed alone from the Netherlands, away from her security. She hugged her loving parents farewell, her father embracing her mother, their arms raised in blessing on the same docks where she and Nico had waved her Dad off just seven years prior.

Diny departed on the ship *Oranje* for her three-week journey to Indie, to marry Nico in the New Guinea Christian Reformed Church. Diny was willing to follow Nico to Indie. Her route entailed traveling by boat for 3 weeks, from the Rotterdam docks west to England, then south, down the coast of France and Spain, through the Strait of Gibraltar, along the Mediterranean, through the Suez Canal, to the Red Sea, and across the Indian Ocean, first to Australia, and then to Indie. This was their means of travel, with no commercial airplane flights available.

As she sailed on her journey, Diny considered her beloved Batavia, which she had not seen in almost eight years. Much had been lost and destroyed, including their former home and all their possessions. As much as Dad attempted to set away their most beloved items, he assumed their home was eventually taken and occupied by a Japanese officer, and later, after the war ended, assigned to another family. Property was not important, for they survived. And what are possessions without survival?

Mam always seemed to have a clear sense of priorities, keeping her possessions simple enough to travel and collecting her belongings into a steamer trunk to traverse the world. Diny was raised similarly: to value relationships and experiences over possessions and belongings. She was skilled at packing quickly and settling into a new place proficiently, eager for sewing clothing, establishing routines, finding markets for shopping, planning a garden, and running their home. Every move with Dad and Mam over the years provided them a challenge at those tasks, which never seemed burdensome, but delightful. They could explore new corners of the islands, enjoy blossoming friendships, and examine challenges as exhilarating. Their togetherness solidified, bonded over the depth of trial and forged through the pain of loss.

Diny suspected Dad's harsh mistreatment at the hands of the Japanese forever soiled Mam's view of the Indies. Had they returned, Mam would be burdened with the task of forgiveness and integration, and the complicated culture of racial tensions and shattered idealism.

Japan refused to acknowledge any involvement or responsibility in the Pacific during the war, instead telling the Dutch, "This was your country, the

Dutch East Indies, and your city, Batavia. We had nothing to do with what happened there during the war." Japan bowed away from responsibility.

Nelly had balked. "Then who imprisoned our father?" Diny also wondered, aghast, and considered the Japanese surely felt torment in their hearts for an outrageous falsehood. How could an entire country fail to admit their mistakes?

Not until Diny sailed into her inevitable destiny did she realize the complexity of emotions Mam harbored for Indie. She wondered about their loyal servants who cared deeply for them during their time together. Had Indie changed so much she would not recognize the place or the people? Perhaps she was blinded to dangers, but her sense of adventure had not dulled, and she eagerly anticipated the future she would nurture with Nico.

The three weeks of travel on the *Oranje* ship passed graciously, with favorable weather, smooth passage, and hearty conversation to pass the time. She enjoyed tea and meals, movies and events designed to help socialize the passengers. Each person aboard seemed on the cusp of some adventure they hoped would carve their new life, with wives married by-proxy and meeting their husbands, or husbands involved in business and setting on ahead of their wives.

Diny held the railing as they sparkled through the familiar Batavian waters. She closed her eyes and suddenly she was fifteen again, leaning into her father's shoulder, sitting on a bench in the harbor, the day they bicycled to the *Tanjung Priok*, as they watched a round of men unload two-masted sailing ships full of timber from another island, then loaded the vessel with rice to depart. She smelled heavy scents of wood, varnish, and spices intermingled with street vendor food, and mangrove forests, as though nothing had changed. Diny opened her eyes and felt satisfied that her memories of Batavian's port *Tanjung Priok* were about her dad.

The great sailing vessel *Oranje* brought her from Rotterdam to Batavia, and she recognized the ports and docks were the same as before, seven years prior. She recognized Batavia had burned and shifted, with modern ships, rebuilt docks with new wood, and a larger flurry of busyness with imports, exports, and travelers. Once in port, she was approached by a Jacobson Van den Berg representative, who handed her a telegram from Nico, notifying her of his transfer away from New Guinea, and of her new boat to Makassar (Udjung Pandang) on the island of Celebes (Sulawesi).

She was surprised, but relieved to know they would begin their married life in a more populated location on Celebes, instead of the remote New Guinea. She changed in Batavia to a smaller boat heading to Makassar, with the inter-island shipping company *Koninklijke Paketvaart-Maatschappij*, KPM (meaning Royal Packet Navigation Company, established in 1888). However, her boat rocked furiously with a storm, and all the passengers remained inside as the rain challenged the fortitude of the ship's captain.

When Diny arrived in Makassar in the rain, the captain encouraged the passengers to exit quickly. All the ship's inhabitants set forth, yet Diny lingered, standing at the rail, expectantly gazing out above the crowd for Nico, trying to determine his face among the sea of people welcoming their loved ones. Finally, she set forth down the ramp. Even in the roaring rain, the port was a frenzy of movement and reunions. Diny could not find Nico's face in the crowd, as all the men wore dark hats and carried black umbrellas. Diny stood in one spot on the dock until everybody at the harbor found their companions and left. However, Nico was not to be found!

The wet benches were empty, and even the ship's crew exited the vessel. What if Nico changed so much, she did not recognize him? Did he wander the entire quay and miss her in the port, then go home? For three weeks on her boat journey, she imagined him waiting for her, and for years she envisioned their happy reunion. Deeply disappointed, Diny returned to the empty boat and sat along a row of empty chairs, to wait for Nico, eventually laying down and weeping. Diny could not restrain her disappointment.

When Nico drove home on his bicycle during lunch time, he passed the harbor and saw the KPM boat already docked there from Batavia. He jumped off his bike in a panicked state, ran aboard the boat, and heard a young woman sobbing, which led him to Diny howling on the seats.

"Diny, here you are, *Schatje*!" Nico cried. "Oh, my darling, welcome back to Indie!"

Diny covered her face and turned away, as hiccupping sobs escaped from her mouth.

Nico's face paled. "Why are you crying, my sweet *Lieverd*?"

"Where were you, Nico? I waited on the quay until everyone left." She sniffled loudly. "I had this vision of you on the dock awaiting me after all these years apart. This was our glorious reunion, but you were nowhere to be found!" She covered her face with her arm.

He kneeled beside her, stroking her hair. "I wanted to be here to greet you, my love, I honestly did. In fact, the KPM man promised me that your boat would arrive tomorrow! I ordered flowers and had a gift and fancy suit all prepared for tomorrow." Nico sighed, then stammered, "I called for lunch reservations at a special restaurant. The KPM man assured me."

She groaned.

He continued, "After all this time, and after all we have endured, did you think I would abandon you? We are married now, *Dien*! Well, almost…we just have to marry at church." He held her close. "I built a house for you, darling."

"How exciting!" she cried.

"It remains in New Guinea," he said flatly.

"I see. How is that possible? When will the house arrive here?"

"I worked for many months on the Guinea home, and then I was transferred to Makassar, but at least it helped me pass the time until you arrived." He offered a half-smile.

Perhaps Diny should have felt sorry for him, and should have been more understanding, as he planned surprises for her arrival and had built a home in New Guinea (which she would never see), but she was deeply disappointed. In her mind over the last year, she inflated their reunion to be as glorious as Nico planned, with flowers, sunshine, and togetherness, instead of riding his bicycle in a monsoon. Yet she quickly rebounded as she realized they had survived the unimaginable war.

He extended his hand to help her stand. They embraced for the first time in more than two years, and while soaked and exhausted, throats raw with emotion, were relieved to reunite! Again, as the first time they met, Diny flushed with a dizzy excitement and giddy eagerness.

Nico ushered her off the boat and onto his bicycle, then delivered her to Joop and Jan Saarloos' home to clean up and dry off. Joop retrieved towels while Nico nervously paced around the sitting room and queried Diny about their by-proxy wedding. He asked about her parents and siblings, and his cousin Jacob. She dripped and shivered on the entryway tile, suddenly noticing Nico's physique, as tall, lanky, mysterious, and contemplative as the moment they met, seven years before. During their absence, she forgot the warmth of his embrace, the way his entire frame enclosed upon hers in a hug. He was taller and broader now than seven years prior.

"Are you feeling okay, *Niek*?" Diny blushed with anticipation.

He nodded, his lively, tan face gleaming.

"I have so much to share with you, *Grietje*!" His glowing face and enthusiasm reminded her of a stormy afternoon seven years prior, early into their courtship, when she retrieved him from his Friday train amidst a rain storm.

She asked, "Remember how you looked after that crazy rainstorm seven years ago?"

"That was the start of everything, Diny — my feelings, hopes, dreams with you."

Back then, they huddled closely on her bicycle as Nico pedaled, and she leaned against his back as she entrusted his ride through rain. They journeyed through the ropes of rain to her Hilversum home, then warmed beside the wood burning stove, mesmerized by an unexpected situation and by their maturing relationship. His lively blue eyes glowed in the light of the blaze with fervor and possibility, and that same innocence now emerged.

He nervously cleared his throat.

Her mahogany eyes danced, and she sighed, "I am so relieved to finally be home."

Nico was initially stationed for work in New Guinea and built a small wooden house for their first home together. He labored each day and on weekends, enlisting the help of coworkers and new friends, until eventually, the home was complete. At the last minute, Nico's job location changed, requiring a move to Makassar on Celebes. Diny would never walk through the house he had lovingly built, nor enjoy tea on the veranda, since Nico received those new orders while Diny sailed on the ship from The Netherlands to Indie. Their reunion required a reacquaintance with each other, as they matured into adulthood over the war years, as Nico was 30 and Diny 25. When they met, they were nearly 23 and 18, both floundering through life and ambition.

Over the next week, Diny remained at the home of friends Joop and Jan Saarloos, eating delicious meals, and preparing for the wedding. Jan worked with Nico at Jacobson Van den Berg, while Joop was a housewife. Nico visited for lunch together nearly each day, their courtship resuming after years apart. Joop and Jan also survived the war in Japanese camps while on the island of Java, each in their own camp.

During lunch one afternoon, Joop said, "We observed many strange occurrences in the camps. Some camp locations were European homes filled with dozens of people and fenced off, with Indies living just outside the fences, as though we did not exist. And other camps were filthy barracks with little food and grueling labor. From one camp to the other, we were resigned to accept new challenges and blessings; I became the cook at one location and was excused from railroad work, which probably saved my life. A positive optimism helped us survive, too."

Jan nodded, and agreed, passing around his bread basket. "We both witnessed friends who sought the good, even small, daily victories, and they survived. Some found scraps of paper to write or draw upon, and others read a book, which brought purpose each day. We knew musicians who continued playing, usually a performance for a Japanese commander. But those concerts gave them single-mindedness and hope."

Diny smiled.

"What Jan says is true," Joop agreed, "and some of his friends became deeply depressed, and their health became poor as a result. Many of those people did not survive the war. Positive, cheerful attitudes sustained us."

"We were separated by the war for four years," Joop told her, "and yet we both held onto the promises of God and trusted that the other would remain alive." Joop and Jan looked warmly at each other, foreheads touching, tears forming.

"I am fortunate Jan survived, and I also endured until liberation day," Joop concluded.

Diny considered the wisdom of the Saarlooses and the compassion they demonstrated. They would prove to be trustworthy mentors as Diny and Nico began their married life.

Their official wedding date was their by-proxy date in the Netherlands, of 12 September 1946. After 6 years of war, Diny would now step into married life, with her love Nico. Her emotions surged from discouragement in the length of time required to arrive at this day of marriage — four years after their engagement — with genuine gratitude for God sparing them. Since Nico and Diny married by-proxy in the Hilversum City Hall, they would exchange vows before God in the church.

For her wedding day, the beaming bride Diny wore a delicate white long-sleeved dress. The V-neck bodice was fitted, wrapping around on the side, with draped sleeves fashioned with lace. The dress lengthened to the tops of Diny's white shoes and she felt elegant. Her veil was sewn together by Koenie Martinot, a sweet friend who also lived in Makassar, who made the veil from *"klamboe gaas,"* mosquito net mesh, a practical wonder. Diny carried a bouquet of fragrant flowers and the broadest smile. Cheerful and eager groom Nico was attired in a fancy new white suit with a light striped tie, a brown belt, and shiny brown shoes, handkerchief in his chest pocket, sprig of flowers on his lapel, and Bible.

Nico and Diny married in Makassar Christian Reformed Church on 26 March 1947, the ceremony officiated by Dr. Bergema. As the *"trouwtekst,"* or wedding fidelity Bible text, Dr. Bergema preached from Romans 8:31b, "If God is for you, who can be against you?" It was a strong promise to hold onto through their whole married life. Nico's company Jacobson Van den Berg arranged a nice party for them after the wedding, with colleagues and friends celebrating the newlyweds. Nico acquired a hotel room in Makassar to spend the night before they departed on their honeymoon. After many years of war and separation, they were finally alone, together, and married.

They were glad they had remained chaste and pure for each other, despite the greatest challenges of war and survival, and were delighted that their most intimate desires and experiences were reserved for each other alone, for the marital union. He enveloped her with security, and she vowed herself to him. Those proposals which had slowly built in anticipation were no longer unfulfilled longings, but finally realized in the beginning of their marital felicity.

The next morning, they set forth on their honeymoon. Jacobson Van den Berg offered them the privilege of a mountain honeymoon in Malino, Central Sulawesi, at the foot of volcano Pegunungan Pompangeo, providing transportation to the location and all the arrangements. At the wedding reception, Nico's boss assured him, "Everything has already been planned and taken care of! A chauffeured car and house await you and Diny for your honeymoon. Do not worry about anything! We have prepared a wonderful honeymoon!"

Nico and Diny were escorted to Malino by a chauffeur driving them in a jeep, along with one man directing the driver and several other men keeping watch, armed with guns. They explained the armed escort to the uneasy couple: the countryside remained unsafe in early 1947, just after the war, as snipers remained, especially in remote mountains. When Nico and Diny arrived in Malino they stopped in front of a large building and in no time, they were surrounded by Chinese and Indie children, who greeted them happily.

"Dag Oom! Dag Tante!" (Hello Uncle! Hello Aunt!)

What a welcome! The air was humid, but the mountains were slightly cooler, with rain and shade amidst verdant green foliage. Their special honeymoon resort consisted of small individual dwellings on stilts, due to the monsoon rains and their steep hillside location. The site was owned by a

Chinese man who wanted to provide a sense of normalcy to those starting out afresh, after the war. Their meals were shared in a common building, with all three meals each day cooked by excellent chefs who provided unique feasts. All those other dwellings were taken by other couples also on honeymoon, and they all sat together around tables during meal times.

Nico and Diny's lodging encompassed one small room containing a singular chair, a large children's bed (but not long enough for Nico, because his feet stuck out the bottom of the bed), and a single electric outlet hanging down from the ceiling but no lightbulb present.

"Ah, you should have brought your own light bulb," the resort's owner told them.

"I see. Thank you." Nico nodded. Aside, to Diny, he said, "Nobody at Jacobson told me of this. We surely are off to a rocky start, now."

She laughed, "If they had mentioned it, you would have thought they were sending us to some jungle honeymoon. After all we have survived, four years without electricity, this is no big deal, Nico."

Another couple also on honeymoon was nice enough to lend them a light bulb. There were no places to put their clothes as there were no closets, but a clothesline was tacked from one end of the room to the other to hang garments. The little room contained a children's bed, a chair, a lightbulb, and a clothesline. But they did not despair.

The war was over, but traces of troubles still echoed along the jungle paths. They took long walks together on the mountainous property, enjoying the peace and tranquility of nature, sharing about all their lives had entailed and the wonderful miracles God had performed over the past few years. With each step were several Chinese and Indie children following as they ventured out and explored, wanting to talk and play with them. Not an easy start for a marriage.

Chapter Twenty-Eight
Makassar, Celebes, Dutch East Indies, 1947

When they returned from their exhilarating honeymoon, rested and eager to begin their lives, Nico collected Diny's belongings from Joop and Jan Saarloos' home, and thanked them for allowing her to stay with them for the weeks leading up to the wedding. Then he set out to assist Diny at becoming situated with their home in Makassar, to become accustomed to living as husband and wife.

They would move into new roles within the company every two years, with a promotion each transfer, and a Furlough every 4 years, depending upon his position and their moving schedule. Jacobson Van den Berg paid Nico a comfortable salary to afford daily home helpers, and would employ a household staff of *Djongos, Kokki, Baboe, and Keban* as paid servants.

Diny welcomed each morning breakfast on the veranda with her cup of tea, while Nico savored toast topped with a fried egg, another toast with jelly, and coffee with hot milk. Nico read the newspaper then escaped to work while morning coolness persisted. He began a long cigarette in the morning, slowly inhaled, savored. He would stare at the newspaper, his eyes warming to the day and absorbing world news, sometimes within a smolder of his own, while Diny carefully watched him, chuckling to herself at his routines.

Her own toast topped with chocolate sprinkles and another toast with cheese suited her each morning. Her palate was inclined toward creams and cheeses after years of living in the Netherlands, particularly Gouda and Edam, and she marveled at eating chocolate for breakfast. It was reminiscent of her desire for dessert before dinner all those years ago as a toddler when her father instilled a clear direction for a life of balanced moderation. Without a refrigerator, she could only procure cheese for rare occasions, and not every day.

Diny's mornings were established as soon as she arrived, and one of her favorite moments involved early walks, sometimes along with her friend Koenie Martinot, as soon as Nico departed to the office. Koenie showed her the city. They might meander along a shoreline, and sometimes Diny explored the market with *Kokki*, who picked out a fish for their evening meal, meals based on whatever seafood was special at the market. Sometimes they walked, if the weather was fair, and hailed a *becak* for their return home, allowing the pedaled taxi to offer them a break from the heat or monsoons and a place to set their bags of purchases.

Monsoon season signaled a change, borne from months of monotony, suddenly shifting. Rain poured heavily, relentlessly from thick clouds. It was as if a necessary thirst had settled into the land and the heavens yielded to the beckoning command. The water swirled through trees and churned into eager soil, below estuaries and into rivers now swollen with rainwater. If Diny ventured out to linger in her garden as clouds formed, she might be caught in the storm. Banyan trunk hollows offered a cave-like hiding place for her until the rain slowed into a drizzle, and the warmth of the sun noted the departure of the storm.

When Diny returned home to clean up, she bathed with a soap called Maja, smelling fragrances of citrus, lavender, clove spice, and woods. She found the Maja soap by chance at a street market, which was impressive as it boasted being imported from Spain. While she held it, the distinct fragrance captivated her, and moreover, she marveled at the box design: a Myrurgia swirl of a confident woman dancing, round soap wrapped in black and red paper. Even hours after her bath, the spices in the fragrance lingered in the balmy air.

Nico reserved Saturdays for exploring their island on a hike beside a river or lake to reflect. But once immersed into the bird-chirping wilderness, with shade of thick trees and benches to sit upon, they realized the world offered none of the serenity they sought, and only a momentary solace. Only Christ offered true peace, as only God bestowed upon them the sort of love which traversed the senses. Ephesians 2:14 was a balm to their souls, reminding them, "He alone is our Peace."

Their time in the early months in Makassar felt especially sentimental, a reunion, and they were amused at reacquainting, discovering peculiarities about each other, and learning to live with someone for the first time, balancing each other's temperament, personality, and interests. They also felt fulfilled in accomplishing their dream of Indie and sought to learn the new topography and lifestyle of Celebes. This colorful, vibrant culture still felt preserved in beauty and enchantment. It was tucked away from the rest of the world at times and they would remain explorers, pioneers, and adventurers of the varied landscapes.

As during her childhood, fruits dripped syrupy sweetness like maroon guava, bright yellow mango, purple passion, spiny reddish rambutan, yellow papaya, lime breadfruit, bright pink drops of dragon fruit, and carambola, those yellow waxy star-shaped fruit. Diny recalled her parents' love of the gardens, remembering Dad amidst the swaying flamboya trees with red blossoms.

Those banyan trees offered Diny shelter and branches reached toward the heavens, as though praising their Creator. Rubber trees swayed and creaked. Nutmeg, cinnamon, and cloves were cultivated from the islands. Bamboo, orchids, banana trees, teakwood, sandalwood, and ebony all lined forests and backyards, intermittently offering scented wonders of spices. Diverse gardens greeted them, blooming about their Celebes yard and Indie world with remarkable enthusiasm. Diny lingered in their garden, and to the sanctuary she discovered, to the unsullied peace and serenity found there.

Nico returned home each afternoon for lunch, in the tranquility of the veranda, and then went back to work to finish his day. Later in the evening, after settling the cares of the day and within the coziness of their veranda, Nico found respite after a long day of work, a rejuvenation reserved for dinnertime, for lively conversation together with Diny. If the weather was mild and welcoming, they lingered well beyond their meal, watching the blazing sun drop behind the trees. Their veranda served as an outdoor sitting room, a portal into the beguiling wilds of the tropical rainforests, while still enclosed by three walls into a nook at the front of their home.

Nico lined the veranda bookshelves with his favorite authors like C.S. Lewis, G.K. Chesterton, and Dietrich Bonhoeffer. On the top shelf, crossword puzzles and several decks of playing cards awaited, intended for lively after-tea games. On a lower shelf, stacks of records served as background music to their lives and activities with musical selections like Bach, Mozart, Wagner, and jazz records from the '20s like Count Basie, Ella Fitzgerald, and Louis Armstrong.

Mam had gifted Diny her most valued records, "to provide the atmosphere of learning and togetherness," she told Diny. Perhaps those composers reminded Mam of other, difficult days, or of their nostalgic existence in Indie before the troubling war years began. Mostly, Mam told her, she hoped Diny would enter a lifelong love with Nico, accompanied by great music, which soothed, encouraged, and inspired. Composers like Schubert, Handel, Bach, Mozart, and Brahms felt like traveled friends, and music full of Wagner's operatic movements, Beethoven's dramatic overtones, and Vivaldi's cheerful melodies in *The Four Seasons* orchestrated their activities.

In evenings on the cooled veranda, after sunset, Nico read the newspaper or a book, while Diny cross-stitched decorative artwork, or knit mittens, hats, and scarves for their Dutch Furlough. They listened to radio programs or enjoyed the tropical silences. Sometimes she joined Nico in a hearty card game, and at least weekly they hosted dinner, drinks, and board games for another couple, usually a colleague from the office. Most of Nico's co-workers came from the Netherlands to the Indies. Daily routines would follow Nico and Diny through each location, in each role on the islands, of the husband leading the way and the wife dutifully following him.

Nico and Diny walked together through the black veil, permanently torn for them and all who believed, which humans could never break through, as 1 Corinthians 13 described. Unable to bridge the gap to God, Jesus tore the division, bridged the abyss. They only witnessed a partial view of eternity, and someday would see clearly, fully, face-to-face, and after death, passing through that thin veil, invited in, to dine with Christ forever.

The air remained unsettled during monsoon season, humidity enveloping them into an afternoon haze. Quiet evenings suited him as of late, and Nico leaned over the veranda railing.

"I am unable to possess… I do not have the ability…" he stammered, then thought for a moment, composing himself. "I am unwilling to forgive my friend Henk," Nico admitted to Diny one stormy evening. They retired early, settling inside amidst a rainy stretch, their veranda soaked. Their wicker chairs dripped with water in cadence with the terrace clock, which pulsed lightly, cutting into the evening stillness.

In the house, Nico sat on the couch and continued, "I traveled so far as Henk's doorstep after the war, before racing away, feeling sick."

Diny could not fathom his pain. "Still, we are called to forgive, despite how strenuous the exercise," Diny said, pouring Nico's tea.

"Yes. I feel convinced that the time apart, post-war, might persuade Henk of a lesser guilt, burden, or responsibility." He took a sip. "But I wonder, if the Netherlands as a country has moved ahead, maybe Henk and I could also do so while avoiding the inevitable conversation."

Diny whispered, "Moving ahead is still not forgiveness, Niek. It removes the work of emotional vulnerability."

They discussed the theory of a human's inability to forgive apart from Divine assistance. God would help them, offering the ability to forgive, providing them grace without bitterness or revenge. Yet Nico must first forgive himself and receive God's grace and forgiveness for his own indiscretions.

Monsoon rain stopped, and they again moved out to the veranda. The sun softly emerged from clouds in time to streak pinks and oranges across the sky as the sun set behind mountains, and frogs began *ribbetting* as darkness settled into the air.

Nico sighed, his eyes clouded with pain. "I know Henk made some mistakes and although he faced court hearings, and eventually a prison sentence, I could not visit Henk before I left to come to Indie."

She pondered her next sentence but sat quietly, discerning, folding her hands in her lap. "*A newlywed wife would do well to not question or challenge her husband,*" she was warned by recently married friends, months ago.

Diny rose from her seat to refresh Nico's tea, then stood opposite Nico. "I also found myself unable to forgive after the war," she confessed, her voice lowering. She looked back at her cloth napkin, unable to look in his eyes. "Those men who imprisoned my father were like beasts to me, like wicked men unworthy of God's love."

"They were so cruel to him," Nico agreed.

"While the hatred entrenched into my heart over five years of pain, building slowly, compounded by my own grief and loss, it was a wildfire of resentment. But then when Pap returned to the Netherlands, I recognized his completely opposite reaction, his choice to love. He decided to only tell us the positive blessings of his time away and refused to dwell on anger or discouragement. Dad shared about a Japanese guard's gift of bread with jam, which tasted like grace to my father."

Nico nodded, "Your dad has demonstrated incredible grace, for sure."

Diny continued, "All the bitterness and hatred diminished from Dad's face, and only through the work of the Lord was he not destroyed by a lack of forgiveness. He lost so much, yet felt blessed to survive, and compelled to forgive. Even though he was not certain why we had to endure trials, he knew the Lord is good, and would provide for each need, each day. God could erase the hurtful memories and replace them with a joyful hope; he felt certain of this. And Dad's burden was lifted."

Nico lit a cigarette and leaned against the railing. "Your father always seemed a wise man of strength and restraint," Nico began, exhaling, the air clouded up around his countenance, then wafted into darkness. "And his ideas do hold great merit. What difficulties he faced, and with strength and perseverance! I shall write and ask for his source of motivation for forgiveness."

Six months after they married, they moved again: in September 1947 Jacobson Van den Berg transferred them to another job in Menado, the far northeast corner of the Sulawesi island (also on the island of Celebes, now Sulawesi Utaro, near where they traveled for their honeymoon in Malino) where Nico would replace another salesman. Makassar, southernmost point of Sulawesi, seemed small and remote as they drifted on a boat going north to Menado, situated in the far upper eastern portion, 2,000 km away.

A unique environment was theirs to explore. Jacobson Van den Berg again provided a home for them to rent, called a *contractpension* (contract boarding houses) which was simple, clean, and comfortable. Only Jacobson employees had lived there, and as Nico moved into the new role on Menado, he also moved into the home of the former employee, who had also moved to a new location for a job promotion, as though a precise game of dominoes propelled an employee from one role and home and into the next, each striding into their own challenging location and situation.

Nico befriended local men on *koffietijd* breaks wherever they traveled, as though each person could be his friend, and possibly explain their part of the island and the new realm of Indie, and in the length of a conversation, Nico might sell his product. Yet most of the conversations never ventured to his employment, except him merely stating his career, and at the least, he obtained a friend.

Friendships were an important fabric of their time in each location, as Diny often invited women over for tea. Eventually, when those friends moved away or Nico and Diny were transferred, friendships grew over letters. She met wonderful women at the Dutch social club *SOOS*, and enjoyed conversations with other wives of salesmen, developing a friendship based on their husbands experiencing many similar challenges and blessings. In social gatherings, Nico remained shy and reserved in large groups, but when he shared, he spoke with a composed posture, wisdom, and charm.

"I do love our island nation, and the people," Nico began, folding up the newspaper one morning before work. "However, I had hoped for all ethnic backgrounds to find resolution and community. I do not see these changes have been accomplished since the war, with a new revolution at hand." He held out the paper to Diny, who scanned the front-page article concerning ethnic clashes and fighting, race relations strained under the fragile post-war social climate.

"We always planned to enjoy a long life raising our family on these islands," she conceded, "and I think we are on our way toward being successful. The Indie people already renamed Batavia into the new capital name of Djakarta, but we see no fighting in our streets. I hope independence means freedom for all." Diny handed the newspaper to Nico, who set it aside.

He considered, "There are outbreaks of violence, riots, protests, and uprisings, but we are largely sheltered from those events. There is no need to worry, Dien."

Batavia, which was the former capital of Indie, was no longer the same as it was, and the country was called "Indonesia," a longer, more fluid word combining the "Indie" of the Dutch title for the country, with the "Asia" influence of its location. As time progressed and the country grew in nationalism and pride, they knew additional alterations would arrive as the country progressed toward freedom.

Now, after they journeyed into married life, they were permitted to know each other fully, more freedom than ever before, as possibility hovered before them, while complete acceptance found in commitment propelled them forward together. Indie returned changed for Diny, varied, with a new tone and outlook on the culture. She viewed the country now as an adult, as a married woman instead of as a child.

Meanwhile, Nico's ruminating moods counteracted Diny's optimistic enthusiasms, as they attempted to find a balance. These steps into marriage included new responsibilities and challenges, and she embraced her role as a wife. Her primary task was caring for her husband, growing in wisdom, abounding in love, and thriving in an atmosphere of grace. Those years away from each other altered their perceptions and matured their ideals, primarily the last few difficult years of the war.

Her secondary task consisted of setting up their home and creating a safe, cozy haven together. Her past had vanished, like intricate sand formations demolished after a wave. The early years in Indie disappeared, she reasoned, with no remnant remaining. The Dutch who remained during the war and survived labor camps gathered the few items still in their possession. They felt relieved and blessed to have escaped the devastation of death and attempted to move forward with life. The only concrete evidence of Diny's early life in the Indies were a few photo albums Mam brought with them on their 1939 Furlough, along with an assortment of photos their family members benevolently collected for them to piece together scrapbooks of childhoods for Diny, Nelly, and Jan.

In letters from her family, she sensed her dad's sentimentality about Indie, even after his banishment. Pieter still grieved for his life interrupted and wished he could return to the Police work. Yet after the war, nothing could persuade or tempt Cora to resume life in these islands. Even Diny hesitated to return to hostile territory, except for her husband Nico, her enduring memories, and their plans to raise a family on the islands. Her life was split into neat sides, of a "before-war" emotive naïveté and innocence and a "post-war" stature of reality. Much in her personality was altered, grew in depth, and found steadiness through maturity, loss, and suffering, despite her wish for those rewards without the sorrow.

Her future with Nico shined bright with hope. Warm evenings on the equator with a humid climate, offered a consistent opportunity to hear frogs, vendors clanking their carts down the streets and other familiar night sounds, and the soothing music of their lives. They danced on the veranda in the evenings, amidst fragrant spice winds, swaying to rounds of classical or jazz music on the phonograph, laughing into nightfall.

"Vivaldi tonight, Diny!" Nico called, racing inside the veranda after his evening stroll.

"Sounds good to me!" She slid a record from its paper covering and gently placed it in the gramophone slot, then aligned the needle with the beginning of the record. Diny glanced around the room and tidied up, then smoothed her dress and turned to face her partner. He pulled her close and they were one, fragrant of spices and lavender, whispering together.

At times, Nico tapped his way to the other side of the veranda, caught up in his own rhythm. Other times, she played Mozart, and he waltzed with Diny until the music halted, the record completed its cycle, only scratching pulses interrupting their interlude.

His face looked more wrinkled than when they first met, but at peace. Dreams previously discarded in the war now seemed attainable. Near the end of 1947, Diny sensed a swirling change within her, an alteration of sorts, a burgeoning garden of her own keeping. One evening after work, candles were lit on the veranda, and their finest dishes and silver set on crisp linens, as though a celebration was anticipated. Diny pulled Nico's hand to her stomach, and both marveled at good news from her doctor.

"You will be a father next year!" Diny exclaimed. They cried at God's gift of a baby.

He gasped. "A miracle! Do you feel okay, or can I bring you anything, *Schatje*? Sit, my Darling! You should be resting on the sofa, and not dancing!" Nico attended to his bride and sought to protect her from any upsetting incident, but she laughed him away.

"*Niek*, I am fine! My doctor says the heartbeat sounds strong, and we can expect a baby in late May, perhaps." They telephoned their families with the happy news.

Later into the night, Nico paced into the gardens, pondering his journey of becoming a father. The only glitter cutting the dark sky was a small orange ember alighting here and there as he smoked his cigarette. The cigarette burned down, and a whisper of gray smoke unfurled into the air only visible to Nico.

Chapter Twenty-Nine
Menado, Celebes, early 1948

In the beginning of 1948, Jacobson Van den Berg moved them south, through the inky Moluccan Sea to the small island of Ambon (Maluku), part of the Moluccan Islands. Nico ventured ahead to prepare the home and begin his import-export job there while Diny concluded their work in Menado and later arrived alone by boat, eagerly chatting with other passengers. Diny was six months pregnant with their first child and felt overheated. The boat docked enroute to Ambon while the Captain accepted a few new passengers and his staff took a break on land.

Diny peered over the side of the boat, admiring a clear broad lagoon near the shore.

"Oh, my! This lagoon looks incredibly refreshing!" a woman exclaimed. Diny had befriended the Dutch woman on the boat, who was also relocating in the islands.

"Yes! A cool reprieve from this stifling heat!" Diny cried with a longing look, as she wiped her brow with a handkerchief.

"We should take a brief swim," the woman offered. But she was not sure there was time.

"Just a quick swim, eh? A moment of relief, right? Before we start up again?"

The woman nodded, smiling, a glimmer of mischief in her eyes familiar to Diny. They left the boat together and swam in the lagoon, enjoying the cooler waters and appreciating a respite from the humid air. With her hair already upswept into a caramel-colored bun, Diny could wade into the water up to her neck! Diny floated on her back and stared at the sky, her head soaking and cooled, feeling lighter from her current pregnant state.

The loud horn of the boat sounded, a signal they would soon depart.

Quickly, Diny and the woman swam back to shore and raced onto the boat, dripping wet and exhausted, where the Captain lectured them at the dangers of passengers unauthorized to leave the boat.

"We almost left you behind!" He huffed angrily. "And then what would your husbands say in Ambon? Silly wives! Next time, stay on board for the entire journey!"

They agreed, apologized, and dashed out of sight until they arrived in Ambon, giggling and dripping on their way back to their rooms.

Nico prepared their Ambon home and Diny arrived impressed with his work. She moved slower now, her tired body swelling and rounding at every curve and angle with the magnificent grace of pregnancy.

"What a blessing this little one will be for us!" Nico marveled soon after her arrival, holding her round frame until he was required to leave for the office.

Diny's eyes lit up as she, too, anticipated their new life with children. "You will be a wonderful father, Nico, I am convinced." He lurched for his briefcase.

"Really, Niek," she reminded him, "You had a truly loving example while being raised here, and I wish Father Pouwels could see you as a dad."

He smiled weakly. Nico's responsibility increased in this new career and included small boat excursions from one island to another which consisted of weeklong adventures, as one week per month required travel for cross-training and expansion.

As he kissed her farewell for a weekly excursion, she nervously fumbled with a frayed hem. "Now take care to return home when our baby arrives," Diny warned. "I would be devastated if you missed the birth. I am all alone, and whatever would I do without you?"

He assured her, "I will try to delay my trips in May. Would that be sufficient?" He pulled her close and kissed her. She did not want to inhibit his work. Still, they desired to live as a family. He met fascinating people along his travels, the time rambled along quickly enough to remain busy and occupied. His first goal as a salesman in any arena was to offer a level of comfort. Once he unlatched any anxiety or uncertainty, he could proceed.

"Personal pleasantness first, and then down to business," he said, which contradicted the Dutch directness and immediate professional practices of business first and congeniality only second. The islands often operated on *rubber time*, or general time frames for business, and he soon learned to value relationships first. Some weeks entailed more office work or training new hires, in morning training sessions and afternoons practicing in markets, bartering in busy squares, chatting with tourists and locals, and later in villages and homes. He urged the staff to learn the style of those they were meeting, to relate their methods of unique living for this island.

Diny settled into their new home on the small island of Ambon, and as with previous locations, established her household. They enjoyed the multitudes of bird species indigenous to the island, along with the lush landscape. She had never seen so many butterflies in her life! They fluttered between trees, among bushes, and through the branches of trees, flickering through light. Nico and Diny strolled the long stretches of open beach, collecting abundant seashells, including tortoise shells which washed along the shore, all while awaiting their child's birth. They stood side-by-side, watching the sun set into the west Banda Sea.

Diny hired a compassionate nurse for this location. Ada Oudega was a kind Dutch nurse who lived with them in Ambon to deliver their first child. One late autumn day, Diny's labor began, and together with Ada, Diny sweated through the contractions and delivery. On 22 May 1948 in Ambon, their first child Corina Francisca was born, and they telephoned their families in the Netherlands with the good news, humbled at God's gift to them.

Diny's joy of motherhood felt purpose-filled as Corina's primary caretaker, even though some friends hired a Baboe to care for their babies. Diny was never raised by a Baboe, as her parents actively participated in raising their children. Likewise, Nico and Diny would raise their children on their own. Diny was thousands of kilometers from her family when her first child was born, but she was not alone. She felt comforted by God's hand of love and direction. Diny gently rocked and comforted Corina in the nursery, and listened to tiny breaths and heartbeat, wondering at the grace of such a gift.

Their early years of marriage were marked by a return to the love of the land of the Dutch East Indies, their affection for the languages, customs, and friendships with marvelous people, all intriguing and mesmerizing for years before, separately, then together in Hilversum, when they decided to return. Yet the tone was decidedly secular, as they did not attend church services. There were no church buildings — either Dutch Reformed Church or other denominations — and those who met together resembled more of a social club, like the *SOOS* Dutch club, complete with a clubhouse and luxurious setting on the coast. The church in which they married back in Makassar was an anomaly and one of few in that area. If they did meet for a church service, there was no pastor, and someone always volunteered to share a Bible message. Occasionally, Nico preached, as did other men in their community, on the rare occasions they did attend church, like Christmas and Easter.

Diny looked to Nico for guidance and spiritual leadership, as her dad actively provided, but when her husband was quiet and more reserved — even more on personal matters — she simply waited patiently for his leading, without verbalizing her need, although she hoped to raise Corina as a Christian. After his parents divorced in 1930 and Nico remained another six years in Indie, his beloved Father Pouwels raised him in a secular way, encouraging him with experiences and adventures, activities and games. There remained little discussion for Father Pouwels concerning spiritual investigations, as he had already decided upon Atheism for himself, and Mother Pouwels was a Christian.

Nico's own personal journey of a relationship with God was as delicate and individual as every other aspect of the mind or emotions, best pursued alone. Yet as his sister Jopie assured them after the war, they would reunite with Father Pouwels in Heaven and felt incredible hope. Nico wished he could have seen the changes in his father's heart and experienced their connection as brothers in the Lord. As Diny befriended women, she encountered all realms of human nature, including objectionable qualities. She prayed for the bitter or unlovely and sought to help others see their potential and not their status, an important quality she hoped to teach Corina.

"Every person has some element of beauty," she told Nico, while her foot pedaled the sewing machine one evening, "and everyone is beautiful in their own special way." She always beamed when she conveyed these ideas, noting, "What lovely eyes," or "radiant hair," or "delicate hands."

Diny held up Corina's tiny burgundy dress, and Nico nodded his approval. She placed the dress on her sewing table and inspected it for flaws. However, when Corina would wear the dress, no doubt those around them would only admire her beauty in the outfit, never noticing a misplaced stitch. Her view and opinion consisted more of some personality trait — or flaw — which illustrated after a length of acquaintance. A jealousy or gossip which permeated was viewed negatively. She never spread those discoveries, though, holding back from gossip or malice. Instead, she chose to believe the best about others.

Diny felt emboldened in letter writing, her mind unfettered and her thoughts conveyed in a more carefree conduct, sharing most deftly with her dearest friend Lenny ter Haar. Their friendship had rarely altered over many years and she developed habits of conversing on paper, of extended discussions and delights, a closeness derived from those generous exchanges.

Now, much had been altered in Diny and Nico's lives, and the difficult war years festered an ache inside Nico's soul, a division upon his heart, severing a relationship with his friend Henk, which would take incredible forgiveness to heal. Nico's decision to remain spiritually quiet, press forward to work efficiently, and allow nothing to hinder his efforts seemed easier than floundering in grief over his father and friends lost in the war. Concentrating on his vocation seemed easier to manage than the emotions surrounding loss, devastation, and pain of the war.

After all, what use was he as a man burdened by emotions? His efforts to provide financially, achieve success as he progressed into higher positions, while creating a life of promise and the reality of tangible benefit, would better serve Diny and Corina, he suspected. Diny's enthusiasm shined an example of loving encouragement, especially concerning the ways Nico's life was spared during the war. Few spoke of the war years. Those war years were blurred by moral codes, although they both sought to follow the Bible.

After dinner, Nico smoked, read the newspaper, and drank coffee while eating a cookie or biscuit. Evenings might be spent socializing with other Dutch transplants, attending SOOS clubhouse social events, or dancing with Diny, gazing into her dark eyes.

Nico recalled moments of mercy as an unexplained relief, an adventure intermingled with the holy. He could not rationalize how he had been spared from death so many times, but felt grateful. Even after living through those experiences, some of the enchantment faded into routine, as the sparkle, much like the golden air lingering just before sunset, dimmed slightly. Those months just after the miracle were infused with adrenaline and purpose, which further propelled him into survival, serving others, translating, helping with ration cards, strong-arming leaders in factories for supplies, and other Dutch Underground efforts.

Remarkably, he was spared. Nico marveled at his inexplicable safety from being arrested. He was never forced to enlist in the German army. He still shuddered under the weight of the miracle of stepping off the train just minutes before it was bombed. When a train was set to depart at 6:31 a.m., it departed at that moment, for any disruption hindered other train lines.

Yet the war timeframes were ambiguous, which is how he viewed the entire occupation of their country. The day of the train bombing, he was upset to keep Diny waiting after months of separation. After the train exploded, people scattered everywhere: shoes, clothes, bodies. He stopped to help, to aid the dying, assembled groups of volunteers, transported the injured to hospital, and then slipped back into the east.

With rail lines severed, travel west was impossible, and he remained in Arnhem to continue as a translator. He was near the "bridge too far" during the bewildering moments of Operation Market Garden, with parachuting soldiers. He collected a parachute discarded by a soldier, which he hoped would be useful during the war. Nico was equally confused and terrified during his three days hiding in the baker's oven during the height of battle, a frightening horror for fear of being discovered by either side. How could they remain in a precarious location, unharmed, with just enough strength?

Some full Sunday afternoons were spent on their veranda, in silence, with Corina napping in her pram near the divider, resting and intermittently awaking to eat, then burping in Nico's arms while he stared at her in amazement, her tiny body encompassed in his arms. When she dozed off again, he placed her in the pram. Diny spent time knitting for her Dutch family or mending the outfits she sewed for Corina, as Nico sat reading quietly in another wicker chair, a *gezellig* togetherness.

Diny remembered Dad's war recovery only began with love, with charity and devotion from Mam, from her loving touch care. Dad knew his world outside the veranda was as wild and untamed as the landscape, but within their patio enclosure he would experience peace. In the same way, Nico was entrenched in thought, encamped into an idea, a memory, a vision, and her love might mend his wounds, their home a haven from the world.

Eventually, Nico became the boss in Ambon, which brought them joy and delight.

Diny's way of expressing her love to her daughter each morning rang out with the cheery greeting, *"Dag lieve Grietje!"* She loved to sing songs and take walks with Corina down their shady paths each morning before the heat of the day. Corina sat in the kinderwagen for walks, and Diny read the Bible aloud on the veranda during lunchtime. When Corina was not even a year old, Diny was already pregnant with their second child, a new life within her again, a delight for Nico to provide for his growing family.

Every four years, Nico received a 6-month paid Furlough to the

Netherlands. In July 1949, the family took a 6-month Furlough to the Netherlands, and Diny was again six months pregnant while traveling on a boat, although this expedition lasted three weeks on the seas. Her doctor warned her against the trip, certain Diny would deliver her child on board! During their journey, Nico shared about his independent travels many years before as a young man.

Once, when venturing back to Amsterdam, he traveled up through the Red Sea and across the Suez Canal area, then disembarked at the mouth of the Nile River, and explored Egypt for a length of time, riding camels, touring ancient pyramids and desert communities, and escaping the sharp teeth of crocodiles and grip of slithering snakes, before boarding another boat to continue his journey. He arrived in the Netherlands tan and buoyed in spirit, much to Mother Pouwels' relief. Diny eagerly listened, even amid company over dinner on their ship. The charm of sparkle and enthusiasm with which he told stories captivated his audience, including his wife, even though the story was known to her.

Diny was afforded time for social interaction on the ship, along with contemplation. After prayer and thought, Nico decided to set right his relationship with Henk, who had returned from his prison sentence, and Nico joined Diny to visit with Henk and his wife Janneke. For many years, Nico sought to share Christ with his friend, but Henk consistently insisted God could never forgive the horrible sins he had committed. Plus, as a man of science and reason, the entire premise of an intelligent and benevolent Creator seemed lofty. Henk again respectfully rejected Nico's testimony, instead preferring to live as he chose. Complete rejection of the Gospel hurt Nico tremendously, but Nico placed Henk before the Lord, asking for Him to reach Henk and Janneke as only He could.

Their families in Hilversum welcomed them home and marveled at Corina, with Nico and Diny's affinity for parenting. Diny chuckled, her body swollen with her second pregnancy, ready for delivery. They had only arrived a month earlier when the time arrived. On 23 September 1949, their second daughter Margaretha Caroline was born at the hospital in Hilversum, with broad smile, blond hair, and a sweet disposition. Days were spent caring for their girls in a townhome they rented near Opa and Oma Dekker. Their families enjoyed spending time with one-year old Corina and newborn Margaret, with Mother Pouwels insisting they baptize the girls in Dutch Reformed Church, which Pieter and Cornelia also attended.

The girls were brought before the congregation and prayed over, then baptized. The minister blessed them and covered their heads with water, and both girls cried in their parents' arms. Afterwards, Mother Pouwels held a lunch reception in her home to celebrate her granddaughters. They remained in the Netherlands through Sinterklaas Day and New Year's celebrations, before departing again, steaming southeast to begin the tropics of Indonesia.

In January 1950, upon returning from Furlough, Jacobson Van den Berg moved them to Palembang (island of South Sumatra) where Nico became the boss of that location. To celebrate, Nico brought home a puppy for his daughters, a sweet pet for all to enjoy, named Cocoa. Lenny ter Haar and her Australian husband Romeny visited them in Palembang while on holiday and Diny enjoyed hearing stories of how God spared them during the difficult war years. He was a member of the Australian Army and helped liberate Lenny's internment camp. Through the months which followed, they fell in love and relocated to Australia. Diny was again reunited with her best friend, and although living a continent apart, their hearts remained close.

Diny again mentioned the Bangka Island prison camp of Muntok, the resting place of Father Pouwels, only a three-hour boat ride away from their new location in Palembang. Nico halted, claiming he would not discover peace in Muntok, only haunted memories. They received a photograph of the grave marker, and Nico experienced hope in Father Pouwels' decision to follow the Lord, so he was adequately healed without needing to visit the island.

Meanwhile, uncertainty and outbursts of social unrest and politically charged violence continued to surround them in brief flashes, without resolution, and largely away from home. At times, the echoes traveled up the river and they heard distant clashes. The Indonesian people were fighting for their independence from Dutch colonial rule and from any hindrance to self-government, as there were some colonial holdouts who refused freedom.

Diny's father remained an example of a police officer who aimed to modernize and professionalize to the effect of "good policing." During these revolutionary years, the 1929 colonial police handbook *The Standard Operating Manual for Police Officers,* by Dekker and Tacoma, which also included a history of modern colonial police activities, was a primary tool for many Indonesian officers in training at the Republican Police School in Yogyakarta (and later Mertoyudan). The manual was in use in the context of higher education to the police *Perguruan Tinggi Ilmu Kepolisian* (PTIK, Higher School of Police Science) in Djakarta. The successors of this book devoted full attention to the history of Indonesian police, often omitting the benefits or contributions of the Dutch predecessors.

As the revolution gained momentum, the Dutch realized the transfer of power would happen again, and soon. As Diny's father had predicted, while the Pouwels' were on Furlough in the Netherlands, the police agencies were gradually handed over to the Indie State Police and on 6 December 1949 Chief of Police of the Police Commissioner Jaya promoted Commander TKI Natadikusumah to acting Police Chief Commissioner Jaya, based in Jl Merdeka Square West. Queen Juliana of the Netherlands handed over leadership and reigning sovereignty to the nation of Indie by signing an agreement on 27 December 1949, and they would no longer call the country the Dutch East Indies. These events prevailed as milestones in the history of the birth of the free country of Indonesia.

While they raised their daughters in Indonesia in a similar fashion to Diny's upbringing, the atmosphere of the country had changed. Indeed, an alteration began before the Dekkers departed on their 1939 Furlough, when the system and design of the country began transforming. With war, they lost some of the innocent charm surrounding the land. A sense of wonder was retained while viewing their adopted country through the eyes of their children.

Diny sewed all the children's clothes, and ordered nothing from the Netherlands, because they could buy beautiful, quality fabric in the Indonesian fabric stores. The sewing patterns were shared among Dutch friends. Clothes for children in Indonesia were simple and easy to make: loose sleeveless dresses, clean designs, and children always looked presentable. The outfits kept them cool in the tropic heat. There were no washing machines or refrigerators, yet they could afford to employ staff members to help with their daily chores, which assisted them in a wild landscape as Indonesia.

Their lives were filled with routine, moving, and the constants of time socializing with others. Nico took Diny dancing, waltzing through celebrations, swirling on the dance floor, each mesmerized in the other's gaze. After an evening of delight, the morning arrived, with hungry daughters, an active puppy, resuming responsibilities. Time continued through that dynamic year with two babies in diapers and a busy husband charging forth in his career. Lenny and her family visited again, and she and Diny marveled at the sight of their daughters all playing together.

Chapter Thirty
Palembang, Sumatra, Indonesia, 1950

One bright September morning in 1950, Diny remained in bed beyond sunrise, hiding in the darkness from a headache, her head and body faint in illness. Her doctor had removed her right thumb nail the day before, which was infected beyond repair. Diny's right hand was wrapped to protect the open skin. Her hand and head pounded with a throbbing ache. Looking at Nico's handsome wedding photo, Diny whispered a prayer for Nico as his "big boss" was coming from Djakarta to inspect the office that day, and Nico prepared to make certain the office was running smoothly.

They would welcome the boss for dinner and an overnight visit before a morning departure, and Diny needed to ensure the guest room was well-appointed, and all meals arranged with Kokki. However, Indonesia celebrated a national holiday, so all their servants had the day off, and she would complete all the preparations on her own, from preparing the meals to serving their guests. The house silently slumbered on that morning, too quiet.

Suddenly, Diny heard a clamoring noise out front with screams, and stumbled out the front door, the bright sun blurring her vision. Their neighbor in the street scooped up Diny's bleeding dog. Someone had run over their beloved dog Cocoa and continued along the road! She felt great consternation in her heart with her husband's important visitor, her dead dog, her throbbing thumb, and the prospect of a long, lonely day. Her neighbor, seeing the shock and dismay on Diny's face, took Cocoa to bury in the backyard.

What horrible circumstances today! Hopefully my daughters will bring joy and smiles to my already-tragic day, Diny thought. She raced to check on them, as Corina always bounded out of bed, eager for the day ahead. She wondered at their silence. Little Corina lay still, perhaps tired or growing and needing extra rest. On hearing Diny's voice, she called to her mother, claiming she could not move her body.

"I cannot move, Mother," Corina cried. Diny laughed as Corina repeated, "I am stuck."

Diny was adamant, chiding her. "We need to get going, to begin our day, Corina! I need all your help today for your father's special visitor. Our helpers are not here, so you must help me set the table and cook meals," she urged her eldest, believing her child might be acting in some dramatic fashion. Then she left for the kitchen to prepare breakfast.

Corina screamed with a terrified shriek still foreign to Diny, even after two years of mothering. Margaret awakened, also sobbing. "Please help me, Mother! Help my legs move!" Corina squeaked.

Diny raced into the room, and stroked her daughter's mottled face, but could not inspire her limp, feverish girl to move, as though all muscles lost their ability to operate. Every time Diny held Corina up to walk, Corina collapsed back into bed. Over and again they tried, and her daughter fell, limp and flaccid.

Panic ached Diny's stomach. She doubled over with the gasp of lost air, grief traveling up her spine and into her head, again blurring her vision. She steadied herself and looked into Corina's eyes, where her fear was matched. She must act quickly and without hesitation, praying aloud as she sprinted for the telephone.

Diny called for their doctor, and then Nico, and both arrived quickly. After examination, the doctor grimly led Nico and Diny outside. He removed his protective mask and gloves to speak with them.

"Your daughter has *poliomyelitis*, and will not recover on her own," he warned them. "This very infectious disease spreads easily. You may have read in the papers the terrible outcome of some polio victims."

Nico paced and probed, "What is it? Polio? *Polio*! Doctor, are you certain?"

The doctor nodded while cleaning his instruments, and motioned for Diny's hand, inquiring at her damaged thumb. She shook her head and pulled her hand away, crossing her arms.

Nico asked, "Dien, have you heard of this disease?"

Diny collapsed into a chair. This mysterious disease called polio had taken over Corina's tiny frame, at only age two and a half. "Could this be meningitis?" Diny ventured.

The doctor frowned. "No, her full body paralysis lends itself toward *poliomyelitis*. But you are right. Both illnesses have inflammation of sorts." He held his hand out for Diny's hand and removed the old wrapping. He inspected her thumb and placed ointment and a gauze wrap around it.

"There. Now rest your hand, Diny." He sat down and rubbed his chin. "Let me think. Has Corina gone to a swimming pool recently, in a public place?"

"Yes! We always go to the Palembang pool."

"Ah, I see. That explains it. Another little Dutch girl may have it, but an Indie boy was just diagnosed. They are still very ill. We are still figuring out this polio business, and none of my colleagues here understand what the best treatment is, either."

Even the doctor seemed baffled. He stopped at the edge of their veranda and clutched his bag. "I must quarantine you all immediately, so you do not infect others. Six weeks here, and no exceptions — your servants included — you must call them back from their holiday. We cannot risk an outbreak."

Nico went pale, then sprinted inside to his daughters. Diny remained on the veranda, where the doctor urged, "Rest, my friend, and try to stay calm. We will deliver food and supplies to you, so not to worry. The entire city is uncertain what this *polio* truly means for your daughter, but I will ask my superiors in Djakarta, and find some answers for you. Some say an Iron Lung can help the worst of the patients. I pray little Corina will not need an intervention."

Diny returned to her daughters' room where Nico was on the floor next to Corina's bed. Diny held Margaret close, and mourned, "What will we do, Nico? What if she —" Diny sobbed.

Nico stood and took Margaret into the kitchen to feed her before moving her into their bedroom, while Diny sat on her daughter's bed as tiny Corina slept. Over the course of the day, Corina's fever persisted and spiked. She drenched the sheets in sweat. As Diny tended to Corina, her heart filled with fear. She sat beside Corina's bed, unwilling to move for hours and unable to comprehend the diagnosis, until she was able to care for her daughter, bringing water, broth, clean linens, a cool cloth for her forehead, and love.

Diny's face was swollen from tears, sobs which found no relief. "There must be a special river in Heaven filled with all my tears," Diny wept. As darkness settled four days into the illness, exhaustion invaded her mind, and Nico ushered her to bed.

Diny sighed, "I am sorry about your boss, *Niek*, I did not have him over for dinner this visit."

He pulled her close, "Hush, *Grietje*. My boss understands. He went back to Djakarta immediately, and was certainly glad to not join the quarantine. All is well in my office, where I am not needed. Here I am most needed, and here is where I want to be." He tucked her into bed, and she slept while he tended to their girls.

The whole family remained under quarantine for six long weeks, including their servants, who had returned from their national holiday celebration to a household filled with deep sorrow. The idea of total paralysis horrified the Pouwels' family. They were helpless to assist Corina or bring healing. Diny brought Corina into her bed at night for comfort and security, and still, Corina cried from great pain.

Eventually, Corina provided a few hopeful smiles through the pain, but remained in a state of peril, only starting to regain the use of her arms. They were uncertain if her paralyzed legs would regain any feeling or use. She eventually healed from the polio, and never required an Iron Lung to breathe, as other unfortunate children had, but her body remained weak.

None of the other family members contracted the illness. Corina eventually learned to crawl around, right next to one-year old Margaret, and both started to walk precariously, together holding onto furniture for assistance. Corina tried to strengthen her body, and Diny challenged her. The girls played as they grew together, both along the same physical ability, until Margaret surpassed Corina's ability for motor skills.

Initially, Corina's doctor prescribed various treatments: electrical shocks three times a week to stimulate stagnant muscles, therapeutic massages, and swimming every day, as a rejuvenation therapy to restore her muscles. They were blessed that she survived the polio when so many did not, and some who remained alive were required to live inside a hospital with a machine breathing for them. Diny marveled at Corina's bravery.

They were also thankful God provided them with faithful servants who cared for Margaret when Diny took Corina to hospital for treatment and therapy sessions. Corina rode on Diny's bike to the hospital, holding tightly, and Diny recognized Corina's little heart feared the treatments. Unable to pay extraordinary hospital costs, Nico and Diny felt despair at times, but Jacobson Van den Berg generously helped the family pay the high medical bills.

After a while, Diny felt another stirring within her, and again discovered she was pregnant. She and Nico rejoiced at God's goodness with the hopes of another child, yet fear threatened to overpower her at the idea of another sickness to overtake her children.

The Pouwels family discovered Corina's polio therapeutic massage treatments could not continue because the masseur was moving back to the Netherlands. Nico's company asked around and was unable to find a qualified masseur in Palembang but discovered a skilled masseur in the city of Bandung. Normally, they might take a train for treatment, but Bandung was on another island. Palembang was in the eastern portion of Sumatra, followed by the Sunda Strait waterway, and Bandung was situated in the western portion of the island of West Java. With water between them, a full 800km separated the cities.

Nico remained in Palembang as he was the boss at that location, so Diny went alone, again quite pregnant and traveling on a boat, with Corina and Marge to Bandung, and they rented a bungalow to live in during Corina's intensive treatments. The Bandung masseur was a kind and loving man, and Corina improved with treatments. Time progressed through Diny's pregnancy, Corina's therapies, swimming each day, and to the market for groceries, and the park for exercise. Still, it was lonely without Nico, caring for two children while pregnant. Their separation weighed heavily on her mind.

While alone in Bandung, Diny went into labor, and sent a telegram to Nico to hurry along to Bandung for the birth, although his journey took hours and she knew she might deliver their third child alone. The kind masseur and his loving wife took care of Corina and Marge while Diny was in the hospital. Diny gave birth to her third daughter on 29 September 1951. She wept at the Lord's goodness in providing a healthy child! Nico arrived via airplane to see his little daughter, and sat at the edge of Diny's bed, admiring his wife and daughter. Diny held their child to Nico's face.

"Well, she is a girl. We only have a boy's name, so I think we should decide on a girl's name," Diny said. "I like Nicolette."

"No, she must not be named after me!" Nico chuckled.

"Okay," Diny said, "you go ahead and think of names."

Nico offered ideas from Alice to Zelda, but he could not come up with anything. They happily settled on naming their daughter Nicolette Christine. Nico stayed the weekend and returned to Palembang. Post-delivery, Diny became ill, an intense sickness which failed to subside, and she could not care for her baby. The doctors diagnosed Diny with malaria and she stayed in the hospital for ten days after Nicolette's birth.

Nico visited them on weekends, since he worked during the week. To travel that distance, he took a Friday morning ferry between the islands of Sumatra and Java. When Sunday arrived, Nico returned to Sumatra and Diny remained alone, to care for three tiny children, feelings of agony, helplessness, and despair overwhelming her.

When Diny's illness weakened her for a time, with a newborn child and two other daughters, Nico would tend to Corina and Marge in the gardens, a blanket on the grass for lunches outside, so Diny remained indoors. He assembled a table, chairs, and tablecloth underneath a wide-spreading tree, to sit in the yard together to play. The two older girls were crazy about their little sister Nicky and helped Nico and Diny with her tiny diapers. They could carry Nicky or sit with her on their laps. They watched as Diny nursed Nicky, careful to protect her in every way throughout each day.

Eventually, the masseur decided Corina progressed enough to return home, and they bid their new friends farewell, finding a new masseur in Palembang to continue Corina's therapeutic massages. Nico was elated to have his family return home, as his responsibilities were immense as the head of that office. A typical day in Palembang included daily treatment for Corina's polio, so Diny took her on bicycle to the hospital, while Marge and Nicky remained home with the servants. They returned from therapy for a warm lunch and nap.

Diny filled her hours of the day with those therapies, caring for her small children, sewing clothing, and keeping correspondence with family and friends, time together outside on the veranda, and stooping down for kisses from her daughters, who rarely settled into a chair next to her until tea time.

On the days Corina did not have treatment or massages in the hospital, Diny took all three girls to the Palembang swimming pool. Nico assembled a basket/seat on the front steering handles of Diny's bicycle for Nicolette to sit in, and a long wooden board on the carrier in the back, a plank on the *bagagedrager* (luggage rack), for Corina and Marge, sitting in a tandem straddle position, with a strap around them to keep them on the bicycle. Diny placed Nicolette in the front seat first for balance, then held onto the saddle, and hoisted Corina and Marge in the back; otherwise, the whole bike would tip over. Quite an acrobatic adventure every day, and it must have been quite a sight. They received many astounded remarks when she bicycled with her three young girls!

As they were preparing to relocate again, Diny heard the sad news that her father's colleague, Johan Henry Smith, had died in January 1951. Pieter and Smith wrote the police handbook together when Smith was the head of the Soekaboemi Police Training Academy and Dekker served as Adjunct-Chief Superintendent of Police and Inspector. The Dekkers and Smiths flourished in the Javan mountains, and moreover, they remained friends over their years and travels, and steady companions in the internment camps during the war. Diny always asked for a flaming plate of bananas when Smith was their dinner guest.

After surviving his own horrors in the war, in 1946 Smith retired and returned to the Netherlands. Between 1946 and 1951, he wrote textbooks, articles in police journals, and gave lectures to officers. Diny felt sorry her father lost more friends and connections to his former life in Indie. Even as Diny thrived there, her dad could never return; they were powerless to return the perceived innocence to those islands.

In 1952, Jacobson Van den Berg moved Nico and family to Medan (northeast coast on the island of North Sumatra, 1400 km from Palembang), where he worked just underneath the head of that location. When they arrived, their home was not ready for them, so they started in a hotel, occupying one big hotel room on the ground level, complete with a sizable patio, where Corina and Margaret played. Beside the front patio was a sandbox under a tree, where they created sand cookies and tarts, socializing with other neighbor children as well. Nicolette napped in her pram in the shade while Diny cross-stitched or sewed.

When the house was prepared for them to move in, the Pouwels family employed a married couple on staff — Rapin the *Djongos*, and Samira the *Baboe* — and the family felt blessed with a special convenience of a refrigerator. All the customs and routines were resumed. Diny bicycled all three girls to the Medan swimming pool each day for therapy and exercise. Nico and Diny played tennis a few times a week if it did not rain, and the children came along to help retrieve the balls. She also set up a badminton net along with croquet when they entertained guests outdoors at their home.

Nico was not the boss in his Medan work location, as the region was very large; he was second in charge but required to do most of the traveling. This routine would last two years. The untouched, unprotected soul is a fortress, indwelled by Christ and in greater measure than before. Diny longed to anchor into a home, and yet their Home was God, despite the fleeting length of time in locations. With each move, their equilibrium jostled, but eventually evened, usually as they grasped God's faithfulness and longstanding love.

Nico and Diny preferred the veranda, increasingly called a "patio" (*platje*) after Nico returned from work at half-past four, after their invigorating tin-bucket bath, then "tea hour," drinking tea or lemonade (*air djcroek*). The children received a cup of tea with milk. They spoke of their day, sharing the latest struggle which presented itself and marveled at how the Lord would work out those details. At times Nico read the newspaper while Diny embroidered or created something (pillowcase, dress, decoration, or doily) and their daughters played around them joyfully, content with dolls, riding their bicycles, or frolicking in the gardens.

On 31 January 1953, they heard on the radio the sorrowful news of a great North Sea Flood of 1953, which soaked a great deal of land, mostly in Zeeland, but also England and Belgium. Dutch fatalities in the *Watersnoodramp* were 1836, with much land to recover and rebuild. Nelly and her husband Anton were devastated by this event, which altered their neighborhood in Rotterdam. The Delta Works project was initiated to sustain the country from future flooding disasters and the rebuilding took even more than a year for some communities. During that time, the Netherlands made a startling discovery, pumping out water to reclaim more land uncovered Allied airplanes and German bombers, all on the muddy bottom of the North Sea.

Later that year, Corina began her education at a Dutch school, and Diny sent her off with encouragement and love, certain her daughter's bubbly disposition would earn her many friends. She encouraged Corina to remain determined. They vacationed for a week in Prapat on Lake Toba, in the middle of North Sumatra. Nico with his three girls took the canoe into the peaceful clear lake, rowing out so the girls could swim back to Diny at the shoreline. They continued rowing and swimming, then turned the canoe over and sat upon the hump of the canoe, like riding a whale. Each girl took turns leaping off the upside-down canoe into the water, and again paddled over to Diny sunning on the shore.

When Jacobson Van den Berg transferred the family to Padang in 1954, their married couple on staff (Rapin, the *Djongos*, and Samira, the *Baboe*) wanted to come along with the family, which was a great blessing. However, they found out that was not possible, because upon arrival, the locals of Padang would not accept a Medan couple into their local society. They were only moving 800 km away, to the southwest coast on the island of West Sumatra. Even amidst the attempts of Indonesian independence as the country transformed from an overwrought, prolonged colony into a multicultural democracy, some islanders refused to accept those from another area, even though they were still on the island of Sumatra.

Rapin and Samira mournfully returned north to Medan to work for another Dutch family there, and Nico and Diny hired another round of staff to help them in Padang. With this move, Nico became the boss of his company there, the head man in charge. The city was larger than other Indonesian cities and had a vibrant Dutch Christian Reformed Church. Nico served as an elder of the church and helped perform the lengthy communion ceremonies around tables.

Also, in Padang, they met a wonderful family, Sylvia and Ruud Benink, who were lovely neighbors with two daughters. Nico connected with Ruud, and Diny found a kindred spirit in Syl, exchanging stories, recipes, and sewing patterns. They were tremendous companions and a help with getting established in the neighborhood, with the social club and schools for the children. When the Pouwels family went on Furlough, they knew their home would be well tended by the Beninks.

Chapter Thirty-One
Hilversum, 1954

In 1954, they again went on furlough — the 3-week boat trips were a highlight. Diny often thought back on those trips, and the delight throughout her life from childhood to adulthood. Nico's company Jacobson Van den Berg paid for the 3-week boat trip there, along with their entire stay for their 6-month Furlough in the Netherlands, and 3-week boat trip back to Indonesia. The amazing experience they took for granted, because all the big Dutch-owned Indonesian companies provided luxuries for their employees.

Diny created crepe-paper dresses for each of her daughters, which they wore for a Sinterklaas "costume" party for children, where they could win a prize with the best costumes. The design of the contest was utilizing crepe paper and their imagination for a dress. Diny took a picture of her girls, and all three looked so miserable, because it was hot, and the crepe paper was wrinkled and itchy, so the dresses were uncomfortable. Diny felt terrible for them. That was the only time she made crepe-paper dresses, and they were not a success. After all the effort and discomfort, nobody in their family even won a prize. Diny found oranges for her children, which was a great treat, as they never ate oranges in Indonesia, a worthy consolation for not winning the dress contest.

While on Furlough, they lived in a rented, fully furnished house in Hilversum, the Netherlands, and Nico rented a car. They visited family and friends, and one time went with friends to Austria for a few days. They had found a highly recommended home for their three girls to stay in Austria. Nico and Diny would stay elsewhere, nearby, with their traveling companions. The friend who suggested the place to them was pleased with the people who took care of their children. This idea turned out to be a complete disaster, and Nico and Diny felt terrible about it. The three girls were crying when Nico and Diny picked them up and they never understood why this family was so highly recommended. It bothered them, as they really thought their girls were cared for with love.

Also during their time in Holland, Corina faced her first operation. Their Medan masseur gave them the name and address of an orthopedic children's hospital in Leersum, the Netherlands, 30 minutes southeast of Hilversum. The hope was the doctor there might provide more advice for Corina's condition. Diny encouraged Corina to be strong and brave, and ensured Nico would be at Corina's side for the recovery process. Corina's first surgery at age five was a success, although her fear and discomfort were evident. She remained in the rehabilitation center for six weeks, on the Hoogstraat. Nico, Diny, and Opa Dekker visited Corina as much as possible. Other family members lived far away from Leersum and telephoned when they could, "Zij leefden met ons mee" (they sympathize with Corina) and offered prayers.

Diny realized Corina would just be differently-abled than her other daughters but hoped to inspire Corina to strive for the best recovery, striving to strengthen her weakened muscles and solidify her self-esteem. She promised to remain in prayer for Corina and to support her in any way possible, just as the Lord would strengthen her and offer peace. When Corina returned home after six weeks, Diny created a feast for her. She assembled the couch in the front room with a sheet, pillows, and blankets for Corina to rest, along with Corina's favorite dinner to bring her cheer. She wrapped Corina's leg with plastic for a bath, so her healing wound would not get wet. Diny urged her daughter to work hard for a quick recovery.

Marge started school in the Netherlands as soon as they arrived. As soon as Corina healed, she also attended classes, and Nicolette was too young for school so she stayed home with Diny. Evenings were spent visiting family. Diny sewed three identical dresses for her daughters. With matching saddle shoes and bobby socks, her girls looked like triplets, although their varied heights did reveal they were sisters.

Plenty of time was spent in the Hilversum home of Pieter and Cornelia, called Opa and Oma Dekker. Oma sat in her cushioned chair with her feet in warm slippers (one blue and one red, because the other ones wore out), and a foot warmer. Pieter and Cornelia were older, but content to reside in the blessings of grace and hope the Lord had afforded them. Sometimes the intense quiet in their house, the stillness during nap time, was unbearable, and the only sound their granddaughters heard was a grandfather clock ticking away. Moreover, eating proved interesting, as Oma Dekker was placed on a salt-free diet and their food tasted bland.

At the main entry hallway stood a large hollow elephant's foot which held umbrellas. The toe nails and elephant's hair on the outside of the leg brought any child a fright. The stairs leading up to the bedrooms creaked, and the grandfather clock chirped and chimed at strange hours. Upon a wardrobe inside Oma and Opa's bedroom was a glass case holding a colorful bird-of-paradise.

In the main level sitting room, Opa's chair was close to Oma's chair, opposite the wood burning stove. Nearby, a stuffed crocodile hung on the wall. Diny recognized all those Indie details anew through the eyes of her daughters. The backyard whirled with tall trees near Opa's garden shed, and the courtyard ended in a gate toward the woods. They lived near a large pond, where Opa took his granddaughters to feed ducks. On Sunday mornings, the girls would hold Opa's hand the entire walk to church, his large hands encompassing theirs in security and love.

Opa Dekker maintained a morning routine of drinking coffee, "Strong enough to put a thick mustache on my face," he chuckled. His breakfast was toast with butter, and *hagelslag*. Oma Dekker boiled milk in a saucepan on the stovetop.

"Children, I take the skin of the milk, like a pudding skin, and place it on top of the hagelslag, resulting in a creamy milk and chocolate sprinkles toast breakfast for Opa." The granddaughters stared at Opa's unique breakfast, and then Oma prepared chocolate *hagelslag* for everyone.

They drove to visit Mother Pouwels, her body shrinking with age and fragility though her spirit remained steadfast. *Moeder* loved her grandchildren and welcomed them with food and cheer. They later visited Oma van den Bout, her body aging yet her mind flourishing, living in a retirement home in Amsterdam with other older women. Both the great-Omas were vibrant and loving despite their age, but Diny realized she might not again have a chance to visit with loving matriarchs, so she savored each conversation.

In late June, Nico and Diny took their daughters on holiday to Noordwijk, a beach just west of Leiden. They splashed in the North Sea, walked along paths, and hiked up dunes and dikes lined with tall grass. Later they gathered to watch sailboats glide smoothly, white sails fully engaged. In the evenings, fishermen returned to shore, their boats full of herring, cod, and haddock.

Later that summer, Diny and Nico left their girls with Opa and Oma Dekker and visited Paris for several days. They enjoyed moments of tourism in France, which was still rebuilding. It was only four years after the war, but France gained momentum in growth. One evening in Paris, they ventured to the Moulin Rouge, where the windmill out front seemed like a misplaced Dutch antiquity, and lights along the edges of the buildings glowed warmly along wet streets. Charming double-lit street lamps guided them to the entrance, a curious place in a quaint neighborhood. The women at Moulin Rouge seem bawdy to Diny, but the stage was lit to obscure the meager clothing, draped elegantly on the dancing ladies. It seems so artistic and natural, this nudity. Much like a "Men's Only" smoker's lounge, lights were dimmed, and round tables intimately situated with jarred candles to illuminate faces, the table, and their night. After a few days away, touring the Eiffel Tower, the Louvre Museum, and other Paris charms, Diny and Nico returned to their girls.

When they left on Furlough, they took suitcases with clothes and unique presents from Indie (wood work and colorful sarongs) for their Dutch family. For the return to Indie, they filled their suitcases with special Dutch treats and items to introduce their servants to the Netherlands, their possessions stacked and stored on the ship for the three week journey home.

Padang, Sumatra, Indonesia, 1954

After Furlough ended in 1954, Jacobson Van den Berg stationed them in Medan again where Nico worked under another man. While that man managed the local Medan office, Nico did much of the traveling. A year later in 1955 they were transferred to Padang (island of Sumatra), where Nico again was promoted to boss. Like the streets of any bustling city, Padang teemed with movement. Merchants offered colorful fabrics, tobacco products, and local ready-made foods. Others sold jewelry, trinkets for tourists, and carved wooden treasures. Men sat on the dirt under the shade of a tree, carved in silence, knives scraping away into smooth, rounded movements, etching scrollwork onto dark Sulawesi wood.

While strolling on a Padang street one afternoon, Nico requested three sizable panels of wood: one depicting the planting of a field, one expressing the harvesting of it, and one examining the threshing of the grain. The undertaking required time, but Nico was pleased with the man's detailed efforts, with the presence of scene, the active depiction of a working Indonesian farm. Nico placed the three wooden panels in a row in their hallway, and each time the children passed those wooden scenes, they were reminded of diligent work.

They welcomed an excellent *Kokki* named Siti, a delightful and compassionate Indie woman. She was older, with white hair, and beginning to slow with age, although her meals were always appetizing. Nico discovered her squinting and unable to read Indie writing, signaling she had vision problems, so he drove her to the eye doctor, who prescribed glasses. Then she could read again without headaches. Many hired helpers had neither health insurance nor the money for doctor appointments, but Nico insisted on paying for doctor visits. Siti's vision and life was so improved, she could crochet numerous doilies and placemats for the family. Diny paid for the materials, and Siti found a pattern from a Dutch crochet magazine. Although Siti could not read the Dutch instructions, she studied the picture and skillfully constructed the piece, which turned out terrific!

Moreover, Siti specialized in preparing elaborate *Rijsttafels,* and often the family would have a dozen friends and colleagues over for meals, to enjoy her cooking, always including their gracious neighbors Ruud and Syl Benink. Kokki prepared prevalent dishes like Nasi Goreng (fried rice), vegetable dish Gado Gado, Lodeh (jackfruit and vegetable coconut soup); Javanese dishes like peanut Saté Babi (skewered grilled pork) with Katjang Saus (peanut sauce), Kip Saté (skewered grilled chicken), and Babi Kecap (pork in sweet soy). They ate Balinese Chicken, Sumatran dish Rendang (dried meat, coconut milk, chili, and spices, which preserved the meat for weeks), Saté Daging (marinated chicken on bamboo sticks), fusion foods like Filipino-influenced Loempia (meat/vegetable egg rolls), and Bamie (Chinese wheat noodles with meat). Dinners also included Atjar, a cool, crunchy cucumber salad to soften the spicy Sambal bite (a spicy relish), and kroepoek emping crackers (shrimp chips), and concluded with fragrant Pisang Goreng (fried banana fritters).

The various textures, flavors, spices, and temperatures of their foods provided a more rewarding — and colorful — dining experience to enhance the senses. Gathering for food, for joyous occasions, provided a bonding, and heightened their well-being. Saying grace remained an important aspect, to include God in their thanksgiving feasts.

Also, with Ruud and Syl Benink, they were part of the *SOOS —* "Society," Dutch social club in Padang. They spoke Dutch, ate delicious food, and their children grew close. Nico brought a large bag of freshly fried kroepoek emping, shrimp chips, a special treat, the scent of *trassi* (shrimp paste) lingering in the air. Diny became accustomed to Syl's familiar mannerisms and easy-going temperament, her gentle way of speaking, and her generosity. When gathering with the SOOS, they congregated in a clubhouse right next to the ocean, and occasionally on the ocean side, someone yelled, "Shark!" and everyone gasped and ran to the windows to see the fin of a shark slicing through the water.

The untamed beauty of the beaches, with sea shells, and jungles with monkeys splashing on the shoreline, could often be dimmed with the danger of sharks gliding close to the edge. Monkeys swinging from trees and geckos scurrying on walls were normal occasions. Their family times were especially memorable at the edge of the water. When the tide was out, they walked toward the ocean, collecting pristine seashells from the shallow banks. Nico walked with their girls as far out as possible, looking for shells, crabs, and other critters. They loved sea cucumbers, because when they stomped on them, the cucumbers popped. They liked to see how far a sea cucumber would squirt into the water.

As a child, Diny appreciated the quiet and serenity of nature, along with the joyful bird songs and majestic flowers in ways she was unable to as an adult. Perhaps the busyness of her life, raising children, attending to daily physical and emotional needs, seemed to swallow up her former self, *the daydreamer, the wanderer, the gardener*, if only for a season of busyness. She utilized her skills as a nurse and wondered at a life with that dream realized.

Diny felt a sense of accomplishment through mothering, and discovered ways to express herself through floral arrangements, and by creating welcoming gardens reminiscent of her childhood home in Batavia where her dad meandered. She wisely established a place of solitude for silence and prayer.

On nights of a volcanic eruption, the darkness was sliced by fire, the bright red flow of lava descending the distant mountain. Corina was fascinated by the majestic destructive nature of a volcano, reminiscent of Diny's childhood fears and awe at God's creation. Earthquakes were common, but not large. Nico warned his children to not stand underneath a coconut tree during an earthquake, or a coconut would bump them on the head.

Diny's mother Cora telephoned on 17 June 1955, with the sad news of Oma van den Bout's death in Amsterdam at nearly 85 years of age. Pieternella Jannigje den Breejen van den Bout passed peacefully. Diny fondly remembered their times together making Stroopwaffels, snacking on Queen Wilhelmina peppermints, and baking together on snowy days. Riding in Opa's river boat together. Oma's enthusiastic, outgoing spirit, which Diny inherited, was passed along to Nicolette.

Less than three months later, Nico received a telephone call from his older brother Piet, sharing about their beloved Mother Pouwels' death at the age of 74 on 15 September 1955. Klasina Aaltje Van de Wetering Pouwels had been ushered into the presence of God, and Nico sadly realized he was now an orphan and must navigate life without the love and leadership of parents.

After another year in Padang, in 1956 Nico and Diny moved their family to Surabaya (Java), where Nico was promoted to boss, working his way into a new job and location which seemed suited to him, finally arriving into a comfortable place to thrive and build a real life. To celebrate another successful move, Nico brought home a dark brown puppy for his children, and they called him *Chocolate*. Their puppy was a welcome addition to their home, playing with the girls and bringing them laughter. On Friday evenings, Nico took Diny dancing at their Dutch social club, and their daughters stayed home with Kokki Siti, who stayed late to create something from the crochet books, such as doilies or placemats, and earn some extra money for her own family. The children slept peacefully until their parents returned home from dancing, when they wanted to hear stories of dancing.

Every move for Nico's job brought a promotion, so at last in Surabaya Nico was the absolute boss of Jacobson Van den Berg there and would not require travel, but could settle into his role and raise his family there. Nico was a good salesman, always efficient and charming. He had worked diligently and now after ten years had become accomplished with the company, so he could finally reap the benefits of all the challenging work and effort. No sooner had they arrived than Diny felt a new life growing inside of her and was expecting their fourth child. Nicolette started school in Surabaya, and all three daughters attended Dutch schools in Indonesia.

On 28 December 1956, Nico's son Peter Huibert Pouwels was born, fulfilling the heritage for more than two hundred years of each generation of the Pouwels family producing a son and naming him "Pieter Pouwels." And God had blessed their marriage richly with four beautiful children: Corina, Margaret, Nicolette, and Peter. There was an incredible sense of satisfaction for Diny to watch her son and daughters grow and mature in the country she loved. This was indeed a dream realized, a marvelous upbringing with cultural experiences, a graceful atmosphere, heat and humidity tolerable to them, and wonderful diversity of events in their lives.

They felt secure, settled, as now in Surabaya they prepared to stay, to fashion their life there permanently. Jacobson Van den Berg was a solid company with tremendous benefits. As compelled and attracted as Diny was to safety and the relative comforts of home, the thrill of travel and adventure surged her forward. This was now a new world, called *Indonesia*, an altered and varied landscape, and days stretched before her like a promising purpose. She could see the generations extending beyond her in the dappled sunshine of the verdant islands.

She and Nico dedicated their purpose toward a genuine love for God and felt committed to the greater plan for Indonesia despite the political chaos islanders embraced in a battle for independence. After months of riots and unrest creeping closer to them, darkness pervading and revolution in other cities, they realized the unavoidable, unalterable change. Nico and Diny's plans had been etched in their minds, but faced an atmospheric shift. The conflicts were described in the newspapers and radio programs, warning of chaos and trouble.

A revolution was growing on bustling city streets and toppling an empire. The situation in Indonesia increased in violence and danger. When Queen Juliana of the Netherlands handed over leadership and reigning sovereignty to the nation of Indonesia by signing an agreement on 27 December 1949, everything crumbled. Nico attributed the differences to World War II, but thought the skirmishes would eventually settle, and they could safely remain in the country.

The government under President Sukarno would be called Indonesia thereafter; they worked up to the moment on 5 December 1957 in which all Dutch and other Europeans were expelled and required to leave the country. Thousands of Europeans would be forced to leave and resettle. By Sukarno's decree, white people were forbidden in stores, movie theaters, and other public places. Local Indonesians threw rocks at Diny as she bicycled with her children; rocks smacked her legs and left large bruises. She dared not stop, for fear of what would happen with young Indonesians pelting them with stones and screaming for them to leave. In public markets, people tossed raw eggs at them, and overnight painted profanities and other unpleasant things on their homes and cars (like, "Go home, dirty dogs!").

"You cannot come in here anymore," an Indonesian shop owner said to Diny. She had stepped into a small grocery store where she frequently shopped.

"Why? I have always paid you, and I am always good to you."

"That does not matter any longer. From now on, I need to see your passport to see if you are Dutch. And if you are Dutch, I will not sell to you."

Diny pointed to her face. "Can you see I am Dutch?" She cried.

He shook his head, ushered her out, and locked the store door.

Their beloved servants, whom they respected unconditionally, always considered family members, were not allowed to come to work in European homes any longer. Late one evening, Kokki knocked at the door and offered to shop for them at the *Pasar*, the market, and to leave the groceries on their front steps. Diny gave Kokki money to shop and felt grateful for her friend's support and compassion to help her shop for the family. The servants visited one last time to say farewell, a tearful goodbye for them all. The Pouwels family prepared to depart their beloved Indonesian home for an uncertain new life in the Netherlands.

Chapter Thirty-Two
Hilversum, December 1957

They realized they must leave Indonesia permanently. Diny wished to gather dark handfuls of soil into bags, jars, or urns to keep with her, yet she knew their personal items were limited, and after all — dirt is just dirt. She thought of the idea in the night, a sweaty horror dream waking her to alertness. In the morning, the depth of terror subsided, and she packed necessities for their exodus. She left behind the precious soil, for if she gathered clumps and soil settled under her nails, she would soon be required to wash her hands clean of the place.

What would a jar hold but memories of ordinary soil? Just as tropical fruits and flowers would flourish nowhere else if transplanted, the heart might wither from lack of a temperate climate. Diny reminded herself she must always cultivate what may grow. Her beloved paradise slipped away, at first slowly, unnoticed, as lyrical and enchanting as swaying to music. As in the sultry heat the fragrances of flowers waft through thick air and later subside, so her homeland shifted, an earthquake of circumstance and liberation for some and departures for herself and her loved ones.

In December 1957, Diny sorrowfully left Indonesia with their four children, bringing along minimal luggage. Nico stayed behind to liquidate his business, since he was the boss in that location. He could no longer care for their little puppy, Chocolate, and gave him to a staff member. They were not allowed to take much with them — no extra money. Nico bought some special jewelry for Diny, instead of leaving much money there. From the things they could take with them, a lot was stolen by the people who had packed their stuff. Diny could transport some heirlooms inside a giant wooden chest with a ship carved into the dark Sumatran wood, and packed wooden serving trays for coffee and tea time, and other local traditional items.

When Diny and her children left Indonesia, Corina was 9, Marge 8, Nicolette 6, and Peter almost 1-year old. They departed on the boat *The Waterman* for a three-day boat trip from Surabaya to Singapore, packed full of people who had to leave Indonesia. Their entire boat was wretched and disconsolate, including islanders who sat on their haunches, watching the Dutch with distrust. They all left their lives for the unknown, a future encompassing change and fear. Diny had one cramped boat cabin for the 5 of them, and it was so hot, without a window or fan, just miserable three days tightly situated together.

In Singapore, they were assigned to a World War II concentration camp. The design of the camp included long rectangular buildings which were wide open inside each building with no privacy. The camp had no baths, and no baby food for Peter. They slept on army cots with blankets, and it rained tropical monsoon rains the entire time. They ran between buildings to get to a cafeteria to eat, tracking along the mud inside with them everywhere they ran. The girls received their own cots, with a folded army blanket at the foot end, and on the blanket, was a box which contained their own knife, fork, and spoon. Late one night, Corina urgently needed to use the restroom, which meant they all had to go quite a way through the rain without an umbrella. Diny pointed her eldest toward an awning. But Corina snuck around a corner and found a dry place outside the barracks.

As there was no baby food for Peter, Diny received graham crackers and bananas, which she mashed together for her one-year old son. Corina, Marge, and Nicky became inventive, and with cots and blankets made tents, then later played "robber." They were considered outcasts, thrown out of a country, and were required to fend for themselves.

"Everybody for his own, and God for us all," Diny reminded them. Feelings of desperation came over them but Diny was always determined to make the best of it.

"Does this time in the barracks remind you of the war, Mom?" Marge asked, her eyes wide and innocent.

Diny smiled and held her daughter close. "Yes, but thank the Lord we never went to a concentration camp. We had to push through our feelings, even then, *Grietje*. During the War, there were few opportunities to feel sorry for ourselves. We had to stay alive, and it formed us. It did not make us hard or bitter, but it did make us strong. Dutch-strong!"

After 3 days in the camp, they flew from Singapore to Karachi, Pakistan, where they were surprised to see some friends who lived there. Their friends met them at the airport and brought them home for a shower, food, and for cleaning their clothes. What a blessing that was, an unexpected provision in the desert! Every night, their friends would go to the airport, and wait for the Indonesian arrivals, to see if they knew someone immigrating back to the Netherlands. They were unaware of who was on the plane, but knew the Europeans were banned from Indonesia and routed through Karachi for the halfway point. Their friends felt determined to help those friends caught in the troubles. And then Diny and her children flew on to Amsterdam. The trip from Singapore to Amsterdam took 36 hours.

Once in Hilversum, the Netherlands, the family was assigned 2 rooms in a large boarding house (*contractpension*) on the Utrechtse Hoofdweg. Diny knew they were only "passing through," until Nico arrived, when they could look for a house. The boarding house was a haven for children, with always someone to play with in the safety of the boarding house. For the parents, however, it was more difficult: a long line for the only bathroom on each floor, and few toilets, which were often stopped-up by toilet paper. The families had to figure out how to line dry their washed clothes inside small areas of their room. They were fortunate to have heat, because it was winter and bitter cold, but the heat was pumped through pipes, and not a general heat source.

Diny washed their clothing in the kitchen sink and dried it on the conduit (pipeline) which went through the room and produced heat. Peter's many diapers, with the general laundry of four children, produced a great deal of wash, with clothes lining every pipe in the room. The camp complex in which they were temporarily situated had many children to play with and activities like hula-hooping, marbles, playing in the snow, making forts in the woods, and putting on dramatic shows for the parents.

Every morning for breakfast, large pots of oatmeal and cream-of-wheat were delivered to their door. They had to provide their own lunch, and dinner came in stackable square tin containers called *Rantang*, sometimes thick stews, potatoes, meats, and dessert. Diny could scarcely remember when the Netherlands provided her a hearty meal like this! Diny's children all wanted to deliver the tins to the elderly couple on the second floor, since the couple always tipped a sweet candy. Whichever girl delivered the Rantang and received the candy ate it immediately, the sweet luxury a tasty reward.

Every other Friday they ate macaroni and cheese with onions, and opposite Fridays they ate pea soup (*erwtensoep*). There was no refrigerator, so they stored milk and yogurt in glass bottles on the cold tile by a side door with a draft, in front of Nicolette's bed. One morning, a yogurt bottle accidentally fell from Diny's hand onto Nicolette's head, cutting her in the process, with milk and glass scattered. They all cried as Diny bandaged Nicolette's head!

Even though it was a large boarding house with many rooms, each family only had two rooms as their entire home, except for a large family with nine children, who lived in the whole attic, occupying each corner of that space. The children ventured outdoors even on snowy days, and Diny warned them not to gamble with the thin ice covering the nearby pond, as the Netherlands had not encountered a deep enough freeze that winter for ice skating. The *Elfstedentocht,* or eleven cities tour, the 200-km ice skating race through all eleven towns in Friesland, was deemed a special treat to watch — and participate in — and Diny hoped to someday take her children to witness the dashing event.

Nicky rebelled anyway and dashed out toward the middle of the lake, then promptly fell through the ice, into the chilly water. Marge and Corina, spectators to Nicky's rebellion, pulled their sister from the lake. Nicky shivered in her soaked clothes all the way back to her room and Diny fumed in anger and with fear of Nicky's foolish actions.

Every time she was alone, Diny accepted her situation and decided not to fight it. Those moments were a necessity and in many cases in life she realized she had to face hardships and disappointments alone, independently, to reach her goals. There was no other way. Her entire childhood, her father instructed her in matters of character and faith, reminding her God would journey with her. Those times alone were not easy, and she missed Nico terribly. They attempted to handle each challenge at a time and do their best, and Diny was thankful when Nico arrived in April 1958, after his long journey by boat from Indonesia. He had quite a story to tell.

In the Suez Canal near Egypt, another large boat crashed into his ship, although he was not injured in the smash, and the result was a big mess. All the passengers were rescued from the damaged ship and transferred to another boat. The crash had been all over the news in the Netherlands and they worried Nico was hurt, since they knew his boat traveled the Canal around that time. They were delighted when he arrived safely in their midst. Nico was welcomed by four children with "mottled" faces, because all four had the chickenpox at the same time, and were miserable, scratching messes. Young Pieter was in bed, miserable, with cardboard toilet paper rolls over his arms, so he would not scratch the chicken pox. Mercy!

Their years in Indie, their land which would always be *Dutch East Indies* in their mind, their own paradise, remained in Diny's memory as delightful and special, in spite of all the heartaches and troubles they experienced. She was especially ecstatic to return to the country where she was born and had spent the first 17 most beautiful years of her life. Diny and Nico lived in Indonesia from March 1947 until December 1957. Only ten short years had been afforded to their dreams. Even as their brief decade passed, and the family would no longer live in Indonesia, they carried those memories with them. They had matured and raised a family for a decade on those islands.

Nico lost his job and the Jacobson Van den Berg company was liquidated, as their primary business in Indonesia was within the import-export industry. However, upon return to the Netherlands, Nico worked as a salesman with the company he had worked for during the war in Elst. They were overjoyed to see him, as they had plenty of work for him! The company was Taminiau Jam Fabrieken, a jam manufacturing company, and he had served as a salesman.

In 1958, Heinz bought Taminiau Jam Fabrieken, and they merged together, and expanded. The company provided him with a corporate car and began building a house for them in Schiedam, just west of Rotterdam. In the meanwhile, they lived in another contractpension, until they moved to a furnished house near Zuiderhof park on Moerbeilaan in Hilversum for four months, a brick row home with white window frames and red clay roofs, clean windows, and marvelous front gardens. Then finally, they moved to a furnished house on Bilderdijklaan.

Corina, Marge, and Nicky were reacquainted with friends and attended a church retreat. The girls grew in friendships at their Christian school and blossomed. The Pouwels family visited Diny's siblings Nelly and Jan and their families, along with Tante Sluis, Jacob, Stien, and others. Nico and Diny occasionally met with Nico's older brother Piet and his wife Annie and their children.

Many residents in the Netherlands were displaced people, overcrowded into public, subsidized housing, with the government stretched financially, and with few in their ideal place of employment. Some citizens accepted jobs beneath their pay grade or expertise due to an influx of people returning from Indonesia. There were too many people and while rebuilding post-war was necessary work, eventually they found there were not enough sustainable jobs. And the weather, the bone-chilling cold, snow, and ice, was not to their liking. They longed for the tropics.

Nico spoke of this to Diny, of his ideas concerning their life in the Netherlands, after their children were asleep.

"Shall I play some music, perhaps?" Diny smiled, with refreshed lipstick and perfume, ready for an evening with her husband.

She swayed in a bright red skirt and soft white sweater and held several records out for Nico to choose. Their home on Bilderdijklaan boasted enough space for them to play music and dance in their sitting room.

Nico shook his head and slouched into the couch, loosening his necktie, and tossing it onto the coffee table.

Diny placed the records on the shelf. "What happened at work today, Nico? What can we discuss?"

He nodded and stared into the distance, deep in thought, so Diny brought in a tray of hot tea and crispy cookies.

Nico held her hands, beaming at her. "Diny, let me first say, you are an angel; you truly are! God has brought us through so many trials, and you have weathered them gloriously. You take wonderful care of our children and manage the home so seamlessly. Thank you for standing beside me when all seemed lost." They embraced.

Diny smiled, and replied, "All my pleasure, and my love, Nico. You know, I prayed for you for many years, for a strong man of courage. And the Lord answered my prayers and beyond. How could I ever imagine how blessed we would be, with four delightful children, and living so close to our families! But I see something is amiss with our return here." She took a bite out of her cookie.

Nico set down his tea. "Indeed. I feel blessed by you, Dien, and our children, certainly. And so fortunate to work again for Taminiau Jam Fabrieken, as the pace and job is comfortable. I know how to do the work and became very successful in this vocation before the war, learning to barter, trade, and persuade. The time spent as a jam salesman developed my character."

"Yes. You developed your business ideals there and the work sustained you during the war. I am glad you had that opportunity, even if it kept you away in the East when we first met!"

Nico's eyes brightened at the memory of their courtship, and he chuckled. "But I am older now, Diny, more than fifteen years older than when I first started this exact sales career. I wonder how this is progression, for it seems I am going backward! The company was purchased by Heinz, and many things have changed."

He shared the details of some changes, along with a rumination on his job in Indonesia. "Even all I learned for Jacobson Van den Berg seems irrelevant here, without a place to use my profession in import-export trading. Perhaps I would fare better in Rotterdam, in the trade business there, where advancements are steady and expected. I feel haunted returning here, turning every corner and encountering another war memory."

Diny glared at him. "Taminiau Jam Fabrieken has been generous with us, Niek. Please do not shirk that reality. I lived here too during the war but this is a new life, with us, together! A new home. Surely that counts for something? I understand your heart, and your drive. If import-export suits you better, we can ask Nelly's husband Anton about Rotterdam's prospects."

He crossed his arms. "Perhaps, perhaps. At the very least, I know here, in jam, I have no place for advancement, no means for improvement in rank. Moreover, I wonder if our children will have the same opportunities in this country, due to overcrowding. And Corina's doctor warned us the Netherlands does not lead in post-polio therapies or medicine."

"Really? Where is another alternative?" Diny wondered how she missed a detail from Corina's doctor.

"America."

"*America*?" She blinked, and he nodded again. Her brown eyes lit up. "Sure, I know the place; a number of our friends moved there."

Nico nodded, adding, "And I think the medical advancements there are substantially greater than here. And the freedom of opportunities for our children." He faced her. "We should pray about moving to America."

Her mouth dropped. "Pardon? Are you serious?"

"Sure, why not?"

"Well, to begin with, our children are finally settled here, after two years of challenges, not to mention our exile from Indie and the pain they suffered there, and then moving around — this is already our third home in the Netherlands, but we are settled, and it remains our own. They love this home, their friends, the schools and language — and our families are here."

"Right, Diny. All good reasons to remain here, and we would have a decent life here. A comfortable life. But let me ask you this: have you ever considered what you are missing out on there, on the other side, and the wonderful opportunities Over There? Or do you only consider what you might miss here, in the Netherlands, should we decide to leave?" His eyes twinkled.

She sighed, pushing down the emotions which surged in her throat. "Everything, Nico, all you mentioned. I admit I loved the adventure of moving when we were younger, but I have enjoyed establishing roots since our return. As a woman and mother, I value developing deep friendships, and having family nearby has been a blessing, with all the cousins to play with and enjoy!" She wiped away tears.

Nico offered his handkerchief and assured her, "We only understand the 'known' and cannot fathom all God might have for us. I believe in America, our children will have more opportunities than here in the Netherlands. We can pray about what the Lord would have us do. I can investigate medical opportunities for Corina, and the jobs and housing prospects. To begin, I will telephone our old neighbors Syl and Ruud Benink from our Padang days, to ask their opinion on America. They live in California now. They said the weather in Southern California is like Indonesia: always warm, sunny, and fragrant."

Diny nodded, remembering Syl's optimistic letters about their life there. She felt tired and overwhelmed by the prospect of moving to yet another country. Later, while lying awake in bed, Diny considered the alterations in the Netherlands. The country had changed since 1947. In the previous decade people moved quickly and tried to rebuild their lives. Many Rotterdam streets and storefronts in Nelly and Anton's neighborhood seemed foreign and contemporary to Diny, but Rotterdam was bombed during the war and the country needed to rebuild; yet they marveled at the modern growth of the infrastructures of communities, of the stalwart determination of the Dutch.

Even Hilversum had transformed into a new community, with innovative homes. The country seemed more progressive, even more advanced than those household conveniences allowed, and in rebuilding they sought efficiency instead of charm. The comfort of larger grocery markets with more products felt lavish, and new homes were constructed where bright seas formerly splashed, a seeming impossibility of reclaiming the Sea.

The home Taminiau Jam Fabrieken was building for them in Schiedam seemed like an unnecessary luxury. Diny discovered some items Nico purchased in Indie were still missing, as she was looking for something and never found it. Nico shrugged and mentioned those who had helped them pack, and that they had lived in several locations, including public boarding houses. They lived without those items before and could live without them now, whether stolen or misplaced. As Diny drifted into sleep, pondering America, she considered the way God always supplied all they needed, granting grace and provision for each day. He would bestow all they needed.

Nico knew God would always provide. Profound faith was embedded into the fabric of his character, more closely knit to his soul than other abilities and fondness for activities like field hockey, salesmanship, or water polo. He walked with peace and spoke clearly and deliberately. His charisma was affectionate, his strength inspirational, and his smile endearing. He was the same strong-hearted man in the Netherlands as in Indonesia.

They loved spending time with family and especially Diny's parents. Opa and Oma Dekker remained in a townhome in Hilversum, where the Pouwels family frequently visited for dinnertime. The three girls loved to bake little treats with Oma Dekker and when she grew weary or cold, Opa Dekker would guide her to her special chair in the front room, and she smiled while letting Opa do for her what she requested. He would lovingly fill up her copper and wood foot warmer with hot coals from the fireplace, so she could keep her feet toasty warm.

Later, the grandchildren would listen to Oma elegantly play the new piano in the sitting room, singing along together, or they would snuggle on Opa's big lap, and examine his bushy mustache and dark puffy hair, his bold laughter exuding every encounter. He recited a little rhyme while bouncing his grandchildren higher and higher:

"Een dames paard, een dames paard; een heeren paard, een heeren paard; een boeren paard, een boeren paard!" A gentle knee bounce for "A ladies' horse, a ladies' horse;" a sterner bobble for "a gentleman's horse, a gentleman's horse;" and a rocky, wild bounce for "a farmer's horse, a farmer's horse." Opa trotted gently at first and by the time he reached the farmer horse rhyme, he nearly dropped his granddaughter off his knees, much to her delight.

Later, Opa Dekker chased them in their patio garden, their gentle bear of a grandfather roaring with delight and humor. While Pieter's ample but lean frame still commanded a tall presence, a gentleness seemed to prevail over strictness. He softened from his war years, instead of becoming bitter and full of revenge. He seemed sensitive to the groaning pains of life.

"How do you remain so hopeful, despite all the pain you experienced?" Diny asked her dad on the patio. He shrugged and smiled.

She continued, "Now I know more of what you experienced, but cannot fathom how you emerged so victorious and with such kindness. I am not sure I would remain so forgiving," she admitted, looking down.

Dad chuckled and pulled her into a sturdy embrace. "Oh, Diny!" he bellowed, "God sustained me in a way only He could. I survived those years of suffering but realized my own sin nature and need for forgiveness. As a result, I know the sweet refreshment of joy and contentment. When God spared my life in Indie, I promised to forgive others, and asked Him to heal me." Pieter Dekker dwelled in the safety and blessing of grace.

Despite the loving times with their families, Nico and Diny prepared for a life in the United States. Nico called Ruud Benink in California and discussed opportunities in America, and seemed encouraged by several possibilities, although the process might take a long time. They spoke on the telephone more frequently, and Nico developed a plan for moving, and decided upon jobs and locations to raise his family in the Los Angeles area. He wrote a list of negative and positive aspects concerning the Netherlands versus America, and together with Diny, prayed about the idea. Nico seemed hopeful about a move, and Diny realized the merits of relocating, especially with America's booming post-war economy.

Slowly, Diny warmed to the idea of America and became convinced when Corina's post-polio medical treatment in the Netherlands halted and stalled. Their eldest daughter needed ongoing physical therapy and additional surgeries, and America was more willing to perform those necessary actions. Then, through the Marshall Plan, the United States assisted the Netherlands in recovering post-World War II and allowed for economic growth and restoration. It seemed fortuitous the USA would again provide help for Europe.

Finally, John Orlando Pastore, a Senator, and Mr. Francis Eugene Walter, a Congressman, made it possible for the people who had to flee Indonesia to emigrate to America more rapidly than normal (called the Pastore-Walter Act of 1958). Their status was changed from "repatriates" to "refugees".

The World Refugee Year Law of 1960 also provided a quick entry into America. The congressmen recognized housing and employment were difficult for the displaced Dutch to find, with the Netherlands occupied with thousands of additional families, plus other nationalities fleeing Indonesia, and America held prospects for those looking for promising jobs and housing. The Pastore-Walter Act allowed the Dutch and Euro-Indonesians to enter the USA, and churches helped in finding homes and sponsors for them. The majority of the 30,000-60,000 Dutch Indo refugees were sponsored by Church World Services, an organization representing 37 Christian denominations, and the Catholic Relief Service, which represented thousands of churches. These two large organizations found churches all over the USA to sponsor families, which is why Dutch and Indos began settling all over the country. The majority moved to Southern California and found both the varied culture and the temperate climate favorable.

Usually the immigration process required about six years, but for the Pouwels family, it only took six months. Nico and Diny felt eager to join their adventurous friends who immigrated to America. Moreover, the medical advances in the United States undoubtedly would provide Corina opportunities in her therapies and with future surgeries. Freedom, hope, and promise for their children were suddenly tangible options. When Nico shared his plans with his boss, Mr. Taminiau sat him down for a discussion.

"Pouwels, you left me once, just after the war, when you wanted to move to the Indies and start a life there. When you returned here, after Indonesia's independence, and applied for this job, I knew you would leave again." He saw Nico's abilities and drive, felt no ill will against him, and blessed them in their endeavors.

Their extended family was sad, believing Nico and Diny might remain in the Netherlands forever, but understood they wanted to spread their wings again for prospects. Diny knew little of California apart from the tremendous gardens and orchards her friends were growing. If they had any hesitation or doubt of the months ahead, their four children were unaware, and slept in peace without any sense of change. For the three sweet girls and one trusting boy, the world surrounding them was changing. Much of what they learned of their original homelands was from stories. Their parents realized this opportunity, a chance for change, and scooped up a hope for freedom, accepting their destiny.

Chapter Thirty-Three
The United States of
America, December 1959

On 1 December 1959, family and friends waved goodbye to Nico, Diny, and their four children at Schipol Airport in Amsterdam. Nico was 42, Diny 38, Corina 11, Marge 10, Nicolette 8, and Peter almost 3. Nico knew the most English and promised to help them during the transition to America. So many opportunities lay ahead, Diny felt a sense of hope and refuge surrounding their move. She dreamed of connecting with friends and in a church, of a promising career for Nico, and good schools for her dear, trusting children. Faithfully stepping forward in love and commitment to her family seemed easier than running from troubles. She knew their promise remained in God — whether living in Indie, the Netherlands, or America — but their most encouraging hope was for America.

However, Diny spoke little English and remained unfamiliar with running a household on her own. She feared she might lose her connection with her Indie roots. Diny loved dreaming in Malay, the Indies language, smelling balmy fruits, earthy mustiness, tasting dripping mangoes and papaya, and hearing the calls of birds. Her dreams brought comfort, echoes of her parents' voices, images of their warm, smiling faces. Diny wondered if her own grandchildren would know the magnitude of their sacrifice, or did that matter?

They flew from Amsterdam to New York. As they were approaching the airport in New York, Nico pointed out the Statue of Liberty, a mint-colored statue on an island, a beacon of optimism and promise for those entering the harbor. If they were arriving by boat, Diny surmised the sight would be even more grand and glorious, moving in spirit and soul. Nico shared with his family how Lady Liberty was a symbol of free America. The Statue of

Liberty represents hope, as Lady Liberty faces toward the ocean, welcoming those arriving, offering her light of compassion and freedom.

From New York City, they took the train west to California. Their journey stretched from New York across three thousand miles, numerous states, and countryside — *their America* — with spacious skies, amber fields of grain, and purple mountain majesties. The smell of oils on the metal track, with wooden planks supporting the track, intermingled in Diny's senses, wafting up into the train as they boarded. Inside the wobbling train, however, were stagnant fragrances, of perspiring people huddled together in tight spaces for travel, little fresh air, pungently-scented food brought for the journey, and perfumes merged in the moment.

The disappointments were a simple reality of life in a new land with a foreign language, as they were unable to discover six seats together, and found plenty of unsociable people. Nico found four seats in the middle and two in the back and requested a couple who sat across from the four seats to trade with them. His face smiled as he inquired, "Would you please exchange places with us, so I can join my wife and children and sit together as a family? We have found two seats for you at the back of the train."

Yet the couple only stared at them and sternly replied, "No! Find other seats!" and turned away. This was an unexpected non-welcome to their new surroundings, an unfriendly entrance to a new country. They decided not to dwell on disappointments, and instead, looked forward to the future of their new life in California.

The expedition delivered them through New York meadows, tree-lined states in the middle, and dormant pastures brown in the winter as cows grazed and gazelles leaped fences. Thick populations thinned as they traveled west, homes appeared aged from wind and weather, trees submitted under snowfall. As the journey continued, the entire family became sick, which greatly dimmed their optimism, as stomachs lurched and fevers rose. They hoped for their wobbly journey's end as soon as the three days began. They tried to enjoy glimpses of the countryside along the way. Nico paced the length of the train, his lanky legs stretching as best as possible, while Diny held a sick child on her lap and stroked away the tears, anxiety, and stress of the move.

Beyond rivers they went, over bridge girders. All three girls held their baby dolls closely, protectively. Before they left Europe, Diny bought each of them a portable bassinet for their babies. Hours of entertainment were found from playing with the dolls in their bassinets. When they stopped in Chicago,

Nico realized there was no food to purchase on the train. Diny originally purchased food in New York, unaware they were required to buy items for their entire journey. So far, their food had lasted 24 hours of travel.

The other passengers were fully aware of this reality of bringing meals along for the trip, and with various cultures represented, fragrances abounded. Fortunately, Nico found American food vendors in the terminal at the Chicago Union Station and purchased food. From there, they transferred to a Santa Fe train which rambled faster, and slowed over the Mississippi River girders, as glinting water splashed around ferry and cargo boats dotted along the murky waters. They picked up speed near fields, through canyons and villages, cities fading into a sparse population, beyond river crossings, beyond the East, transforming into the West.

The engine roared through Denver, then chugged slower through the rugged snowy passes of the Rocky Mountains, and zoomed beside landscapes of red sandy rocks and spacious deserts boasting a hazy sunset. The gleaming promise of Los Angeles, California loomed ahead. Row-after-row of orange groves lined beside the tracks, orchards breezing beyond their windows, welcoming them to a prosperity they imagined from Hollywood movies. The station in Los Angeles was hectic, the destination for many on a similar journey to begin life anew.

In Los Angeles, they arrived on 5 December 1959, which was Sinterklaas Day! None of them felt well enough to celebrate, with fevers and queasy stomachs persisting. Diny guessed the children would rather celebrate once they settled into their own home. Dear friends Syl and Ruud Benink and their two daughters warmly greeted the Pouwels family at the train station. They were ready to rest in the comfort of those who had navigated this journey ahead of them. Ruud cared for all the baggage, piling it onto rolling carts; Syl linked arms with Diny, steadying her to their car. They marveled at the breadth of downtown Los Angeles, traffic snarling their drive, and the suburbs offering a peaceful situation near the large metropolis.

The Beninks considered everything the Pouwels family might need, as their own emigration journey remained fresh in their minds. They reserved a hotel room for the Pouwels family, who collapsed into beds, sleeping long hours that first night, relieved they arrived, while uncertain what the life ahead of them would entail. At the least, a comfortable bed and warm shower were a welcome respite. Nico and Diny had a nightly invitation to dinner at Syl's mother's house (who was an excellent cook). Every morning Ruud picked them up at the hotel. The whole family piled into the Benink's large station wagon and Ruud drove them around to find a place to live. The sickness the Pouwels family experienced on the train struck Diny and she was ill in the motel, with miserable stomach pain, with nerves from moving and all they went through.

Their sponsoring church in Los Angeles provided a list with several rental addresses, but some of the homes were dilapidated or in disappointing neighborhoods, so by the time Diny felt well enough to join the crew on the daily jaunt around town, when they came to an address situated on Delta Street in San Gabriel, they were so tired and worn out, they liked what they saw and decided to move into the rental house. On 12 December, the Pouwels family moved into the house on Delta Street, and with few possessions, plenty of memories, and determination, were strong-minded to hold no regrets about their move. The gray two-story structure was not a beautiful house, yet served their needs, and quickly became home to them all, with memories accumulating as soon as they arrived.

Never quite their dream home, but suited to housing them, providing shelter, and a place to connect and host friends. With cleaning and bright flowers, it could become a real home for them, a haven from the stresses of life. Upon entering the home through the front door was the kitchen, and each return through the front door they were encountered with warm and savory aromas of Diny's cooking. As the hub of their lives and activities was often situated around the breakfast and dinner table, the dining room was directly behind the kitchen, serving as the back of the house.

Their living room was also in front of the house, where they entertained guests and joined as a family in the evenings, laughter and hospitality radiating from the room, a fireplace offering heat in the winter. Behind the living room, the den and bathroom were next to each other, along with a narrow spiral staircase leading upstairs. The upper level was above the garage. The front upstairs bedroom was for Corina and Peter to share, and the back bedroom Marge shared with Nicolette. Down the staircase again, and just situated at the complete back of their home (behind the den), was the master bedroom.

The master bedroom appeared inside-out, because it was the original outer back wall of the home, as an open-walled, roofed patio, leading into a backyard at one point. Later the owner enclosed it as a bedroom for the home. The entire feel of Nico and Diny's bedroom was one of an enclosed veranda. Multiple screened windows lined the wall and allowed for a clear view of the back yard. The exit into the back yard was also situated within their room.

Nico purchased a screen door to add to the original wood door, for summer breezes into their bedroom, the familiar *slap-slap* of the door a comforting sound each season. To reach the back yard, family and guests alike traveled through the master bedroom, and down four concrete steps with an iron railing. The garage had a door to the yard, yet the home exit was more utilized.

If Dutch are straightforward and preferred front-yard *verandas* to catch sight of company arriving to visit, while observing the happenings of the street, Diny surmised Americans must be private for placing their *patios* in the back of their home, facing their yard, within the confining fenced-in comforts of solitude and isolation. She hoped the Americans would be more social than their patios. Although it was completely enclosed, their veranda served them well, and Diny frequently opened the windows to receive cool breezes on sunny days.

Their house, the gray physicality of that structure, was not of her foremost desire or first choice in taste of appearance. She noted the building was drab and unoriginal.

"Renting an affordable place is important," Nico laughed, "and not the color of the home or walls." He declared, "Diny, our love can permeate walls, with good cooking and laughter in the air. Be sure of this: you always turn a house into a home."

She replied, "I suppose you are right, Niek. The idea repeats in my mind of 'creating a home,' and forging a place of our own to welcome others. I will adjust my expectation, and am happy God answered our prayers for a place to live." Diny imagined she would work sunny afternoons when spring arrived in the garden, lingering under the spread-wide trees, and digging into the soil. Her childhood was in Indonesia, she was a caretaker in the Netherlands, then for a decade a wife and mother in Indonesia, and now matured into womanhood in America.

Morning sunshine cast a shadow, encapsulating the house in backyard shade. Buds rolled inside their protective shell, awaiting expression. The gardens felt tranquil in dew until dazzling afternoons, as buds opened, thirsty for watering. A winter season of rain would no doubt yield a more vibrant spring.

After they settled into their Delta Street home, Nico took their daughters to their classrooms to begin school. Corina's sixth grade teacher was playing a film, and all the lights were out. When the teacher stopped the film, and turned the lights on, Corina became strangely aware of her short hair and physical limp as she found her seat. All the twelve-year-old girls in class had long hair, and some wore makeup, which surprised Corina. Her teacher showed kindness and respect, welcoming her to sixth grade. Due to her being different — a foreigner — many kids tried to talk to Corina.

All she could say in response was, "I do not understand you."

Still, they stared. And just watched her.

I do not understand you: five simple English words Nico taught his children, so others would recognize their need for help. They all had Dutch-to-English dictionaries for reference as they learned, and for as bewildered as Corina felt, she remembered to rely on her smile and outgoing personality to fill in any gaps in language. Similarly, Marge was welcomed to her fifth-grade class, and students studied her smooth short hair, freckles, and sweet smile. Marge's fifth grade classmates took her around the school and explained, in English: "chair" and "table" and "door," which seemed to help her at least navigate, and at age ten, could try her best to learn another language. Still, she often responded, "I do not understand you."

Nicolette assimilated into her third-grade classroom quickly, with her enthusiasm and friendly demeanor, her eight-year-old smile beaming with dimples and charm.

Corina found American children more readily willing to accept her handicaps, but she was frequently greeted with stares, or was simply avoided.

Tante Syl extended herself to help in many ways, escorting Diny and little Peter to the department store to buy dinner plates and glasses, some furniture, and other immediate household items like silverware, towels, a mop, and an iron.

"*Dien*, look: big dish towels which dry quickly!" Syl marveled, holding up a cream cloth with stripes.

Diny nodded and crossed one item off her list, then grinned at her friend. "One item down, dozens to go."

"Well, at least we found the store together!"

"Yep." Peter jumped with his arms in the air and Diny scooped him into the shopping buggy to sit with her purchases. Syl thought of everyday details which assisted their life into a more seamless transition, and her English proved fluent enough for traversing the stores, although they chatted along in Dutch every moment they could.

Any way Diny considered the move, she felt determined to navigate their new life with as few troubles as possible. Their friendly neighbors offered some assistance, as Mr. Williams across the street allowed Nico his lawn mowing machine in the beginning, until Nico could purchase one. Until they could afford all the necessary pots and pans, neighbor Moonie lent Diny pans with special instructions on how to clean them. Yet Diny was baffled as to how to properly clean cookware, becoming accustomed to a servant in Indie; moreover, Diny could not read the English instructions on the soap.

Her children reminded her, "Rinse off the soap completely under a steady stream of hot water before drying the dishes with a towel, Mam!" Corina demonstrated for their mother how to rinse the dish, and Marge giggled as she grabbed a towel for drying dishes.

"Sometimes the soap resurfaces when wet!" Nicolette added, and illustrated by filling a glass with water, and the water completely foamed up the insides of the glass; she poured out the water, rinsed several times, and handed the glass to Marge. They all laughed. Diny thought she cleaned those dishes properly — and she had. She had scrubbed the dishes and just allowed the soap to dry.

"Well, now you know how to wash dishes," Corina sang to their Mam, who blushed and hugged her girls, then replied to them in Dutch, "I do not understand what you are saying."

CHAPTER THIRTY-FOUR
SOUTHERN CALIFORNIA, LATE 1959

Since the family arrived in Southern California on Sinterklaas Day, the Pouwels family decided to celebrate Christmas on the 25th of December. For their first Christmas in 1959, their first month in America, the neighbor kids brought over presents of games, books, puzzles, and so on, to add to the dolls and bassinets the girls brought along in the train.

Arriving in America meant new language and customs, and some new surprises, like washing machines, refrigerators, and one evening Nico and Ruud brought in a big box called a television set to watch news and entertaining shows. They all marveled at the television, which was an exciting substitute to the radio programs they all grew to adore. Those luxuries served as additional blessings. Meanwhile, their four children desperately missed the love of their grandparents.

"Can we telephone Opa and Oma for American Christmas?" their girls begged. They were extremely close to Opa and Oma Dekker and longed to hug them. Certainly, the granddaughters could correspond through letters and telephone calls, but the closeness diminished, and they promised to not allow the relationship to fall absent. They wanted to live closer to their grandparents.

Nico replied, "Those wishes for family togetherness are not always possible. You can write them as many letters as you can, and I suppose we can telephone them occasionally."

Diny agreed, "Dad is right. We miss our families but have wonderful opportunities here, especially for Corina's medical care."

Classical music filled the air for the New Year's Eve celebration, with the elegant sophistication of George Gershwin embodying the pioneer spirit. Diny prepared a roast chicken and vegetable dinner, followed by sparkling cider toasts at the turn of midnight, along with sweets of *oliebollen*. She shimmered with gratitude for all God had provided them. Their music always served as a soundtrack for each place permeating an important evening of remembering.

Indonesia sounded like the creaking of frogs, scratching of Tokays, clicks of tjitjaks, swooshes of palm fronds, shrieks of wild monkeys, and the snarling of distant tigers. The humid tropics seeped around each corner, with clanking food carts and rumbling volcanoes establishing the beat of the percussion.

The Netherlands resonance was more classical with interludes of nature, soothing snowfall, with fluttering tulips and whirring crescendos of windmills, swishing clattering ice skates on frozen canals, gentle winds purring through the countryside, and splashing canal boats amidst Amsterdam's waterways.

America's musical undertone was now a crescendo: a reminder of Batavia's ferns, flowers, and warm climate, an interval of Dutch scenery with a multicultural tone, and a new, lively, undiscovered seasoning, the beginning of a melodious masterpiece still to be discovered.

As the new year of 1960 began, Nico introduced himself as "Nick" to American neighbors, yet remained "Nico" to Dutch and Indonesian friends, who spoke various languages with him, feeling more like brothers than just fellow countrymen. At first, Diny was surprised, and later felt disappointed at her husband's desire to Americanize his name. She brought it up as they tidied their room for bedtime.

"Nico, who are you now, calling yourself Nick? What is that name? Reminds me of Willem DeMunck at church who asked to be called 'Bill.' Can you believe it? You know in Dutch, Bill means —"

"Buttocks or, rump. I know, Diny." He smiled at her and closed the curtains. "The name Jan in Dutch sounds like a 'yawn' in English, and have you heard the joke about Joke?"

She chuckled, then became serious. "The name 'Nick' loses the Dutch appeal, not to mention your family heritage of the name, and seems so… ordinary. But you, my dear, are anything but ordinary!"

He crossed his arms and looked down his sloping nose at her. "Thank you for calling me extraordinary, Diny! But remember, my family seems attached to the name 'Pieter.' For two centuries and many generations there has been a *Pieter Pouwels*, not 'Nico Pouwels.' And as the second-born son, I was given a lesser family name, not the one made of two hundred years —"

"Yes. I understand you are the pained younger brother. Believe me, I have one."

"But the real point, *Grietje*, is that the name 'Nick' sounds more Americanized."

"Why does that matter?"

"That name is easier for Americans to remember, especially when speaking with an accent." He set his glasses on the dresser and continued. "In telling someone my name, at that moment, I do not have to explain my complicated heritage, describe how to spell my name, or feel like an outcast." Nico rubbed his eyes and turned off his nightstand lamp, settling into silence. "That is the point, Diny, and the only reason. I love being Dutch but prefer to feel accepted and not an outsider." He lay in the shadows of Diny's bright lamp.

She lifted her eyebrows, then chuckled aloud.

"Pardon?" he frowned.

She confirmed, "Ah, well, that makes sense. People ask me how to pronounce and spell my name too, and they think *Dee-knee* is a body part! When I tell them my name, *Gerardina*, and roll the r's in my name 'Gerrr-arrrr-dina,' they stare at me with their mouth open!"

They laughed and Diny turned off her lamp. Then she sighed, "If that is what you decided, I will respect your wishes, my love. But at home, I would still like to call you *my Nico*."

She quietly pondered Nico's name choice, recognizing they each encountered a great deal of change while adapting to their new country. His accented English words already alluded to a foreign upbringing, so perhaps he desired equal footing in America. She refused to overthink something so ordinary, this minor act of her husband's change into a new life or assume anything except her bright and industrious husband also longed for real community and connection with others in California.

Delta Street, San Gabriel, California, Spring 1960

The front azalea bush and camellias bloomed with rich shades of pink, soft blushes tightly bundled blooms expanding, all accented by green leaves. She had nurtured the lavender hydrangeas and watched yellow roses attract bees and aphids throughout seasons, from a thorny brown bush into a lush assortment of growth. The front walk of their beloved rented home on Delta Street swirled with fragrance and various colors of rhododendron lined their driveway with bright orange and sunny yellow hues. Lemon trees and blackberry vines were common in many yards, while orange and avocado trees grew wild around almost each corner. They were nestled in the Los Angeles suburb of San Gabriel and lived among many who loved the temperate weather of California.

In her gardens, Diny found peace and felt alive with the mixture of shadows and sunshine as breezes moved through the trees. The purity Spring provided offered redemption, and enhanced scents, sounds, and memories. California mild weather stretched year-round, with plants and flowers blooming in the garden. Unlike an unrelenting Dutch winter, even a California February shade of green could be discovered.

The family had settled into a rhythm in the mornings before work. Their children assimilated quicker, perhaps due to their transitory lifestyle their entire childhood. Each morning, Diny boiled milk on the stovetop and skimmed off the top, the skin, which Nico placed on top of a fried egg on toast. His other slice of toast was topped with jam, which he enjoyed with a strong coffee. Diny's most important task was assisting Nico to work and her three daughters to school, with preparing hot breakfast and packing them all a healthy lunch.

When her children left for the day, walking down the driveway toward school or another activity, they could always see their mother's happy smile from her kitchen window at the front of the house, waving them along to school, her shining face wishing them well for the day ahead. They prayed together before leaving for school, Diny urging her girls, "God be with you today!" Her beaming smile warmed them cheerily all day. Peter's tiny hand flapped excitedly as they waved at the window, sending off his older sisters, who blew kisses to their boy.

After Nico and their girls left each morning, Diny turned her attention to Peter, who followed along to accompany her in daily chores and activities. She read colorful rhyming books to him, both practicing their English as they read, and then set him up with something to do while she studied the Bible. When Peter napped, Diny worked at her desk along the back windows of her bedroom, praying, jotting notes in the margins of her Bible, then logging prayer requests into a notebook. From the vantage point at her desk, Diny viewed the entire back yard, of birds flitting and butterflies fluttering. The world was her cinema, mountains in the distance, with sunshine warming her face, illuminating ideas. In correspondence with family and friends, she shared and received a measure of needs and difficulties, with blessings, and contemplated those issues before the Lord. She journaled into a notebook and later marked the date her prayers were answered.

Diny found more time to garden because of the modern appliances available to them, she could wash clothing, clean the floors, cook, and keep food chilled at a better rate of efficiency than in the past, especially in remote areas of Indie. She separated her tasks into daily chores to manage the work. Diny loved fine sunny weather to dry their clothes on the backyard clothesline. Their world had changed and many household tasks were learned in the war years, and Diny could still saw down a tree if she needed, joking to Nico they could find a Christmas tree in the forest and haul it home.

On Mondays, Diny vacuumed and changed sheets, and then ran laundry, lining wet, clean clothing on the rope lines stringing along the back yard. On Tuesdays and Thursdays Diny dusted and changed towels and might run laundry again. On Wednesday, she cleaned the bathrooms and mopped all their floors, and on Fridays, she vacuumed again. She and Nico attended AVIO club (Dutch Indo club) on Friday night, and gardened every afternoon if the weather was appropriate. Family day remained on Saturday, and Sabbath rest on Sunday, which they reserved for church, a hot lunch at home, *gezellig* family togetherness, and entertaining friends.

If Diny participated in a church Bible Study during the day, she telephoned Mrs. Skelly or Janet Verdell for a ride. Diny and Peter would pull along a little metal luggage cart to Beaches Market about five blocks away, fill the cart with food and pay using the cash Nico provided, then tote the cart home. Peter always begged to ride atop the cart.

Their local *Hollinda* (Holland-Indonesia) food market and restaurant imported sweet and savory treats. While it was a longer walk to that specialty marketplace, Diny recalled the tastes of home — of her parents and siblings — when she bought pea soup, chocolate letters or coins, meats, cheeses, breads, and more. She sometimes found Griotten licorice, a sweet, soft licorice, which came in a light square cube coated with sugar. She ate one square and savored the taste, relishing the flavor of the Netherlands. Lumpia, a wet rice mixture with ground beef and curry, instantly brought her back to Indie and provided a warm lunch treat to share with Peter, nourishment for their walk back home.

To allow adequate gardening time, Diny felt motivated to quickly complete her household tasks each day, which also provided her with exercise. She sometimes gardened just after her girls went to school to take advantage of cool morning air, especially days when the heat settled in humid bands around their grass and underneath trees. Most of the time, her schedule varied according to toddler Peter's needs, and he joined her in the garden, content to pull weeds or lay on the grass after racing around the yard at furious pace, determined to catch birds.

He is such a rambunctious little boy, Diny thought, marveling at all she learned while raising her young son. Peter set out each day with his trains and trucks, crashing them on the kitchen floor as Diny cooked, dancing around his train tracks. Or climbed the oak tree while Diny gardened. He helped harvest fruit from blackberry bushes, strawberry patches, and lemon trees. Other times, Peter compliantly "read" books while she wrote letters. He spent nearly all his waking hours keeping her aware of his vigorous mind and active temperament.

Nico and Diny liked to play tennis a few times a week, and their children retrieved balls. She also took the children swimming as often as possible, and set up the badminton net in their backyard, along with a croquet set when they entertained guests. Games lasted for hours beyond their evening meal together as the sun escaped their view and backyard torches lit as guests continued enjoying their games together. Diny no longer sewed her children's clothing, but mended and updated some of the pieces, especially if converting trousers into shorts after the youngest (Nicolette or Peter) was too tall for the long pants. Evenings with Nico were still passed by engaging in cross-stitch or dates out for dancing and refreshment at the *SOOS* — "Society," Dutch social club.

Throughout her day, Diny pondered her days in Indie, reflecting on nostalgic memories from a long-ago time. She remembered clacking Tokay geckos, monsoon rains pouring down thick-banded greenery, the Saté man's clanking cart passing by their home, calling out, "*Saté!*" and spicy peanut sauces wafting into the air.

When the children heard Nico returning home from work, they happily sprinted to him. Diny prepared with a fresh coat of lipstick, a spray of perfume, and a quick comb through her hair. She shook her apron out and hung it for the day, smoothed her skirt, and made certain the home was tidy for his notice, with dinner prepared. Their children's homework was completed and tucked into bookbags for the next day. Some evenings she set a record on the player, a delightful orchestral movement or somber piano solo, London Symphony, or perhaps a Christmas rendition.

In the evenings, Nico and Diny walked the backyard while their children stayed inside to get ready for bed.

"Those together-walks are meant to solve problems, make decisions, or talk things over in the privacy of our yard, away from eager, curious little ears," Nico explained to his children.

At first, their strides seemed a jumble of confusion, but only later — as Diny surmised her parents experienced — did their steps begin to align and shoulders match, voices calming and regulated. Sometimes their arms grazed each other, as each began to say something, but Nico gently grasped Diny's elbow and steered her along, her pace quickening to his idea, his warm breath sweetly brushing against her neck.

Nico always assumed the responsibility of leader in taking steps, in making decisions, and Diny was willing and gracious to accept his headship, thankful to share the amble through life with an honorable man.

Chapter Thirty-Five
Southern California, 1960

Now settling into America, Nico started to work for an upholstery company in Los Angeles, a thriving business and a suitable challenge for him. He still worked import-export, selling *kapok* (cotton-like material) and webbing and textiles for furniture upholstery. Everything from the various fabrics of the outside of the sofas and sedans to the inner stuffing could be manufactured and then delivered to him to be assembled in Los Angeles.

This work remained in the textile industry, a field he knew well and thrived in negotiating. Nico could glorify God by providing working-class families a solid deal on fabric and upholstery, transforming their worn, frayed couches into renewed, classy masterpieces. His chief aim remained to provide for his family and then secure a deal for his customers. Nico never made a lot of money because he always returned his profit toward his customers, many of whom drove more than an hour to see him in Los Angeles. He negotiated with factories in other countries which paid fair wages to their employees, so he could obtain the materials for his furniture. When the material arrived in kilos, he quickly decided whether the price was fair when converted to pounds, priding himself in mentally translating the cost from kilos to pounds for his American audience.

During his lunch break, Nico walked the streets of Los Angeles, regularly searching for a homeless man along the way to invite him to share a meal together at McDonald's. He looked for a man with a sign, sitting on the roadside, a man in need of food or work. It seemed a better alternative to handing out money, as a relationship intermingled with a shared meal could provide comfort and the start of a friendship.

During their first year in America they encountered challenges, yet Nico and Diny promised each other to remain faithful to the move, and they kept their promise. They often discussed the unique challenges of transferring countries and lifestyles, and the desire to teach their children their heritage, while remaining open to the customs and holidays of a new country. One evening, over the soothing record Diny placed on the record player, they recalled God's goodness in carrying them through difficulties.

Nico considered, "Well, Dien, our family was thrown out of Indonesia, where we had a good living, the place we always imagined growing old together, building a family, and life, and where we loved to live. Afterwards, we moved to the Netherlands where we were not happy, yet our family was nearby, and we all loved that comfort, and felt blessed. Then suddenly, as though God listened to our request for direction, we received the opportunity of a lifetime to move to America within 6 months instead of 6 years, so when we sat down and prayed for guidance, we received an answer."

Back then, in the Netherlands, they thought about, and wrote down, the advantages and the disadvantages as much as possible, realizing moving again would not be easy. They recognized the need to give up Nico's promising job, release the house his company built for them, and disperse the closeness of family nearby. They knew the English language might be a struggle in the beginning, as would be the whole way of living in a different country, but together with God they were bound for triumph.

Nico and Diny were still young, at ages 42 and 38, respectively, and were willing (if it was God's will), to make the best of it. They promised each other, as Nico pledged then, "From the beginning, we will learn about the customs and culture, and will accept our new lifestyle and not look back constantly, and never compare our situation with *what had been*, because that would not be fair."

They were victorious before, surviving the war and thriving in Indonesia. For a decade, they instilled the wonder and charm of the country into their children, who equally loved the tropics and grew well there. Now, in America, every possibility seemed promising and they were filled with great hope for their children, and for future generations who would benefit from their steadfast grit and determination. They thought their children would have a better opportunity in everything in America, from career choice to the quality of living along with opportunities for growth, learning, and freedom. While it was not easy, they were together as a family, and that was important.

Upon accepting their emigration opportunity, the Pouwels family promised to act as sponsors for other families to live in America. Their sponsoring program felt it vital that families receiving assistance toward beginning a new life should also extend hospitality for other arriving families, and they promised to co-sponsor at least three families. Additionally, the Pouwels' home always remained open for many friends and family.

Their first family to co-sponsor was Henny and Hans Carmiggelt with their two children, and they arrived 17 March 1960, and stayed for 6 weeks. Three months after the Pouwels family arrived in America, Hen and Han flew into Los Angeles as new arrivals. The Pouwels family relied on the Beninks for help with their first sponsorship. Ruud and Nico drove Hans to find a rental home, while Syl and Diny helped Henny find dishes, cookware, and other household items.

Each family member helped with the sponsorship and they realized they only had so much room in their home when hosting other families, and everyone must contribute to helping the home run efficiently, even the children of the sponsored family. There was an air of excitement, as though they recalled their first days there, like they were reliving their experience as new settlers, yet with the eyes of time. Wisdom would be passed along to their friends, to those they sponsored, who they truly loved. The children moved around at home to allow the sponsored family Corina and Peter's bedroom, lining up bed mats from wall to wall. Corina stayed in Marge and Nicolette's bedroom, while Peter slept on a floor mattress in Nico and Diny's room. Their home was crammed with 10 people, but nobody complained.

The Carmiggelts provided money for the supermarket, which helped to defray the food costs. The ladies cooked meals and enjoyed a special tenderness from the unique experience, reminiscent of large *rijsttafel* events. Diny enjoyed a daily companion in Henny, a friendship strengthened by time together. While the children were in school, Diny and Henny worked efficiently, quicker together than alone, remaining in the familiar Dutch language.

One advantage included their expansive backyard for children to play and explore. With little rain from April through November, they spent most of the time outside and held pleasant memories from those times, and with youth and energy could accommodate larger parties and gatherings with ample space. They played outdoor games of ping-pong, darts, croquet, and badminton. Inside, they gathered around a table for *Sjoelbak*, the Dutch shuffleboard game.

Nico was always there to support Diny, to step into any role she requested. He drove their sponsored men around to find a home, found ads in the newspaper listing house rentals, and other details settling the men into their jobs. Diny took care of the rest, running the household. They worked together as a team, remaining open to communication and to the experience.

On 12 March 1960, Nico and Diny celebrated the milestone of having been married for 12 ½ years. They decided to have their big wedding anniversary party — a Dutch custom of celebrating the halfway point to 25 years. They invited people from church and Dutch friends who also celebrated, so their party at their home was a success, and included Syl and Ruud Benink, who welcomed the Carmiggelt family with gusto. All the women prepared *rijsttafel* dishes and Nico barbequed the *Saté* meat outside while chatting with the men. After a lavish spread of food was enjoyed by all, Nico gifted Diny with a gold ring with a ruby jewel in the center as a reminder of his love for her. She always wore the ring on the hand opposite their wedding bands. They still wore their wedding bands on their right hand ring finger, a custom of the Netherlands.

Their children developed friendships, finding others around them who also navigated the migrant journey without any prior scope of English and perhaps remembered the stumbling pain of starting afresh. These new friends daily assisted the girls while looping through routines, as those classmates shared everyday words — "chair, door, teacher, desk, bathroom, class, friend" — until words were commonplace, and sentences flowed easier with a more natural inclination.

"I feel relieved for my children, now that we have finally arrived in America," Diny told Syl in Dutch over a cup of hot tea in Syl's living room one morning.

"Relief?" Syl howled, startling Diny. "Dear, do tell me, where is this relief you find? I still feel a giant sense of shock and awe at this busy place!"

Diny scanned the pristine, clean living room, but realized Syl meant their new country. "True. Los Angeles seems bustling and overwhelming at times, more crowded and fast-paced than Batavia. And Southern California is faster than the easy pace of our Padang days! City block after city block — gracious!"

"Well, those Padang markets were colorful — and busy. Sumatra still seems quaint and unconventional and we still seem to carry forward our Dutch social club, even now." Syl always loved the *SOOS*, engaging others in conversation in her congenial ways. She motioned for Diny to continue.

Diny mused, "I just keep reminding my daughters this difficulty will not last forever. Eventually, even these enchanting neighborhood gardens in Rosemead will seem familiar, or the drive to church not so foreign, and they will easily navigate their school campus. Even the English language grows stronger in their mind every day. In each new step, we leave something of our old countries behind."

Syl's face dropped, and she set her tea cup down, before refilling it.

"Yes, Diny, that is partially true. Unfortunately, younger generations may lose their native language. But who we are — our character — was formed long before our location deemed us so. We are loving, hardworking women because of how we were created and how we choose to live with grace, not where we do our living."

Diny narrowed her gaze, quieted her thoughts, and closed her eyes.

Syl stood and hummed her way to the kitchen to heat additional water for tea.

Diny had long decided to identify herself with her place, Batavia, and not a character trait like grace or love. She longed to belong to a place with as much ferocity as longing to belong to a group of people. She always felt connected to Batavia and to her fellow Dutchmen. Somewhere along the way, the marvels of Dutch fortitude and strength overtook any location and she determined to deliberately remain optimistic no matter her location.

She lived in Hilversum during a world war, and yet always longed for Batavia. Perhaps that desire helped manage the terror of tragedy and war. Eventually, her place of belonging was beside Nico, moving every few years, developing friendships quickly, and carrying them forward over miles apart. But it mattered little whether they resided in Batavia, Hilversum, or America. Nico was her place of belonging.

The hot water kettle whistled in the kitchen, and Diny could hear Syl refilling the pot with tea bags to steep. She hummed her way back beside Diny and rattled the tray to signal her return. "Wake up, Dien!"

"Yep! I need a moment to process this change, Syl."

"We shall offer each other grace in the transition. Even grace when my best friend decides to nap on my couch."

Diny chuckled, opened her eyes, and suggested, "We must never forget what it feels like to be new! The confusing bewilderment and lessons developed in heartache remind us to reach out with a caring hand and guide others who are new to America. We should continue to support others after they relocate here."

Syl agreed, "We both serve as home sponsors and mentors for refugees. But have you noticed that many people who move here seem infinitely stuck in their native language, afraid to launch a conversation into English?"

Diny choked on the tea and cried, "Syl, you must be joking! Here we are chatting in Dutch, our own first language! And you speak of others as though they are not us! Of course, we could invite others into our group, like Americans, but then we would have to speak English."

Syl nodded, "Okay, but who would we invite, *Dien*? Our social circle remains intertwined within Dutch, Indonesian, and Eurasian groups." They admitted their church was mostly Dutch.

Eventually they arranged their own social club, with Dutch friends joining them at Syl's house each week to lean into conversation over coffee, tea, and snacks. They spoke of husbands and children, family trials, and joys alike, and discussed their varied abilities in settling into America. Syl frequently welcomed new arrivals to their group. And after some time, Diny was no longer the most-recent arrival to America.

"Once you dream in English, the language and words are your own," their expatriate friends encouraged Diny and the other new women, with optimistic smiles, as they sat together in knitting and embroidery circles.

Diny groaned. "Such is my hope, but I cannot remember how to pronounce many things. I struggled with 'TH' sounds, because the Dutch never use those sounds! 'TH' comes out of my mouth as 'Daaa' to me! I say, 'Why you do dis?' or 'Where did you drow dat?' And people look at me strangely. Dis and dat 'TH' sound is a rrrrreal pill."

She rolled her R's, and everyone laughed. Others chimed in with similar frustrations, and their time paced by quickly with humor and lessons. Their sessions offered life for Diny and encouragement in tangibles and propelled her from surviving into thriving. Still, in this landscape, her voice felt muted or subdued. Unable to properly express her mind within the English language, she often translated to Dutch, then back to English. Dutch, her first language, or Pasar Malay, her second, felt more comfortable to Diny.

Their own friendships, many of which transferred from Indie and the Netherlands to America, were of comfort to Nico and Diny, reminders of the challenge of assimilation, reminders of their heritage and origin, and all the miracles which had sustained them into their present benevolences. In moments of disappointment, feeling as though they may never fully adjust to America, Diny telephoned Syl, and slouched into a kitchen chair.

She sobbed, "This feels impossible, Syl. How can we live well here?

Are we doomed to a life of being different?" Diny expressed her doubts and fears, rattling off her failures.

"*Nay*, Diny, you forget how strong and able you and Nico are, and how resilient your children can be! Remember that God led you here and will provide for you. And I am one of many friends who are here for you!"

"Thank you, *lieverd* friend. When will this feel like home?" Diny sniffed.

"Hmm…. Maybe you are miscalculating the time it takes to adjust and feel integrated."

"Perhaps. But Syl, how did you adjust so quickly?"

Syl laughed on the telephone. "I have always moved, like you, as a child with a father transferred and promoted all over Indie, then into a Japanese camp as a teenager, and later again as a newlywed. Ruud's job did not remain in Padang, but all over the islands. We all seemed to scuttle around over the years."

"Heh. True."

"But remember, Dien, like you, I also lost my childhood home and all our possessions in the war. I suppose I feel at home wherever Ruud is. And if that is not enough, I pray for God's definition of contentment."

"Maybe I became too lethargic in the Netherlands, settling into a place which was impossible to remain," Diny confessed, although she always loved to pursue adventure with Nico, believing they could return to the Netherlands as easily as they integrated into Indie. Syl further discussed ways they both could draw closer into a life of contentment and joy, and Diny found comfort in her friend's reassurance and support.

Syl was on the same journey, yet several strides ahead, having moved to California in the early days of the expedited welcome, sponsored and embracing the new culture. She continued to support Dutch families arriving in Los Angeles, believing she and Ruud could offer insight and help for the process. Their optimism provided great hope for the Pouwels family.

Their friends assumed at least a year would be required to become adjusted to the language, customs, foods, currency, politics, and weather of America, of California, to figure out how to merge the lifestyle they brought with them along with unique situations; to create a balance with the way of life in their adopted land. They felt like newborn babies, floundering at first, totally dependent upon others, who eventually helped them learn to feed themselves, crawl, walk, and run into the newness of their opportunities. Speaking a new language, retraining the brain and mouth to form English words, was like beginning again, a rebirth, an origin of being displaced.

Pungent cooking scents permeated the air at dinnertime during the warmer months with outdoor grilling and open windows. Aromas rose from Diny's *rijsttafel* dishes and fragrant meals. Dynamic parties welcomed them in the gregarious neighborhood, with families inviting all on the block to celebrate an occasion. With so many neighbors also recent transplants from other lands, such as Argentina, the Philippines, Poland, or Mexico, a consensus remained of togetherness, help, and kindness.

Their family was initially sponsored by Los Angeles Christian Reformed Church on 1st & Hoover under the leadership of Dr. Dane. They appreciated all the church had provided in sponsoring them to America. However, after a brief period there, they decided to find a church closer to their home, as the one hour drive each way felt long every Sunday, and they were unable to attend week night events, due to the drive and early bedtimes.

Many Sundays after church in temperate weather, Nico and Diny took their children to the beach at Playa Del Rey, picnicking with a cooler and playing in the water until dark. On days Nico did not like to drive those hours to and from church, he set his children in the backyard, teaching them and quizzing them on Biblical theology and lessons. Eventually, they started to attend the local Arcadia Christian Reformed Church, a congregation filled with young families and immigrants. The church culture was an almost micro-IndoNetherlands culture, with Dutch and European-Indonesian. This was a new occurrence for the family, for they attended church regularly only while living in the Netherlands, and Corina and Marge enjoyed youth retreats in the Dutch countryside.

The Arcadia Christian Reformed Church pastor was Dr. Michael DeVries along with frequently-visiting pastors Dr. Lewis Smedes and Dr. Dane. An occasional visiting missionary rounded out the preaching list. Long sermons and limited children's church meant children stood through three hymns sung from the Psalter Hymnal, and sat on an uncomfortable wood pew for a sermon and lengthy prayers, and were careful not to stick their hands inside the offering plate. They gazed at stained-glass windows which recreated parables and miracles during the laborious Pastoral Prayer. After services, punch and wafer cookies provided a relief just before a hot lunch at home.

The family continued to explore, to seek out adventures, if only for a few days. They traveled on weekend trips to the beach, and immediately loved the coastal village of Santa Barbara, just two hours north of Los Angeles. Nico always set out to provide great delight with each vacation — encouraging them to remain outdoors, taking family walks along the pier and shoreline, swimming, and eating dinner at delightful places like Moby Dick, or at The Blue Onion, the famous restaurant with the tree in the middle. Their children always asked to sit near the tree each time they visited. They walked downtown for ice cream, beside trellises with vines, and meandered the gardens on the steep hills near the old *Santa Barbara Mission,* which afforded an expansive blue view of the bay and adjoining wharf, from the prominence where the bell tower stood.

Nico brought along his games on each adventure, as he loved to play cards.

"A bit of sport, children?" He winked, and they sat around a picnic table for a game. Sometimes when playing double solitaire, he needed an extra space for a playing card, and breezily asked his daughter, *"Lieverd,* just hold this card for me, so I can play another one, okay?" to adequately maneuver the play and win the game. Sometimes they complied, eager to see his talent, and other times they just laughed. Games reminded Nico of a time where all was serene, of times past which were no longer, those luminescent dreams of childhood, reborn as an adult, raising his own children.

Nico set up a backyard dartboard to throw darts each evening as a stress relief after his work in his Los Angeles upholstery shop. Soon, the grass was worn down to dirt on the throwing path. He practiced frequently, aiming for accuracy, his methodic details similar when playing shuffleboard: concise and meticulous. Moreover, Nico constructed an aviary, a little bird house which accommodated various birds from goldfinches to blue robins. In the early mornings, merry, sweet birds chirped their songs, and the happy aviary could be heard from within their home.

Collectively, in accord, their musical concerts narrated the children as they played outdoors, while Diny gardened, but she could not detect any singular song or note, as all melded into one chorus. Altogether, as though in unison, the aviary hummed with music to accompany their lives with certain melodies. And later in the evening after darts or tending his aviary, Nico reclined in his chair by the window, sometimes enjoying a glass of sherry before bed. He also loved that spot for drinking coffee while reading the newspaper.

Most summer mornings, Diny took her children swimming a mile north, at nearby Rosemead Pool, over the long months of June and July. Communities thrived in the public pool system, allowing people to refresh from the summer heat within the safety of a lifeguarded swimming pool. They enjoyed the public resource and felt fortunate for America's assets. Their children flourished in swimming, and Corina found the physical challenge in water a therapeutic exercise to her recovery. Diny refused to treat her any differently, insisting Corina held the same requirements as their other children for education, behavior, church involvement, and practice. She provided extra time for her daughter to dress or travel from one place to the next, but the levels of expectation were great. How else could Corina learn to grow and survive in the world unless Diny pushed her?

At times, Diny caught herself, fearing she was too harsh or lacked compassion for her eldest daughter's plight. She always let Nico take Corina to the hospital for surgeries and procedures, reasoning her role at home was also important. She offered stability for their other three children while running the home. Diny enmeshed herself completely in assisting Corina during the recovery time at home.

If these actions were insensitive or somehow obtuse, she knew nothing else. She had most certainly failed in numerous ways over the years, disappointments in school grades, friendships, or her stubbornness toward her parents. But if Diny could exert the effort to change, she would do so. She encountered distractions along the way but remained as focused as possible. This same work ethic was vital for her children to learn, to hopefully avoid harsher worldly lessons.

In the fall of 1960, when the children had resumed their school schedules, they again sponsored a family to America. Gon and John Van Rij' arrived 15 September 1960 with their three children and stayed 5 weeks. In preparation for the sponsorship, their children again assembled in rooms together: Corina with Marge and Nicolette, while Peter slept on a mattress in his parents' room. Their surroundings were snug, but they never complained. The Van Rij' family helped with money for the supermarket, the women cooked meals together for their families, Nico drove John around to find a home, and all enjoyed a special togetherness from the unique experience. Everybody helped during the sponsorship, and they re-lived their initial experience of being new emigrants, offering wisdom to their loving friends.

During this time, they became more familiar with another Dutch couple,

Co (Cornelia) and Mart (Martyn) Vos, as Co was the sister of John Van Rij'. Co and Mart Vos had one son named Ronald, and among many talents, they made spectacular fried shrimp chips (*kroepoek emping*) and brought some along for the Van Rij' family. From that moment forward, Mart cooked the *emping* for all the *rijsttafels*, as Mart housed a deep fryer in the garage and prepared perfectly crisp chips to accompany those meals. They loved Jesus tremendously and were shining examples of faith and peace in Him. Co and Mart moved to the Long Beach area of Bellflower not long after arriving in America, and joined the Pouwels family for family events, including every *rijsttafel*.

Autumn was glorious, with fair weather and long-lit evenings, so they sent the children outside to explore, and ate barbecue dinners on the back patio. The large backyard was a blessing, and there were always games to play. Lively children helped Nico in his birdhouse. The dads threw darts while grilling meat for dinner. In evenings when Gon and John were up for an adventure, they walked to a local school to play doubles tennis, while the seven children collected the stray balls and played on the swings. Nico and Mart chauffeured John around neighborhoods to find a place to live and Diny and Co took Gon to the department store to find household items. By the end of October, Gon, John, and their children were off on their own, and settled into their home.

As December approached, Nico and Diny urged their children to maintain the Dutch holiday traditions, discussing the idea as they cleaned up after dinner. Nico gathered blue plates and the lacy white tablecloth.

Nico announced, "Okay, kids, we celebrated the American Christmas last year, so now we can celebrate our first Dutch Christmas living in the United States! Who is ready for Sinterklaas?" His eyes lit up with anticipation.

Diny washed dishes, her eyes locking with Nico's.

Nico raised his hands in the air. "Who has their wooden shoes prepared with carrots? Have you been a good little girl or boy this year?" Nico danced around the kitchen, playfully tapping each child on the nose.

Marge frowned, then said, "Dad, we loved exchanging presents on 5th December when we lived in the Netherlands, where they celebrate Christmas on that day. And it was a great tradition when we lived there. But now we want to exchange presents on December 25th like all the other American families."

Marge dried dishes with Diny, placed the silverware into the drawer, then turned to face her dad. "How could we explain to our friends that Santa brought our presents early? And what are we going to do on the 25th, then, if we celebrate three weeks beforehand?"

Corina chimed in too, the kitchen erupting in chatter, and Nicolette also agreed.

Peter piped up cheerily, "Wait — maybe we can have two Christmases, Dad!"

They laughed, and Nico lifted his son. "Great idea, Peter. What do you think, Dien?"

Diny dried her hands and shook her head. "No, Marge is right. We must adjust with the culture here, which celebrates on the 25th. We can create new traditions here and enjoy our family time. Besides, celebrating the birth of Jesus is the most important aspect of Christmas, which we celebrate wherever we have lived!"

They settled that. Nico and Diny realized the Sinterklaas celebration would not last many years — so be it — but they had told the children enough about it, so memories remained.

Nico served as a tremendous provider for the family. He appeared as a quiet man, but underneath, he maintained integrity and honesty in his business practices and all of life. Nico held a deep, immovable love for Jesus which permeated all he did. During their difficult years navigating from Indonesia to the Netherlands and then to America, Nico taught his children about never compromising when it came to a choice between what God says and what circumstances say. Neither Nico nor Diny regretted their decision to go to America, and once they forged a life past the first year, they felt more connected, more secure about their decision. During the challenging war years, and through her Dad's guidance, Diny learned to not linger on things in the past, which were often fleeting moments. Rather, she continued to look ahead for what God had in store next and leaned into the assurance of a promising future, which she knew would be filled with His blessings and surprises.

San Gabriel, California, Spring 1961

Little boy Peter was certainly varied from his three older sisters — with busy energy and enthusiasm. His sweet yet animated temperament reminded Diny of her own younger brother Jan and his love of exploring outdoors. She found her son's tiny hands shoved into the dirt, caked with mud, fingernails never quite scrubbed of dark soil, hair filled with leaves or grass as he eagerly helped in the garden.

Those afternoons he assisted with a watering can and trowel, eyes alighting with accomplishment. Her girls were in school, and this season together with her only son would be brief. After the next school year, he would enter kindergarten and spend his energy on the playground, animated in learning to read. In their fleeting gardening moments, he was her *Peter Rabbit*, excavating the grove, naughty, curious, and keen for adventure. He was her shadow and helper, and she frequently heard him singing along with Nico's birdhouse, interspersed with roars to accompany his little trains.

Their children developed friendships and grew in school. While at times Corina struggled with the physical aspects of daily school life, she managed as best as possible and maintained a cheerful attitude. She established close friends through her magnetic personality. Marge hummed along each morning while preparing for the day, her singing like Diny's song bird, her optimistic disposition a welcoming reception. She received an A during her first report card, while her English was not very good yet.

"My 5th grade teacher, Mrs. Star, just likes me!" Marge exclaimed back then. This new school year, however, she struggled at regaining her footing, and sixth grade was a challenge, especially reading and writing in English.

Meanwhile, Nicky never failed at discovering new friendships at each turn, her gregarious personality providing for lively experiences, a dramatic flair, and boisterous family meal times. Some days, as her daughters returned home from school, exiting the bus, carrying heavy loads of books, Diny would still be working in her garden. The children settled into the afternoon at home with a snack while completing homework, and she collected her gardening, sorted her thoughts, then moved into her most important task of caring for her children.

They always did things together, as a family. On Sundays, after church, if invited to another home for coffee, they always took their children along. But soon they found the other invited couples did not bring children, so the Pouwels children sat between adults, well behaved but utterly bored. So that also did not last too long. They hoped to find families who brought children, to encourage them all to play together.

Finally, they began hosting Sunday afternoon events, inviting families over and sending the children to play outside while the adult couples gathered in the living room. The ladies sat close to each other, holding teacups, intertwined in personal conversation, while the men chatted in patio chairs circling the front yard, alternately meandering as they talked about their jobs, favorite sports teams, or projects at home.

Some immigrant parents were reluctant to give any compliments to their children, for fear of puffing their pride, but the mothers spoke of their children, whispering about establishing friendships, wiping away tears when discussing the unique challenges. The validation motivated Diny to realize her newly-found connection with Mam, of raising healthy children in a foreign environment, attempting to mold them into upright humans.

In the spring of 1961, the Pouwels family again sponsored a family and welcomed Lien and Arie Inthout into their home, along with their three children. The Inthouts arrived 27 April 1961 and stayed 4 ½ weeks, the warmth of springtime a grand welcome to America, and their daughter Wilma became a fast friend of Marge and Nicky. Lien was of the Jewish tribe of Levi, and Arie admitted to reading the Bible frequently, but neither professed a faith in God. As they became closer to the Inthouts, Nico and Diny prayed about how to reach their friends with the Gospel.

By now, the family was settled into a routine with visitors, with sharing bedrooms, making space, and cooking together. In fine weather, they enjoyed outdoor games and dining. After a month, the Inthouts were prepared to set out independently.

If she had questions about the Bible, Diny requested God's wisdom. Diny discovered uplifting radio stations with pastors who illuminated the Bible for her, along with devotional guides to explain Biblical concepts. Diny took notes in her Bible, first in Dutch and later in English, to "fan the flame of the gift God has given you." Her quiet prayer life, which began as a child in Indie and later cultivated in trials in the Netherlands, found full bloom in life in the United States with a prayer journal.

When Corrie ten Boom spoke at their sponsoring church, Nico and Diny eagerly traveled to Los Angeles Christian Reformed Church to hear her message. They were astounded at Corrie's humility. She radiated Christ's love, as her sweet Dutch face beamed joyfully and serenely. Only God could offer Corrie peace and love after enduring horrifying experiences of concentration camps like Ravensbruck, and after the deep loss of many family members.

The ten Booms had acted nobly, hiding Jews and caring for them throughout the war, but found condemnation from the Germans. Their unswerving faith originated decades before the war, many generations of praying family members upholding a vision for ministry and for God's efforts, even weekly prayer meetings beginning a full one hundred years prior to the start of the war. Corrie's message of hope and forgiveness drew people to the Lord.

After her speaking engagement, they waited in line to meet Corrie. As the crowd dwindled, they easily conversed with Corrie in Dutch, along with a few other expatriates who lingered to speak together. Among all present who had survived the war, there were too many miracles to convey in a short amount of time to elaborate completely on all God's goodness. Their conversations stretched into a local restaurant where new friendships were formed, and stories recounted. Their close friendship with Corrie would continue over the years through letters and visits to their Delta Street home

Later, at home, Nico and Diny both realized hatred or bitterness still festered in their hearts against Germans and Japanese, which required the Lord's work to forgive. They had read some of Corrie's writings, including the *Gevangene en toch...* (*A Prisoner and Yet...*), interlaced with pain and forgiveness. It contained elements of hope, which Diny prayed would lead their friends to the Lord. They had all survived the war in varied stages, places, countries, circumstances, but they were all the same in need of a Savior. Still, they sought to reach their friends with grace. Nico was a man of God, full of character and strength, although often quiet about his relationship with the Lord, served as a rich spiritual guide.

When Nico bravely talked about God with his friends, some seemed interested, and debates and dialogue followed. One friend said he did not believe anything existed after death. Some friends were agnostic, atheist, or nominal believers. A few friends, like Co and Mart, were devoted Christians, but Nico remained faithful in sharing God's love with all who listened. Some conversations stretched out over years in Indonesia and never found resolution or changed decisions, it seemed, those debates transferring to America and the present.

Nico told Diny, "They watch us, Dien, to see if God is real. And how we treat them — love them, help care for their children, stand with them during painful trials — speaks to them. If we say we are praying, then at least they know, and maybe in a dark hour, the truth will become real to them."

Diny nodded. "Still, Nico, I wish there was more to convince our friends of God's love. Some took a different path, and they may not choose the same as us."

Nico assured her, "We are called to love, and maybe we can reach them after all!" They had just spent a lovely evening hosting their friends. He continued, "Look at my best friend Henk. Remember how hardened his heart was just ten years ago? While he was in prison, we met with Janneke to pray and encourage her, and he seemed softer when hearing that, more open. I have faith he will turn to God before the end."

Father Pouwels enjoyed playing games with Nico (soccer, flying kites, playing marbles) and established the beginning of Nico's love for playing games, which he often did with his children, teaching them tricks of kite flying and soccer. His mode of communicating love and affection was translated through quality time spent with his family, often through engaging in games, a change of pace from the everyday.

Nearly every summer, the family took a holiday. Diny budgeted a certain amount of money from Nico for groceries every other week after receiving his upholstery shop paycheck. She tightened the list, saved, and tried to find ways to cut pennies in her recipes and spending, purchasing items on sale or planning meals around discounted foods. When Nico's vacation time arrived, he sadly exclaimed they did not have enough money for a holiday. Yet Diny revealed she had faithfully set some money aside each week, and the family could spend it on a fun adventure. She showed Nico the money left over from their grocery budget, and they joyfully took their children on vacation. Diny saved the entire year, anticipating Nico's eagerness at escaping from the ordinary for an adventure. And every year, Nico acted surprised at Diny's frugal nature, even though he fully knew her integrity after fifteen years of marriage.

Saving pennies was a game, an amusing contest with herself; she felt proud for saving on meat or vegetables during a sale. She quickly calculated meals, certain that more discounted meals meant an additional day away on holiday, or an added ice cream treat at the ocean. Diny's deep longing for seeing her parents, coupled with extra care and savings, meant they might be able to return to the Netherlands every four years or so to visit the Dekker side of the family.

Bright white and gray seagulls, scuttling crabs, craggy starfish and creamy sand dollars lined the golden California coast, and tide pools offered purple prickly urchins in emerald waters. Teal water surged forth and then receded at Laguna Beach, and blue water transformed, splashing frothy on rugged rocks. Land jutted out, stretching into cobalt waters. They explored parks with tidy gardens hidden away and walked the edges of lakes as dogs frolicked, chasing ducks.

Nico relished extended moments with his children while on holiday, helping them build sandcastles with moats. He packed sand tightly into a bucket or mold, with sea water soaking through as a concrete, then swiftly pulled off the container, setting the form into shape. He patiently molded each part of their castle, adding buildings, landscapes, and diversity, using water to seal the castle snug. Later, he grabbed handfuls of wet sand and drizzled mud along the paths of his creation to make miniature forests and other details. Their children delighted in Nico's creations, which eventually toppled when the high tide washed his creation away; yet for the afternoon, his kingdom remained.

On trips driving long distances, Nico's intense concentration seemed amplified, as though he reflected upon life. One place of significance which they returned to for a week in the summer over the years was near Sequoia National Park and Three Rivers. That included the highlight of the "walk" on the rocks in the water, the stream behind the cabin which held numerous stones perfect for skipping, and gentle rippling water soothing away stress and anxiety. Or other busy seasons, when an entire week away was not possible, they escaped for a day-long Saturday trip to the mountains, where Nico and their children looked for empty cans. He lined them up, and from a distance they threw rocks to see how many cans they could hit. So many wonderful and precious memories filled their days.

Life seemed busier than when they first met. Courting in early 1940, they worried about the approaching war, the impending storm cloud following from a distance, eventually disrupting every aspect of their lives. In their current situation, raising children was a busy task and contained many diversions, along with necessary lessons and decisions. Most were blessings, sweet musings from their children, sometimes wet kisses and, "Tight hugs, Mother!" They held close as young children, especially those early days in Indie. Then their interlude in the Netherlands eventually loosened their grip. Their son had always known the transient life, having lived in half a dozen homes or more before his third birthday.

"We were not always nomadic," Diny assured Peter, "but your father has always been an ambitious businessman."

Nico agreed. "Yes, my son. Perhaps we long for the change, of dusting off and having an adventure; it remains in our bloodline. My father also traversed the seas for a life in the Dutch East Indies, and during my time there I grew in love with the tropics."

Moving to a new job assignment and being promoted every two years established change as a normal custom. They wondered if their children enjoyed stability, which had been available in the Furlough season and was now their reality. Diny could only speculate if the sense of exploration and pioneer spirit would grow into something new for forthcoming generations, with a draw to embark on the world and engage with new cultures.

CHAPTER THIRTY-SIX
SAN GABRIEL, CALIFORNIA, SPRING 1963

Diny grew to rely upon and respect the changes of season, the variety of blooms maturing over different months during the year, and the way light shifted from winter into spring, a slow awakening into the warmth, which submitted into heat. The same transformation also required careful notice, the temperate alteration from the long indeterminate hot days of summer into a crisp and gentle transition to autumn. In each place, Diny searched for change, attuned herself to details, and in Indie welcomed the transition from monsoon to dry season, or from the frigid winter of the Netherlands into the muddy brisk spring accented by tulips.

The large yard proved a blessing in California. There were always games to play and later they had a small above-ground swimming pool. Peter learned to swim in their pool! Nico threw coins in the water, and they sank to the bottom. His girls jumped into the pool, swam to the bottom, collected coins, and resurfaced, then returned the coins to Nico, who repeated the fun game. Diny sat beside the pool reading or laying out for tanning. After swimming, the children dried off on jelly lounge chairs while eating snacks and drinking lemonade. Neighbor girls brought two plastic bead jump ropes over to play "Double-Dutch" jump rope games. The clicking of the plastic jump rope snapping on the concrete transformed Diny's mind back to Indie, to the methodical clanking noises of the street markets, of clicking peddlers, bicycle pedicabs, and clattering food stands.

They welcomed friends into their home who were visiting America, and enjoyed the community provided by visits with Beebs and Gerritt in April, and then Hetty and Ger in May. That spring, Dutch friends Leen and Anke stayed at their home, and all their Dutch and Indo friends joined them for a *rijsttafel*, a treat welcomed by all. Creating rice-tables of dozens of meals required more than a week for Diny to cook it all, organizing and making food ahead of time and storing prepared dishes in the back of her large refrigerator; yet she thrived on preparing meals for friends, and they had a marvelous time together. Nasi Goreng, Gado Gado, Saté Babi, Pisang Goreng, Babi Kecap, Balinese Chicken, Lumpia, and Sambal surrounded the versatile base of white rice. She made cucumber salad to soften the spicy Sambal bite. (The spicy Sambal chili was Nico's favorite, and Marge also dared to enjoy it.)

Diny's desire to remain the center of attention, coupled with her deep love for people, added to her enjoyment for entertainment. She incorporated Americans, Dutch, Indies, and others into their family unit, from Arcadia Reformed Church, so *rijsttafels* were the perfect opportunity to graft in friends from church into their traditions. Dutch-Americans Nick and Arlene Kopinga joined them, always a cheery part of the family and conversation. They also invited numerous Dutch and Indo friends, including: Lien & Arie, Gon & John, Hen & Han, Co & Mart, Syl & Ruud, Leen & Anke, and Ennie Jantz & Rex Van Delden. Some couples had children and others did not, but all were welcomed around the dinner table.

As a couple in a Bible study, Nico and Diny read Dietrich Bonhoeffer's *Cost of Discipleship* and learned more of God's grace. On summer Saturday mornings, Nico mowed the grass, and trimmed bushes, hedges, and trees. He nurtured his aviary, whispering to his birds. Then he retreated into the house from the heat and sunshine, settling into his favorite lounge chair in the living room to enjoy a Dutch beer, Heineken. He joined his children as they watched cartoons, a friendly competition between the Coyote and Road Runner, which were his favorite pair of illustrated comedians. Diny and Nico marveled at the invention of the television, which enhanced their lives with news and humor.

Some afternoons with favorable weather, Marge assisted Diny in the garden. Yet after a while she tired of activity, resigned to the knowledge her gardening skills were lacking and she felt unable to manage blooms. Her mother seemed to intimately — and innately — comprehend the requirements of gardening. However, Diny encouraged Marge to grow a cactus — which became the only living plant Diny knew Marge would keep alive successfully! Marge also had a parakeet and was proud of keeping that bird alive.

In other weekend moments, their teenage daughters found activities to occupy their time, so they all might be scattered in various places, with Peter playing basketball in the front. As Diny worked spring cleaning, knitting, or baking, Nico watched the Dodgers baseball team play on television. He turned down the television set volume while listening to the radio commentary, Dodger announcer Vin Scully imparting the best information about the team and players. Vin Scully had been the announcer since the club moved from Brooklyn to Los Angeles in 1958, and the Dodgers played at L.A. Coliseum. Transistor radios were the perfect way to hear Scully's crisp and animated narration and truly feel within the action of the event.

Meanwhile, Nico fixed watches, broken items, or untangled jewelry, and adjusted clocks, or tinkered with a project like pinning collected butterflies into a shadow box display, working on meticulous projects while enjoying the Dodgers game. This was always his routine when watching sports, to keep his mind occupied and active.

"Vin Scully makes the game really come alive," he told Diny, who hummed in response, not looking up from her work on the kitchen counter. "Those television reporters just do not describe the game like radio announcers do! Scully sounds as though he is right on the field!"

Nico loved sailboats, the water, the ocean — any boat, really — and might spend an entire baseball game carefully constructing the tedious boat-in-a-bottle. He slid a flat, collapsed vessel through the narrow bottle opening, then "launched" it to full standing position with strings and leverage, patience, and practice. His son was awed with the results.

Corina continued to struggle physically because of the effects of polio, facing frequent therapies and surgeries requiring hospital stays, but could utilize leg braces and arm crutches at elbow-level to support her walking. She worked hard and strived to participate in everything but there were times she fell on the sidewalk or while walking up steps, which was embarrassing. Marge helped pick her up, then tried to bring levity to the situation.

"You are just learning some new dance steps, Corina!" Marge said.

Corina laughed and disagreed, but Marge's love and encouragement infused hope into the circumstances. Marge remained with her, walking along to the next place. Corina, always the conversationalist, interacted with others along the way, talking about life. Others who were also differently-abled captivated her, speaking about their own challenges, which allowed Corina the opportunity to raise their spirits.

Nico's silences sometimes seemed a hesitation, an opportunity missed through fear or lack of ability to share effectively in English or his decision to keep matters as spirituality close to his heart quiet. Bothered by this discovery about her husband, and unable to understand his introverted personality, Diny pestered Nico concerning speaking more openly about Jesus to their Dutch friends, even to the detriment of the friendship. At times, she elbowed him gently, or discussed the matter in the car on the way home from a gathering. Was this mere passivity, or a deeper flaw? Was he just shy or introverted? She could not discern the root of his reservations.

During one drive, he sighed, looking out his window. "Just because it is easier for you to talk about your belief than it is for me does not indicate that I can act as you can act. Yes, you talk about God easier than I can… and even though I cannot, my heart still belongs to Jesus, and I believe in Him."

She began to respond, but Nico held up his hand.

"Diny, do not translate my silences as ignorance, skepticism, heartlessness, or indifference."

He stopped the car at a red light and they both looked down as he spoke, his face obscure in the shadows. "I know my friends and their mindset, along with their need to see us throughout the years as consistent people. Our example speaks more than our mouths."

Diny's neck inflamed in shame at her lack of trusting her husband in the most fundamental way. Her face flushed with sorrow. Diny could see so clearly God was always there — guiding, leading, and protecting them. Although they did not always acknowledge His guidance, she knew He loved them. And only because of God's love, grace, and mercy for them were they able to make it through all the difficult times in their lives. After arriving home, Diny drew Nico into the backyard to mend their quarrel.

At dinner, Nico reminded the family to study for their upcoming citizenship class, which would solidify their inclusion into American society. Citizenship class required extra study beyond schoolwork, yet involved being honored as a new citizen, which Nico deemed a vital step toward grafting into American culture. Diny hesitated to become an American citizen.

"I might just stay a Dutch citizen, because who cares if I am an American? We are a country full of many nationalities." She shrugged, turning off the radio and plating the steaming dinner onto a blue and white platter.

Nico leaned near to her and replied, "Dien, our entire family attended the class and all of us are becoming citizens, taking the test in English, and memorizing passages to recite for the ceremony."

He sat down, unfurled his cloth napkin, and placed it in his lap, then turned to look at Diny with a glimmer in his blue eyes. "Now, *Grietje*, if you ended up the only Dutch citizen in the family and the Netherlands should go to war with America, you would be deported. Alone!"

She gasped, almost dropping a full platter of meatballs, mashed potatoes, and carrots. Diny placed the platter on the table, then wiped her hands on her apron before sitting down to the meal with her family.

Nico abruptly ended the conversation, preferring to focus on more positive events of their day over the dinner table, and instead questioned their children about school and friendships. This veiled threat was all the motivation Diny required, and all six of them took the citizenship test at the same time, which everyone passed to become American citizens, and they celebrated at a fancy restaurant afterwards.

After the test, Diny realized as an American, her speech still held a thick Dutch accent, substituting "d" or "s" sound for most "th" words, sounding guttural on all "g" words and other supposedly-soft American words, but laughing along at her attempts at the language.

"Why you do dat, Nico, some-sing is wrrrong with de car heaterrr," she complained in English, her accent still remarkably Dutch.

Nico adjusted the temperature gauge, then responded in Dutch she should carry a scarf at all times.

Diny had become accustomed to his driving, to his leisurely personality accelerating in both instances of business or driving. In life, he was good-natured and humble; in business and driving, he was assertive, determined, and uncompromising. He sped along too hastily, she thought, peering over at the speedometer of their car. As he consistently tailgated and quickly changed lanes, he retained a certain precision about this discipline as well.

Yet how could she measure his driving without any previous experience? She had never bothered to learn to drive in the Dutch East Indies, as her father only needed a company car for work, and they bicycled, walked everywhere, or took a *becak* when shopping in Batavian markets. In the Netherlands, with bicycles as common as cars, and timely train systems and buses, along with expertly-designed neighborhoods, she never felt the need to bother with a car.

When the war eventually settled into their lives and the inability to learn to drive, she decided a frivolous attempt was not appropriate then, especially without the use of gasoline or a vehicle on which to practice. At twenty-five, she set sail on the ship which delivered her to a new life in Indie, where she traveled on *becaks* around the cities, walked to shops, or bicycled to the swimming pools with the children attached, a unit of four on one steady bicycle. Arriving in America at age 38, she felt obtaining a driver's license seemed foolish and pointless.

Now in the broad expanse of America, she felt secluded when Nico traveled far from home, and while all their children were in school, she was confined to toting her clanking metal cart to the grocery store, to tote home bags of groceries. They were purposeful in their selection of a location for their home, for walking distance to the library, doctor, grocery, dentist, and other shops.

Many Saturdays, they escaped to the mountains for crisp air. Sundays provided an uninhibited chance at *gezellig* social interaction with her friends. Some friends drove to her house for an afternoon coffee in the winter, sitting together in their living room, or for a shady chat on the wooden lounge chairs under the tree, sipping iced tea. If she were to join a Bible study, she solicited a friend to pick her up and drive the palm tree-lined boulevard to church in Arcadia, and then deliver her home again. If her friend was sick, Diny was resigned to remain home, yet she always returned to her writing, corresponding in letters to friends in many countries, and to telephone thousands of miles away, to hear Jan's laughter and Nelly's stories.

Nico recognized raising a son offered its own unique challenges, and did not always decipher equal treatment, but favoritism. With three daughters, Diny and Nico set out to treat them all fairly, yet everyone in the family babied Peter. He was six school years behind Nicky, and raised with four mothers, it seemed, and his solitary escape was his father Nico, who held ideals for his only son's life.

Diny witnessed her brother Jan's lack of fatherly role model from eleven through sixteen, and she was certain he suffered for all they missed together during the war years. Nico esteemed time alone with his father exclusively for his teen years, during which time Father Pouwels' influence was steady, infusing a profound sense of worth for work, being dependable and reliable as noteworthy attributes.

Nico desired a special friendship with his son and realized the importance of the relationship. Together they assembled a basketball hoop on the edge of the garage door and worked on their free-throw precision. Attending Dodger baseball games or Rose Bowl football games provided special opportunities for time together.

On Sundays, they continued to enjoy community at their Reformed

Church. Their daughters were now teenagers, involved in high school and junior high youth activities, appreciating weekend retreat outings throughout the year, to the beach to camp, or to places like Big Bear in the local San Bernardino Mountains, where they stayed at Bellows Lodge. Nico and Diny had friends with a boat and took the kids to places like Lake Piru near Santa Barbara, Lake Powell, Lake Shasta, and other water-borne destinations.

Marge and Nicky spent summers with Wilma Inthout, all three close friends, forged through sponsorship. Fond memories were created in the respite of those mountain escapes. Peter was keeping pace and eager to join his older sisters in their events, yet at six grades behind Nicky he seemed nearly a different generation and displayed tendencies and traits of a firstborn. Their girls enjoyed beach adventures with friends and the friend's parents, and as they were older, ventured to Huntington Beach with girlfriends, spending full Saturdays in the sun.

Sometimes their home was quiet, with their daughters camping or enjoying the water at the Colorado River on Spring Break. Diny felt the foreshadowing of the future, when all their children would join the great wide world as adults. She prepared lunches for her girls to take to the beach, and then the bustle settled. Nico and Diny took Peter on special outings, to the park for play time, or to the ice cream shop for a cone. Later, he might accompany them to collect groceries for the week. Strangers may remark they had a well-behaved son, assuming he was their only child. They smiled politely, thankful. *If they knew the truth,* Diny thought, *they would see a busy household. Today is slower, and we are grateful.*

Diny was never permitted to participate in after-school activities which disrupted her studies as Mam felt their social calendar filled with enough to keep them occupied, especially with her dad's police work. Yet Diny's daughters begged her to allow them to join glee club, pom squad, cheering, and other social groups which met after school.

Marge picked up English quickly in her fifth grade year, but the next year she struggled with the language. She worked in the evenings on her lessons, and vastly improved, but she was also motivated by her desire to participate in extracurricular programs. After they proved year after year their grades would not suffer, Diny and Nico allowed their girls the appropriate freedoms. They attended operas and musicals in Los Angeles, and home football games when Marge cheered, they attended games.

Their children offered to teach Diny how to drive, as Nico had ventured out with each child around the age of sixteen to learn the skill, and she laughed them off. Corina could drive, despite a handicap. She bravely took to the streets, venturing to her part-time job tending orchids at friend Rex Van Delden's local greenhouse, a place called Stewart Orchids. Rex patiently cross-bred orchids and kindly taught Corina about the delicate flowers. He was wise and efficient in his practices and held a great reputation for his work.

Diny was frightened of the velocity of the vehicles and overwhelmed at the swiftness of choices she would be required to make as a driver. Each time her daughters offered to teach her, she shook her head, burning with an inner embarrassment of powerlessness, her stomach raging with mortification. At this age, and with her daughters driving to events or opportunities, what was the benefit from her learning? Her evening activities were with Nico, who delivered them anywhere she asked. And when she was their age, with efficient public transportation in Indie and later the Netherlands, she never needed to drive. It was almost as though her friends, now in their 40s, all had made a monumental decision about driving, and she was left behind.

Soon Peter was permitted to play basketball, and the girls noted this, as he was in elementary school. They discussed the matter one evening.

"Pete is still young, Mother! We had to wait until we were at least teenagers, proving our grades before we could participate in after-school activities!"

They reminded her of those truths, and she prompted them to recall, "When we moved to America, Corina was in sixth grade, Marge in fifth grade, and Nicky in third grade. We all had an entirely new culture to learn and comprehend, and at that time could not adequately understand the language, let alone after-school groups, remember?"

They nodded and sighed.

Diny continued. "Pete benefited from our language now that you girls are older. Simply stated, Dad and I can handle more now, as we understand the country, culture, and language."

They slowly agreed and dispersed upstairs, and Diny marveled at the boisterous emotional swings of three teenage daughters. What she later told Nico, and not the children, was that Diny desired to appropriately funnel some of Peter's abundant energy into a positive avenue, and he was skilled at basketball. Nico warned Diny about favoritism, as he was always hurt by Mother Pouwels' obvious preference for Nico's older brother Piet.

"They will have plenty of challenges in life," Nico noted. "They must know of our unconditional love for all four, equally."

Nico also wanted to be certain his son did not start smoking, as Nico started smoking at an early age and did not desire his son to follow his pattern. Each night, Nico escaped to their back patio for a cigarette, no matter the weather. One evening, they stood in the dining room and started a heated discussion about smoking. Nico was now smoking in the house, and between his thin long fingers, held a lit cigarette, from which he inhaled smoke during breaks from his lecture about not smoking.

"Smoking is horrible for you, son, and you should not start smoking, no matter what!"

During the lecture, Pete looked not at his father, but at the smoldering cigarette. His son's innocent face was clearly confused with the contradiction, and in a moment of clarity and epiphany, Nico realized his hypocrisy. He grabbed the ashtray and extinguished his cigarette. The cigarette between his fingers was his last, and he quit in an instant, as a genuine example to his son. Diny later rescued the final cigarette and framed it on a plaque, which she mounted in Nico's office, so he could be reminded of his momentous decision.

After several years of upholstery work, learning from his employer while offering inventive ideas about work but never receiving recognition, Nico decided to start his own upholstery store. His entrepreneurial skills and business sense matured during his many years as manager in their Indonesian offices, and since their move to America. His English was strong, and he was mesmerized by Americans and the ability to accomplish everything he undertook in this great adopted country, if only he labored long enough.

His honesty and integrity had created a favorable reputation for affordable prices and quality work. The upholstery store seemed promising, but people told him the location of his store was wrong — directly on the bustling thoroughfare of Temple City Boulevard, a busy place, near a major freeway, and not in a location where people expected a business, like Las Tunas Boulevard afforded. Moreover, his location did not hold enough parking spaces.

Perhaps he was allured to begin a new business out of a desire to experience adventure again — they would be stable and live in the same home and the furniture store was a long-term investment. Diny's love provided Nico the courage to begin this business initiative. Now he was the boss of his new enterprise, but his ideas failed to reach fruition. Perhaps he thrived on leading an already-established venture instead of creating something from nothing. Yet this was a new business, and it was in America, the land of opportunity.

However, even his best hopes could not sustain the business, and his company failed. The furniture business was solid, yet its location was doomed. Maybe he would just excel if he maintained a company instead of creating a new one, Diny suggested. *Too bad*, said others, since the people who had warned Nico were right because the business went down. He liquidated yet another business and sold the empty store. Then Nico started to study real estate. He spent several months preparing, passed the exam, and was ready to sell houses.

Nico spent a great deal of time quietly, almost contemplative, and his head whirling with ideas. His blue eyes danced with inventive thoughts, with a shyness sometimes overcoming those hopes. Many of his interests remained unspoken, even to Diny, hidden treasures within. The failure of his business nearly ruined him. The great American Dream presented an imperfect luxury. The wealth they sought resided in friendships and love, the support derived from genuine, permanent acceptance into a new culture.

Not long after his brief furniture venture, Nico and Diny discussed his new career and decided no matter his profession, their primary aim was providing for their children.

"We have an excellent life here together, Dien," Nico remarked, his arm around her as they lounged in the backyard, watching another sunset. Their three girls giggled over badminton and Pete and his friends convened on the front driveway, his basketball bouncing a steady rhythm in their game. "Our children are healthy, successful, and happy, and Corina is finding the medical help she needs. We have many opportunities here. God has blessed us tremendously!"

He leaned in for a kiss, and Diny cried, "Nico, the children!" before submitting to his affections. Then she agreed, "You are correct, my *lieverd*, the Lord has brought us through trials and has provided many joys. What a wonderful life we have in Him!" They watched their children playing joyfully until darkness pervaded, then lit torches around the outdoor patio table and gathered together for board games and stories.

There were still consequences for some trials they had experienced, pains so deep they were buried inside. For the rest of her life, after Diny had survived the dark, bitter cold war years, she would shudder every time she heard an airplane fly overhead. Airplanes reminded her of bombers flying overhead at night, the cold droning of the engine and the waiting; the dreadful anticipation for where bombs might land, which Hilversum family or monument might be destroyed. Fears were a daily indication that at an early age, her temperament and ideals drastically changed, an airplane in the sky replicating those feelings of sorrow. But she believed God could redeem those memories and bring peace.

Her deep affections were realized by passionate living. Her passions were for people, blessing others through prayer and writing and encouragement, and tending for her husband and children. She felt satisfied at gardening, growing with each gleaning season, tilling the soil, fertilizing, preparing the ground for the next bulbs, and storing them in their own hibernation until the following planting season. A glimpse of a new green bud on a branch sent her heart soaring, soft blooms unfurling from trees. She prayed aloud, arranging difficulties or events in her mind, discussing options and ideas with God.

Nico's bird house accompanied her efforts, from goldfinches to blue birds. She was buoyed by sweet birds chirping in their cozy aviary. Their musical concerts narrated her outdoor efforts, but she could not detect any singular song or note. Altogether, as though in unison, the aviary hummed into busy lives with certain melodies.

It was as though each bird had been assigned a precious note to carry, a certain note with which to encourage and bless the world, a voice as unique as their feather coloring and pattern, eye shape, and perch and hop. Without the notes of each bird of the flock, the cheerful tunes of the aviary were altered, the harmonies dimmed, less glorious and spectacular. She crept close to observe the social birds as they mingled and kept busy visiting. They were linteractive, engaged, and industrious.

Diny knew each day presented the opportunity to serve the Lord and care for family and for her garden. Nurturing her brood required persistence, patience, and deliberate attentiveness. She watched years pass happily and could find blessing and worship if she paid attention to tiny details, listened to the needs of her family, and examined their lives for God's gentle hand.

After morning chores were completed, she ventured to her bedroom desk, which afforded the most spectacular views from their home. That part of their home seemed like an enclosed patio, like an attached, screened-in veranda, later enclosed to expand their space. Their bedroom was airy, and her desk aligned with the windows and overlooked the gardens, aviary, and distant mountains, the perfect location to write letters to her parents in Hilversum, to Lenny in Australia, or other dear friends in South Africa, the Netherlands, or even America. She enjoyed keeping those she loved updated on family events.

After writing, Diny set her stationery aside and opened the back door to stand in the doorway, listening to a heavy rain. If she closed her eyes, she imagined Batavia's monsoons, a vortex of energy, with whirling swirls of water falling and slapping on leafy frond trees. It dripped in rhythms around the base of trees, gurgling musical expressions, into a stream. In those musings and imaginings, she was back inside their Batavia front-porch veranda, inhaling balmy mist, floral and dirt. Neighbor's wind chimes jingled in the breeze, orchestrating melodies. In this interval, she opened her eyes and instantly recognized her Delta Street home.

Indeed, this was not Batavia, but California, with backyard patios instead of front-of-home verandas, with fenced-in boundaries surrounding homes. Her eyes filled with tears of joy and wistfulness, a longing to return to the past. *How can we move forward so faithfully? When did this third country transform into home? Home. A foreign word to a gypsy or nomad,* she thought, *and my true Home will someday feel complete. Has anyone on this side of Heaven felt totally settled?* She imagined not.

A single rainstorm could uproot her gardening efforts. How many gardens had she left in Indie every few years? She arranged them to taste and satisfaction, their faithful Kebon labored each day, often silently and connected to his beloved gardens, to align the correct sun positions and climate for each bush and bloom; then they learned of their father's new promotion and moved to another island. Another Dutch family would inherit their gardens, and their Kebon's work. Diny laughed at times, remembering those scenic arenas, and time cataloged in her gardens simply provided her with character growth: of patience, kindness, and perspective.

Chapter Thirty-Seven

Of what country was she now a native? Diny felt adopted into America. She walked several blocks to the grocery store and encountered several transported families along the way. One family from Argentina, another from the Philippines, another from Poland, and a familia from Mexico. Sometimes she felt confused in verbal expression, and yet writing and spelling in English proved a more complicated challenge still. Friendship would be the final graft into this new society, her Dutch transplant friends reminded her, long after they realized one could still feel lonely even when speaking the language.

She felt like an Indie mango grafted onto a California orange tree, something exotic trying to merge with the ubiquitous. With plenty of orange groves in neat rows along highways or backyards, and local homes boasting plenty of lemon trees, blackberry bushes, strawberry patches, or avocado trees in their yards, this American Dream seemed ripe and possible. Diny's beloved homeland was Indie, and those gentle, generous people welcomed her as family. She dreamed in Malay and Dutch, intermingled with balmy nights, light streaming through sheer curtains, a golden hue with small bursts of light.

In partial awareness, she envisioned *tjitjaks* on her bedroom's wallpapered walls and sat up in a flush. Her hair smelled like lemongrass, her mouth tasted of chili peppers, her sheets the scents of aromatic herbs, fruits, and spices. She heard the sizzle of hot flame-grilled kebabs and the calls of market vendors. The feeling of warmth surrounded her body.

Nico startled awake and held her, stroking her hair, calming her visions. He experienced stormy remembrances, convinced he was afloat in their wooden honeymoon suite in Malino, monsoon rains surrounding their house on stilts; paddling a canoe with his daughters in Prapat; or meandering the shores in Padang, the hypnotizing ocean soothing.

Other times, in the humid Southern California summers, stagnant air at night still sultry, the heat transported him to Operation Market Garden, to three days during his hidden journey in the baker's oven, aware of each footstep. If a storm overtook the house, shaking thunder groaning as though it originated in the earth's core, memories took Nico back to delightful days with Father Pouwels, playing games together in monsoon Indies weather, sheltered inside the enclosed veranda, insulated from the outside world.

Delta Street, San Gabriel, California, Spring 1970

One evening, a full decade plus one springtime after emigrating to California, Diny emerged from dreams, in the cool spring night. She sensed a change, an alteration to weather and climate, like previous events, an adaptation in mentality and presence. Scarcely awake, she considered her life, with the sweet goodness God provided their marriage. Their daughters fluttered past the boundaries of home, meant for greater adventures, as Corina married and began her own household with husband Stan, whom she met via other emigrated Dutch friends while cultivating orchids together in Rex's greenhouse.

Marge completed schooling and now worked an administrative and accounting job alongside Nick, building his import-export textile business in Los Angeles again, selling upholstery and furniture accessories, turning his profits back toward his customers. Marge kept the books and conversation going, while Nick marveled that after all these years, he still worked in the import-export and textile industries.

Nicolette started college, moved in with girlfriends from their young people's group, and thoroughly enjoyed her work in a preschool with exuberant toddlers. Peter remained at home, growing taller, playing basketball, and thriving in junior high, spending quality time with his parents. Spring was arriving, with a warm trade-wind breezing through their open window, and the same eerie Santa Ana winds — those from the bone-dry desert, parched with the sun — in weeks awakened their blooms to the full splendor of summertime.

Last summer, on her birthday, *the Americans* landed on the moon (20 July 1969), and the Pouwels family huddled around the television set, to watch the shadowy images of the moon landing in black-and-white. There, on the dusty far-away moon, she was certain the astronauts felt like foreigners, unable to remove the oxygen helmet or protection suit, language unable to describe the phenomenon. *Yet the moon served as a problematic location to live,* she considered, *with dim light, frigid temperatures, and lack of atmosphere or oxygen.* Certainly, *the Americans* would not survive the transfer to the moon's hostile surface.

The Americans, she chuckled.

She always considered herself "Indie," and her children called themselves "Dutch," and now, she considered them all "Americans." She had passed the citizenship class with her husband and children, together standing before the judge in the congregation with others. All graduated into the American dream, bravely calling out oaths of loyalty to the United States, and finally voting in elections, carrying out the duties and privileges of citizenship. She was more of an absolute dweller, inhabiting the Earth. Diny's heart matured in affection for this country, the peculiar language, and the variety of people, the blending of customs from around the world, the merging of many bodies and souls into an invigorating beginning. *All have been afforded a new beginning*, she surmised.

As Diny lay in bed, she speculated what sweetness might ensue this coming summer, this new decade of the 1970s, which stretched before her with expectation. This night was ensconced in hope amid the seasonal alteration, as the English language leapt alive in her heart with contentment and resolution, her spring awakening into the newness of possibility. She walked to the open window, where their bedroom opened to the night sounds, stars, and the full moon illuminating her thoughts. She observed her slumbering garden and hushed aviary, their welcoming yard, envisioning the profound memories of moments there.

A clear sky revealed constellations and a peaceful air. The creamy, swirling Milky Way was magnetic. As her view shifted in the darkness, Diny glanced at her worn Bible. In the dim light, she touched the fading leather, the wearing of the cover. Inside, her Bible narrated her life, papers inserted with church bulletin notes and precious letters holding Scriptural place, intermixed with struggles and triumphs and ideas garnered from Sunday sermons, all scripted carefully in Dutch during earlier years and English in recent years. Words of hope and conviction filled in the margins and blank pages, giving tribute to God's faithfulness over the years.

Even darkness consumed their nights and amid disappointing dreams, God's whisper remained, if only they listened, carving out silence to distinguish God's voice. In the darkness of the night, she remembered the sounds and smells of Batavia, of the saté man calling, the caramel peanut sauce sizzling, his clanking metal food cart, with tjitjaks scuttling on the walls, frogs echoing in the pond, the rhythmic breathing of siblings in the background of neighboring rooms, her parents playing the gramophone, dancing amusedly, conversing into later hours.

Dad and Mam never seemed to finish conversations, and she surmised her life with her beloved Nick was similarly just one lovely passage of time, an extended conversation, always full of exciting developments. She sensed her heritage offering permission for their future, which stretched before her like a lush and bountiful territory.

She glanced over at Nick, who was tucked into his peace, his serene almost-smile. He worked diligently and expressed his love for the family through many avenues, beginning with provision and prayer. If she had been remiss to thank him for his efforts, she vowed to remember, to demonstrate gratitude, to live in the state of thanksgiving.

Diny imagined her sweet aging parents and their round faces wrinkled with smiles. They were exceptionally in love, and just one week ago had commemorated their 50th wedding celebration, remaining in their cozy gabled Hilversum home since their 1939 arrival, enjoying a Golden Anniversary party with loved ones.

She remembered her sister Nelly and Nelly's husband Anton van der Ploeg, and the life they created from the ruins in Rotterdam, rebuilding the city after the war, raising four children together, and exploring the world in their travels through his lucrative flower seed and bulb business. Anton also served as "de Park Wachter," the director and designer for a park called Arboretum Munnike Park, in Zwijndrecht, east of Rotterdam. Nelly would always live in the Netherlands, and her location near De Biesbosch National Park, a wetland of diversity, drawing birds and flowers to its unique landscape, a place of willows and forests felt appropriate, since their dear mother Cora grew up in nearby Hardinxveld, navigating many of those same waterways.

When Diny understood the issues which plagued her beloved sister Nelly, those social challenges which tested Nelly's ability to communicate, Diny's heart filled with compassion. And into adulthood, Diny prayed seriously for a healing between them, to see Nelly through God's eyes and love her the way He loves her. And the Lord answered each prayer, allowing them to reach out through letters and telephone calls, and in better empathy and grace, the rift settled smoothly into love. Nelly and Anton visited them in America, which brought great joy.

Diny considered Jan, her dear younger brother, whom she had previously felt fiercely protective over, perhaps because of her role in caring for him during the war, and later waning as he departed for trade school, and later married, and had three children. He was now thriving in Nijmegen, inventing products for Philips, a large international electronics conglomerate, collecting clocks and colored glass bottles, and tinkering with typewriters, toasters, and other appliances to fix and discover. Jan's life of curiosity and wonder was birthed in Indie, and later nurtured during their difficult war years out of necessity. He was hesitant to visit America, but as Nick and Diny saved money to travel to the Netherlands, she was certain their reunion would be sweet.

Huib was the only one who remained in Indie, buried on a hill in Bandung, his grave permanently overlooking the city, near Pieter's own personal hell in Tjimahi internment camps. *Huib missed out on all the adventures*, she considered, but she would never know what his involvement in the war would have been. Her heart always swelled with remembrance of him, and yet she could not consider the past to suppose any possibilities surrounding him, for Huib was on the Real True Adventure, one she would someday join.

She remembered her tear-filled vow as a teenager to never depart from her beloved Indie. Yet, adventures beckoned her to new landscapes. The exchange of her teardrops and sweat were an ample substitute for a clump of earth. The lofty pledge was like vowing her life to the wild, untamed country, which she eventually traded for the domesticated climate of America. Yet she remained true to her pledge to God to follow Him. She laughed, remembering her certainty: *Nothing will ever force me to leave this magnificent home*, she promised, *and that was certain*. Now, decades later, her siblings were scattered to three continents, with the spread in distance acute yet fixed, but always hopeful.

This was her Promised Land, a place of genuine hope. And unlike Moses, who led Israel to its border and was not permitted to enter, she and Nick ushered their children into a terrain of milk and honey, a residence, following a journey of faith, possessed of potential and purpose. She vowed to surrender her own wishes for the future yet unknown, but shimmering on the horizon, a prospect for forthcoming generations. She did not expect changes in the continent any longer but felt determined to establish deep roots in her newly adopted landscape. Her past swirled around her gently, humming like a warm golden breeze, orchestrated with night sounds.

Then, standing in front of the warmth of the opened window, gazing into the great beyond, she could see her life unfolding over the next forty years, as though a movie reel unfurled before her eyes. As they raised their children, and later welcomed grandchildren — as they would become the *Opa* and *Oma* — she envisioned the scope of their blessings which would entail their *gezellig* togetherness: grandchildren napping in cool bedrooms with open windows, enveloped in the noises of family togetherness, and later playing Dutch games like croquet, badminton, *Sjoelbak,* and *Caroms* with Opa, tending the aviary. Giggling toddlers would help Oma bake *snoepjes* and other treats, dance in the kitchen to classical music on their record player, grandchildren in their arms, stroking their wrinkled hands, with matching golden wedding bands and stories of grace.

When their own four children were growing up, they danced together. Later, when their home only housed each other as their children had matured into adulthood, they continued to sway in a harmony, in unity. They danced in the evenings, on the veranda, amidst fragrant spice winds, swinging to music on the player, laughing into the darkness of the nightfall.

At times, Nick still tapped his way to the other side of the porch, sashaying down the steps, and gliding into the yard as though on ice skates, radiantly caught up in his own rhythm. Other times, he waltzed with Diny for hours or until the music halted and the record completed its cycle, only scratching pulses interrupted their intense togetherness, requiring another interval.

Just as their life consisted of a long and enlightening discussion, a conversation never finishing, Diny was enchanted with swaying along with Nick, certain their dances were simply acts in a musical or scenes in a drama. She was uncertain of where the rhythm would take them, but was determined to enjoy the circling, the swirling movement, the precarious way the dances delivered them, taking great measures to remain in step with each other, paying attention to the nuances and persona of each breath, each look, each moment. Her eyes could not hold marvels, and she wept for the beauty of blessing.

Even Nick and Diny would further their own explorations on numerous voyages to Maui, to visit Hawaii's hidden waterfalls, explore green expanses, and embrace the tropical paradise. The islands reminded her of Indie, of mountain, mystery, and character encompassing lush valleys and craggy shorelines, and she longed to again sink her fingers into the soil.

And their family would also venture out, into their own foreign territories, with stories worthy of their own rendering, of explorations, expeditions, as an inborn sense of creativity, discovery, and exploration surged through the veins of their inheritance. Yet they would always return to Diny, guided by her expressive handwritten letters intermixed with prayers sealed with big hugs and kisses, laughing family surrounding the mahogany kitchen table over delights of coffee, tea, cookies, and language, over merriment and love. They would squeeze together in cozy sitting rooms for plates of sautéed vegetables and smoked meat and rice at *Rijsttafels*, parties, elaborate gatherings, or simple Sunday afternoons.

They were always joined in the hope of the newness God provided, the opportunity to live freely, to experience the grandest of adventures with boundless expectation. For decades, she marched nobly toward the glorious promise of Someday, and realized the day already arrived. The round moon glimmered rays of beaming gold through the window, illuminating her glittering face.

About the Author

If you enjoyed reading this story, would you please write a short review of this book? I greatly appreciate any kind words. Even one or two sentences will help immensely. Reviews are truly encouraging and offer me creative energy for my next writing projects.

Connect with me at: www.carolinemertens.com

A native of Southern California, Caroline Mertens left the beaches and palm trees of Los Angeles to move to the blue skies and mountains of Colorado Springs as a teen. She received her B.A. in English and Secondary Education from Colorado Christian University in Denver. Caroline's most fulfilling career is teaching high school English. She strives to model to teenagers how to nurture a love for reading, and how to write creatively and with purpose. Caroline is passionate about traveling, cooking Indonesian food, and exploring Colorado's Front Range with her family and their sweet rescue dog, a Labrador retriever.

Author's Note

As a first-generation American, I could not speak Malay or Bahasa Indonesia, or any of the other dialects, and I spoke a little Dutch, but craved the sounds of foreign words, languages fluent in my mother's tongue. I grew up in the Los Angeles area, where a wonderful conglomeration of ethnicities provided inspiration and connection with others also newly-transplanted to America. Dutch or Indo chatter lingered in my dreams among fragrant rice-scented moments, memories of *rijsttafels*, unrestricted moments between Oma and Opa's expression of love, in the central block of family togetherness. The immense possibilities for their children — and future generations — certainly abounded. I was raised with a hearty depth of gratitude for my mother's immigration story, and marveled at the gifts bestowed: integrity, hard work, dedication, honesty, love, and sacrifice.

While feeling gratitude for this heritage, it must be stated that this story, Diny's story, is written through the lens of a Dutch woman whose Dutch father Pieter was a police officer and government leader in a Dutch colony. Diny lived a privileged childhood in a time when the world was rapidly changing, and the Dutch East Indies was groaning under the burden of two centuries of inequalities as a colony. Many loving, hard-working, God-fearing Europeans like Diny's family moved there for a promising career in civil service, the military, or other pursuits, and likely did their best to provide a valiant work ethic, but they also lived mostly secluded lives in Dutch neighborhoods and attended Dutch schools.

This is only one story, one viewpoint, one Dutch family who lived there during this timeframe. After Pieter survived the war and returned to the Netherlands in 1946, the Indonesian war of independence was well underway. Pieter, the strong and valiant police officer, faced the repercussions of the war and the transition from colony to freedom. Pieter also realized the necessity of decolonization and independence for Indonesia. His police career was over, and he never returned to service, but his positive optimism remained, along with his faith in God.

In recent years, the Netherlands has admitted they were wrong to colonize Indonesia, and they are ashamed of how they behaved. As such, the Dutch government officially apologized to the Indonesian people. I am aware of these recent changes and purposefully wrote this book through Diny's singular perspective during a momentous time in history. As some characters in novels are static and flat, I hope Diny serves as a round character, as her maturity and dynamic qualities demonstrate both her flaws and her learning about the world as she lived on three continents, raised a family, and sought to grow as an individual.

In transitioning to America, my grandmother Diny undoubtedly faced hurdles while in her late 30s, including the task of quickly learning the English language and American culture, while raising four children, and seeking to support her husband's career and ambitions. I imagine a seasoned, yet calm woman standing at the edge of grace, peering past circumstances and obstacles, stepping boldly into opportunity and freedom. Diny and Nico were normal, imperfect people who survived the war years and decidedly moved beyond the pain they encountered.

I have traveled many of the lands in this novel, from Los Angeles to Amsterdam and back. I walked the same roads as my grandmother Diny in Hilversum, marveled at the bucolic beauty of the region and wooded lands just outside the city, amazed at pleasant places for summertime bicycle journeys or exploration in the heather. I visited City Hall, where Diny married Nico by proxy. Amsterdam held great promise and vibrancy and the shadows of Nico's life there: a city bustling and accessible, both quaint when visiting family in the leafy Jordaan neighborhood, and vast and unrestricted when standing in the broad Dam Square in front of the Royal Palace. Some of my favorite moments in Nico's hometown include strolling cobblestone streets, gliding through canals in an open-air boat, bicycling Vondelpark on a warm and sunny June day, and astonished at the grand scope of impressive artwork in the Rijksmuseum.

When I journeyed to Cora's hometown Hardinxveld and surveyed the serenity of the Merwede River, I picnicked at a cafe and delighted in a steaming bowl of mussels with my Great Aunt Nelly and her dear husband Anton. Nelly and Anton raised four children in an eastern Rotterdam suburb of Zwijndrecht. One of her children, PieterJan, visited their home one day so we could chat, and his likeness to his grandfather Pieter Dekker was great, with his warm sense of humor, familiar gestures, and quiet strength. On another recent visit, we walked the paths of the 19 windmills at Kinderdijk on two waterways and marveled at the beauty of such an important location. Later, PieterJan graciously showed us the charming town of Dordrecht with charming boats and a storied church and government history. We spent an afternoon on a walk of this majestic city, sat beside the confluence of De Lek and Noord Rivers for a coffee, and dined with PieterJan and his wife Caroline in their lovely Zwijndrecht home.

When I traveled north through the Arnhem region, where Operation Market Garden took place in September 1944, I considered the peaceful river and a strategic bridge spanning a tranquil but important location. On that journey, I walked the streets of the tiny village of Elst, where my grandfather Nico was headquartered during the war, when he worked for the jam manufacturing company and as a translator. Later, I visited with my jovial Great Uncle Jan at his home in Nijmegen, a city also valuable to the war efforts; he remained an inventor for Philips for many years and proprietor of many unusual collections, which brought amusement and joy to our conversations. Many descriptions of the Netherlands I attribute to opportunities to visit, and the generous family still living there.

So much of the Dekkers' and Pouwels' lives meant relocating, establishing themselves again and again, and connecting with friends in far-flung lands. The Netherlands felt like home to me: the people, language, customs, and welcoming kindness so familiar and welcome to my soul in the season of life I was blessed to live there.

Los Angeles did not beckon Diny and Nico any more than the general appeal of America — the idealism of a bustling city with genuine opportunity — as simply stated as this. Nothing except the connections of the Benink family, who earlier pioneered the move, urged them to step into California. Those friends were also banished from their beloved adopted country, and sponsored them to Los Angeles, with Southern California a locale with tropical plants and a mild climate like the one they left behind in Indonesia. The war surged a resolve to form friendships and kinship with many types of families, with those who were not their direct bloodline. They recognized God's direction, their intentions were wholesome, and spirit fully devoted to serving the Lord. With open hands and eager hearts, Nico and Diny forged their dreams by

God's design and in humility, directed glory to the Lord. They realized all God gave them was a gift.

As a matter of friendship, Diny grew outwardly in caring for others, and developed her tremendous and keen intuitive hospitality, the "warm, cozy togetherness" Dutch call "*gezellig*," perhaps requiring more than three English words for translating such a powerfully present active verb. The entire emotion of the word *gezellig* is reminiscent of gathering in a sitting room with a roaring fireplace and coffee, tea, cookies, or cakes, and laughing jovially. It conjures some type of connection with another human, on the most comfortable and basic level. If Dutch winters are full of frigid, overcast days, then surely Dutch people are sunshine, welcoming, and accepting, as though hospitality is not a gift, but a lesson taught while children are young, along with table manners and other elements of etiquette.

Nico and Diny's friends were funny, generous, and endearing, and filled with unique eccentricities as in every culture, perhaps borne out of living for many war years lacking any excess. Over the years in California, their Indo-Dutch friends felt like my own, or at least they produced a sense of tender comfort, extending a hug, smile, and kind eyes. Some greeted us grandchildren with kisses, coins, cookies, and mints. Their faces were not marred with tragedy, but wrinkles molded by full-living, laughter permeating more than sorrow.

By not merely surviving, yet flourishing in a rounded life, Oma and Opa and their compatriots from a multitude of countries pursued an excellent existence through adversity. Some had lost entire families in the war, a genealogy taken, a future flickering in the form of just a tiny candle. The flame remained. They hoped, expressing joy through faith. Not all shared the same faith, God, or religion, but could unite as a thriving, sympathetic, and ambitious unit. A new country reset their inhibitions and they pursued vibrant hope and great expectation to experience newness, together.

The ideals surrounding the immigrant story encompass one of hope, even as circumstance remains varied. Global stories must be written, their lives must be recorded. We would all benefit from their deserving narratives. Nico and Diny gave the Lord all the glory throughout their lives, and their greatest joy was in knowing Him; they pursued God's goodness, grace, and love. My desire is that sharing their story will resonate with those who also seek hope and redemption in God.

READING GROUP QUESTIONS

1. Describe how you think Pieter and Cornelia Dekker felt about the Dutch East Indies.
2. What are Pieter Dekker's contributions to the police department? What are his flaws?
3. In what way did Huib impact Diny's life?
4. Which inequalities were the most frustrating for those living in the Dutch East Indies?
5. What may have happened if the entire Dekker family returned to the Dutch East Indies in 1940 (and not just Pieter)?
6. How does Cornelia's illness shape Diny's life and future? How does it change the Dekker family's war experiences?
7. What was the significance of Jan and Diny's journey to Oom and Tante's farm during the Hunger Winter year of the war?
8. How could Nico have reacted to his friend Henk's betrayal? How would you handle a friend who sided with the enemy during a war?
9. Why did Pieter Dekker withhold his war experiences in Tjimahi, the Japanese prison camp, from his children?
10. Describe Pieter Dekker's reunion with his family.
11. Predict what might have happened if the Pouwels family had stayed in the Netherlands instead of moving to America.
12. How does Diny grow and change over her lifetime?
13. What might the 1970s and beyond hold for the Pouwels family?
14. What is a meaningful lesson you will remember from this story?

ACKNOWLEDGEMENTS

The beginning of *In Those Other Lands* originated in Nico and Diny's backyard. As a small girl, I eagerly listened to their stories, and decided my Oma and Opa's accounts needed to be recorded. There was something special about all they survived on three continents, and when my dear Opa Nico passed away when I was only ten years old, I vowed with vivid certainty to accomplish this task. Writing and recording their narratives came together with oral histories passed down to me by family, especially Diny, her melodic voice recordings and thick Dutch accent imprinted on tapes and CDs. She also provided more than two dozen pages of handwritten testimony. Diny's writing style was straightforward, warm, and informal, but I appreciated how she infused God's love and humor into the pages of her life, and tried to incorporate her style as much as possible. Her memory was bright, her mind sharp, and her laughter was my music.

Thus, I am especially indebted to my late grandparents Nico and Diny, for generously sharing with me over countless cups of tea, telephone calls, and love. For Diny, numerous in-person interviews, with sparkling laughter, many tears, and incredible patience answering numerous questions, offering sweet and sorrowful anecdotes, embarrassing and heartening tales which graced the pages of this book; for Nico's ability to share the depth of a meaningful conversation over board games and cards, and the unconditional love and quiet humility he modeled. I am grateful for Diny's sister Nelly, and brother Jan, along with her children Corina, Marge, Nicky, and Pete for allowing me to share glimpses of their stories, as viewed from Diny's perspective. Any details Diny shared which are not corroborated by other scholars or newspapers, I can only suggest her life through her own limited viewpoint, through her unique perception and ideals.

For two decades, I collected findings in notebooks, with details, names, dates, and maps. Where there were divergences in my research, I found Dutch and Indo survivors with similar backgrounds and contacted scholars who specialized in the colonial Dutch East Indies, the Dutch policing practices in the 1930s, the Netherlands in World War II, Dutch war experiences, and so forth. I read books, watched films, unearthed newspapers and other archives, visited libraries in person and virtually, and followed numerous leads. I was always astounded at the records that could be found, and at the readiness of people and organizations around the world, eager to help.

Discovering the stories of my family history required the help of a global community. Thank you to Dr. Marieke Bloembergen, cultural historian and senior researcher at KITLV in Leiden, the Netherlands, for her kind compassion and depth of guidance on Pieter Dekker and his role as police officer and policing practices in the Dutch East Indies, and for the use of her thesis, "Being clean is being strong: Policing cleanliness and gay vices in the Netherlands Indies in the 1930s". I greatly appreciate Jeroen Kemperman of the Dutch Red Cross for assistance with Pieter Dekker's war experiences in Tjimahi, Java; Henk Beekhuis for help on Japanese civilian camps Tjimahi and Muntok; Robarts Library at University of Toronto for camp information; Ria Koster and Kumpulana for numerous leads on Pieter Dekker and Pieter Pouwels; Muntok Peace Museum; and Roos van Borkum at Tropenmuseum for details on the Dutch East Indies.

I am indebted to many marvelous people and offer my thanks. My friends in BEL Literary Society, thank you for the inspiration and support to write and publish, and for your love of literature as we read and discussed great works together. In my formative years as a young child, I was spurred forward by teachers who greatly encouraged the development of my writing: Mrs. Billie Mann, for nurturing my love of creative writing; Mr. Randy Horn, for encouragement in journaling to mature the writing craft; Dr. Elaine Woodruff for uncompromising insights into poetry and life; and Dr. Phyllis Klein for a gentle and saintly practice of prayerful, contemplative living, of viewing writing as a sacred art. I also thank those brave Americans originating the Pastore-Walter Act, which brought my family to the United States. My remarkable Blythe Hunt, dearest friend and fellow author, was the first to read my book; her support from the initial stage to blossoming into fruition was priceless. She challenged me and prayed for my writing. Her keen insights over many years buoyed my confidence and propelled my work to a better level.

For literary help and guidance, I am deeply thankful for my wonderful and talented editor Harvey Stanbrough. A writer, poet, and freelance editor,

Harvey's editing prowess did wonders for my book, and his rich, instructive feedback helped boost my project in a supportive way. Thank you to kind hearted Ronny Herman de Jong for your friendship and sound advice in navigating the publishing world, for guidance and encouragement in marketing, and for your example of bravery in writing your family story of survival, hope, and grace during WWII. You are an inspiration to my work. To the entire Dekker and Pouwels families, thank you for your support. Erika de Jager-Pouwels, your guided insights and detailed information brought renewed perspective to my writing. You were quite helpful in many aspects and I appreciate the intricate research and suggestions you shared to enhance this new edition.

My beloved, cherished friends Tami, Tra'Cee, Erin, Kimberly, and Angie believed in the power of this story, motivated me to press onward, and prayers, letters, enthusiasm, and complete support of my writing accomplishments were stimulating and life-giving: thank you. My bolstering husband J.P., an enthusiast in my writing endeavors, demonstrated patient endurance and provided honest and relevant feedback to positively shape this story. Our three joyful, incredible daughters were delightful, eager readers in the writing process, and I hope this story of faith and redemption develops their courage and ability to forgive and live with kindness, grace, and courage. My in-laws, Kelly and Linda, were supportive and encouraging each step of the way, and I am grateful for your unswerving love.

Finally, a *"Hartelijk bedankt!"* to all my extended family in the Netherlands and America alike. All my love to my devoted family: my kindhearted and supportive parents Ron and Marge; my wise and generous brother Tim (and gracious Jeni, Blake, Logan, and Dekker) and humble, talented brother Daryl (and gentle Sara), my darling aunts (Tantes) and uncles (Ooms): Corina and Stan, Nicolette and Keith, and Peter and Joyce; and dear, inspiring cousins: Galen, Giselle, and Arix; Charissa, Joshua, Caleb, and Emily; Michael, Jennifer, Geoffrey, and Amanda. Your permission to share this story and interest surrounding my writing has been life-giving and redemptive. The story in these pages is also your story, your heritage, and your torch to carry forward for future generations.